THOR IS THE GOD OF THUNDER AND ALL-FATHER OF ASGARD.

IN HIS RECENT BATTLES – THE MOST SIGNIFICANT OF WHICH SAW THOR KILL GALACTUS AND THEN INCORPORATE HIS ANCIENT ARMOR INTO THE ARCHITECTURE OF ASGARD TO HOUSE REFUGEES OF WORLDS GALACTUS HAD DEVOURED – THE ALL-FATHER HAS NOTICED A STRANGE HEAVINESS IN HIS HAMMER MJOLNIR.

AND THE PROBLEM IS WORSE THAN HE KNOWS. FOR WHILE MJOLNIR GROWS HEAVY FOR THOR...IT BECOMES LIGHTER FOR EVERYONE ELSE. EVEN HIS BROTHER LOKI HAS HELD THE HAMMER NOW...

THOR

Prey

WRITER **Donny Cates**

ARTIST **Aaron Kuder** (#7-8) & **Nic Klein** (#9-14)

COLOR ARTIST **Matthew Wilson**

LETTERER **VC's Joe Sabino**

COVER ART **Olivier Coipel** with **Laura Martin** (#7-12) & **Matthew Wilson** (#13-14)

ASSISTANT EDITOR **Kat Gregorowicz**

ASSOCIATE EDITOR **Sarah Brunstad**

EDITOR **Wil Moss**

THOR CREATED BY **Stan Lee, Larry Lieber** & **Jack Kirby**

COLLECTION EDITOR **JENNIFER GRÜNWALD** ASSISTANT EDITOR **DANIEL KIRCHHOFFER**

ASSISTANT MANAGING EDITOR **MAIA LOY** ASSISTANT MANAGING EDITOR **LISA MONTALBANO**

VP PRODUCTION & SPECIAL PROJECTS **JEFF YOUNGQUIST** BOOK DESIGNER **ADAM DEL RE** WITH **JAY BOWEN**

SVP PRINT, SALES & MARKETING **DAVID GABRIEL** EDITOR IN CHIEF **C.B. CEBULSKI**

THOR BY DONNY CATES VOL. 2: PREY. Contains material originally published in magazine form as THOR (2020) #7-14. First printing 2021. ISBN 978-1-302-92087-6. Published by MARVEL WORLDWIDE, INC., a subsidiary of MARVEL ENTERTAINMENT, LLC. OFFICE OF PUBLICATION: 1290 Avenue of the Americas, New York, NY 10104.

Printed in Canada. KEVIN FEIGE, Chief Creative Officer; DAN BUCKLEY, President, Marvel Entertainment; JOE QUESADA, EVP & Creative Director; DAVID BOGART, Associate Publisher & SVP of Talent Affairs; TOM BREVOORT, VP, Executive Editor; NICK LOWE, Executive Editor, VP of Content, Digital Publishing; DAVID GABRIEL, VP of Print & Digital Publishing; JEFF YOUNGQUIST, VP of Production & Special Projects; ALEX MORALES, Director of Publishing Operations; DAN EDINGTON, Managing Editor; RICKEY PURDIN, Director of Talent Relations; JENNIFER GRÜNWALD, Senior Editor, Special Projects; SUSAN CRESPI, Production Manager; STAN LEE, Chairman Emeritus. For information regarding advertising in Marvel Comics or on Marvel.com, please contact Vit DeBellis, Custom Solutions & Integrated Advertising Manager, at vdebellis@marvel.com. For Marvel subscription inquiries, please call 888-511-5480. **Manufactured between 4/16/2021 and 5/25/2021 by SOLISCO PRINTERS, SCOTT, QC, CANADA.**

10 9 8 7 6 5 4 3 2 1

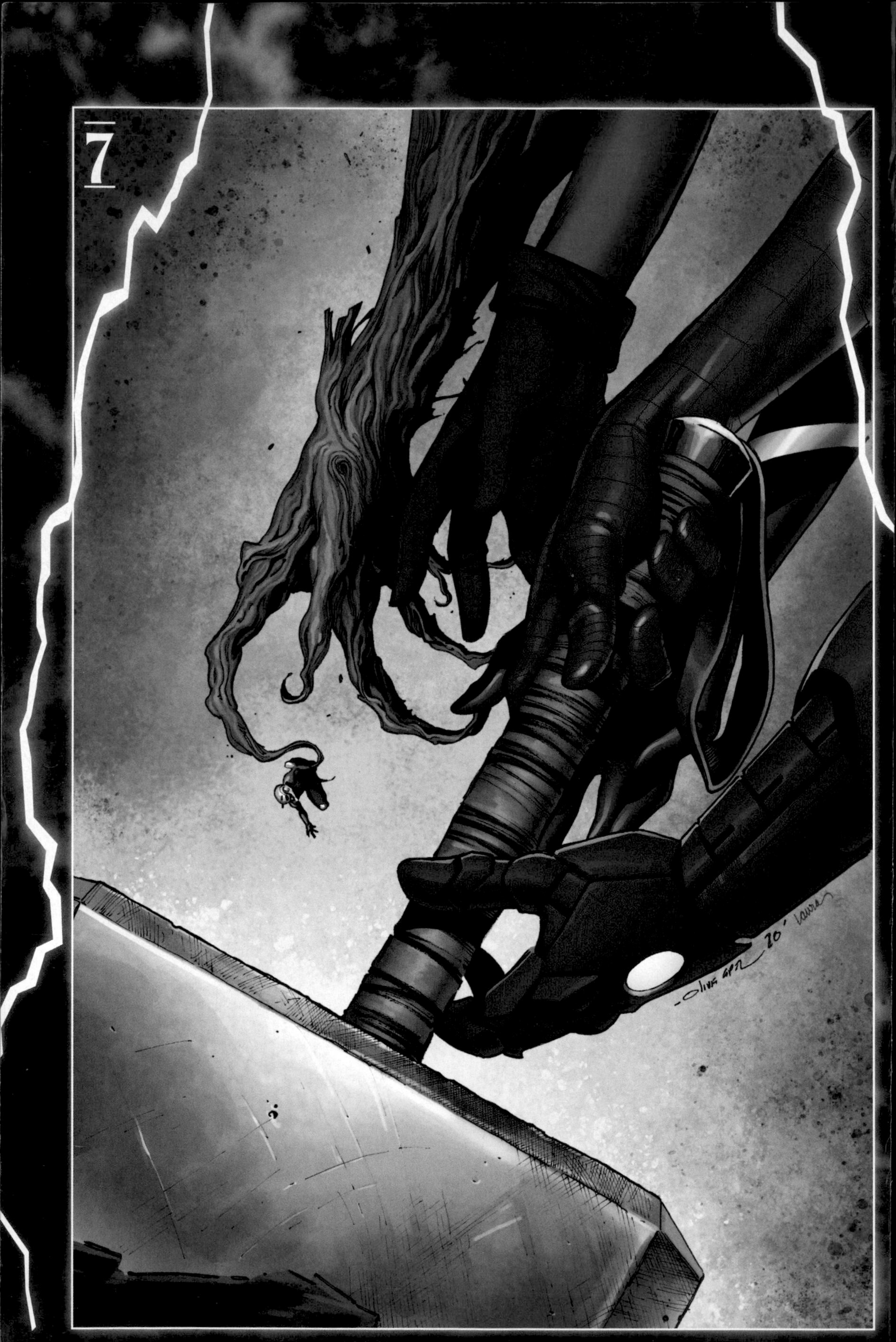
7

"Hammerfall" PART ONE

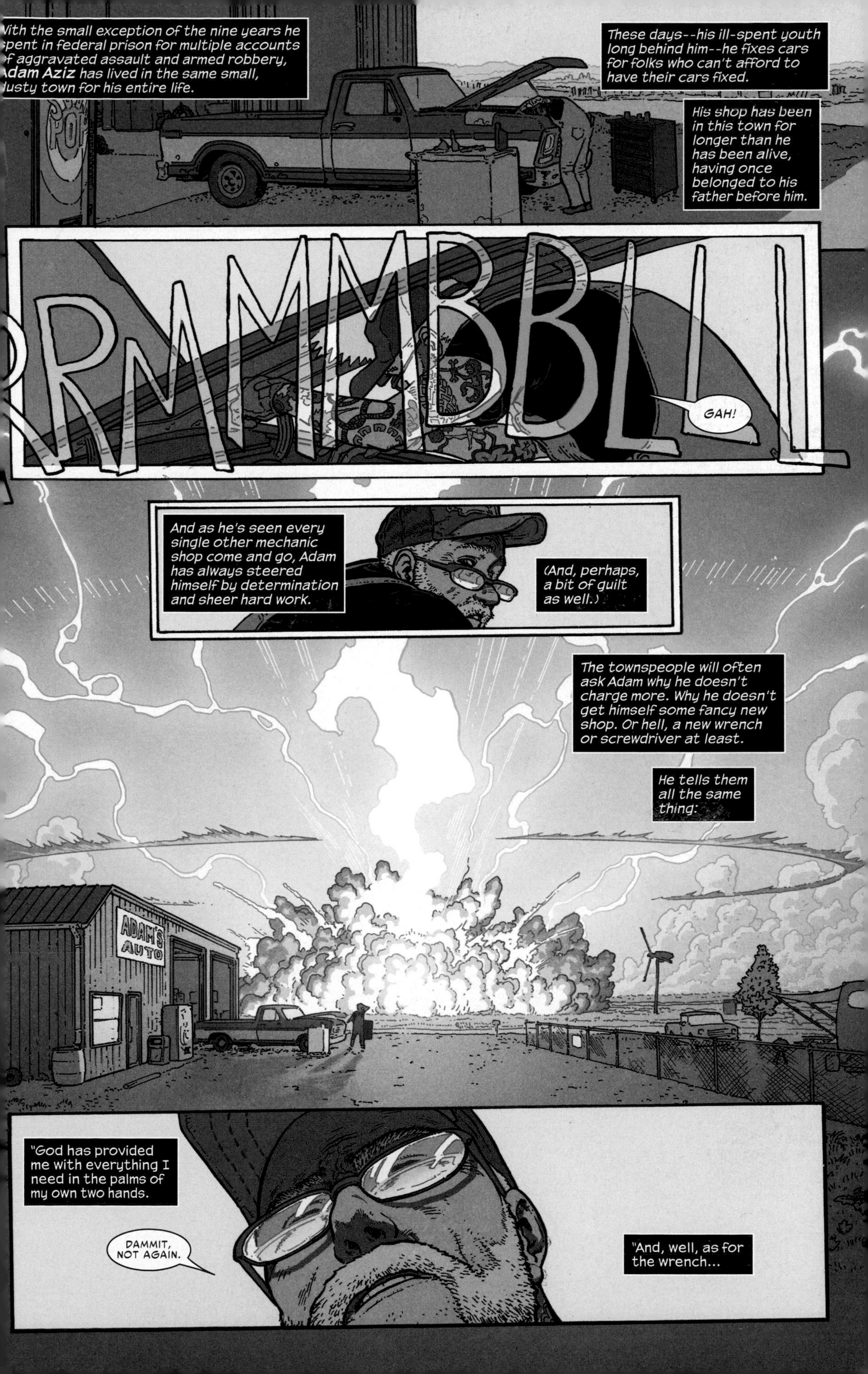

With the small exception of the nine years he spent in federal prison for multiple accounts of aggravated assault and armed robbery, **Adam Aziz** has lived in the same small, dusty town for his entire life.
These days--his ill-spent youth long behind him--he fixes cars for folks who can't afford to have their cars fixed.
His shop has been in this town for longer than he has been alive, having once belonged to his father before him.
RMMBBLL
GAH!
And as he's seen every single other mechanic shop come and go, Adam has always steered himself by determination and sheer hard work.
(And, perhaps, a bit of guilt as well.)
The townspeople will often ask Adam why he doesn't charge more. Why he doesn't get himself some fancy new shop. Or hell, a new wrench or screwdriver at least.
He tells them all the same thing:
ADAM'S AUTO
"God has provided me with everything I need in the palms of my own two hands.
DAMMIT, NOT AGAIN.
"And, well, as for the wrench...

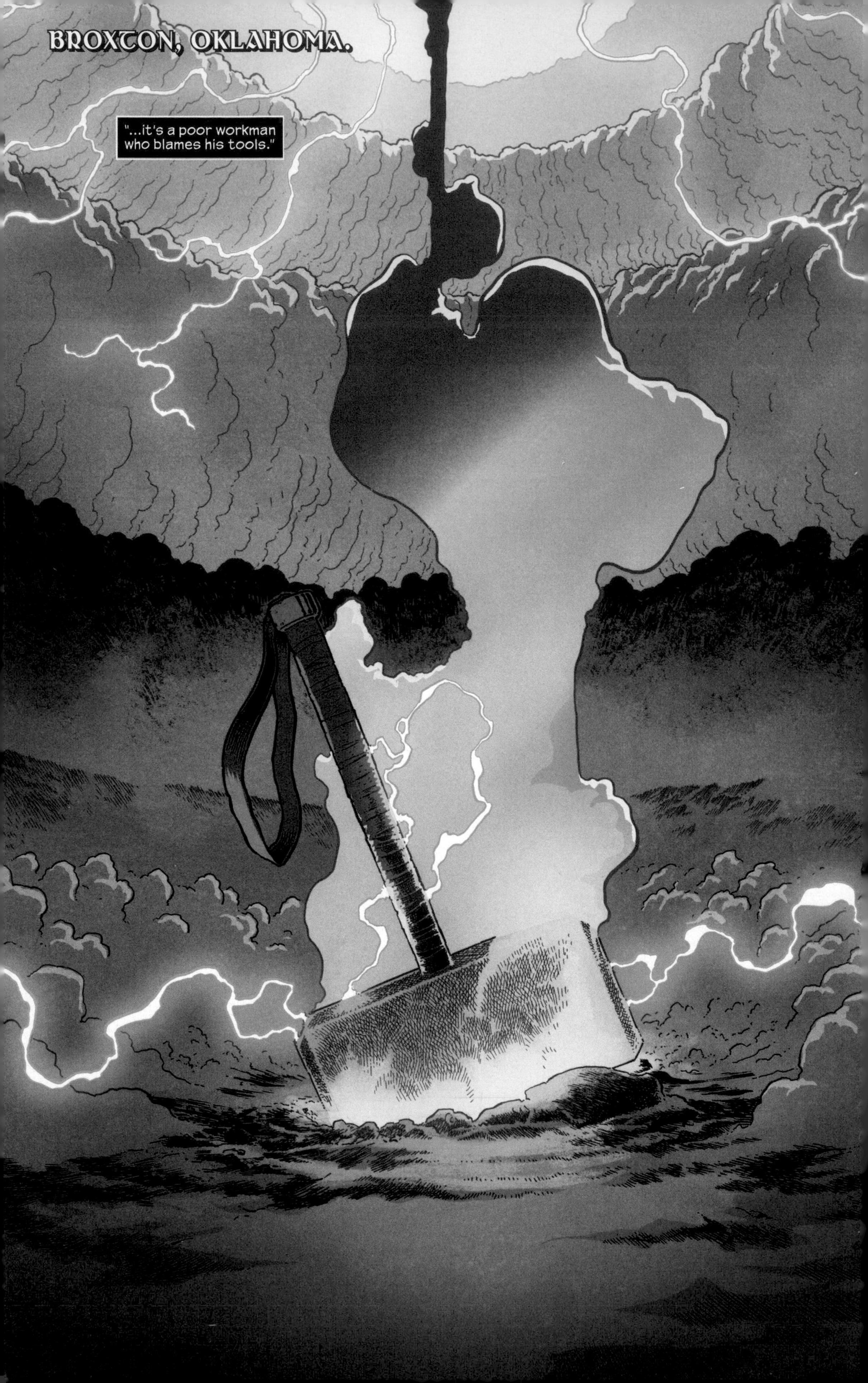
BROXTON, OKLAHOMA.
"...it's a poor workman who blames his tools."

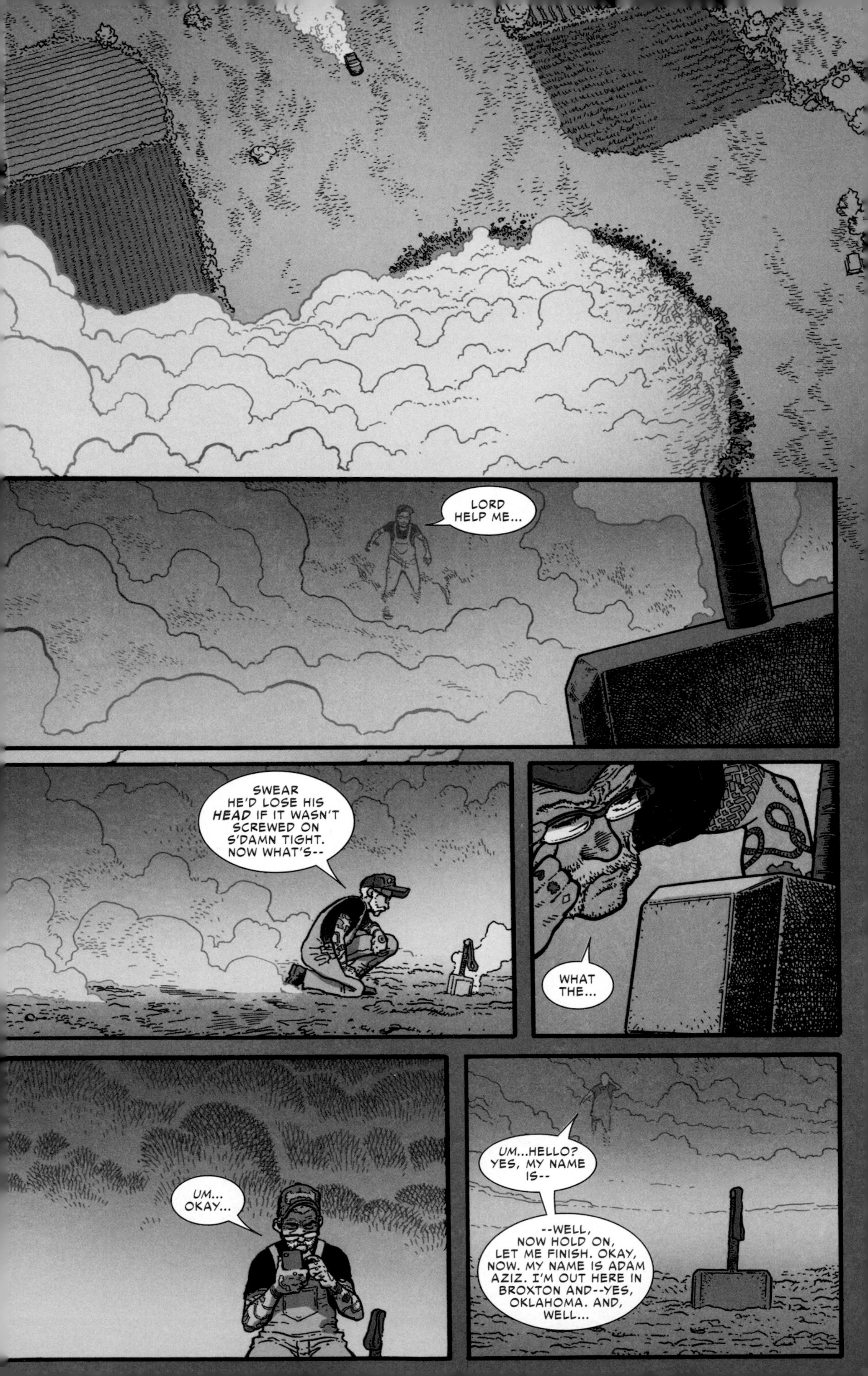
LORD HELP ME...
SWEAR HE'D LOSE HIS *HEAD* IF IT WASN'T SCREWED ON S'DAMN TIGHT. NOW WHAT'S--
WHAT THE...
UM... OKAY...
UM...HELLO? YES, MY NAME IS--
--WELL, NOW HOLD ON, LET ME FINISH. OKAY, NOW. MY NAME IS ADAM AZIZ. I'M OUT HERE IN BROXTON AND--YES, OKLAHOMA. AND, WELL...

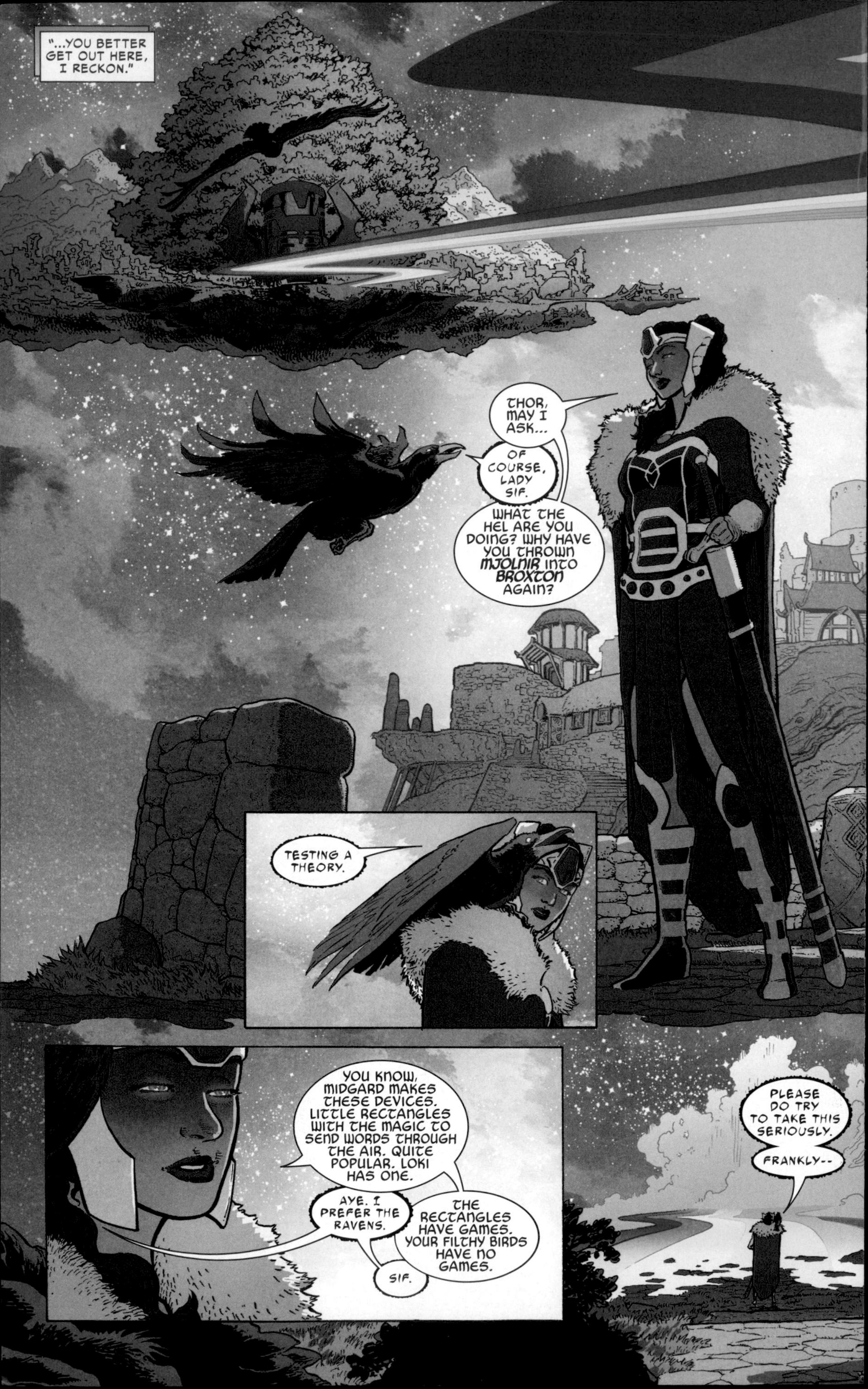
"...YOU BETTER GET OUT HERE, I RECKON."
THOR, MAY I ASK...
OF COURSE, LADY SIF.
WHAT THE HEL ARE YOU DOING? WHY HAVE YOU THROWN MJOLNIR INTO BROXTON AGAIN?
TESTING A THEORY.
YOU KNOW, MIDGARD MAKES THESE DEVICES. LITTLE RECTANGLES WITH THE MAGIC TO SEND WORDS THROUGH THE AIR. QUITE POPULAR. LOKI HAS ONE.
AYE. I PREFER THE RAVENS.
THE RECTANGLES HAVE GAMES. YOUR FILTHY BIRDS HAVE NO GAMES.
SIF.
PLEASE DO TRY TO TAKE THIS SERIOUSLY.
FRANKLY--

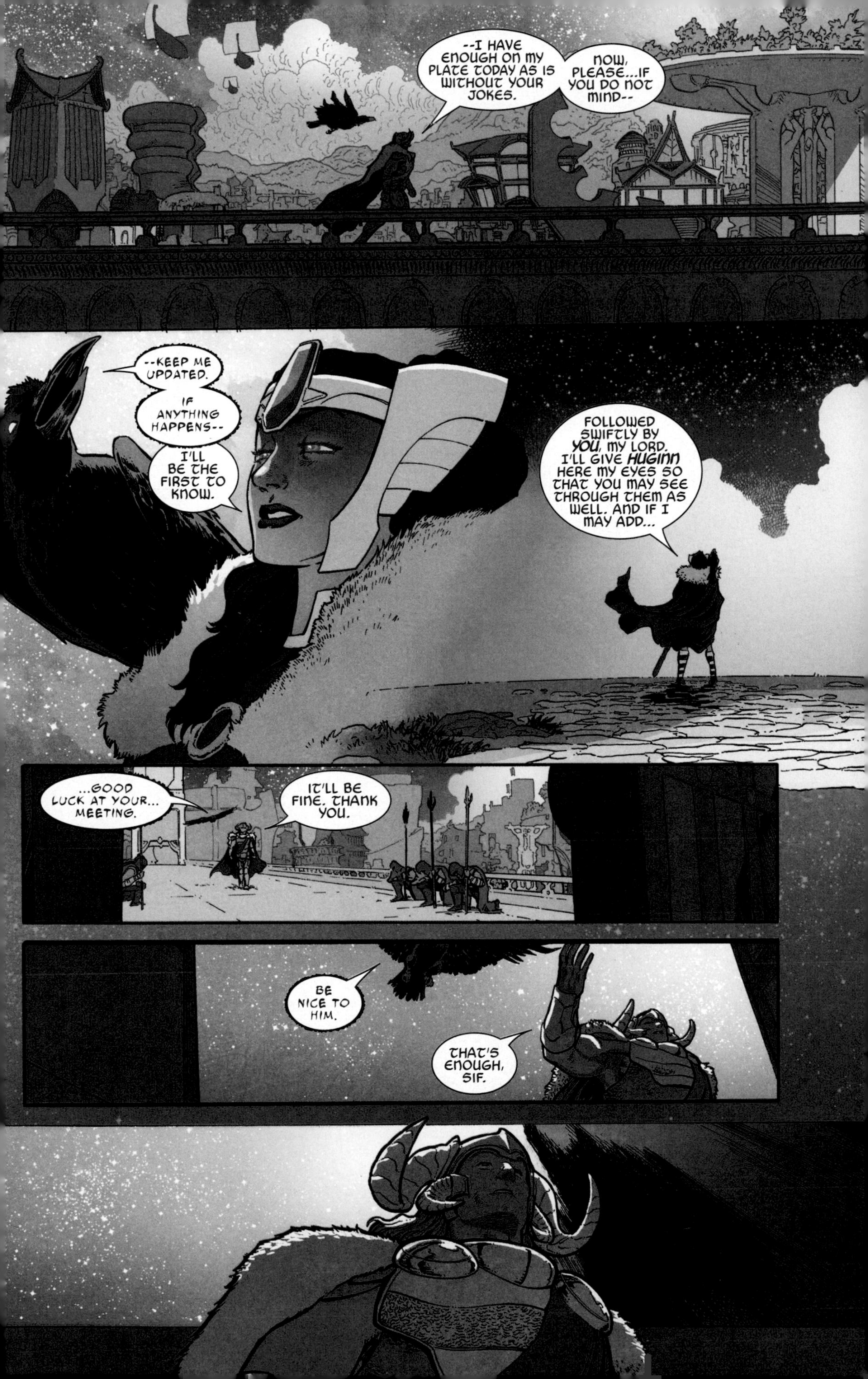
--I HAVE ENOUGH ON MY PLATE TODAY AS IS WITHOUT YOUR JOKES.
NOW, PLEASE...IF YOU DO NOT MIND--
--KEEP ME UPDATED.
IF ANYTHING HAPPENS--
I'LL BE THE FIRST TO KNOW.
FOLLOWED SWIFTLY BY YOU, MY LORD. I'LL GIVE HUGINN HERE MY EYES SO THAT YOU MAY SEE THROUGH THEM AS WELL. AND IF I MAY ADD...
...GOOD LUCK AT YOUR... MEETING.
IT'LL BE FINE. THANK YOU.
BE NICE TO HIM.
THAT'S ENOUGH, SIF.

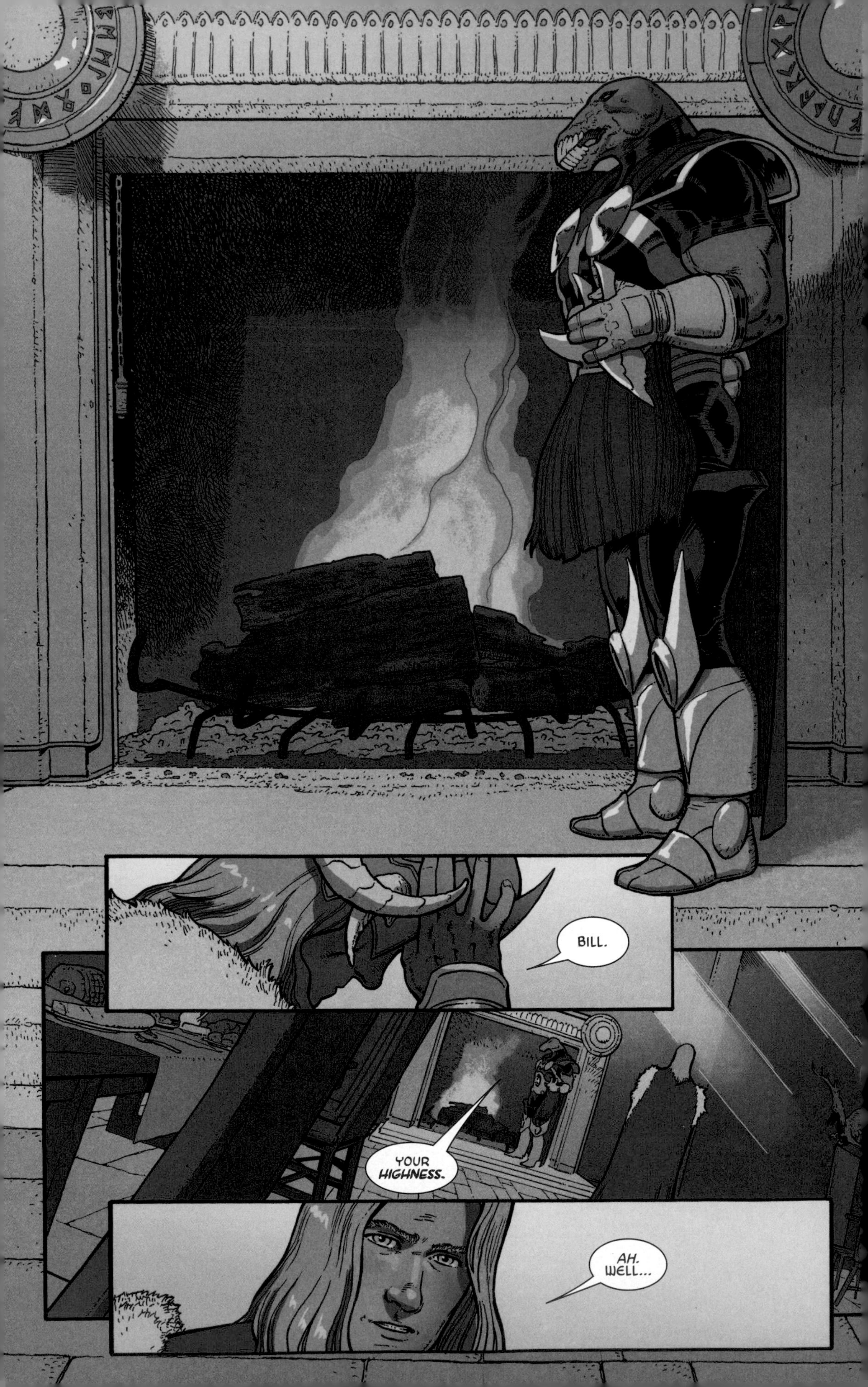
BILL.
YOUR HIGHNESS.
AH. WELL...

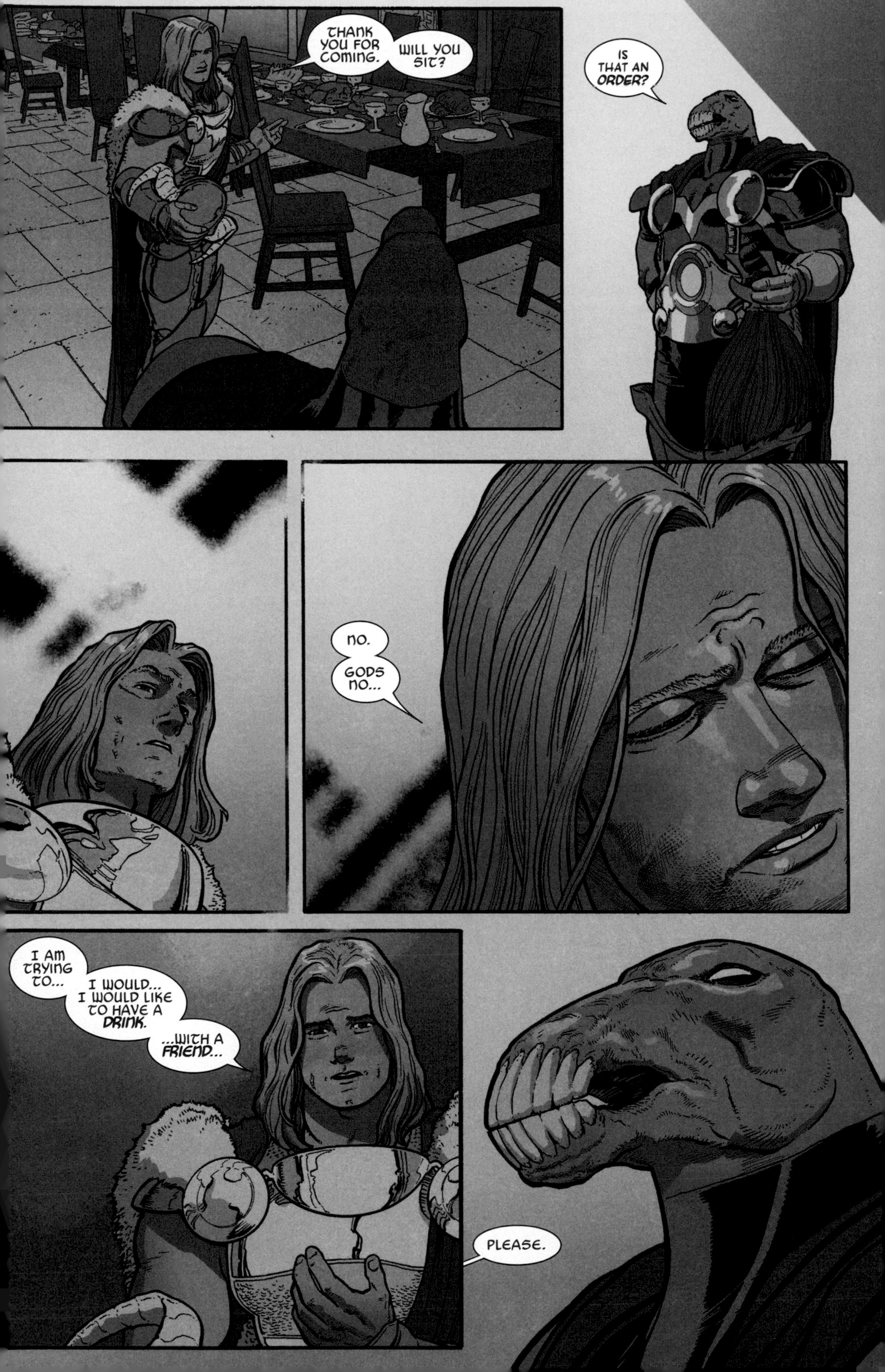

THANK YOU FOR COMING.
WILL YOU SIT?
IS THAT AN ORDER?
NO.
GODS NO...
I AM TRYING TO...
I WOULD... I WOULD LIKE TO HAVE A DRINK.
...WITH A FRIEND...
PLEASE.

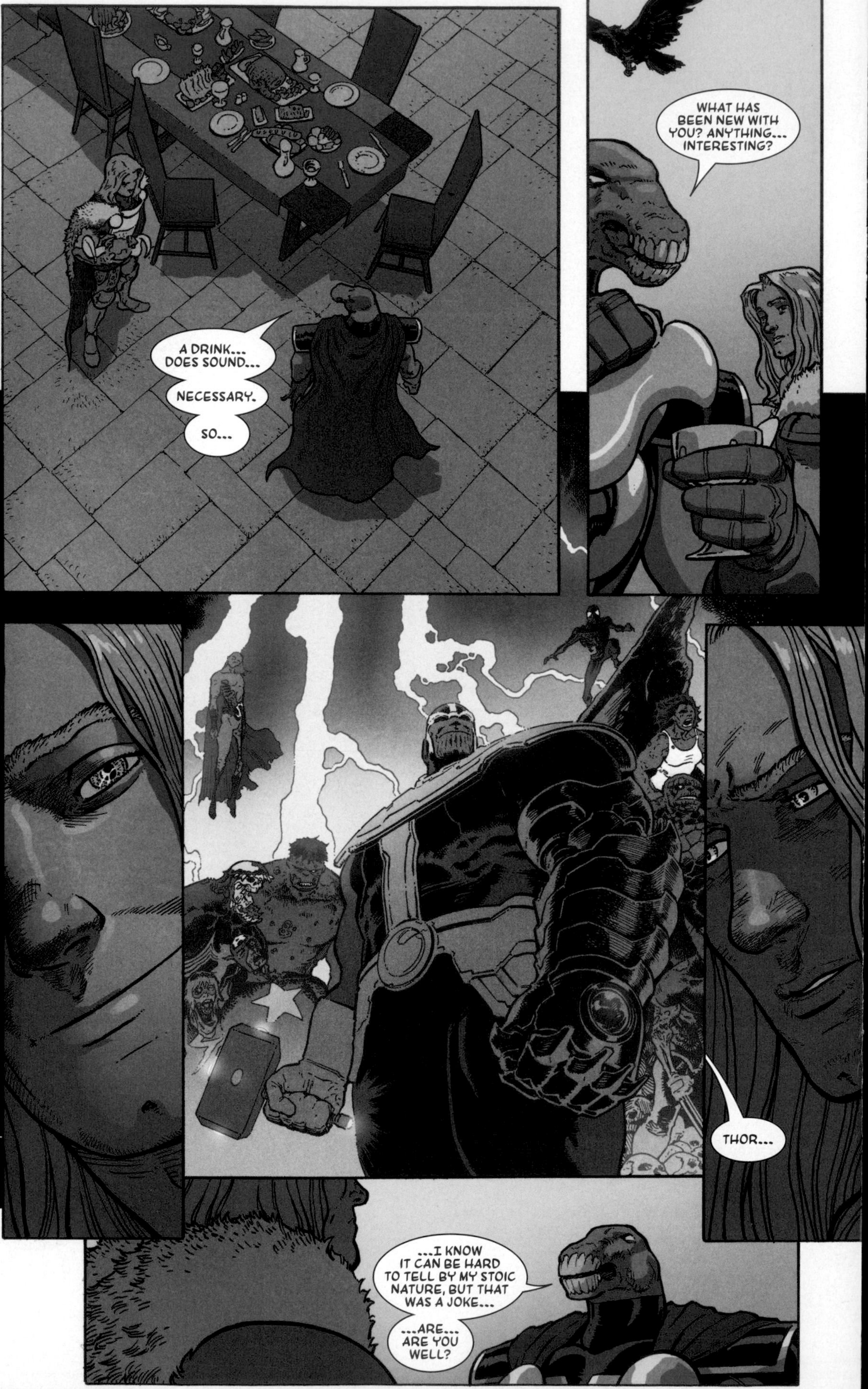
A DRINK... DOES SOUND...
NECESSARY.
SO...
WHAT HAS BEEN NEW WITH YOU? ANYTHING... INTERESTING?
THOR...
...I KNOW IT CAN BE HARD TO TELL BY MY STOIC NATURE, BUT THAT WAS A JOKE...
...ARE... ARE YOU WELL?

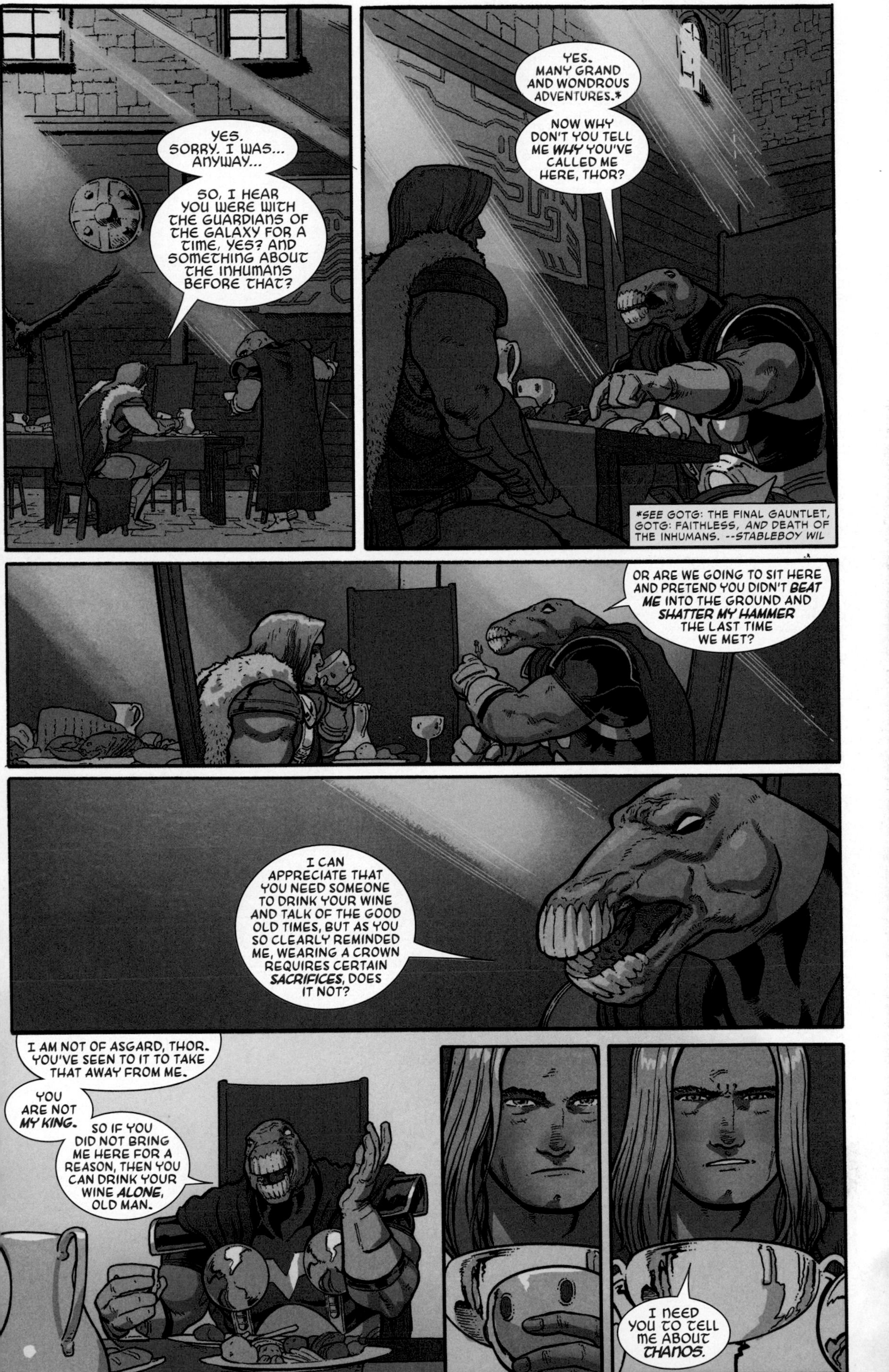
YES. SORRY. I WAS... ANYWAY...
SO, I HEAR YOU WERE WITH THE GUARDIANS OF THE GALAXY FOR A TIME, YES? AND SOMETHING ABOUT THE INHUMANS BEFORE THAT?
YES. MANY GRAND AND WONDROUS ADVENTURES.*
NOW WHY DON'T YOU TELL ME WHY YOU'VE CALLED ME HERE, THOR?
*SEE GOTG: THE FINAL GAUNTLET, GOTG: FAITHLESS, AND DEATH OF THE INHUMANS. --STABLEBOY WIL
OR ARE WE GOING TO SIT HERE AND PRETEND YOU DIDN'T BEAT ME INTO THE GROUND AND SHATTER MY HAMMER THE LAST TIME WE MET?
I CAN APPRECIATE THAT YOU NEED SOMEONE TO DRINK YOUR WINE AND TALK OF THE GOOD OLD TIMES, BUT AS YOU SO CLEARLY REMINDED ME, WEARING A CROWN REQUIRES CERTAIN SACRIFICES, DOES IT NOT?
I AM NOT OF ASGARD, THOR. YOU'VE SEEN TO IT TO TAKE THAT AWAY FROM ME.
YOU ARE NOT MY KING.
SO IF YOU DID NOT BRING ME HERE FOR A REASON, THEN YOU CAN DRINK YOUR WINE ALONE, OLD MAN.
I NEED YOU TO TELL ME ABOUT THANOS.

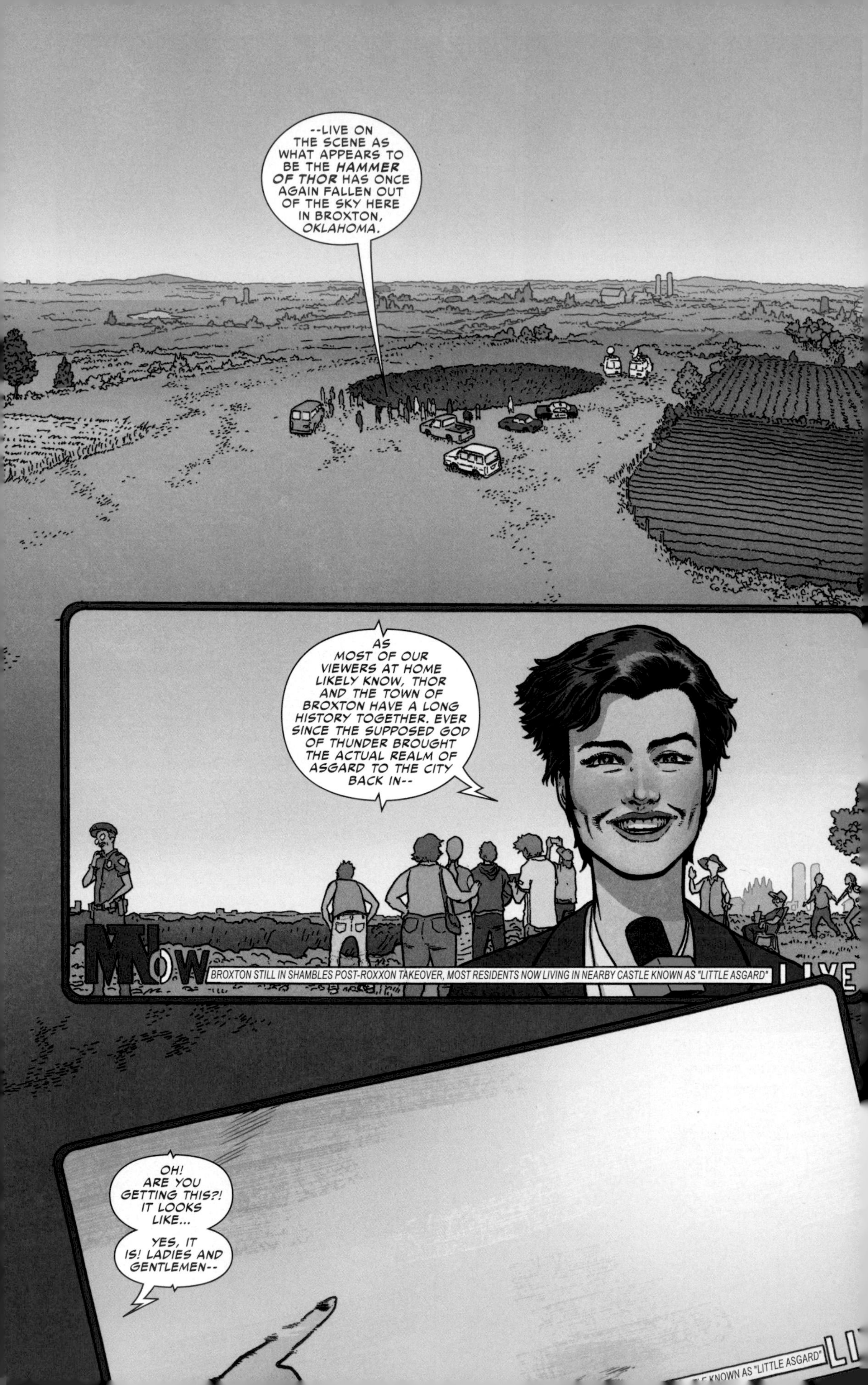
--LIVE ON THE SCENE AS WHAT APPEARS TO BE THE HAMMER OF THOR HAS ONCE AGAIN FALLEN OUT OF THE SKY HERE IN BROXTON, OKLAHOMA.
AS MOST OF OUR VIEWERS AT HOME LIKELY KNOW, THOR AND THE TOWN OF BROXTON HAVE A LONG HISTORY TOGETHER. EVER SINCE THE SUPPOSED GOD OF THUNDER BROUGHT THE ACTUAL REALM OF ASGARD TO THE CITY BACK IN--
MNOW
BROXTON STILL IN SHAMBLES POST-ROXXON TAKEOVER, MOST RESIDENTS NOW LIVING IN NEARBY CASTLE KNOWN AS "LITTLE ASGARD"
LIVE
OH! ARE YOU GETTING THIS?! IT LOOKS LIKE...
YES, IT IS! LADIES AND GENTLEMEN--
KNOWN AS "LITTLE ASGARD"

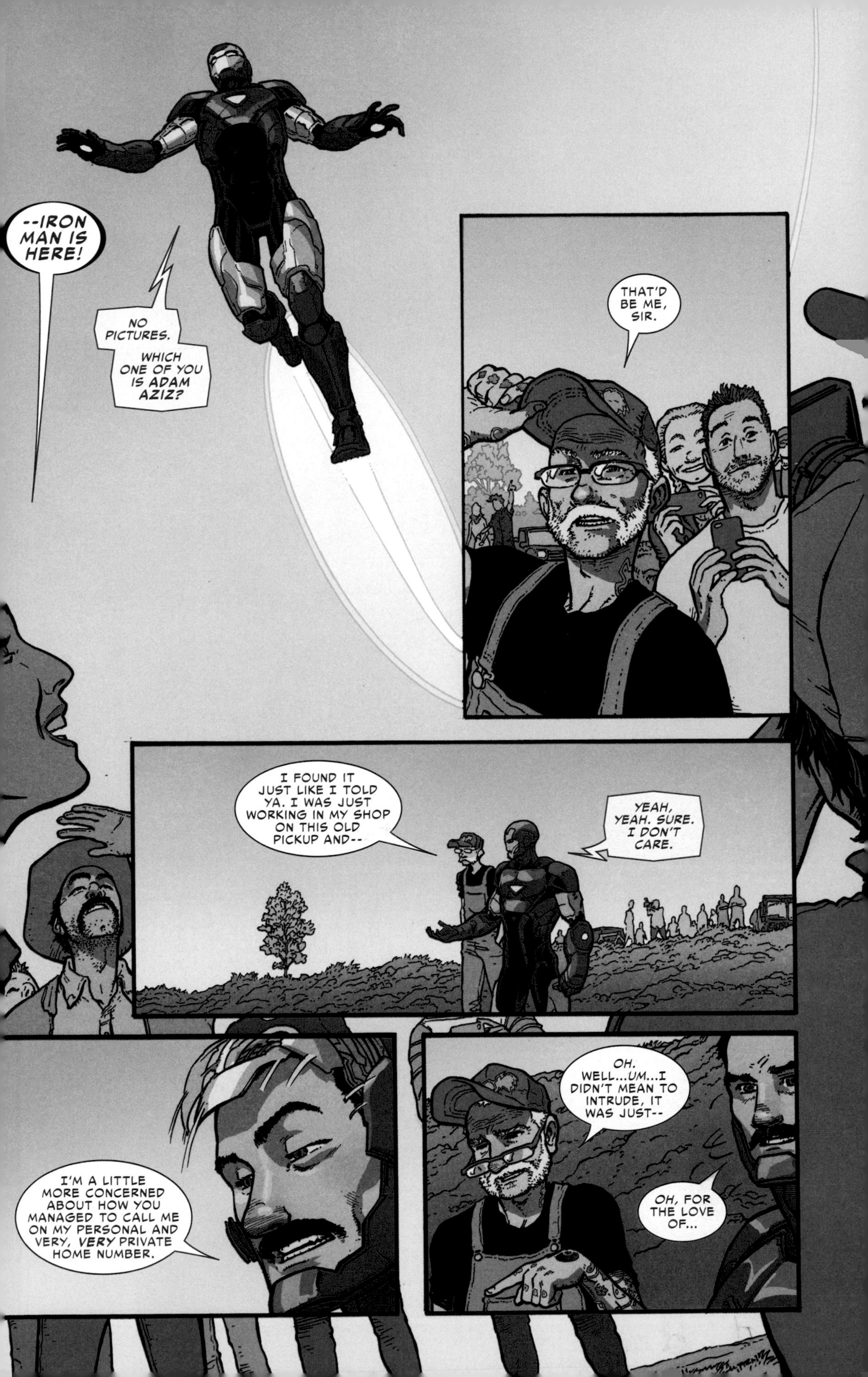
--IRON MAN IS HERE!
NO PICTURES.
WHICH ONE OF YOU IS ADAM AZIZ?
THAT'D BE ME, SIR.
I FOUND IT JUST LIKE I TOLD YA. I WAS JUST WORKING IN MY SHOP ON THIS OLD PICKUP AND--
YEAH, YEAH. SURE. I DON'T CARE.
I'M A LITTLE MORE CONCERNED ABOUT HOW YOU MANAGED TO CALL ME ON MY PERSONAL AND VERY, VERY PRIVATE HOME NUMBER.
OH. WELL...UM...I DIDN'T MEAN TO INTRUDE, IT WAS JUST--
OH, FOR THE LOVE OF...

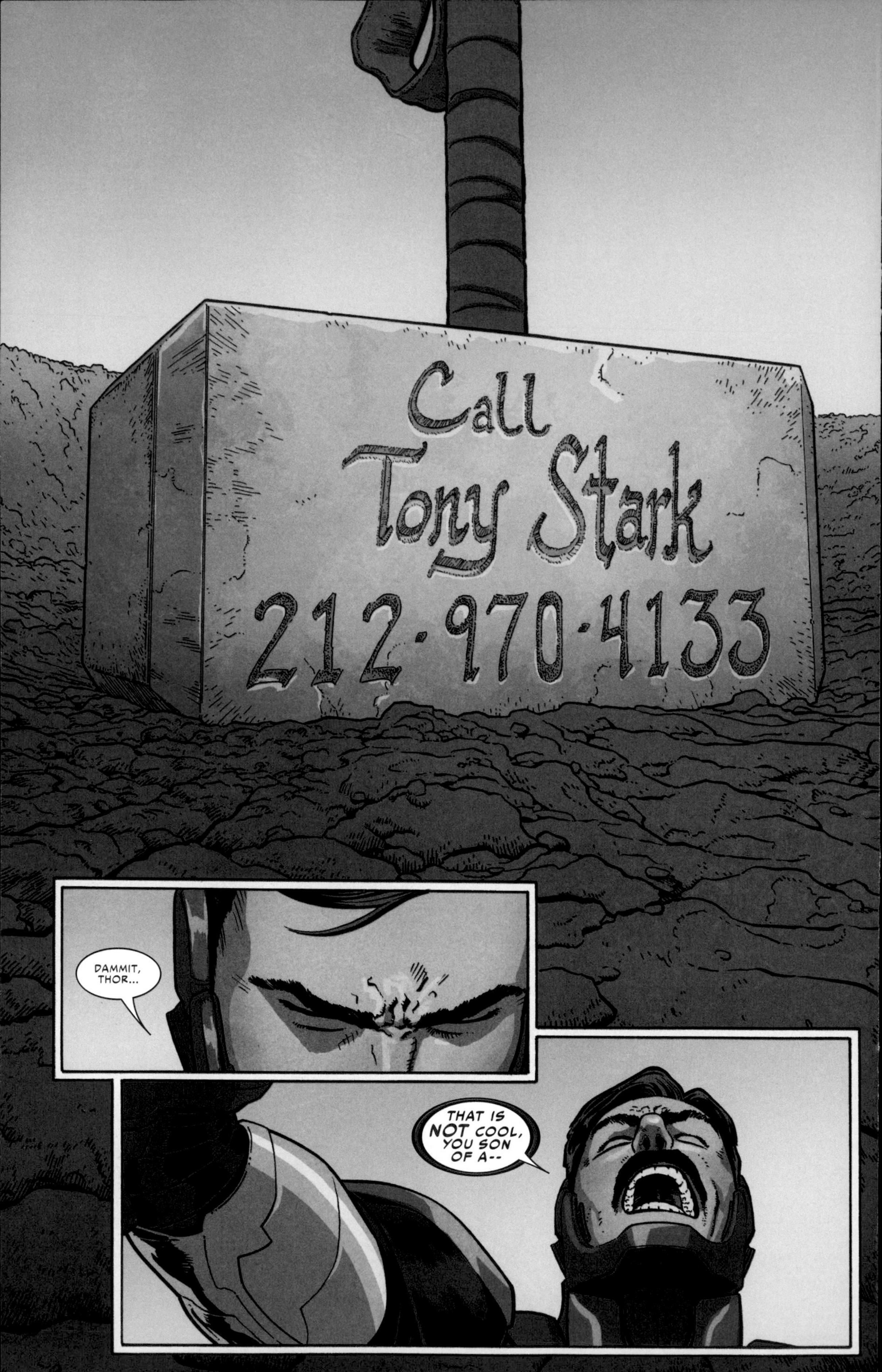
Call
Tony Stark
212-970-4133
DAMMIT, THOR...
THAT IS NOT COOL, YOU SON OF A--

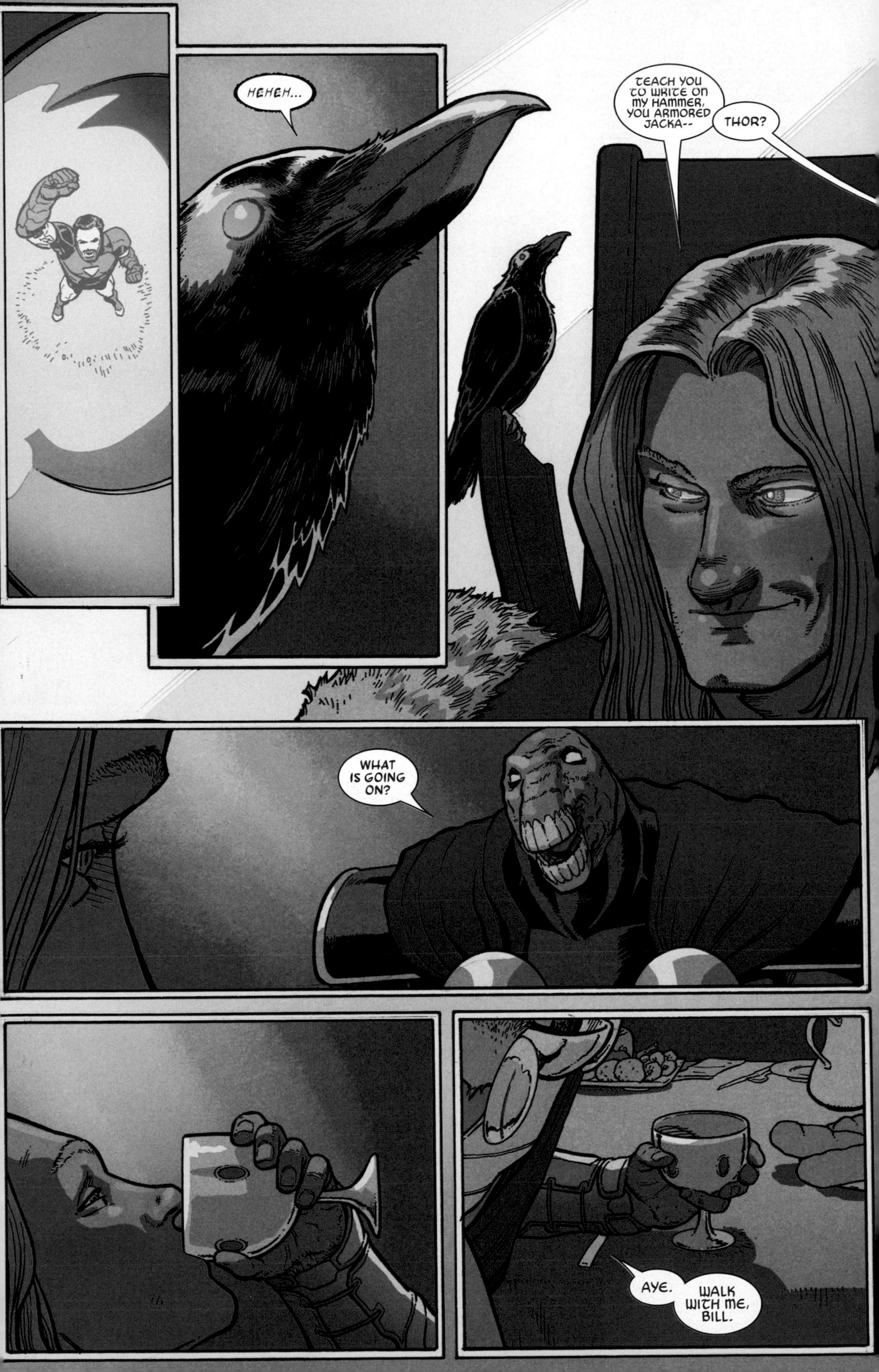
HEHEH...
TEACH YOU TO WRITE ON MY HAMMER, YOU ARMORED JACKA--
THOR?
WHAT IS GOING ON?
AYE.
WALK WITH ME, BILL.

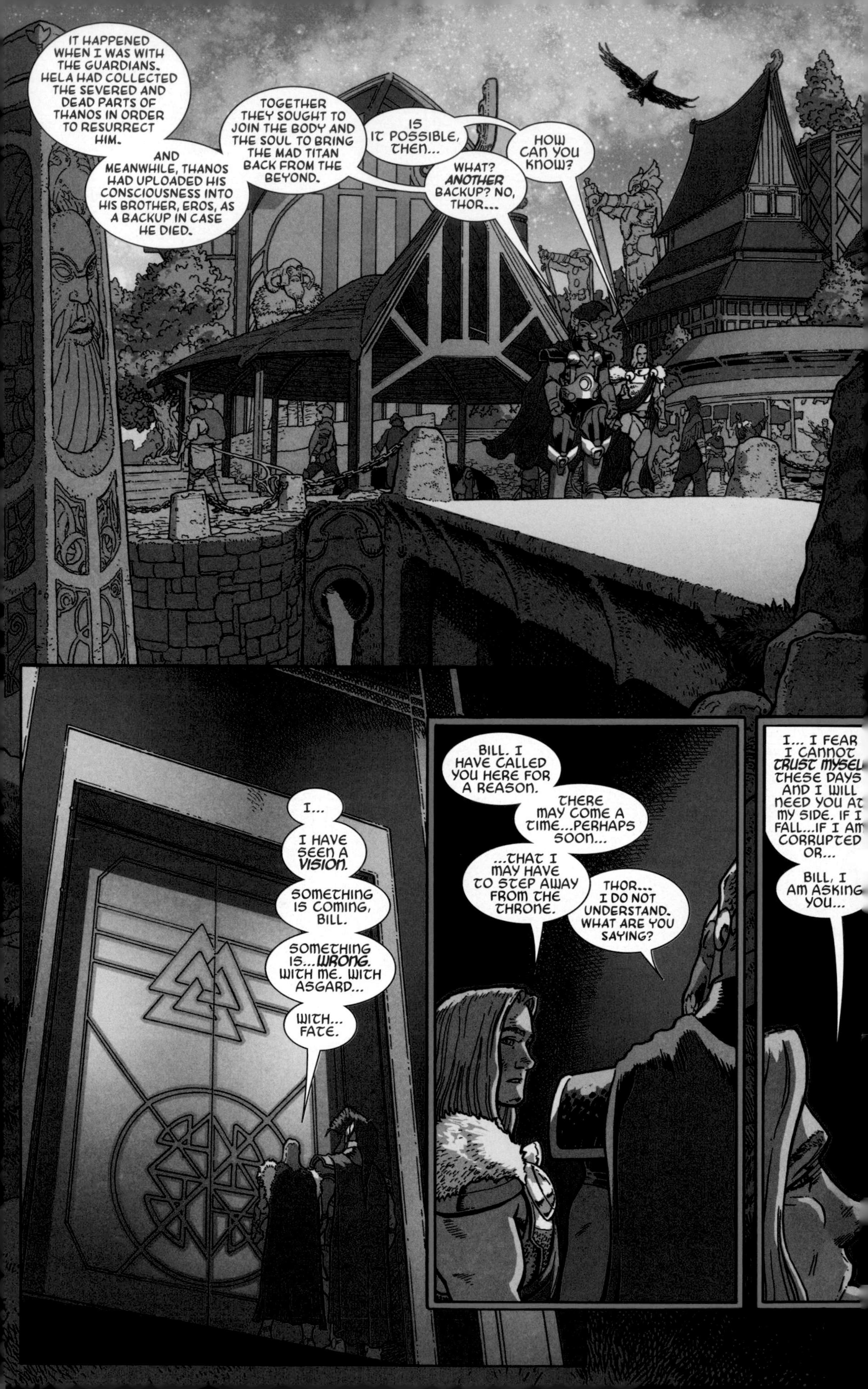

IT HAPPENED WHEN I WAS WITH THE GUARDIANS. HELA HAD COLLECTED THE SEVERED AND DEAD PARTS OF THANOS IN ORDER TO RESURRECT HIM.
AND MEANWHILE, THANOS HAD UPLOADED HIS CONSCIOUSNESS INTO HIS BROTHER, EROS, AS A BACKUP IN CASE HE DIED.
TOGETHER THEY SOUGHT TO JOIN THE BODY AND THE SOUL TO BRING THE MAD TITAN BACK FROM THE BEYOND.
IS IT POSSIBLE, THEN...
WHAT? ANOTHER BACKUP? NO, THOR...
HOW CAN YOU KNOW?
I...
I HAVE SEEN A VISION.
SOMETHING IS COMING, BILL.
SOMETHING IS...WRONG. WITH ME. WITH ASGARD...
WITH... FATE.
BILL. I HAVE CALLED YOU HERE FOR A REASON.
THERE MAY COME A TIME...PERHAPS SOON...
...THAT I MAY HAVE TO STEP AWAY FROM THE THRONE.
THOR... I DO NOT UNDERSTAND. WHAT ARE YOU SAYING?
I... I FEAR I CANNOT TRUST MYSEL THESE DAYS AND I WILL NEED YOU AT MY SIDE. IF I FALL...IF I AM CORRUPTED OR...
BILL, I AM ASKING YOU...

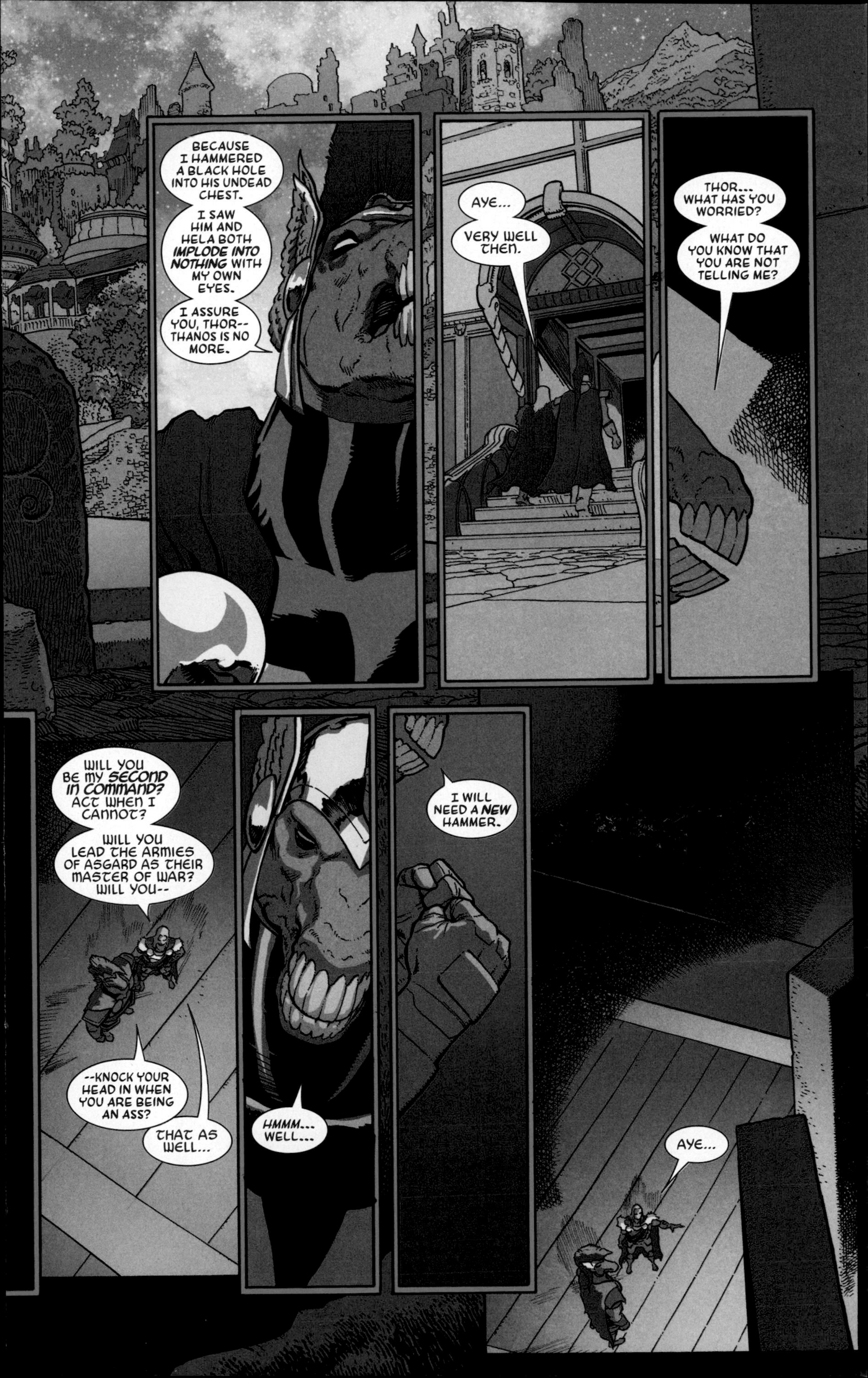
BECAUSE I HAMMERED A BLACK HOLE INTO HIS UNDEAD CHEST.
I SAW HIM AND HELA BOTH IMPLODE INTO NOTHING WITH MY OWN EYES.
I ASSURE YOU, THOR-- THANOS IS NO MORE.
AYE...
VERY WELL THEN.
THOR... WHAT HAS YOU WORRIED?
WHAT DO YOU KNOW THAT YOU ARE NOT TELLING ME?
WILL YOU BE MY SECOND IN COMMAND? ACT WHEN I CANNOT?
WILL YOU LEAD THE ARMIES OF ASGARD AS THEIR MASTER OF WAR? WILL YOU--
--KNOCK YOUR HEAD IN WHEN YOU ARE BEING AN ASS?
THAT AS WELL...
HMMM... WELL...
I WILL NEED A NEW HAMMER.
AYE...

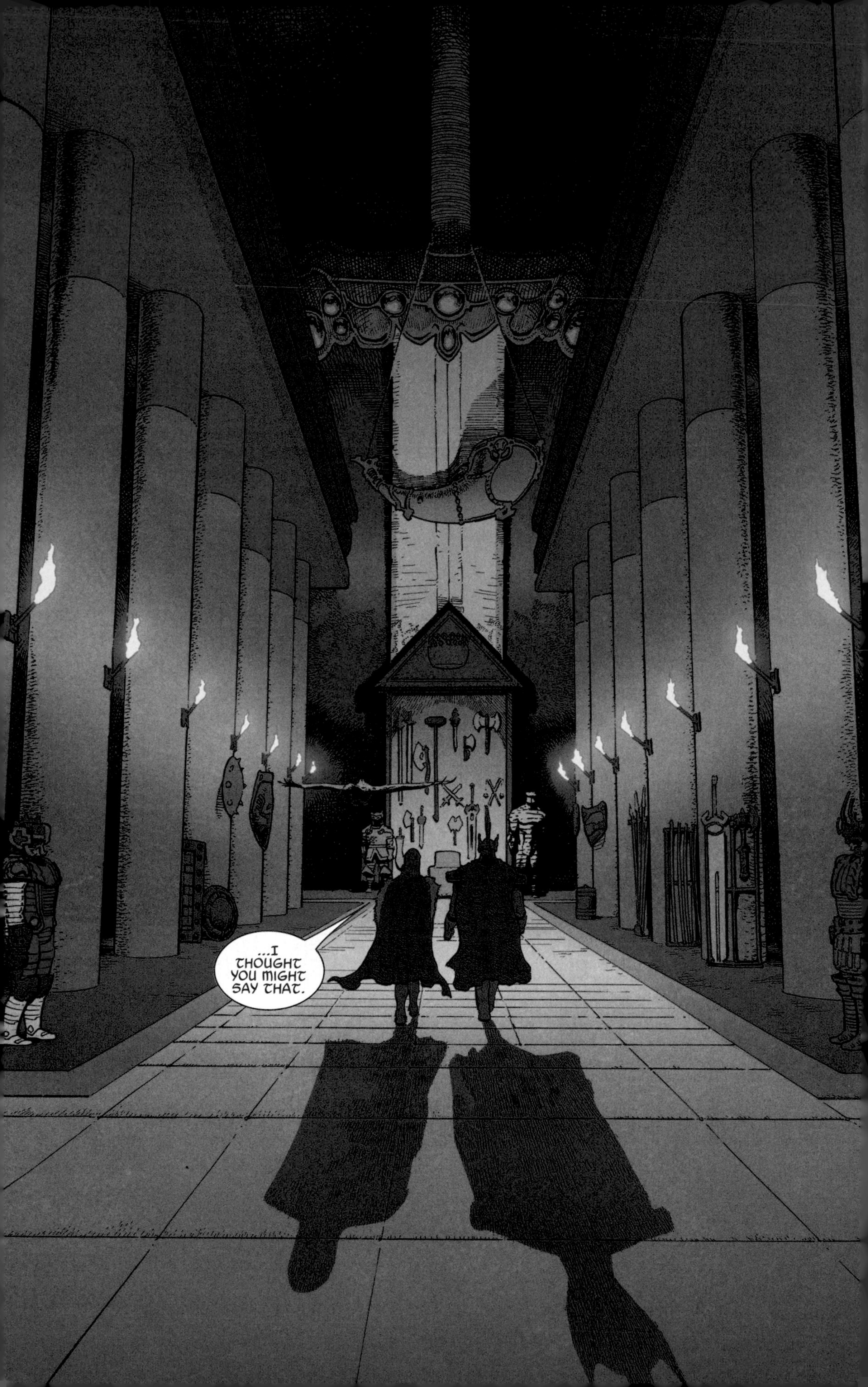
...I THOUGHT YOU MIGHT SAY THAT.

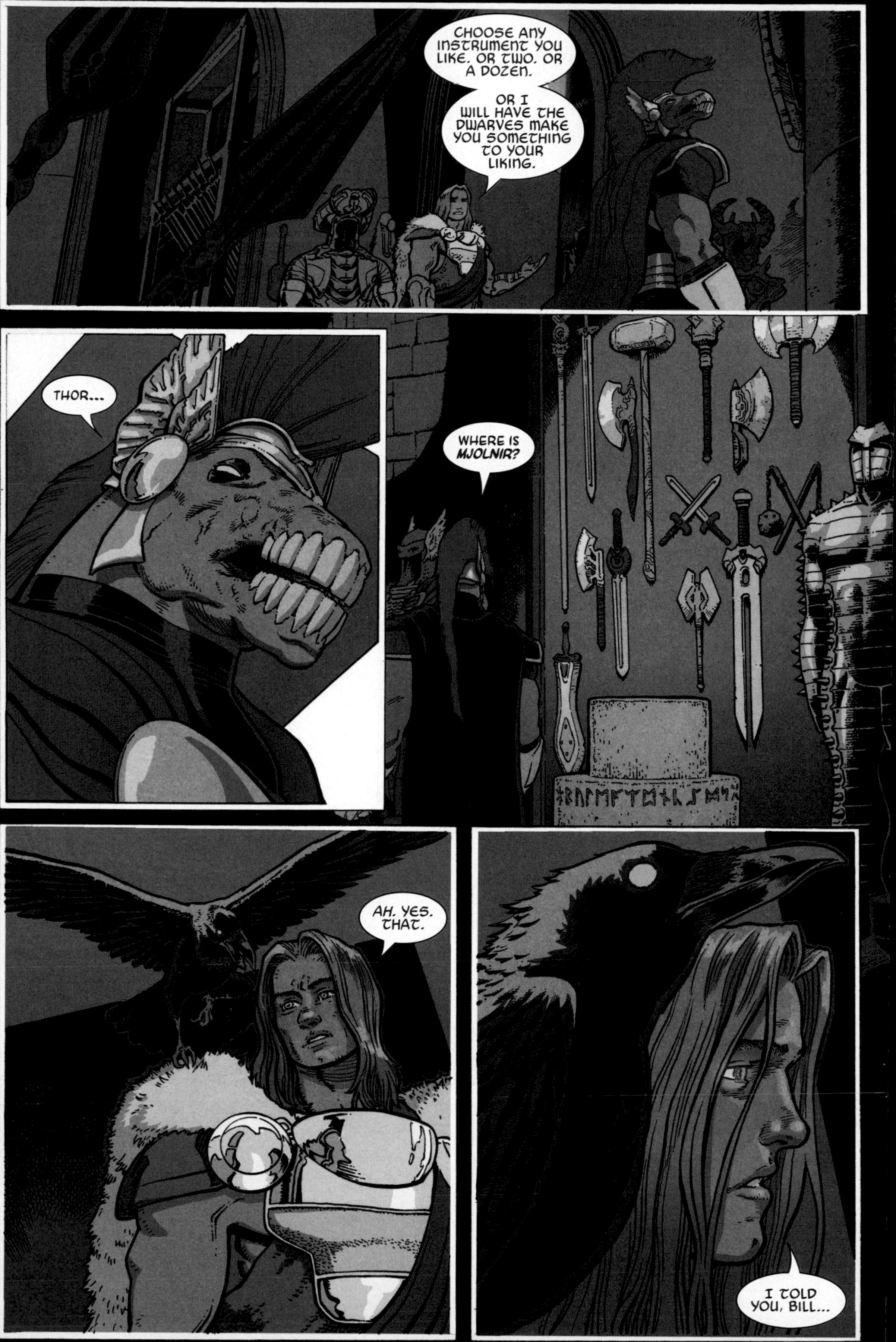
CHOOSE ANY INSTRUMENT YOU LIKE. OR TWO. OR A DOZEN.
OR I WILL HAVE THE DWARVES MAKE YOU SOMETHING TO YOUR LIKING.
THOR...
WHERE IS MJOLNIR?
AH. YES. THAT.
I TOLD YOU, BILL...

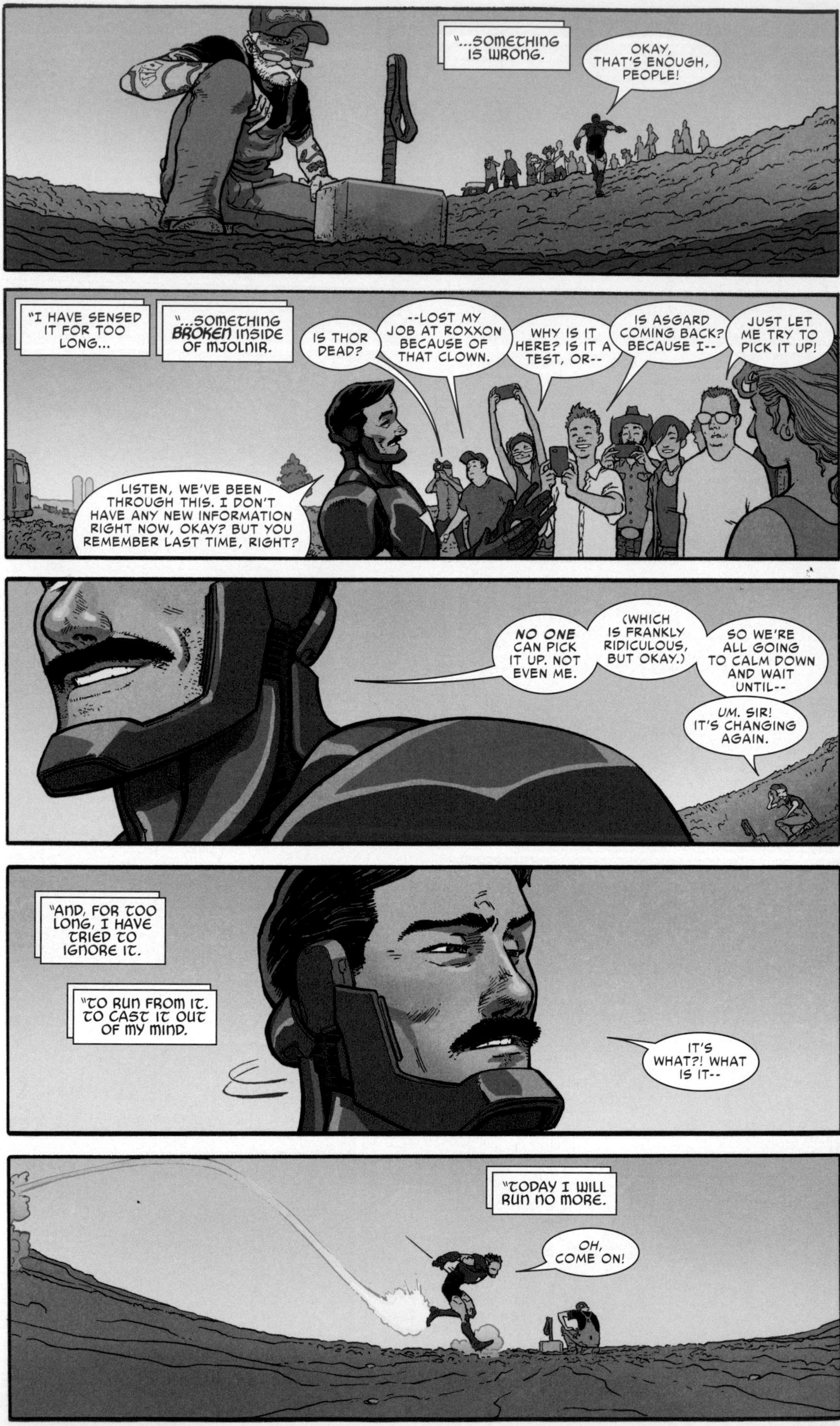
"...SOMETHING IS WRONG.
OKAY, THAT'S ENOUGH, PEOPLE!
"I HAVE SENSED IT FOR TOO LONG...
"...SOMETHING BROKEN INSIDE OF MJOLNIR.
IS THOR DEAD?
--LOST MY JOB AT ROXXON BECAUSE OF THAT CLOWN.
WHY IS IT HERE? IS IT A TEST, OR--
IS ASGARD COMING BACK? BECAUSE I--
JUST LET ME TRY TO PICK IT UP!
LISTEN, WE'VE BEEN THROUGH THIS. I DON'T HAVE ANY NEW INFORMATION RIGHT NOW, OKAY? BUT YOU REMEMBER LAST TIME, RIGHT?
NO ONE CAN PICK IT UP. NOT EVEN ME.
(WHICH IS FRANKLY RIDICULOUS, BUT OKAY.)
SO WE'RE ALL GOING TO CALM DOWN AND WAIT UNTIL--
UM. SIR! IT'S CHANGING AGAIN.
"AND, FOR TOO LONG, I HAVE TRIED TO IGNORE IT.
"TO RUN FROM IT. TO CAST IT OUT OF MY MIND.
IT'S WHAT?! WHAT IS IT--
"TODAY I WILL RUN NO MORE.
OH, COME ON!

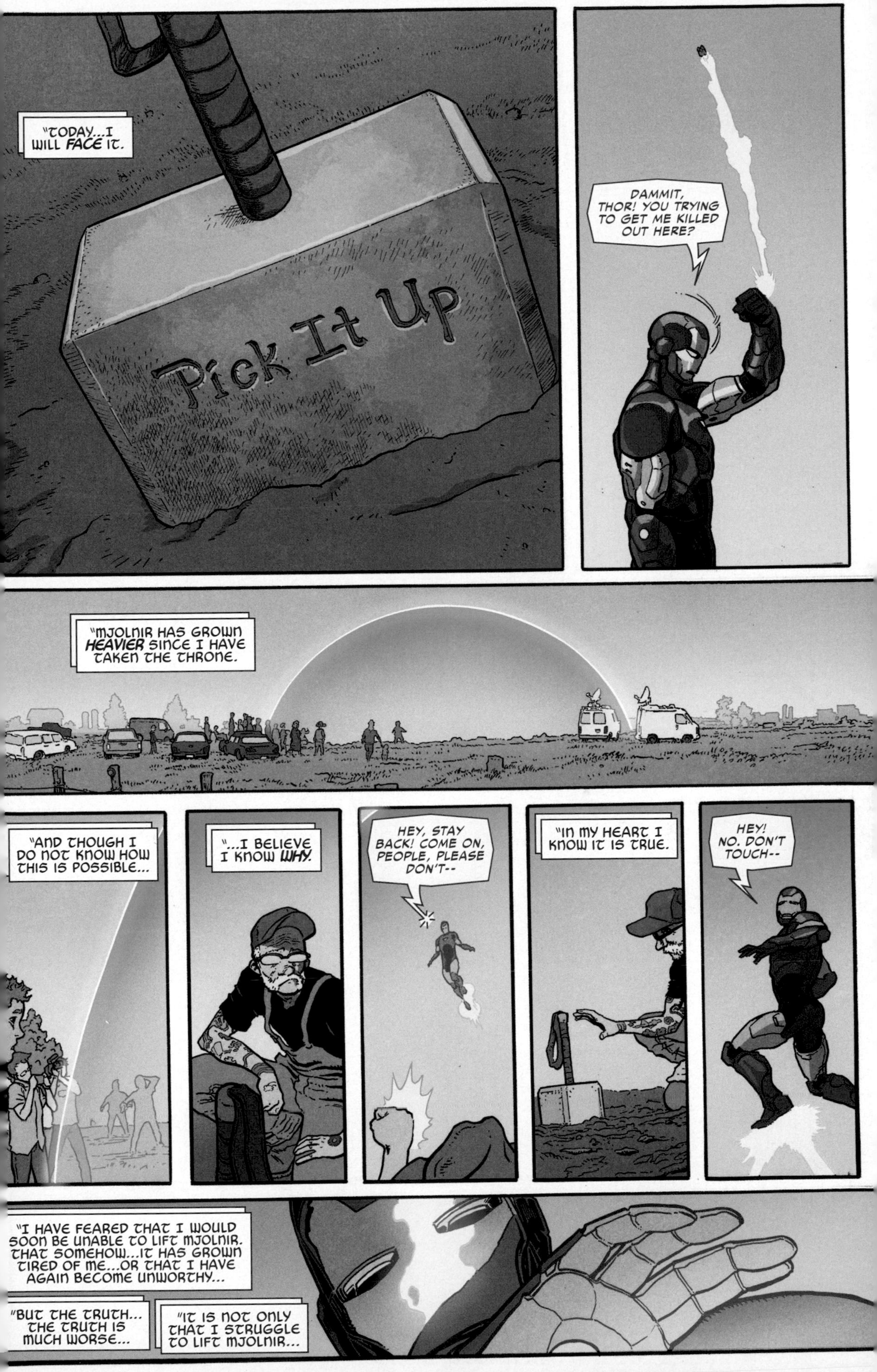
"TODAY...I WILL FACE IT.
Pick It Up
DAMMIT, THOR! YOU TRYING TO GET ME KILLED OUT HERE?
"MJOLNIR HAS GROWN HEAVIER SINCE I HAVE TAKEN THE THRONE.
"AND THOUGH I DO NOT KNOW HOW THIS IS POSSIBLE...
"...I BELIEVE I KNOW WHY.
HEY, STAY BACK! COME ON, PEOPLE, PLEASE DON'T--
"IN MY HEART I KNOW IT IS TRUE.
HEY! NO. DON'T TOUCH--
"I HAVE FEARED THAT I WOULD SOON BE UNABLE TO LIFT MJOLNIR. THAT SOMEHOW...IT HAS GROWN TIRED OF ME...OR THAT I HAVE AGAIN BECOME UNWORTHY...
"BUT THE TRUTH... THE TRUTH IS MUCH WORSE...
"IT IS NOT ONLY THAT I STRUGGLE TO LIFT MJOLNIR...

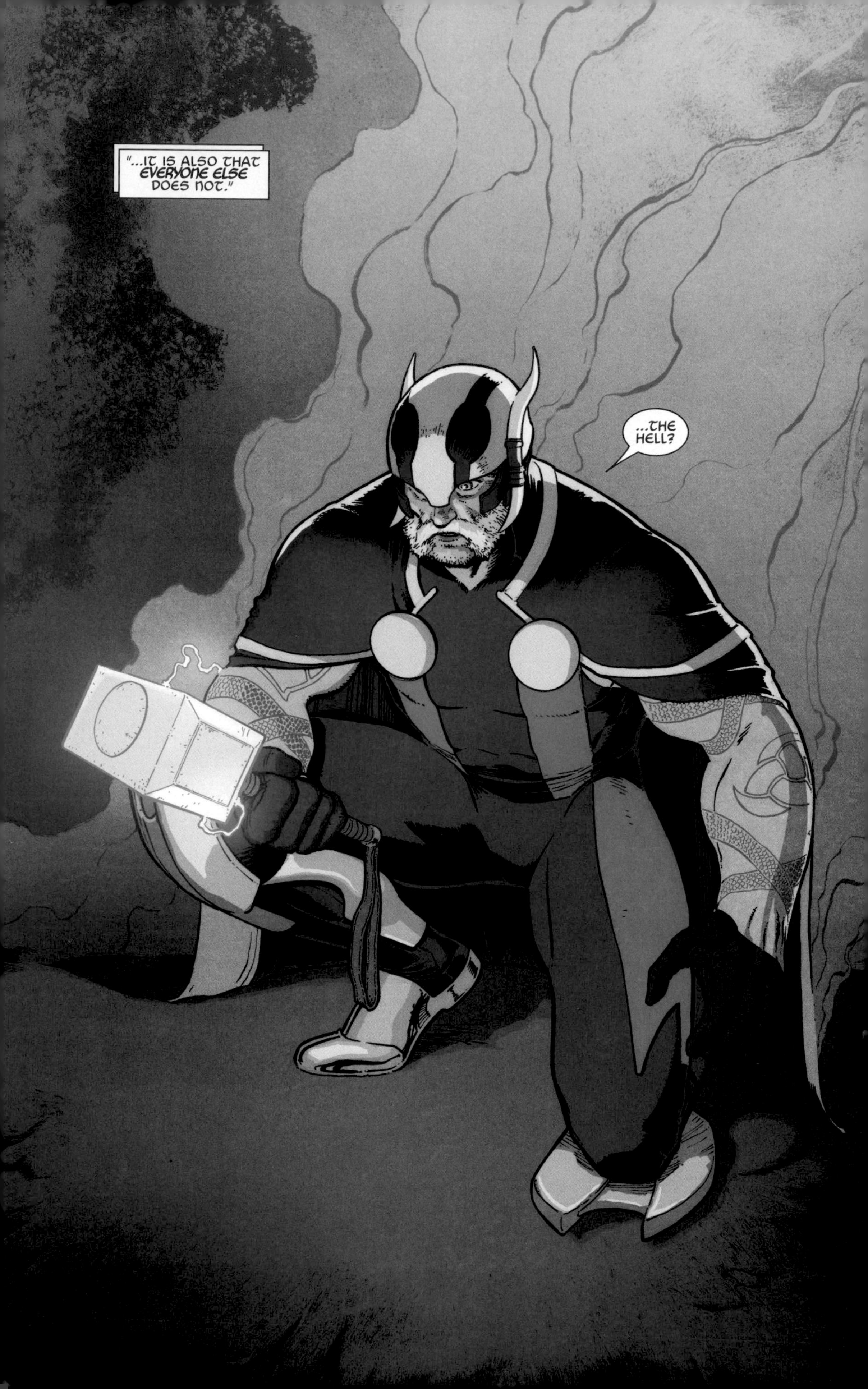
"...IT IS ALSO THAT EVERYONE ELSE DOES NOT."
...THE HELL?

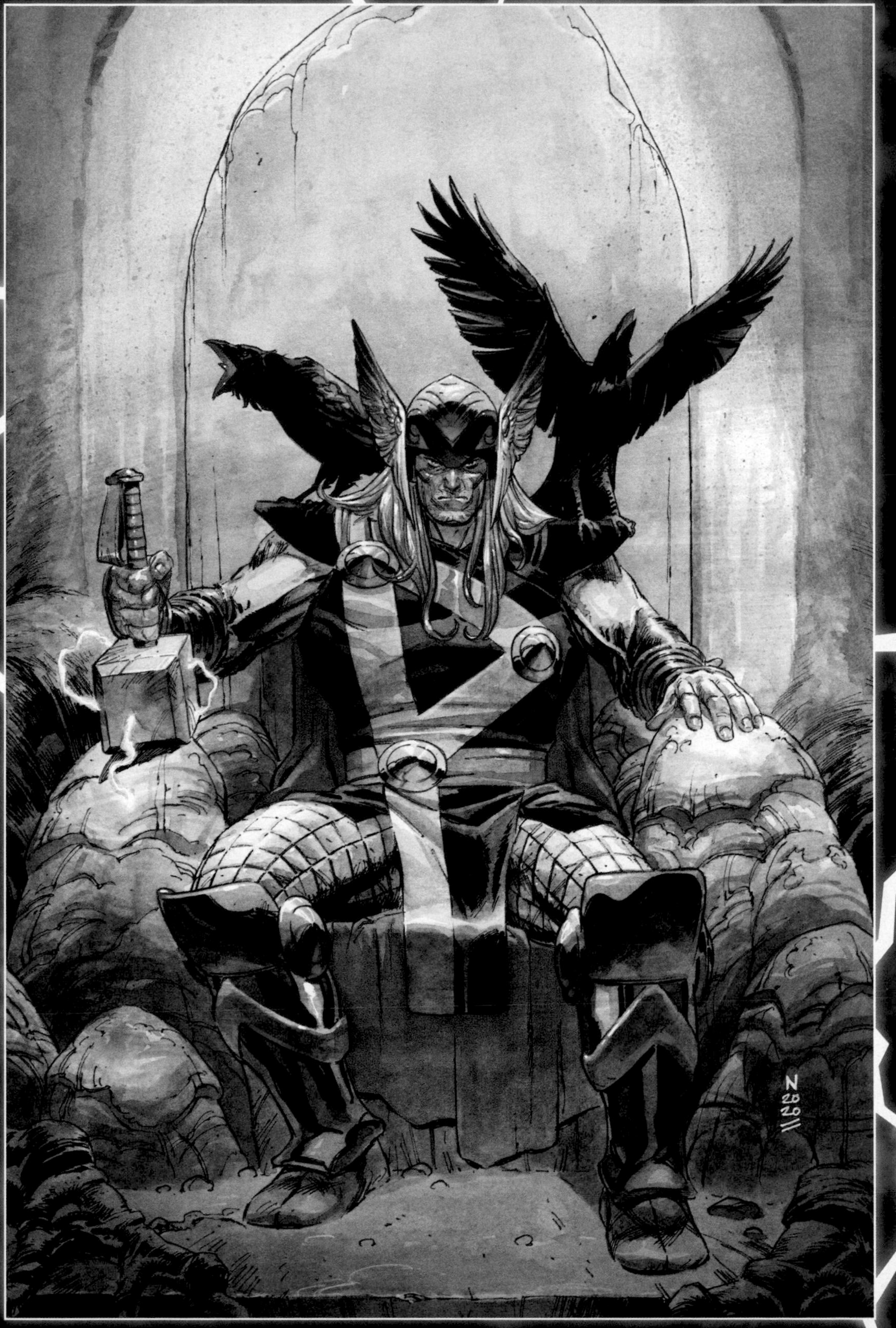

THOR 7 VARIANT BY

Nic Klein

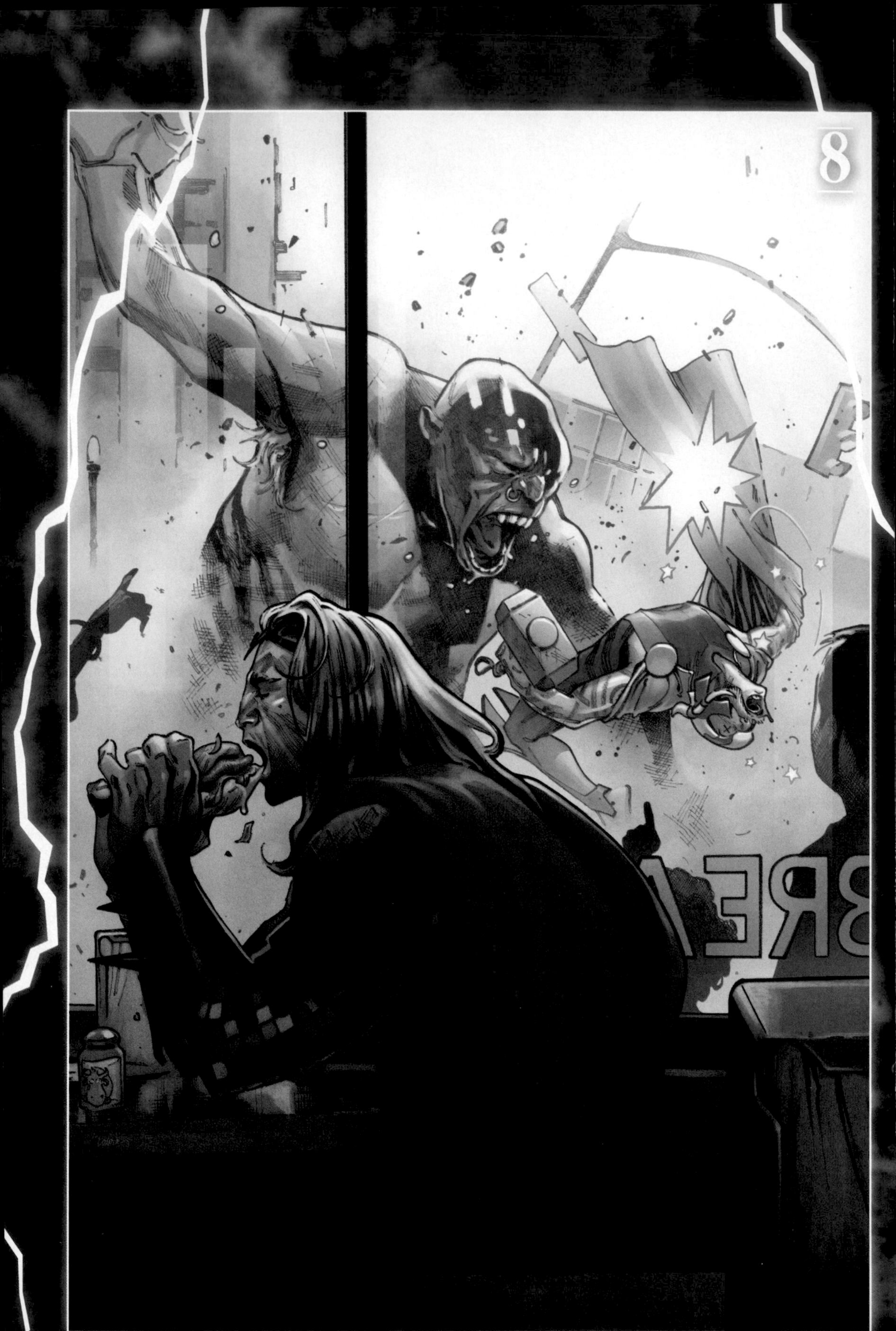
8

"Hammerfall" PART TWO

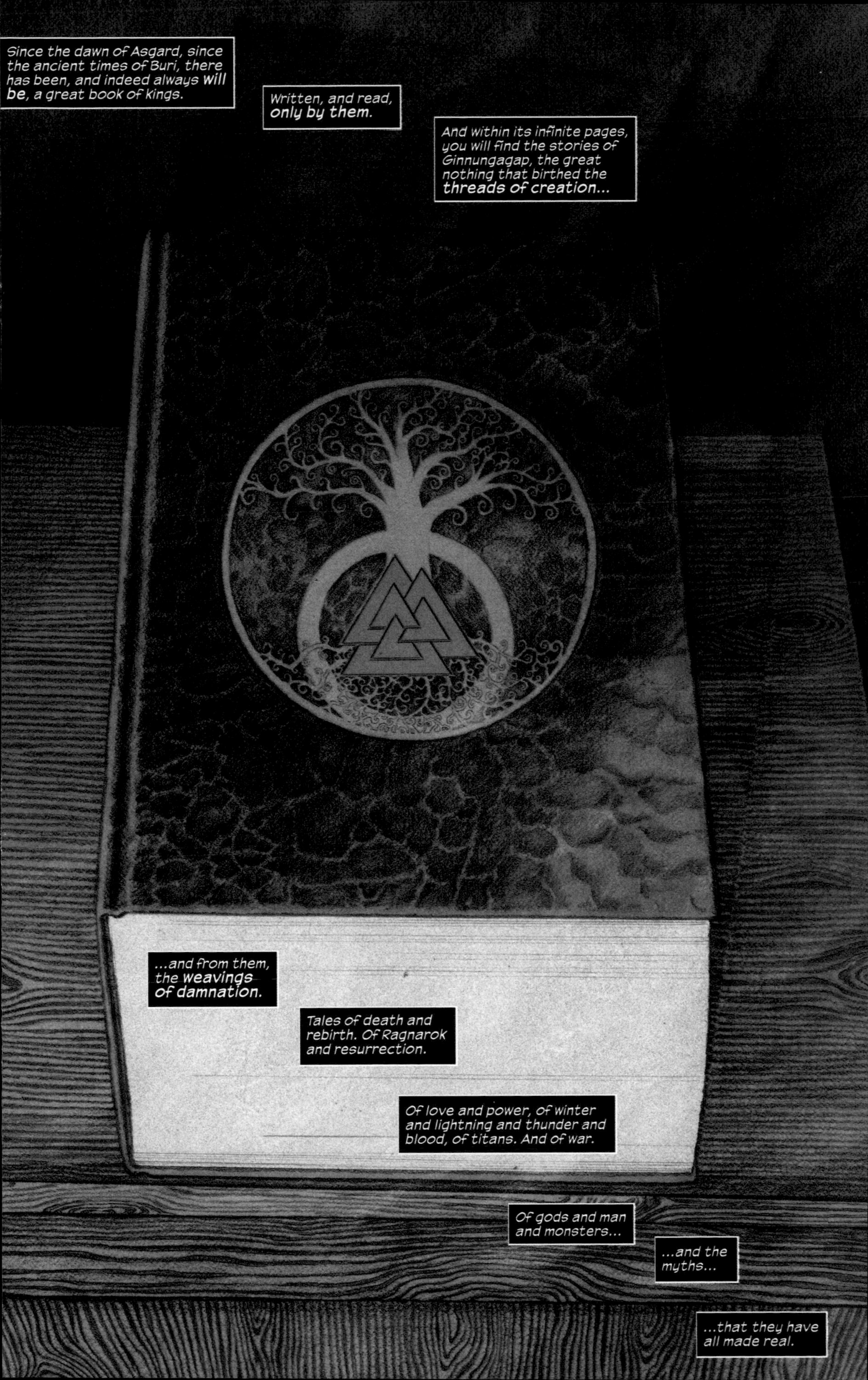
Since the dawn of Asgard, since the ancient times of Buri, there has been, and indeed always will be, a great book of kings.
Written, and read, only by them.
And within its infinite pages, you will find the stories of Ginnungagap, the great nothing that birthed the threads of creation...
...and from them, the weavings of damnation.
Tales of death and rebirth. Of Ragnarok and resurrection.
Of love and power, of winter and lightning and thunder and blood, of titans. And of war.
Of gods and man and monsters...
...and the myths...
...that they have all made real.

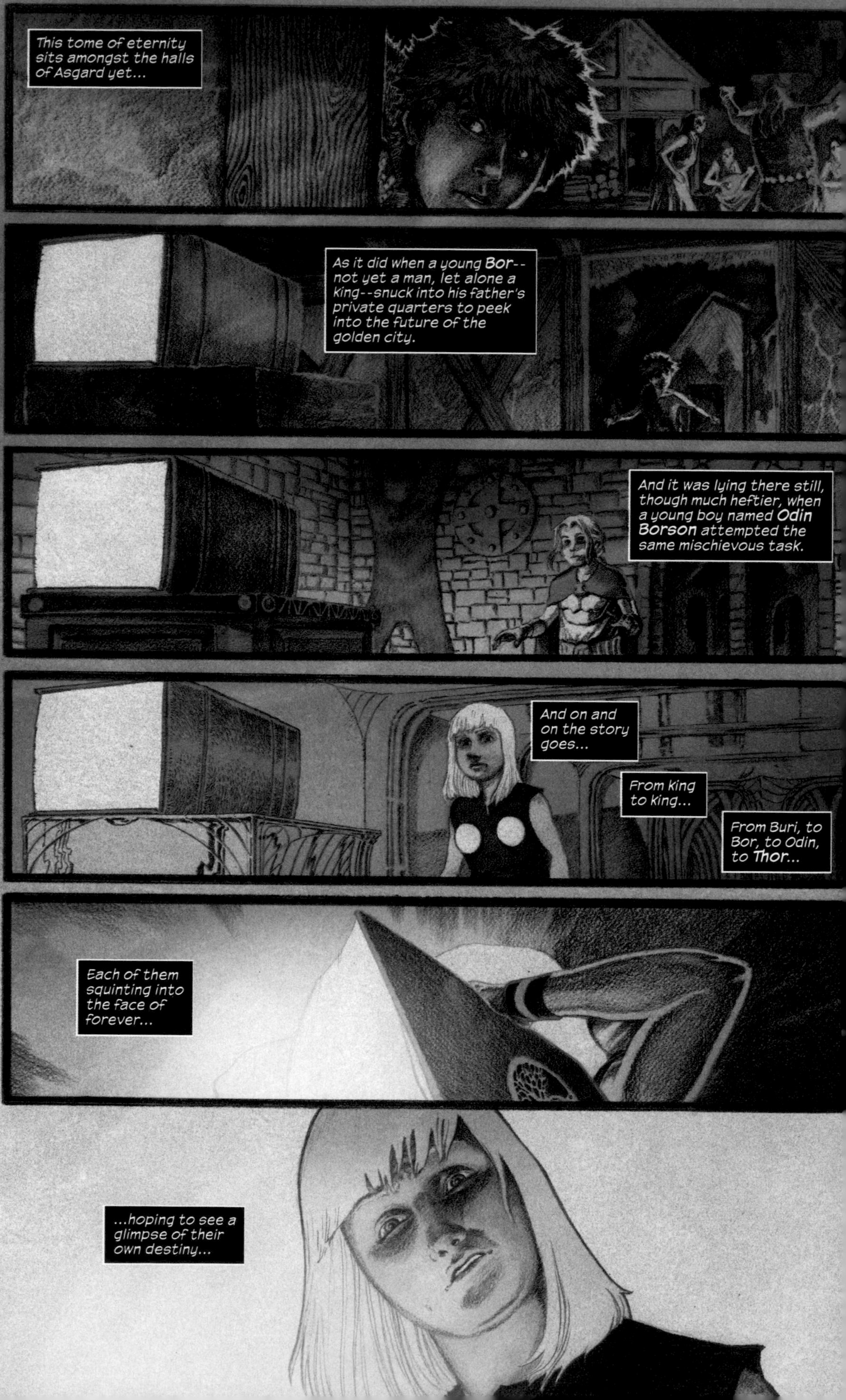
This tome of eternity sits amongst the halls of Asgard yet...
As it did when a young Bor--not yet a man, let alone a king--snuck into his father's private quarters to peek into the future of the golden city.
And it was lying there still, though much heftier, when a young boy named Odin Borson attempted the same mischievous task.
And on and on the story goes...
From king to king...
From Buri, to Bor, to Odin, to Thor...
Each of them squinting into the face of forever...
...hoping to see a glimpse of their own destiny...

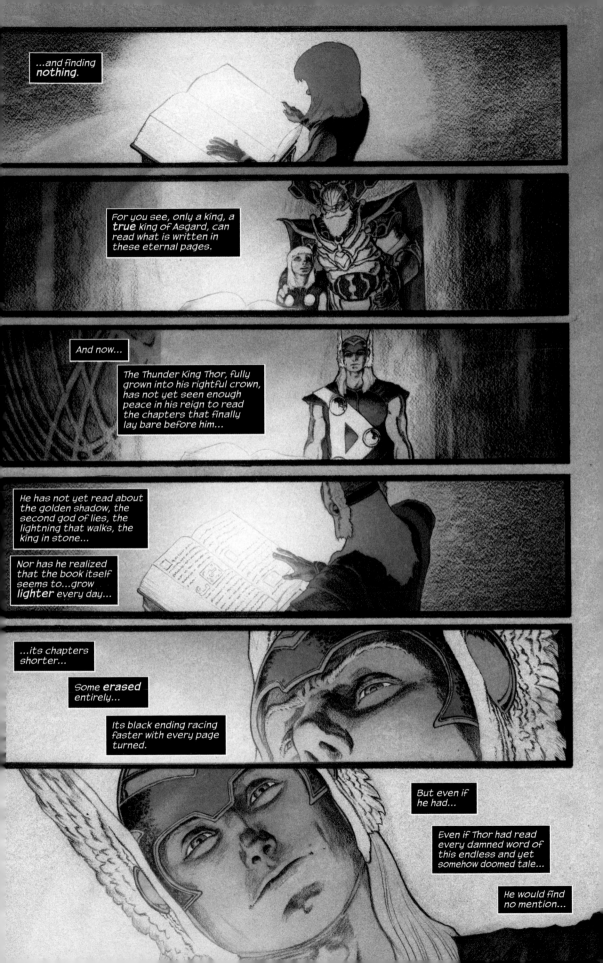

...and finding **nothing.**

For you see, only a king, a **true** king of Asgard, can read what is written in these eternal pages.

And now...

The Thunder King Thor, fully grown into his rightful crown, has not yet seen enough peace in his reign to read the chapters that finally lay bare before him...

He has not yet read about the golden shadow, the second god of lies, the lightning that walks, the king in stone...

Nor has he realized that the book itself seems to...grow **lighter** every day...

...its chapters shorter...

Some **erased** entirely...

Its black ending racing faster with every page turned.

But even if he had...

Even if Thor had read every damned word of this endless and yet somehow doomed tale...

He would find no mention...

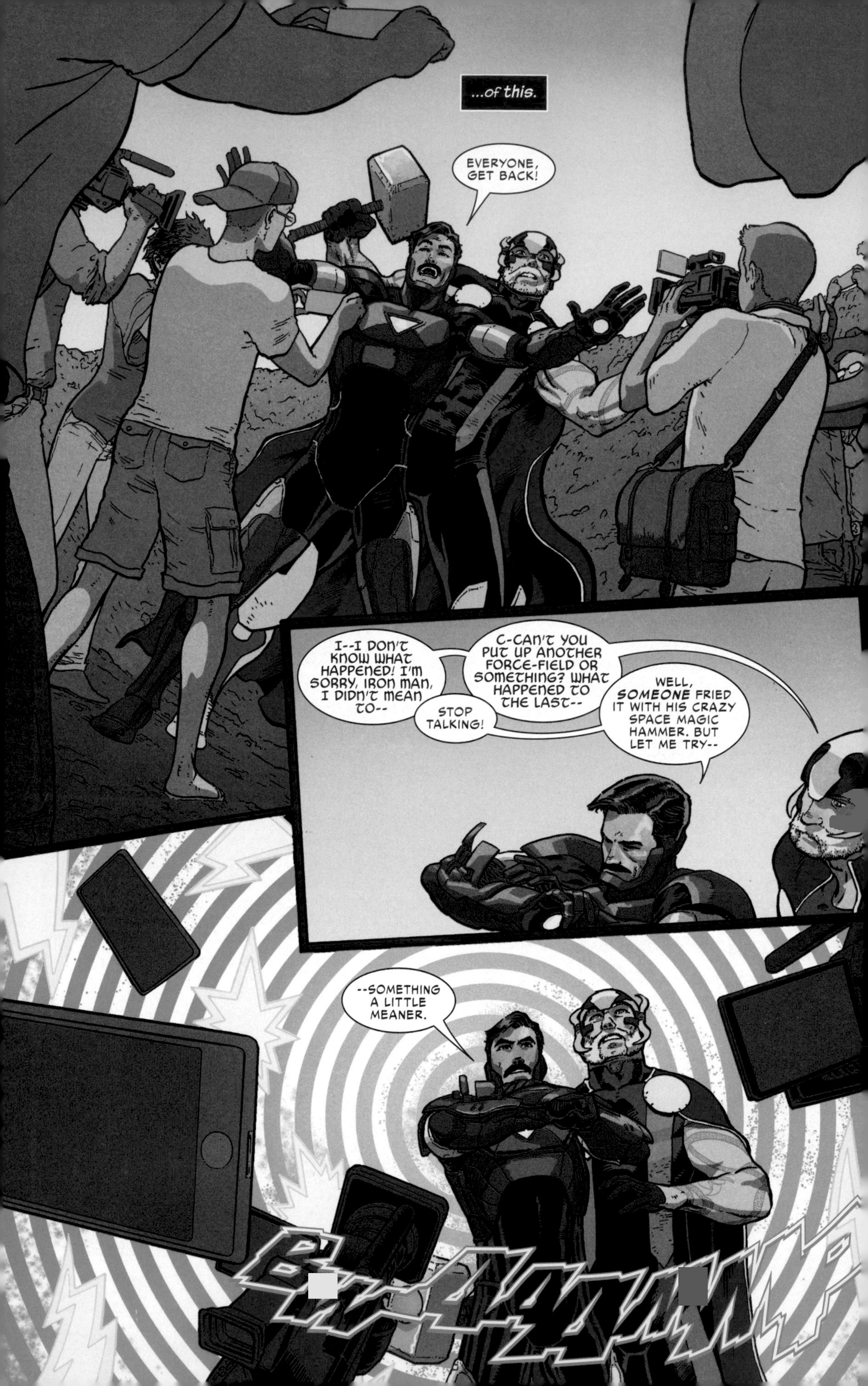
...of this.
EVERYONE, GET BACK!
I--I DON'T KNOW WHAT HAPPENED! I'M SORRY, IRON MAN, I DIDN'T MEAN TO--
C-CAN'T YOU PUT UP ANOTHER FORCE-FIELD OR SOMETHING? WHAT HAPPENED TO THE LAST--
STOP TALKING!
WELL, SOMEONE FRIED IT WITH HIS CRAZY SPACE MAGIC HAMMER. BUT LET ME TRY--
--SOMETHING A LITTLE MEANER.

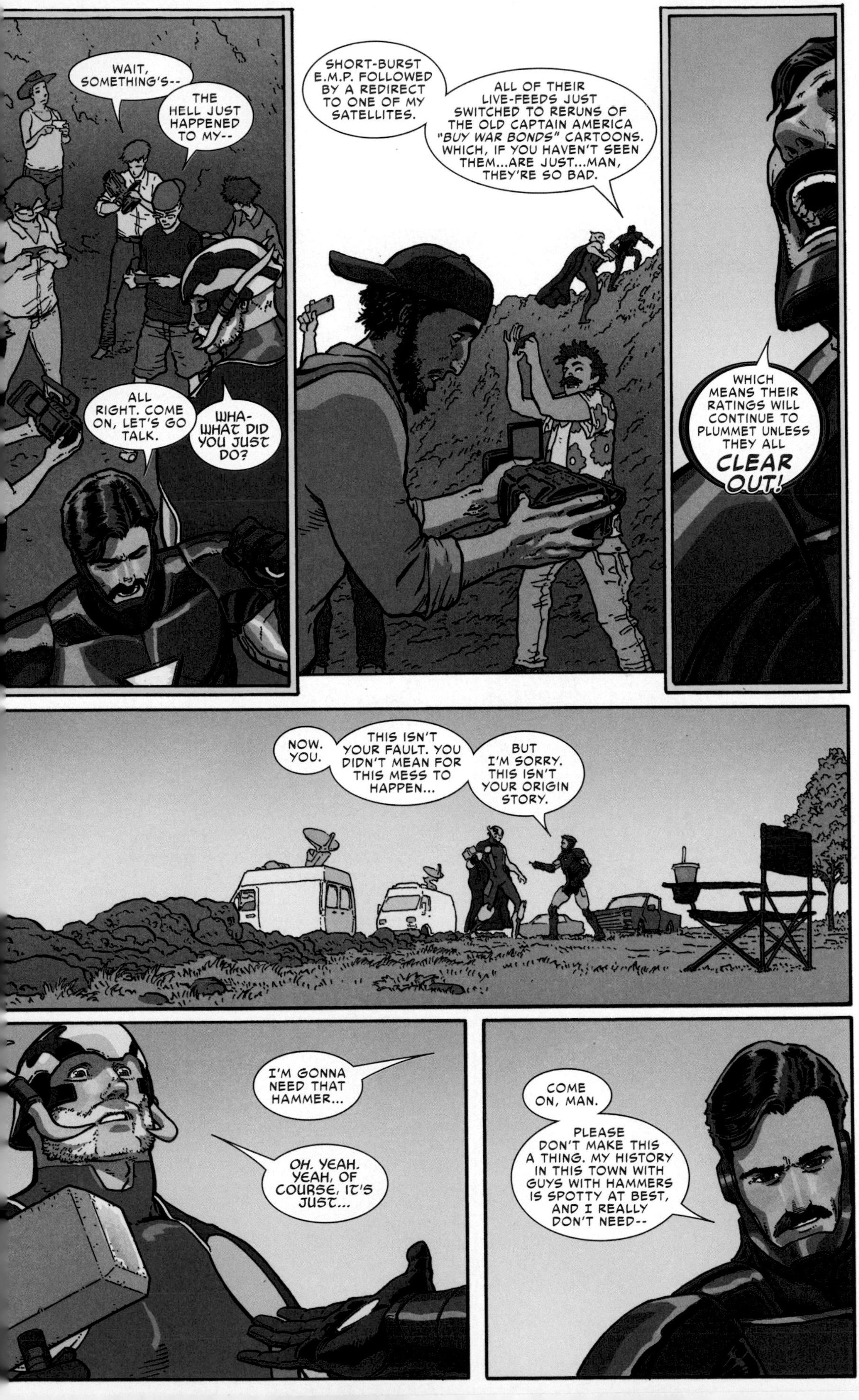

WAIT, SOMETHING'S--
THE HELL JUST HAPPENED TO MY--
ALL RIGHT. COME ON, LET'S GO TALK.
WHA-WHAT DID YOU JUST DO?
SHORT-BURST E.M.P. FOLLOWED BY A REDIRECT TO ONE OF MY SATELLITES.
ALL OF THEIR LIVE-FEEDS JUST SWITCHED TO RERUNS OF THE OLD CAPTAIN AMERICA "BUY WAR BONDS" CARTOONS. WHICH, IF YOU HAVEN'T SEEN THEM...ARE JUST...MAN, THEY'RE SO BAD.
WHICH MEANS THEIR RATINGS WILL CONTINUE TO PLUMMET UNLESS THEY ALL CLEAR OUT!
NOW. YOU.
THIS ISN'T YOUR FAULT. YOU DIDN'T MEAN FOR THIS MESS TO HAPPEN...
BUT I'M SORRY. THIS ISN'T YOUR ORIGIN STORY.
I'M GONNA NEED THAT HAMMER...
OH. YEAH. YEAH, OF COURSE, IT'S JUST...
COME ON, MAN.
PLEASE DON'T MAKE THIS A THING. MY HISTORY IN THIS TOWN WITH GUYS WITH HAMMERS IS SPOTTY AT BEST, AND I REALLY DON'T NEED--

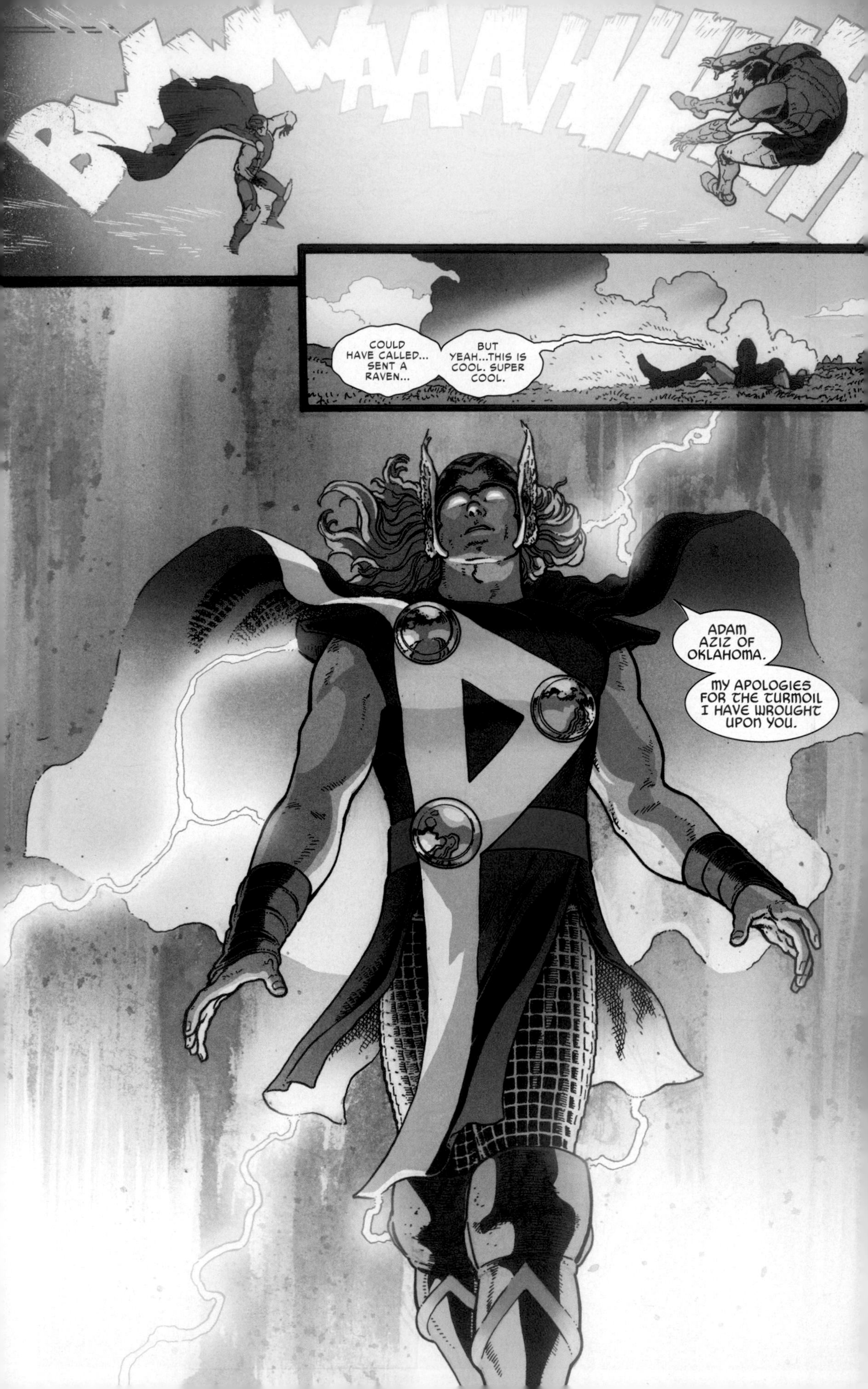
COULD HAVE CALLED... SENT A RAVEN...
BUT YEAH...THIS IS COOL. SUPER COOL.
ADAM AZIZ OF OKLAHOMA.
MY APOLOGIES FOR THE TURMOIL I HAVE WROUGHT UPON YOU.

YOU HAVE EARNED A FAVOR FROM A GOD THIS DAY.

WOW. THOR. YOU'RE...YOU'RE THE *REAL-LIFE* THOR!

I WAS...WELL, I WAS LOCKED UP WHEN YOU GUYS MOVED HERE* SO I MISSED IT ALL, BUT...MAN...MEETING YOU...THIS...THIS IS AN HONOR.

*ASGARD TEMPORARILY MOVED TO BROXTON IN THOR (2007) #1. --WIL

THE HONOR IS MINE.

NOW...IF I MAY?

YES. YES, SIR. AGAIN, I'M SORRY FOR ANY TROUBLE I CAUSED, IT'S JUST--

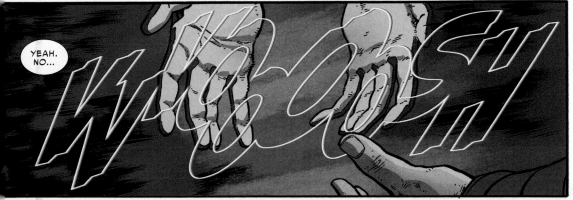

YEAH. NO...

WHOOSH!

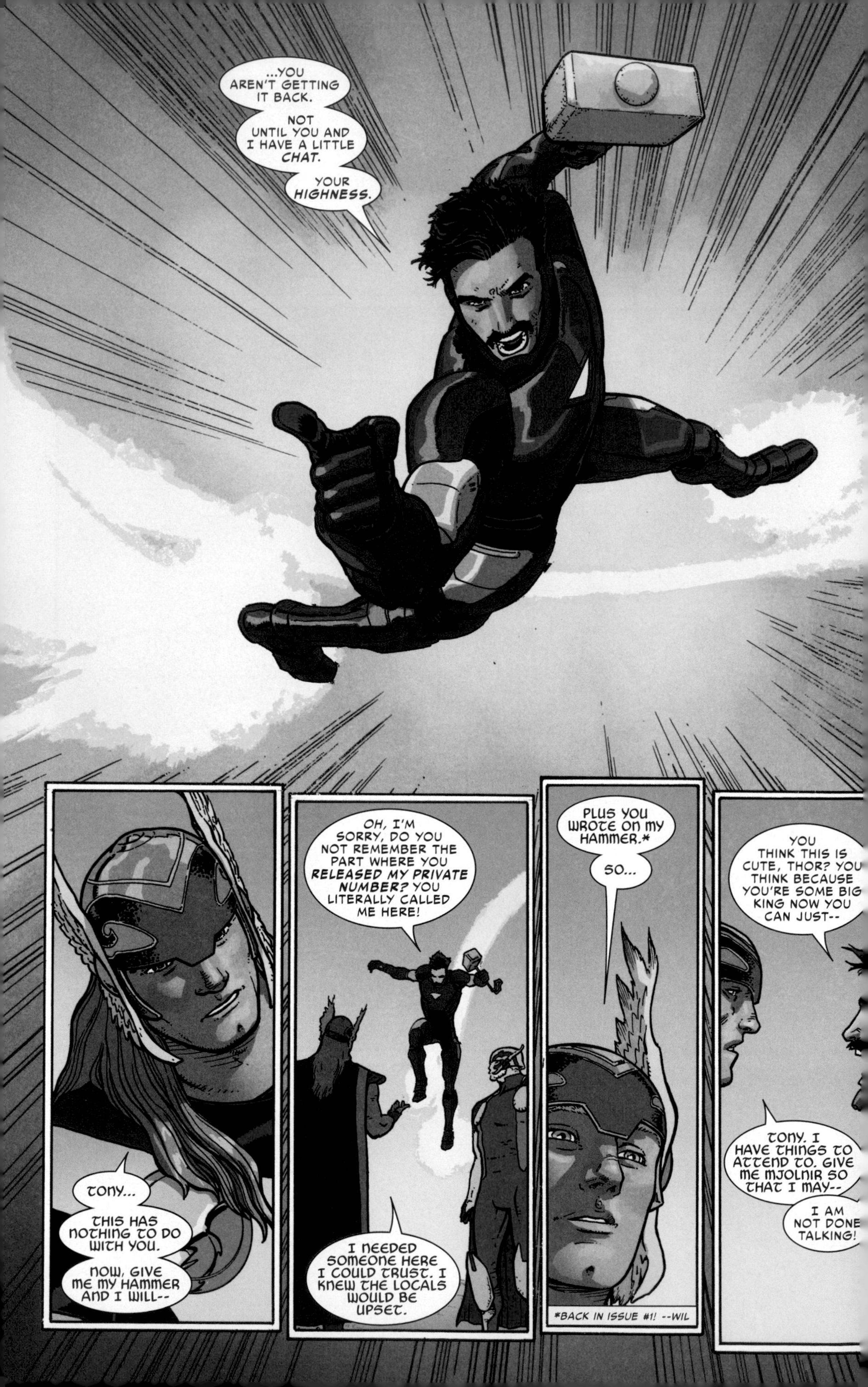

...YOU AREN'T GETTING IT BACK.
NOT UNTIL YOU AND I HAVE A LITTLE *CHAT*.
YOUR ***HIGHNESS***.
TONY...
THIS HAS NOTHING TO DO WITH YOU.
NOW, GIVE ME MY HAMMER AND I WILL--
OH, I'M SORRY, DO YOU NOT REMEMBER THE PART WHERE YOU **RELEASED MY PRIVATE NUMBER?** YOU LITERALLY CALLED ME HERE!
I NEEDED SOMEONE HERE I COULD TRUST. I KNEW THE LOCALS WOULD BE UPSET.
PLUS YOU WROTE ON MY HAMMER.*
SO...
*BACK IN ISSUE #1! --WIL
YOU THINK THIS IS CUTE, THOR? YOU THINK BECAUSE YOU'RE SOME BIG KING NOW YOU CAN JUST--
TONY. I HAVE THINGS TO ATTEND TO. GIVE ME MJOLNIR SO THAT I MAY--
I AM NOT DONE TALKING!

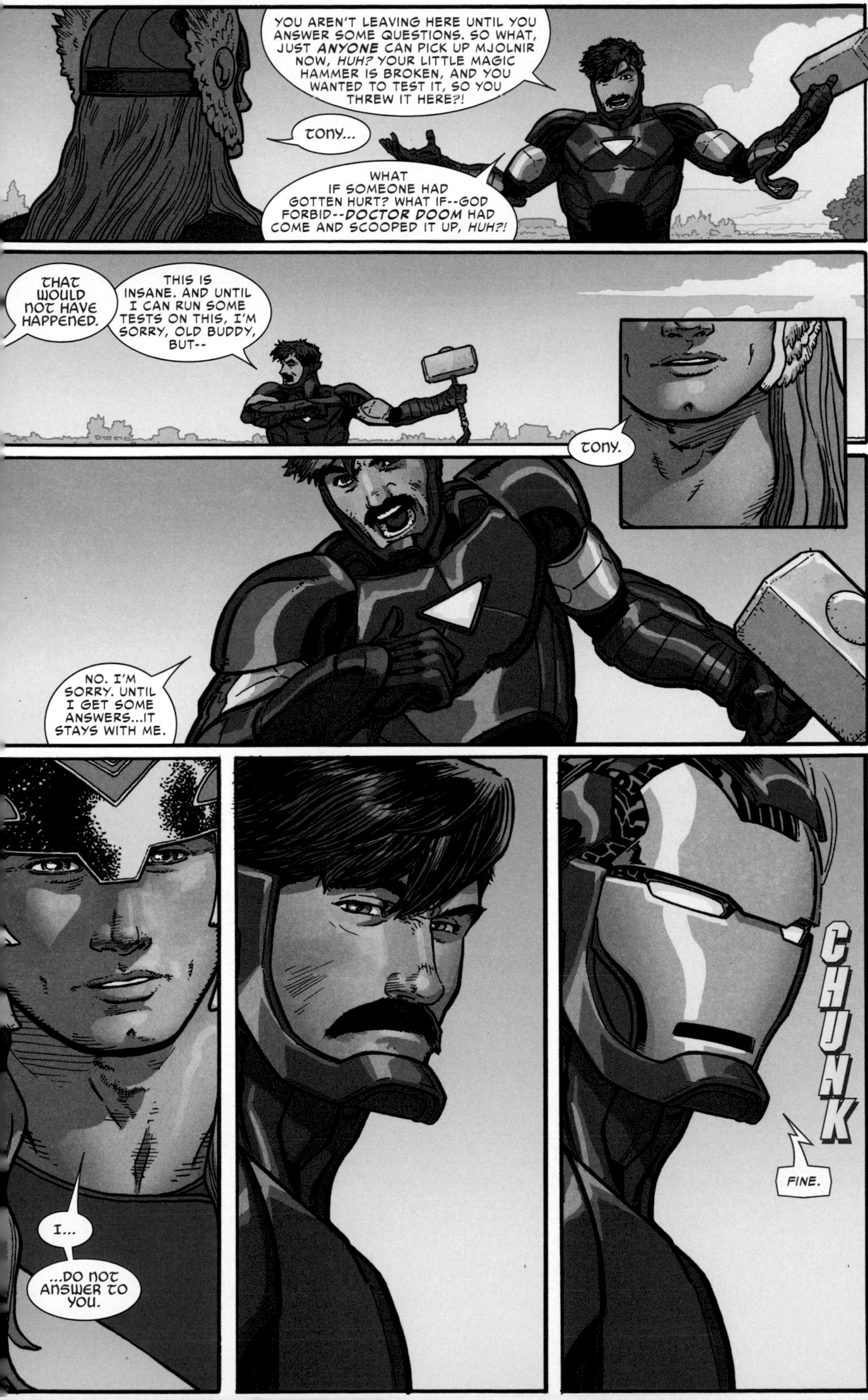
YOU AREN'T LEAVING HERE UNTIL YOU ANSWER SOME QUESTIONS. SO WHAT, JUST *ANYONE* CAN PICK UP MJOLNIR NOW, *HUH?* YOUR LITTLE MAGIC HAMMER IS BROKEN, AND YOU WANTED TO TEST IT, SO YOU THREW IT HERE?!
TONY...
WHAT IF SOMEONE HAD GOTTEN HURT? WHAT IF--GOD FORBID--*DOCTOR DOOM* HAD COME AND SCOOPED IT UP, *HUH?!*
THAT WOULD NOT HAVE HAPPENED.
THIS IS INSANE. AND UNTIL I CAN RUN SOME TESTS ON THIS, I'M SORRY, OLD BUDDY, BUT--
TONY.
NO. I'M SORRY. UNTIL I GET SOME ANSWERS...IT STAYS WITH ME.
I...
...DO NOT ANSWER TO YOU.
CHUNK
FINE.

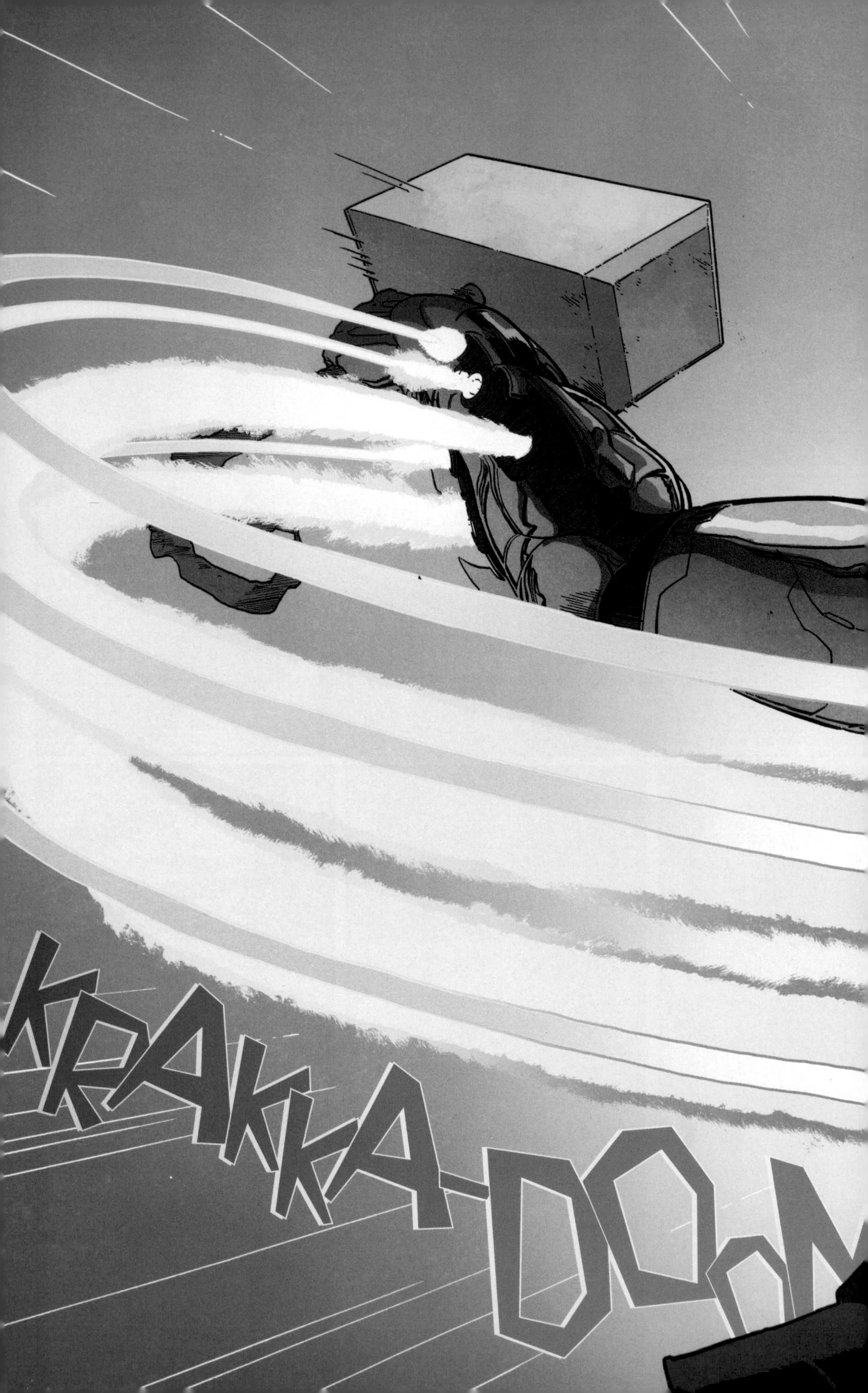
KRAKKA-DOOM

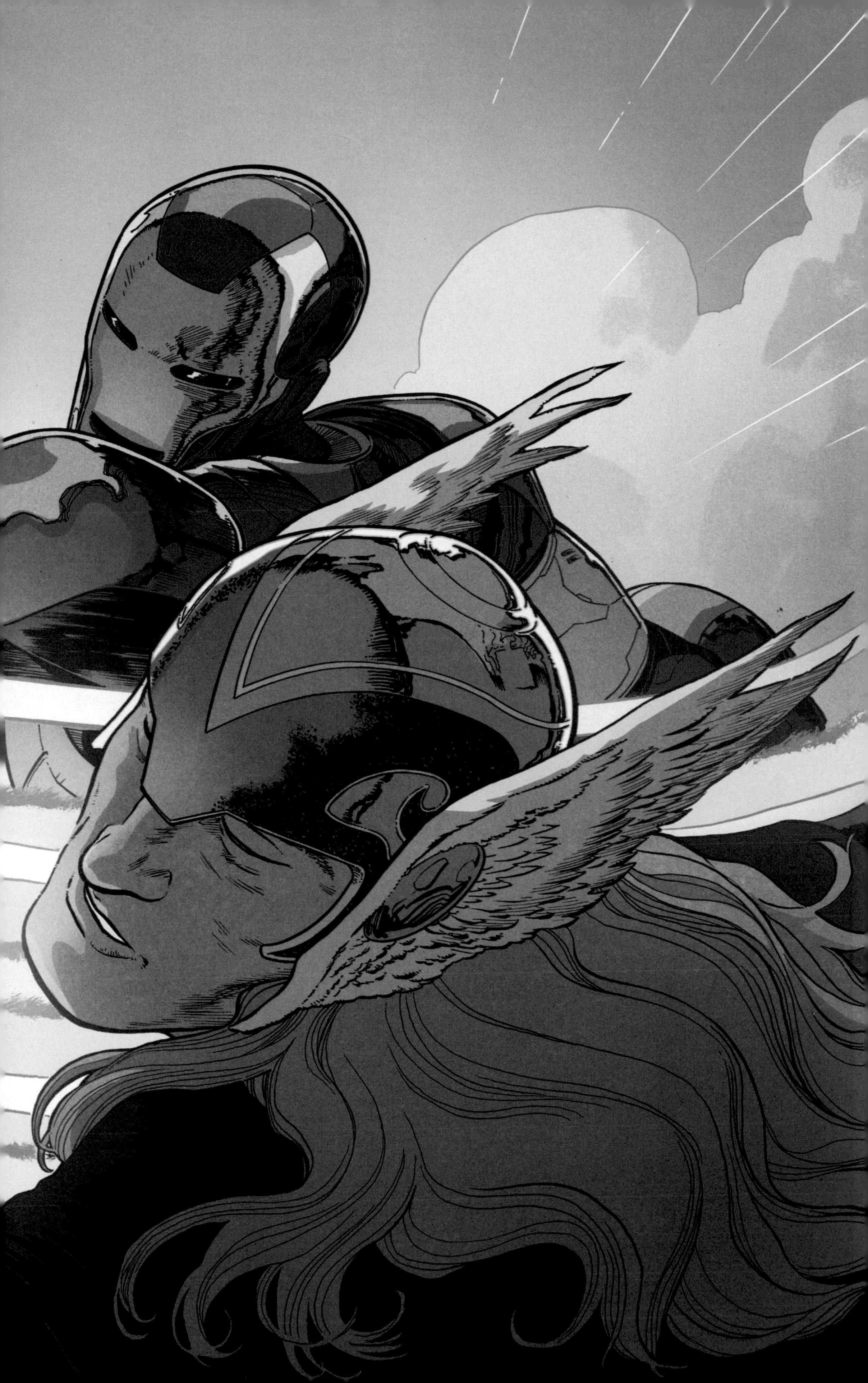

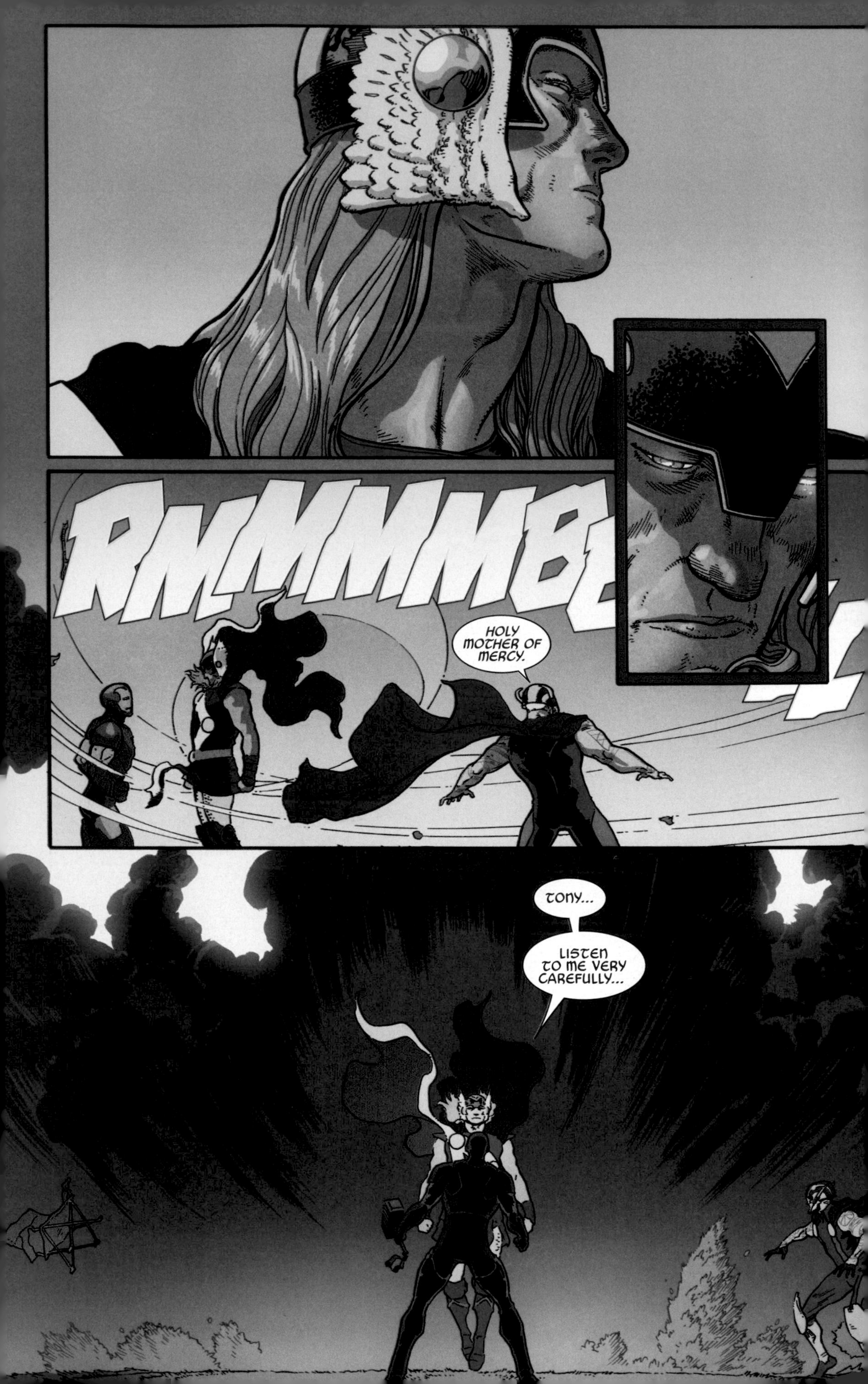
RMMMMBL
HOLY MOTHER OF MERCY.
TONY...
LISTEN TO ME VERY CAREFULLY...

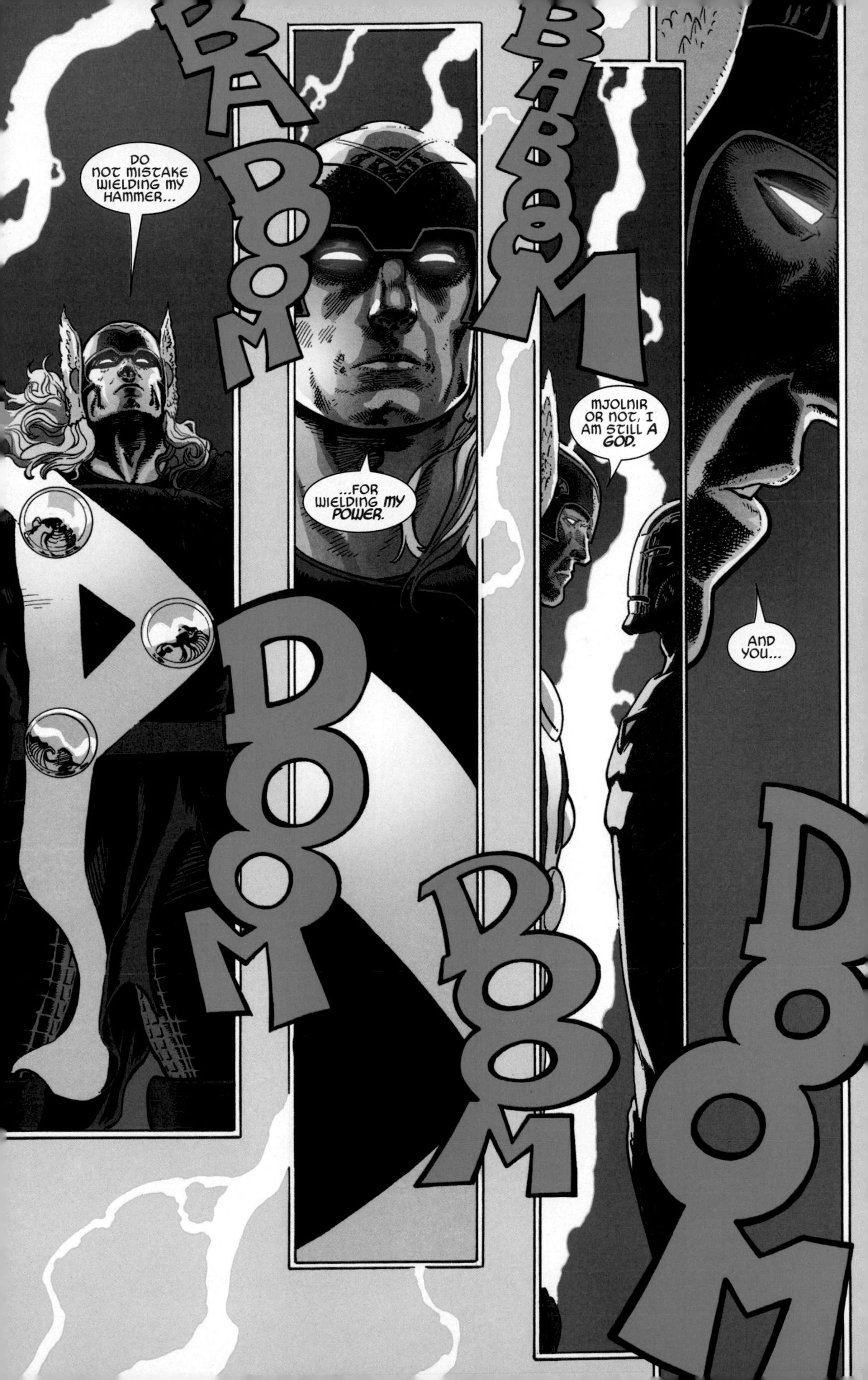
BADOOM
DO NOT MISTAKE WIELDING MY HAMMER...
...FOR WIELDING MY POWER.
BADOOM
MJOLNIR OR NOT, I AM STILL A GOD.
AND YOU...
DOOM
DOOM
DOOM

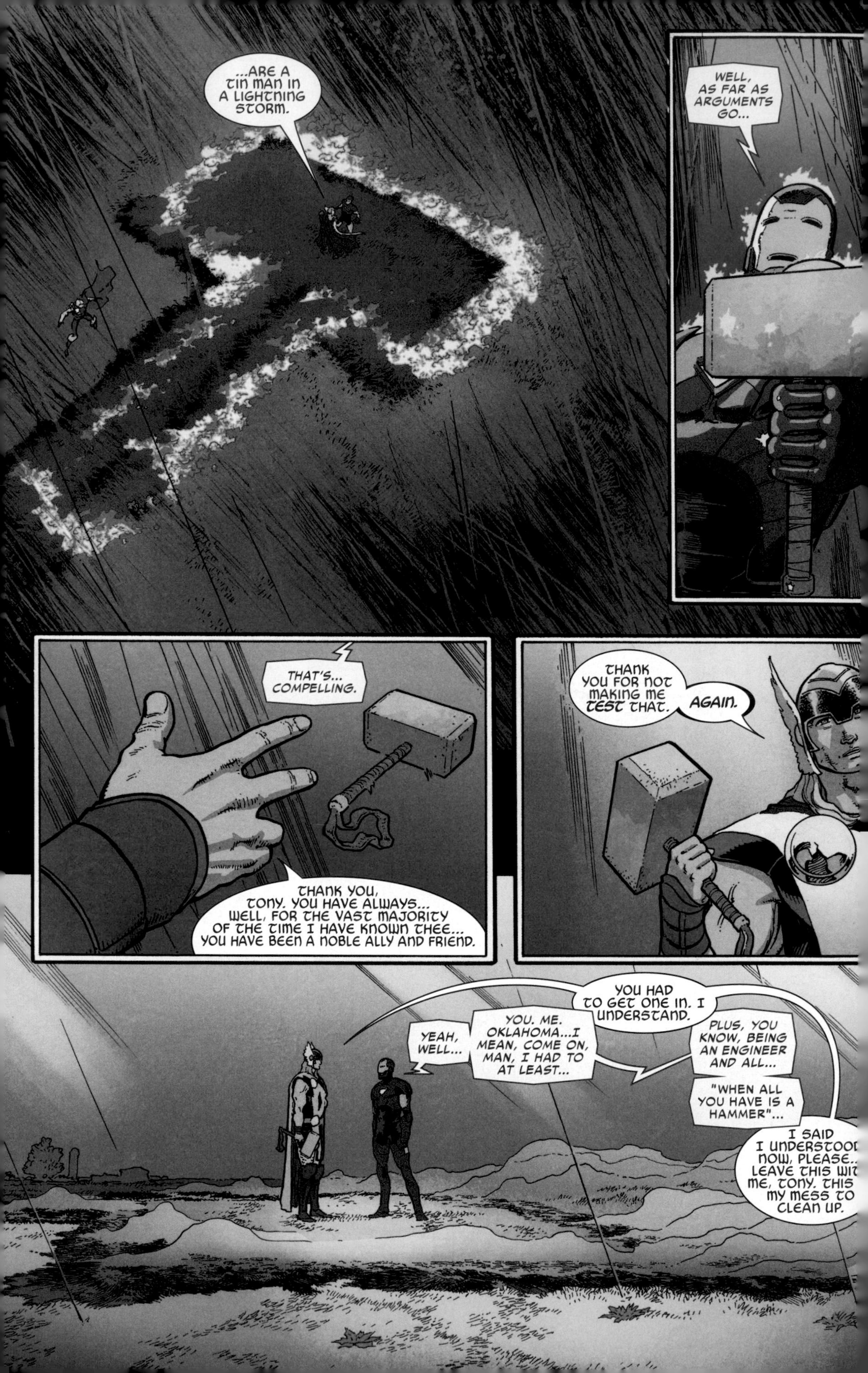
...ARE A TIN MAN IN A LIGHTNING STORM.
WELL, AS FAR AS ARGUMENTS GO...
THAT'S... COMPELLING.
THANK YOU, TONY. YOU HAVE ALWAYS... WELL, FOR THE VAST MAJORITY OF THE TIME I HAVE KNOWN THEE... YOU HAVE BEEN A NOBLE ALLY AND FRIEND.
THANK YOU FOR NOT MAKING ME TEST THAT.
AGAIN.
YEAH, WELL...
YOU. ME. OKLAHOMA...I MEAN, COME ON, MAN, I HAD TO AT LEAST...
YOU HAD TO GET ONE IN. I UNDERSTAND.
PLUS, YOU KNOW, BEING AN ENGINEER AND ALL...
"WHEN ALL YOU HAVE IS A HAMMER"...
I SAID I UNDERSTOOD. NOW, PLEASE... LEAVE THIS WITH ME, TONY. THIS IS MY MESS TO CLEAN UP.

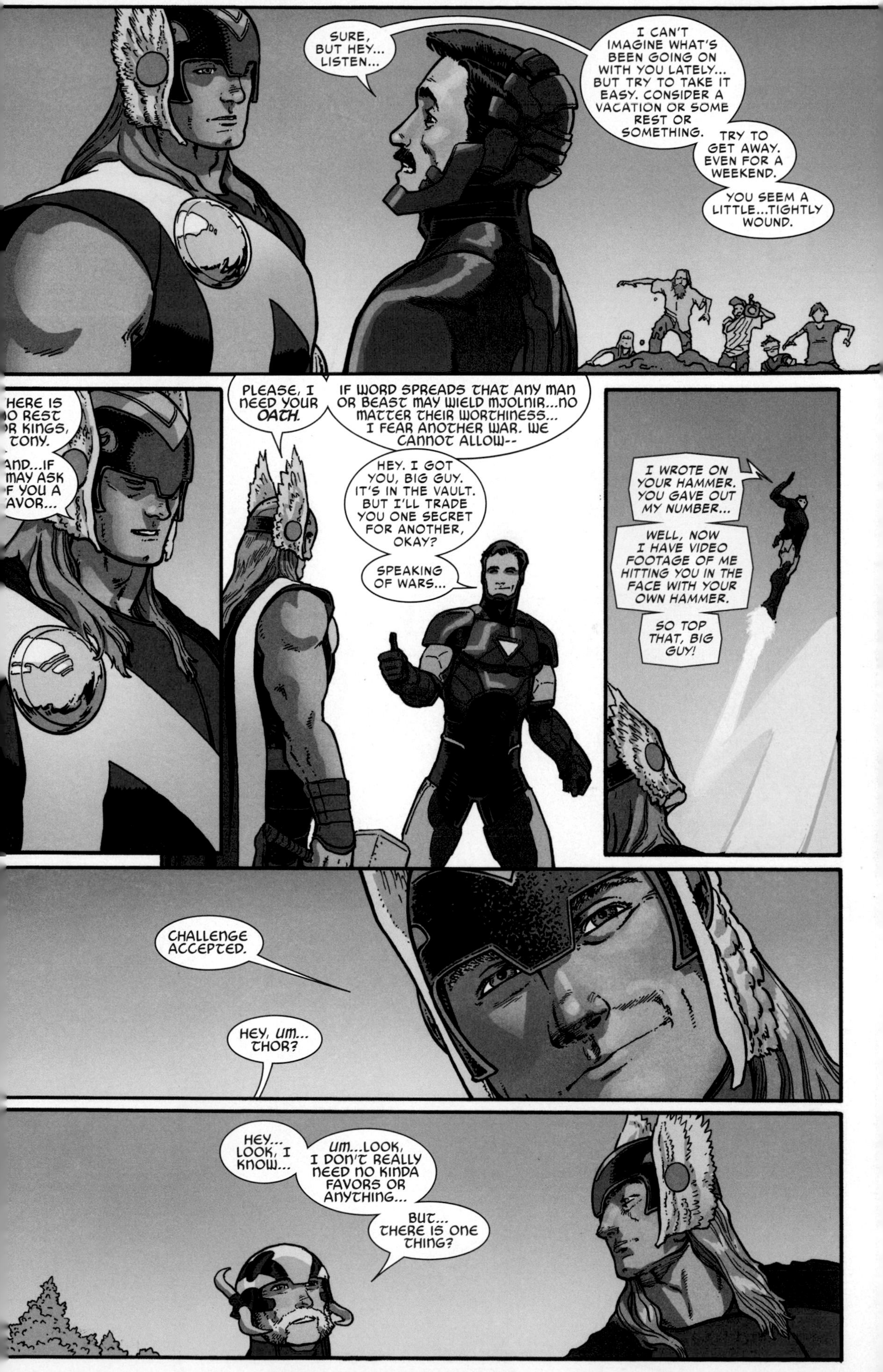
SURE, BUT HEY... LISTEN...
I CAN'T IMAGINE WHAT'S BEEN GOING ON WITH YOU LATELY... BUT TRY TO TAKE IT EASY. CONSIDER A VACATION OR SOME REST OR SOMETHING.
TRY TO GET AWAY. EVEN FOR A WEEKEND.
YOU SEEM A LITTLE...TIGHTLY WOUND.
HERE IS NO REST FOR KINGS, TONY.
AND...IF I MAY ASK OF YOU A FAVOR...
PLEASE, I NEED YOUR OATH.
IF WORD SPREADS THAT ANY MAN OR BEAST MAY WIELD MJOLNIR...NO MATTER THEIR WORTHINESS... I FEAR ANOTHER WAR. WE CANNOT ALLOW--
HEY. I GOT YOU, BIG GUY. IT'S IN THE VAULT. BUT I'LL TRADE YOU ONE SECRET FOR ANOTHER, OKAY?
SPEAKING OF WARS...
I WROTE ON YOUR HAMMER. YOU GAVE OUT MY NUMBER...
WELL, NOW I HAVE VIDEO FOOTAGE OF ME HITTING YOU IN THE FACE WITH YOUR OWN HAMMER.
SO TOP THAT, BIG GUY!
CHALLENGE ACCEPTED.
HEY, UM... THOR?
HEY... LOOK, I KNOW...
UM...LOOK, I DON'T REALLY NEED NO KINDA FAVORS OR ANYTHING...
BUT... THERE IS ONE THING?

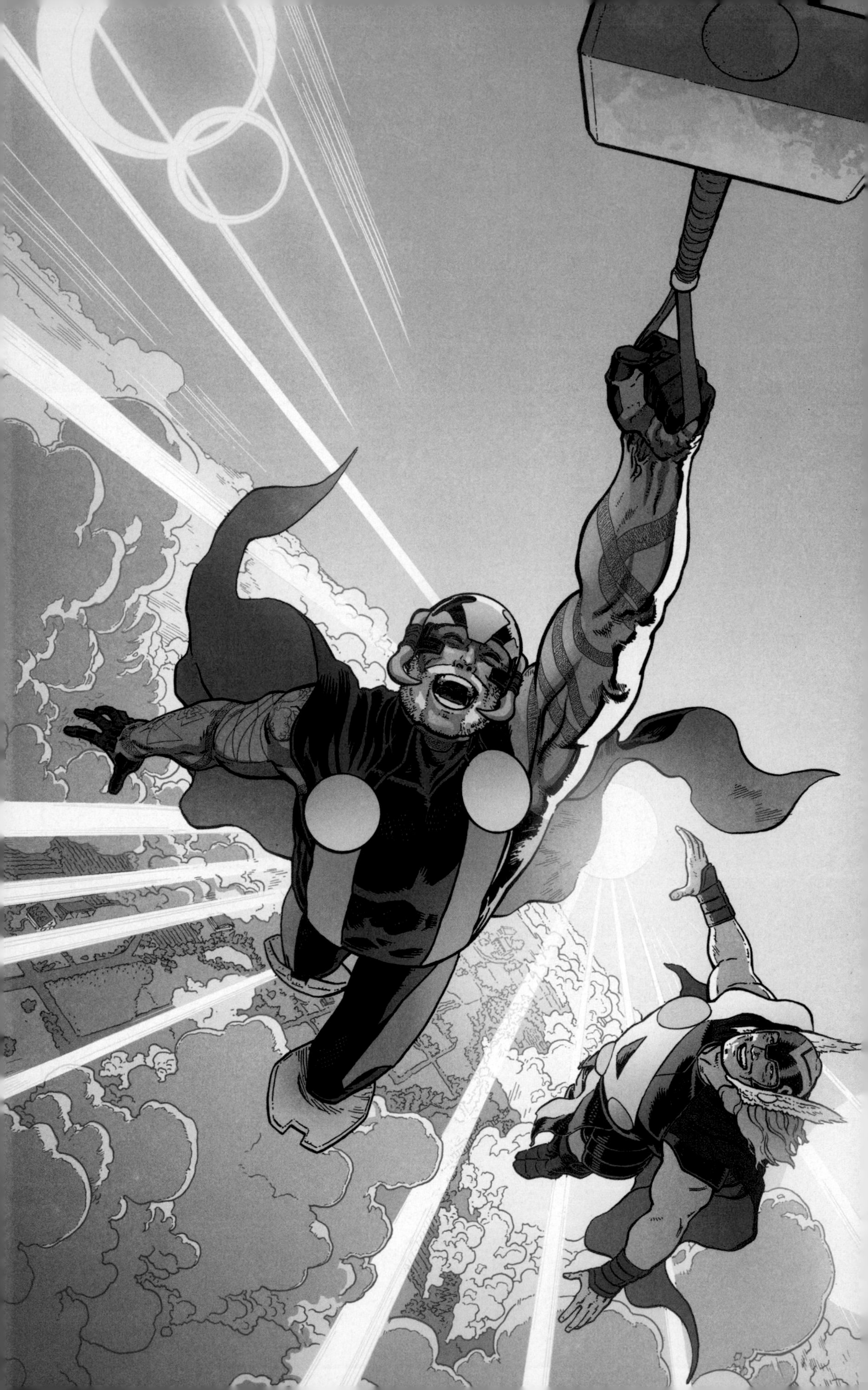

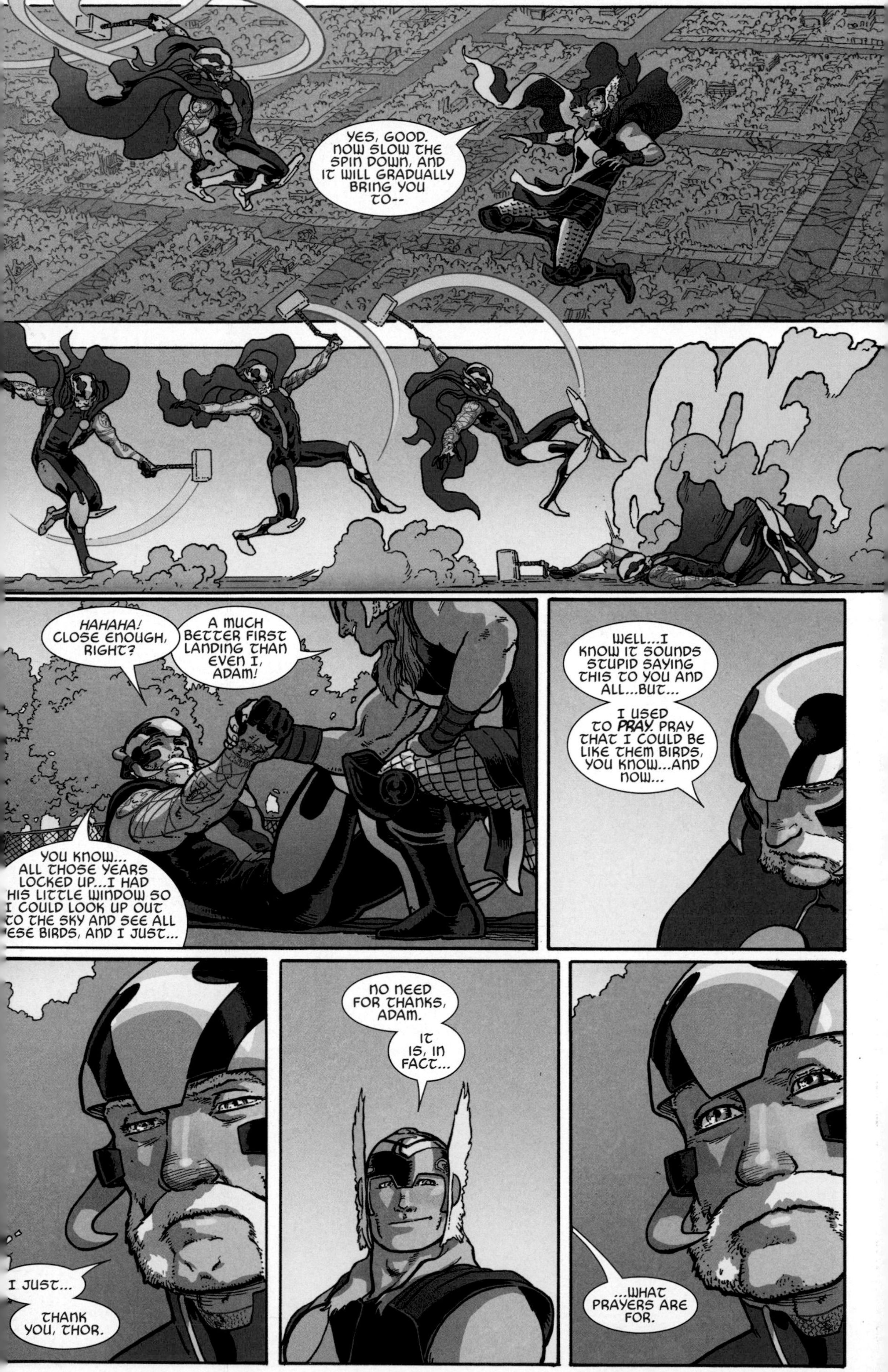
YES, GOOD. NOW SLOW THE SPIN DOWN, AND IT WILL GRADUALLY BRING YOU TO--
HAHAHA! CLOSE ENOUGH, RIGHT?
A MUCH BETTER FIRST LANDING THAN EVEN I, ADAM!
YOU KNOW... ALL THOSE YEARS LOCKED UP...I HAD HIS LITTLE WINDOW SO I COULD LOOK UP OUT TO THE SKY AND SEE ALL ESE BIRDS, AND I JUST...
WELL...I KNOW IT SOUNDS STUPID SAYING THIS TO YOU AND ALL...BUT...
I USED TO PRAY. PRAY THAT I COULD BE LIKE THEM BIRDS, YOU KNOW...AND NOW...
I JUST...
THANK YOU, THOR.
NO NEED FOR THANKS, ADAM.
IT IS, IN FACT...
...WHAT PRAYERS ARE FOR.

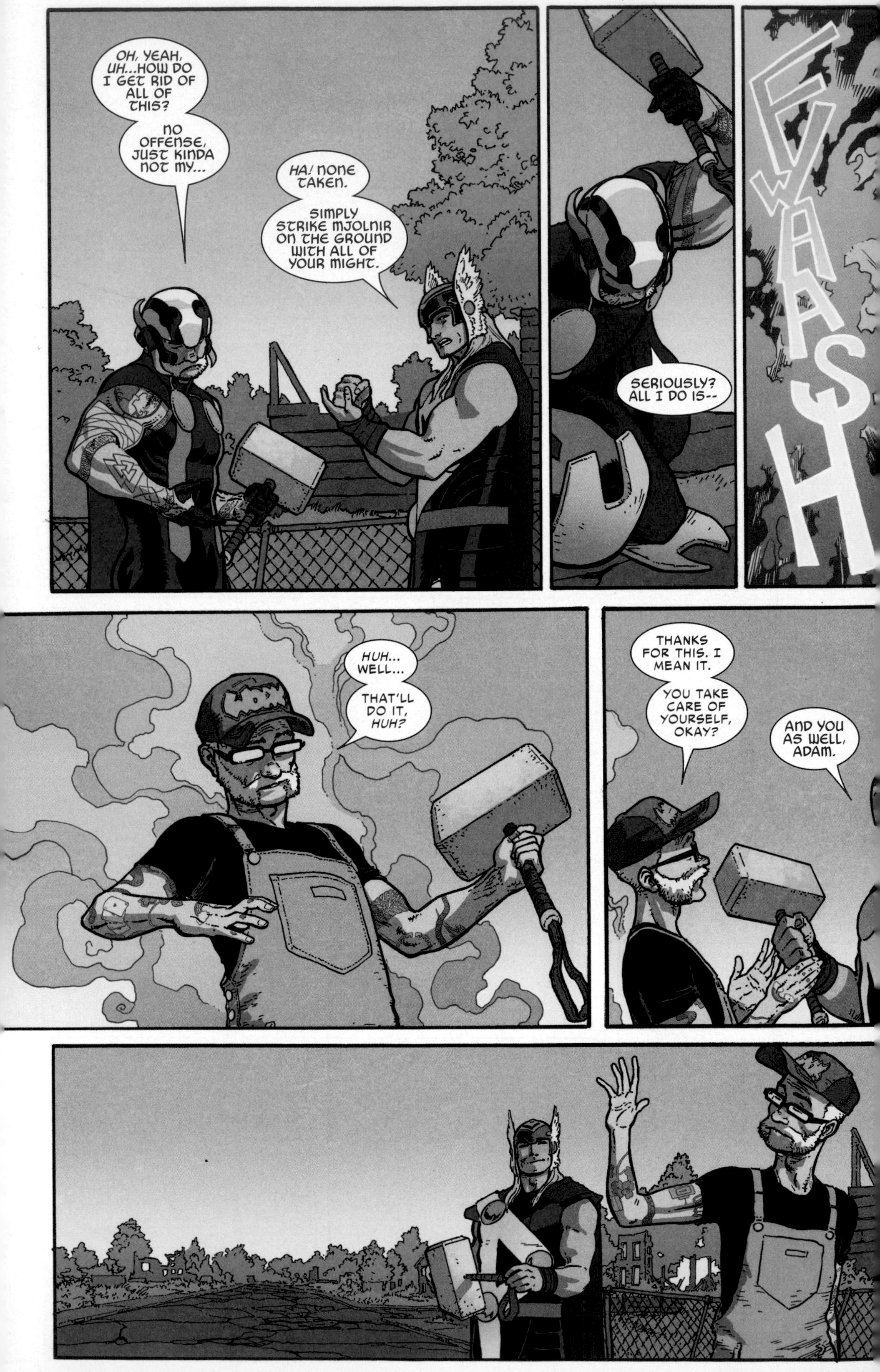
OH, YEAH, UH...HOW DO I GET RID OF ALL OF THIS?
NO OFFENSE, JUST KINDA NOT MY...
HA! NONE TAKEN.
SIMPLY STRIKE MJOLNIR ON THE GROUND WITH ALL OF YOUR MIGHT.
SERIOUSLY? ALL I DO IS--
FWAASH
HUH... WELL...
THAT'LL DO IT, HUH?
THANKS FOR THIS. I MEAN IT.
YOU TAKE CARE OF YOURSELF, OKAY?
AND YOU AS WELL, ADAM.

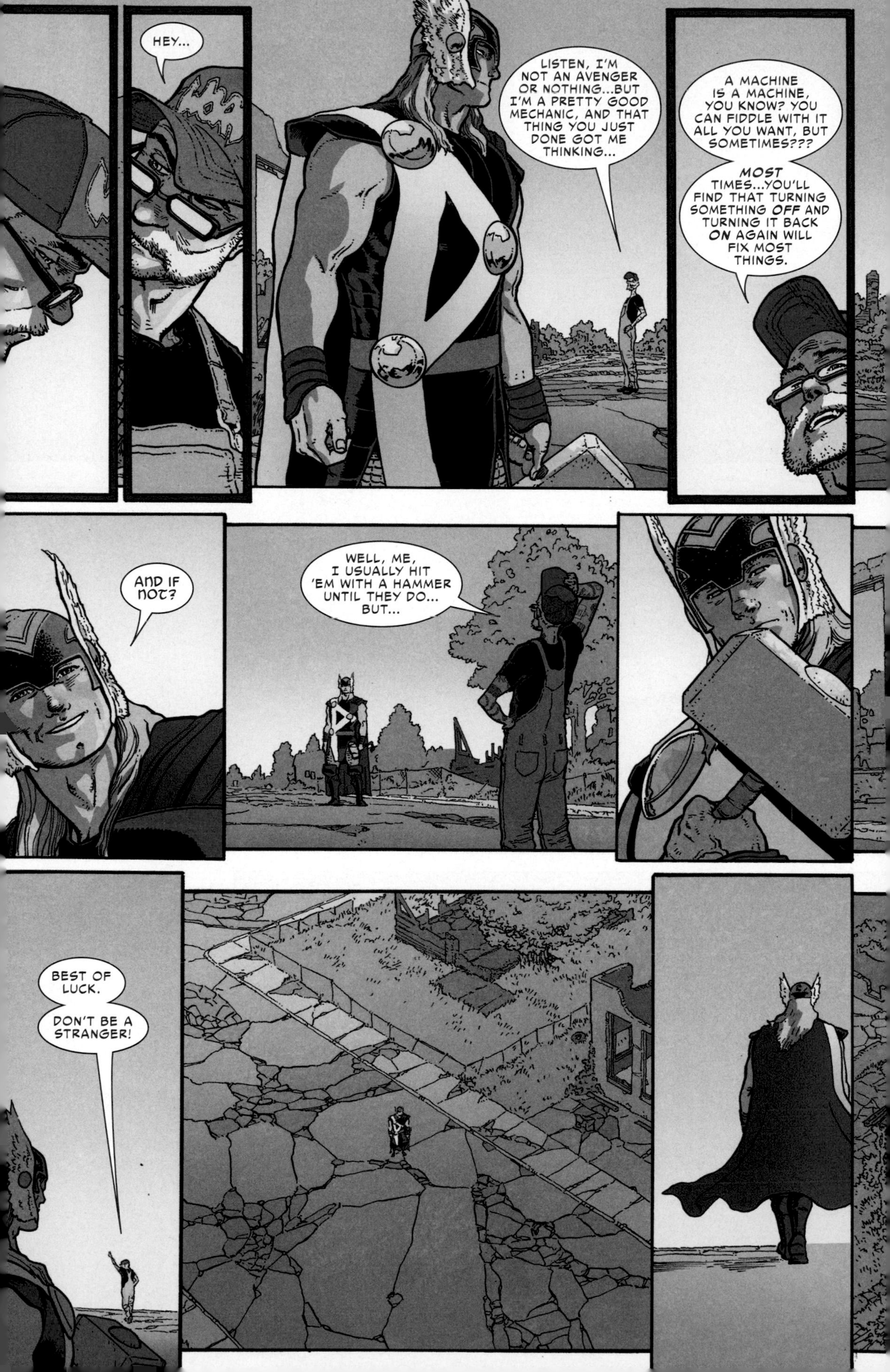
HEY...
LISTEN, I'M NOT AN AVENGER OR NOTHING...BUT I'M A PRETTY GOOD MECHANIC, AND THAT THING YOU JUST DONE GOT ME THINKING...
A MACHINE IS A MACHINE, YOU KNOW? YOU CAN FIDDLE WITH IT ALL YOU WANT, BUT SOMETIMES???
MOST TIMES...YOU'LL FIND THAT TURNING SOMETHING OFF AND TURNING IT BACK ON AGAIN WILL FIX MOST THINGS.
AND IF NOT?
WELL, ME, I USUALLY HIT 'EM WITH A HAMMER UNTIL THEY DO... BUT...
BEST OF LUCK.
DON'T BE A STRANGER!

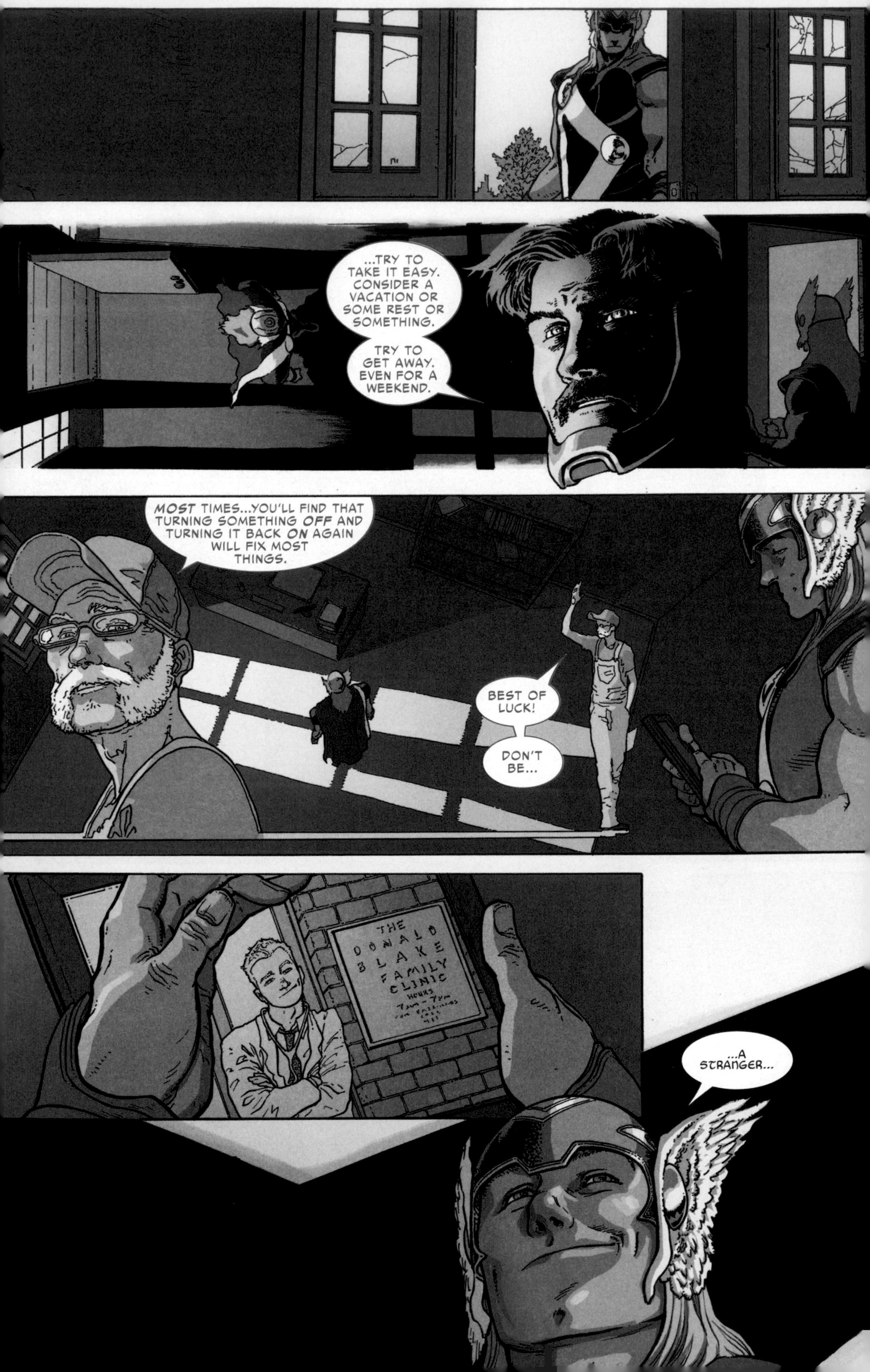
...TRY TO TAKE IT EASY. CONSIDER A VACATION OR SOME REST OR SOMETHING.
TRY TO GET AWAY. EVEN FOR A WEEKEND.
MOST TIMES...YOU'LL FIND THAT TURNING SOMETHING OFF AND TURNING IT BACK ON AGAIN WILL FIX MOST THINGS.
BEST OF LUCK!
DON'T BE...
THE DONALD BLAKE FAMILY CLINIC
...A STRANGER...

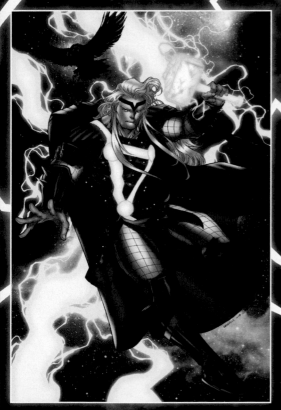

THOR 7 VARIANT BY
Liam Sharp

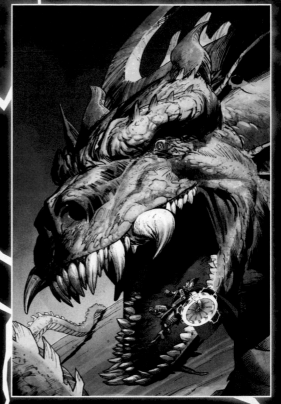

THOR 8 VARIANT BY
Nic Klein

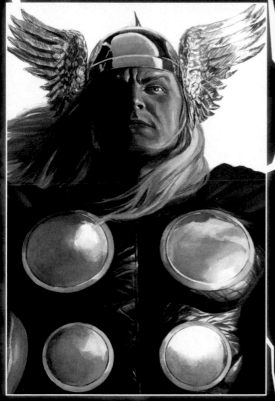

THOR 8 TIMELESS VARIANT BY
Alex Ross

RESURRECTED BY THE VERY LIGHTNING HE ONCE COMMANDED, IT'S...
THE
FRANKENSTEIN
THOR

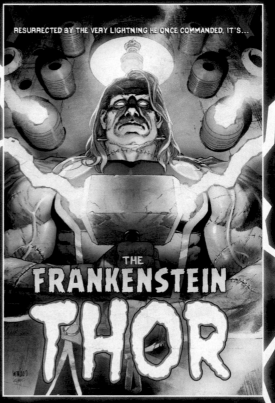

THOR 8 HORROR VARIANT BY
Leinil Francis Yu & Sunny Gho
with Anthony Gambino

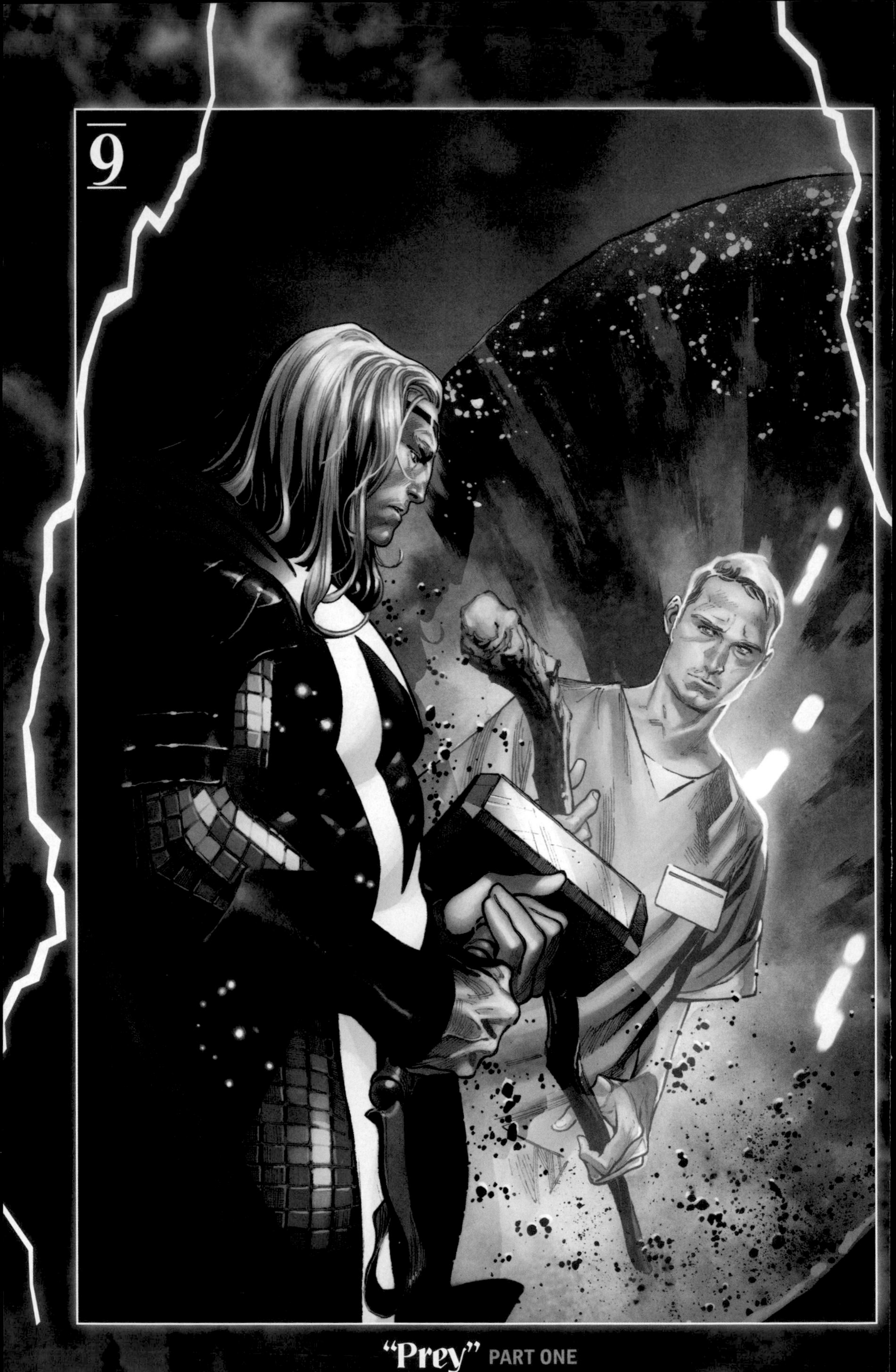
9

"Prey" PART ONE

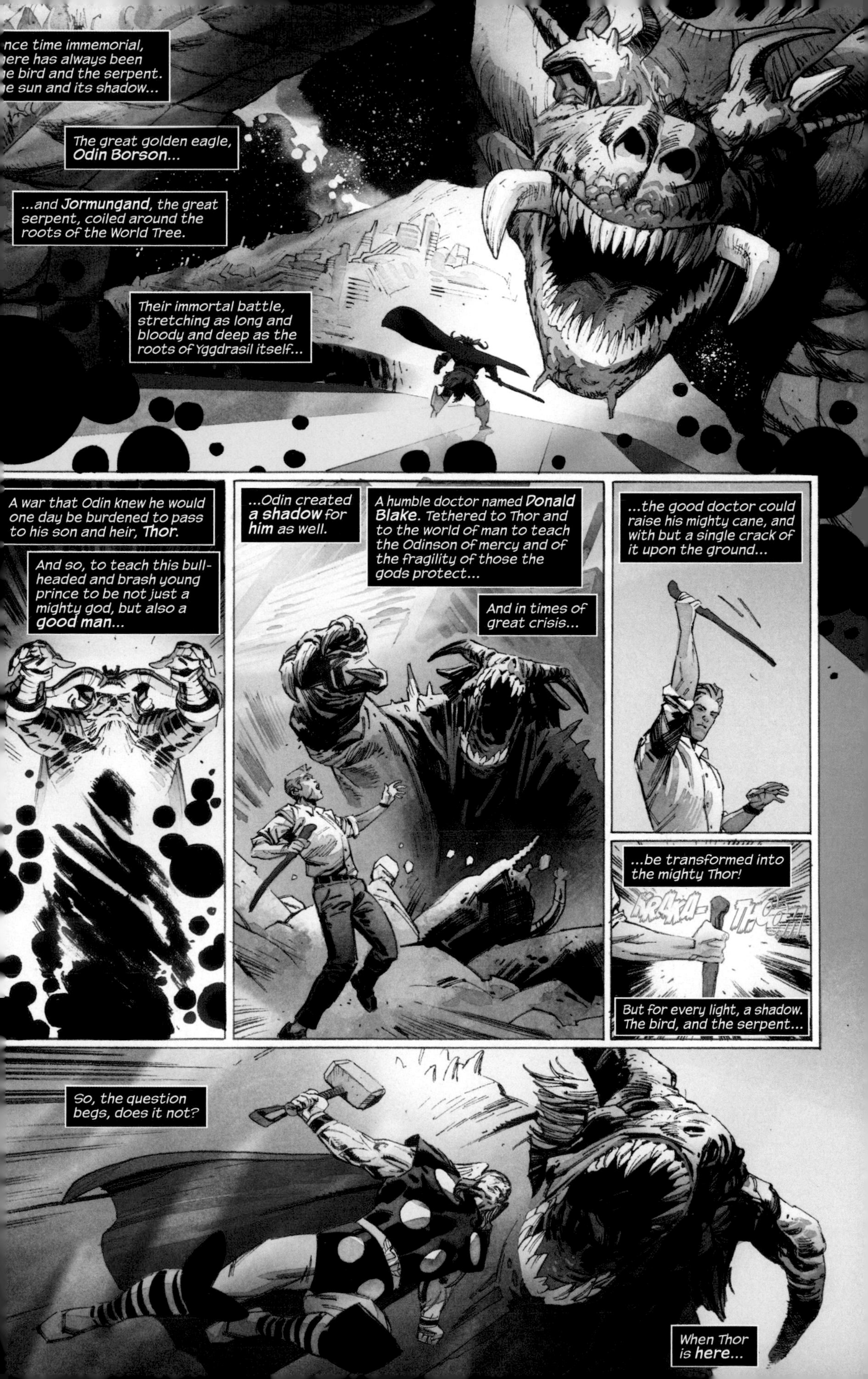
nce time immemorial,
ere has always been
e bird and the serpent.
e sun and its shadow...
The great golden eagle, **Odin Borson**...
...and **Jormungand**, the great serpent, coiled around the roots of the World Tree.
Their immortal battle, stretching as long and bloody and deep as the roots of Yggdrasil itself...
A war that Odin knew he would one day be burdened to pass to his son and heir, **Thor**.
And so, to teach this bull-headed and brash young prince to be not just a mighty god, but also a **good man**...
...Odin created **a shadow** for **him** as well.
A humble doctor named **Donald Blake**. Tethered to Thor and to the world of man to teach the Odinson of mercy and of the fragility of those the gods protect...
And in times of great crisis...
...the good doctor could raise his mighty cane, and with but a single crack of it upon the ground...
...be transformed into the mighty Thor!
KRAKA-THOOM
But for every light, a shadow. The bird, and the serpent...
So, the question begs, does it not?
When Thor is **here**...

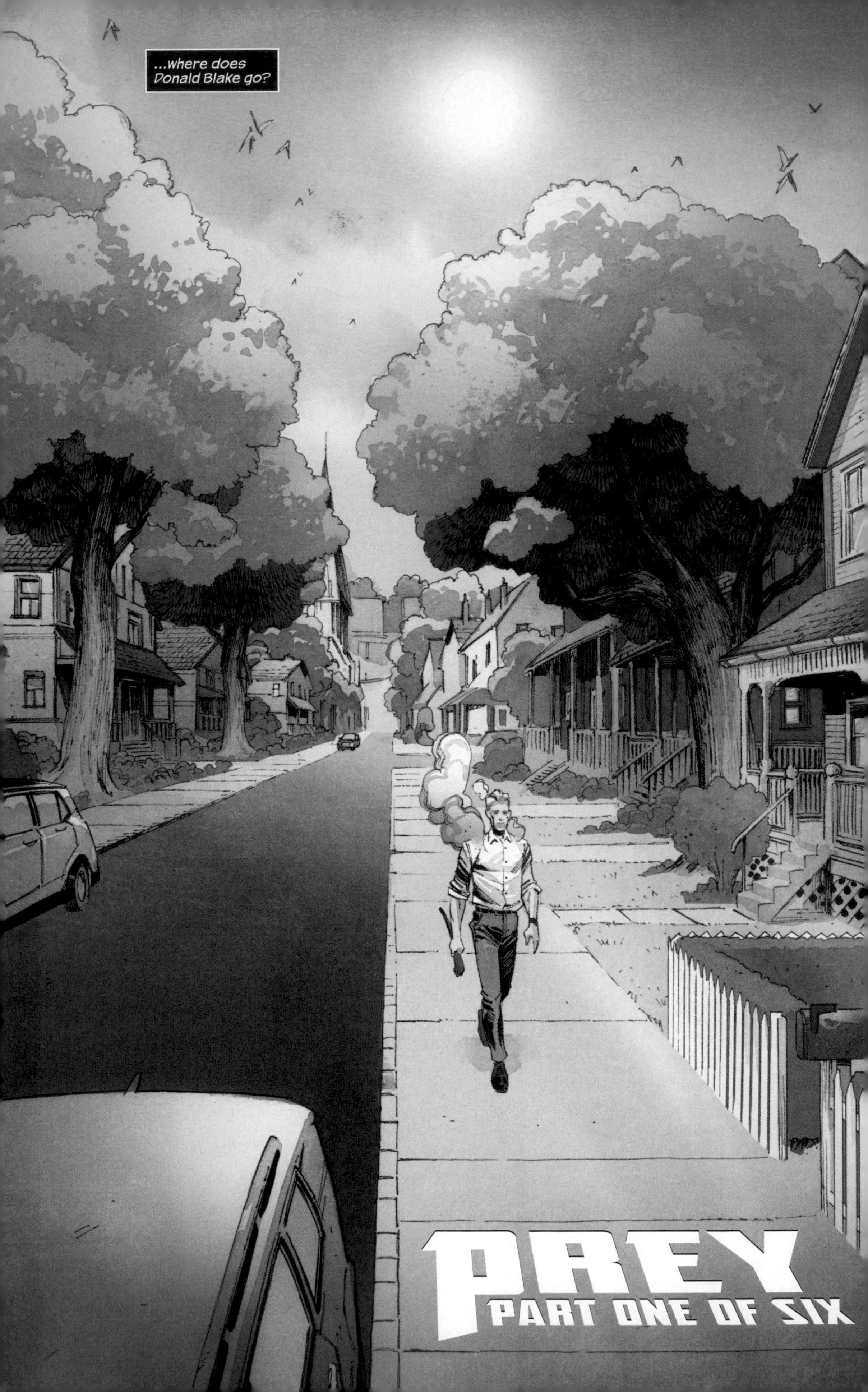
...where does Donald Blake go?
PREY
PART ONE OF SIX

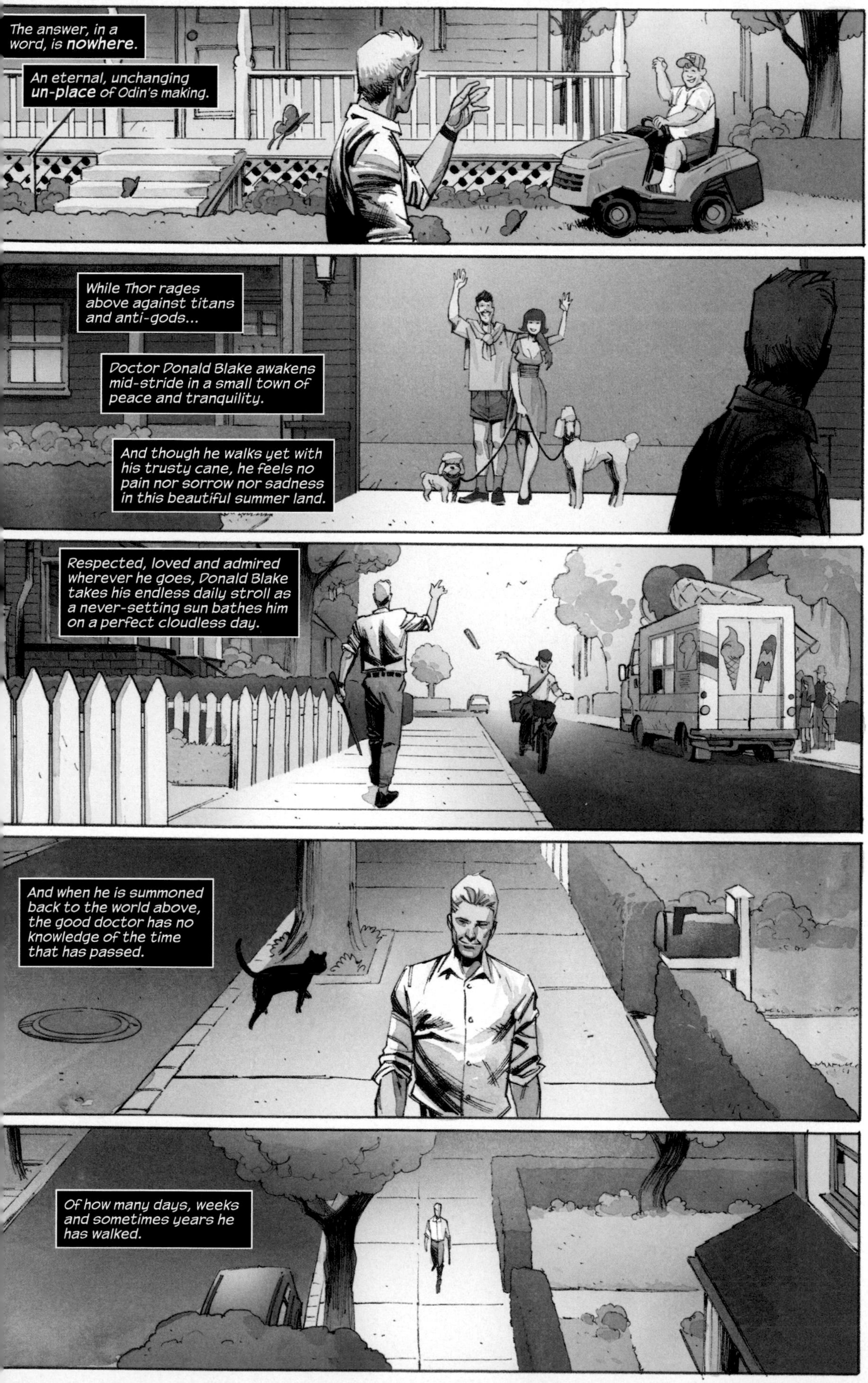
The answer, in a word, is **nowhere**.
An eternal, unchanging **un-place** of Odin's making.
While Thor rages above against titans and anti-gods...
Doctor Donald Blake awakens mid-stride in a small town of peace and tranquility.
And though he walks yet with his trusty cane, he feels no pain nor sorrow nor sadness in this beautiful summer land.
Respected, loved and admired wherever he goes, Donald Blake takes his endless daily stroll as a never-setting sun bathes him on a perfect cloudless day.
And when he is summoned back to the world above, the good doctor has no knowledge of the time that has passed.
Of how many days, weeks and sometimes years he has walked.

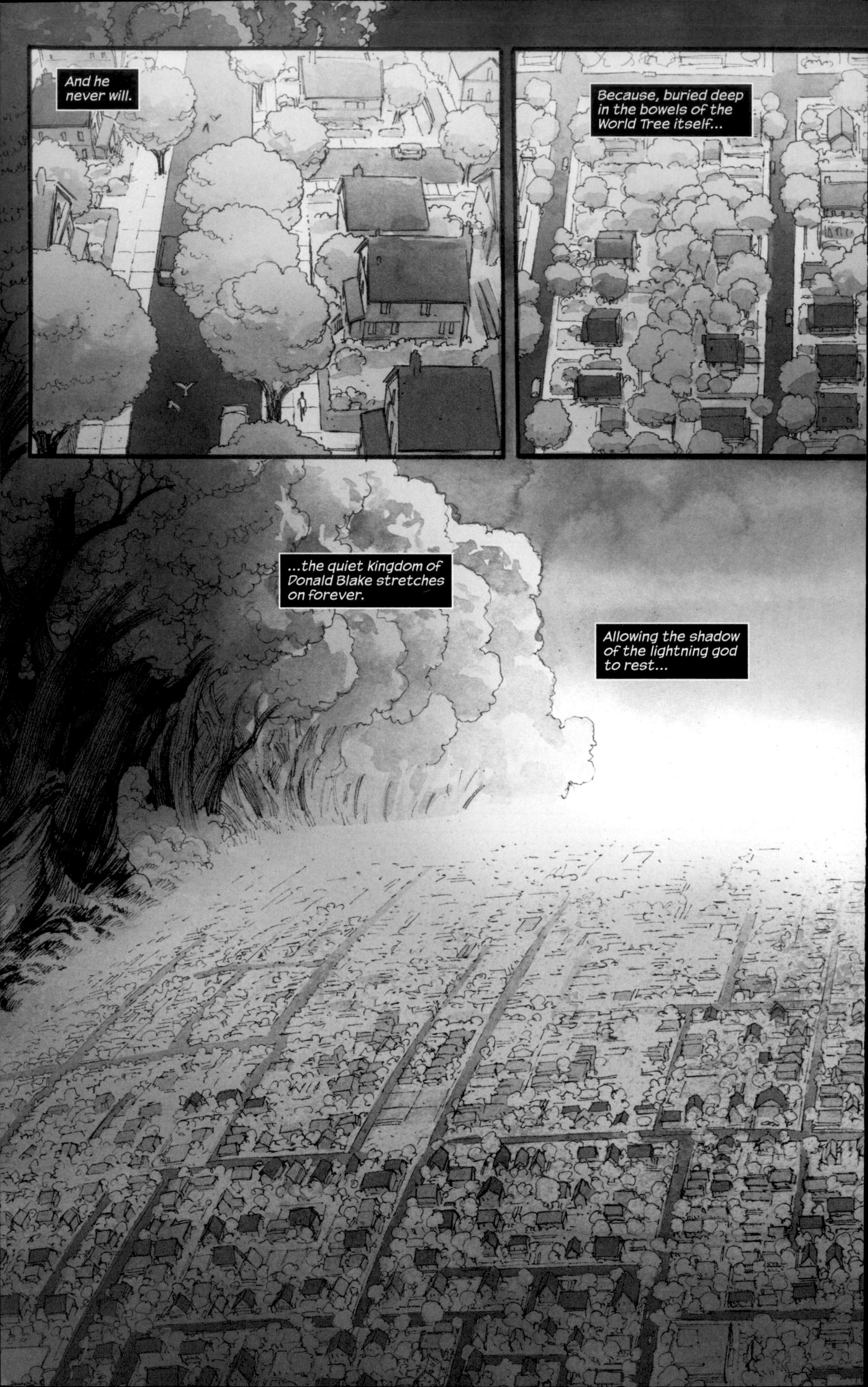
And he never will.
Because, buried deep in the bowels of the World Tree itself...
...the quiet kingdom of Donald Blake stretches on forever.
Allowing the shadow of the lightning god to rest...

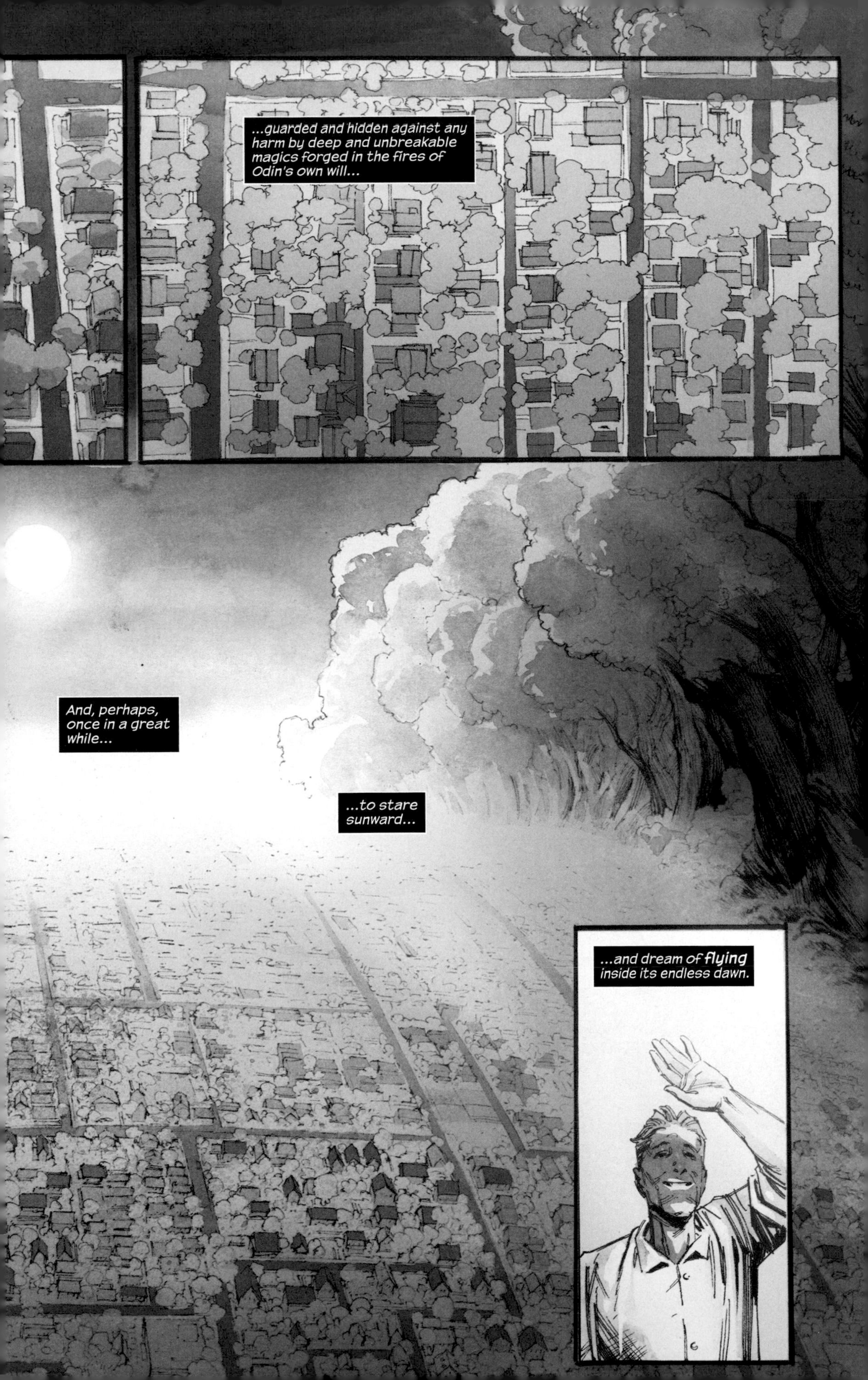
...guarded and hidden against any harm by deep and unbreakable magics forged in the fires of Odin's own will...
And, perhaps, once in a great while...
...to stare sunward...
...and dream of flying inside its endless dawn.

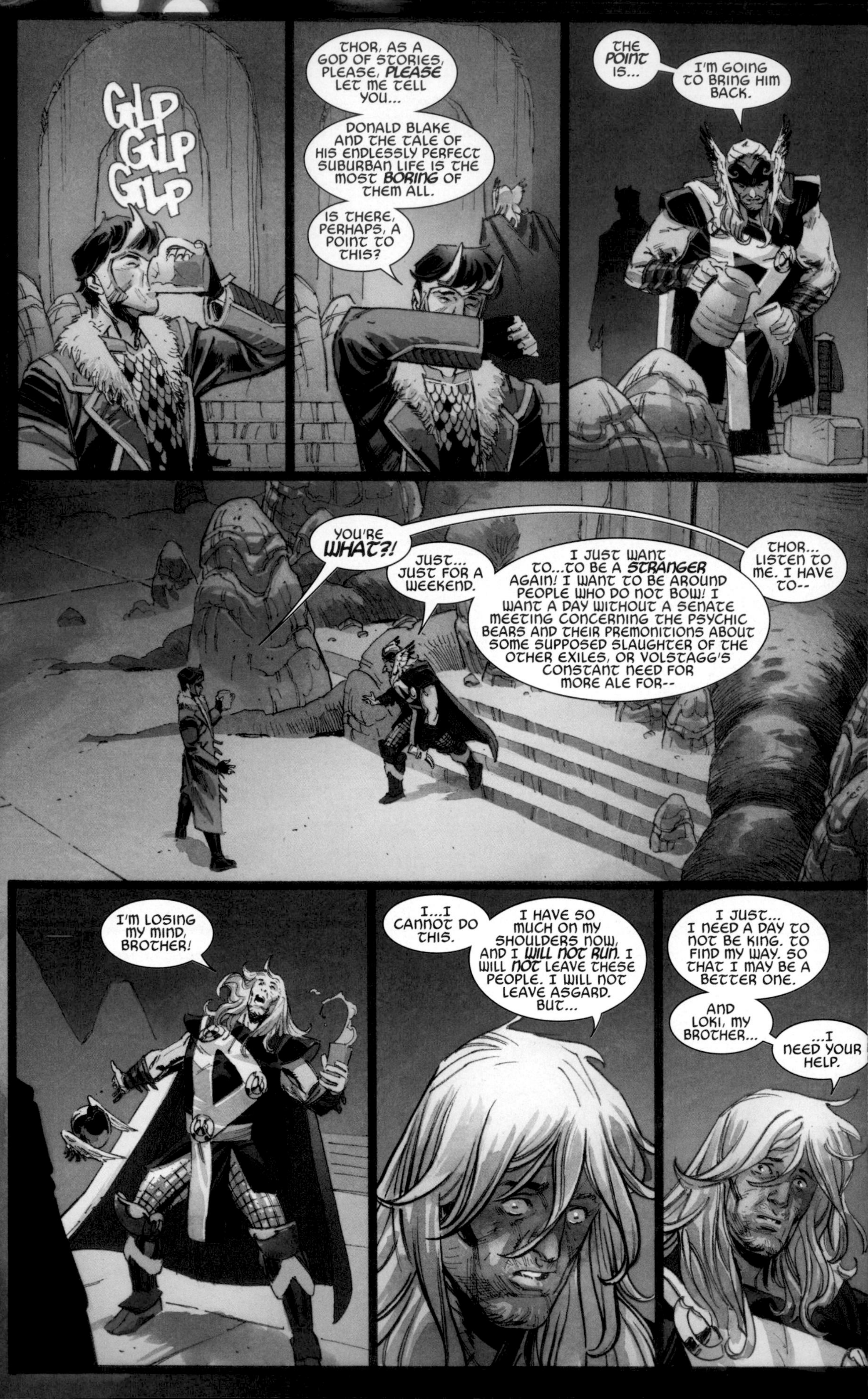
GLP GLIP GLIP
THOR, AS A GOD OF STORIES, PLEASE, PLEASE LET ME TELL YOU...
DONALD BLAKE AND THE TALE OF HIS ENDLESSLY PERFECT SUBURBAN LIFE IS THE MOST BORING OF THEM ALL.
IS THERE, PERHAPS, A POINT TO THIS?
THE POINT IS...
I'M GOING TO BRING HIM BACK.
YOU'RE WHAT?!
JUST... JUST FOR A WEEKEND.
I JUST WANT TO...TO BE A STRANGER AGAIN! I WANT TO BE AROUND PEOPLE WHO DO NOT BOW! I WANT A DAY WITHOUT A SENATE MEETING CONCERNING THE PSYCHIC BEARS AND THEIR PREMONITIONS ABOUT SOME SUPPOSED SLAUGHTER OF THE OTHER EXILES, OR VOLSTAGG'S CONSTANT NEED FOR MORE ALE FOR--
THOR... LISTEN TO ME. I HAVE TO--
I'M LOSING MY MIND, BROTHER!
I...I CANNOT DO THIS.
I HAVE SO MUCH ON MY SHOULDERS NOW, AND I WILL NOT RUN. I WILL NOT LEAVE THESE PEOPLE. I WILL NOT LEAVE ASGARD. BUT...
I JUST... I NEED A DAY TO NOT BE KING. TO FIND MY WAY. SO THAT I MAY BE A BETTER ONE.
AND LOKI, MY BROTHER...
...I NEED YOUR HELP.

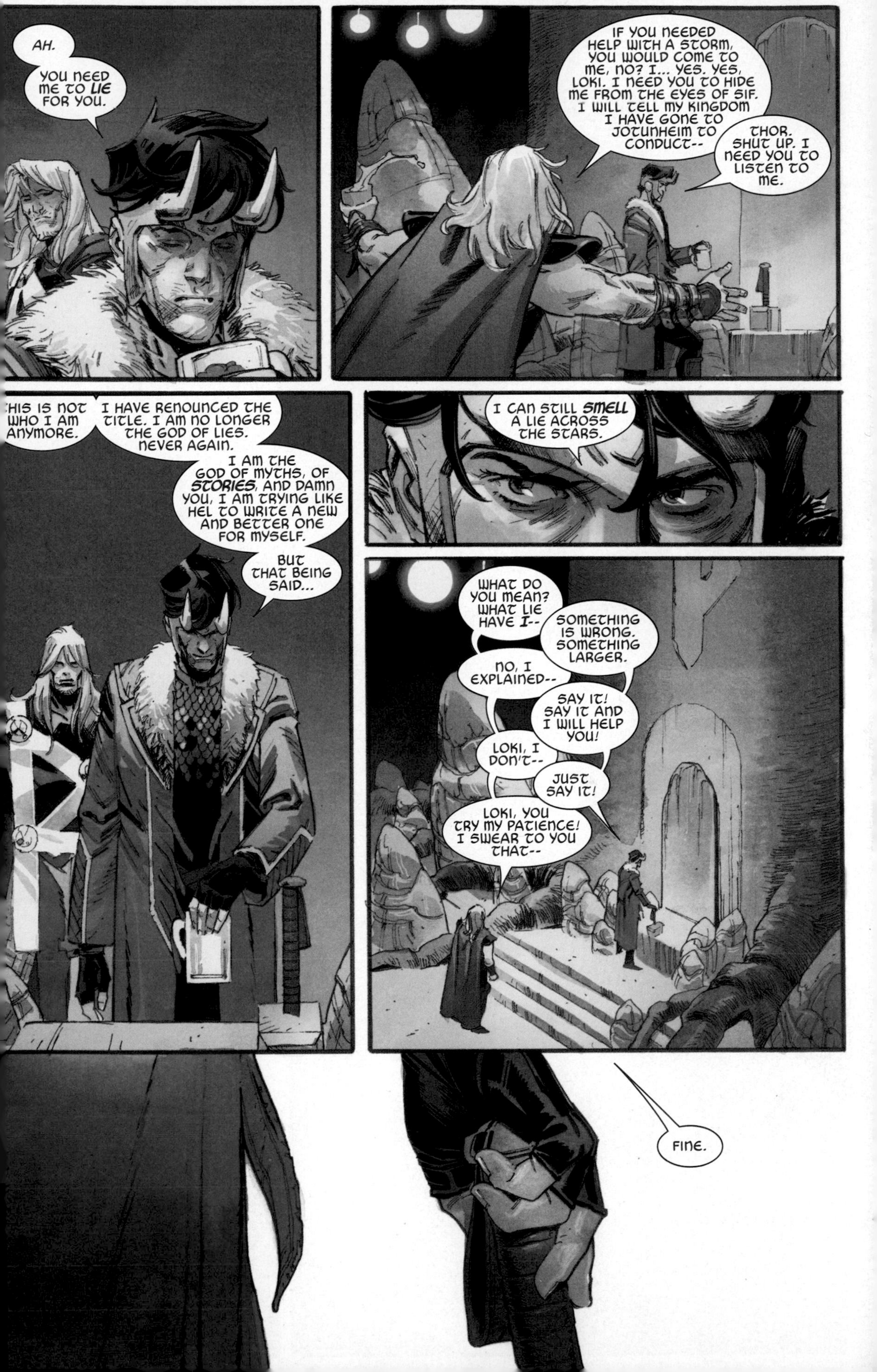
AH.
YOU NEED ME TO LIE FOR YOU.
IF YOU NEEDED HELP WITH A STORM, YOU WOULD COME TO ME, NO? I... YES. YES, LOKI. I NEED YOU TO HIDE ME FROM THE EYES OF SIF. I WILL TELL MY KINGDOM I HAVE GONE TO JOTUNHEIM TO CONDUCT--
THOR. SHUT UP. I NEED YOU TO LISTEN TO ME.
THIS IS NOT WHO I AM ANYMORE.
I HAVE RENOUNCED THE TITLE. I AM NO LONGER THE GOD OF LIES. NEVER AGAIN.
I AM THE GOD OF MYTHS, OF STORIES, AND DAMN YOU, I AM TRYING LIKE HEL TO WRITE A NEW AND BETTER ONE FOR MYSELF.
BUT THAT BEING SAID...
I CAN STILL SMELL A LIE ACROSS THE STARS.
WHAT DO YOU MEAN? WHAT LIE HAVE I--
SOMETHING IS WRONG. SOMETHING LARGER.
NO, I EXPLAINED--
SAY IT! SAY IT AND I WILL HELP YOU!
LOKI, I DON'T--
JUST SAY IT!
LOKI, YOU TRY MY PATIENCE! I SWEAR TO YOU THAT--
FINE.

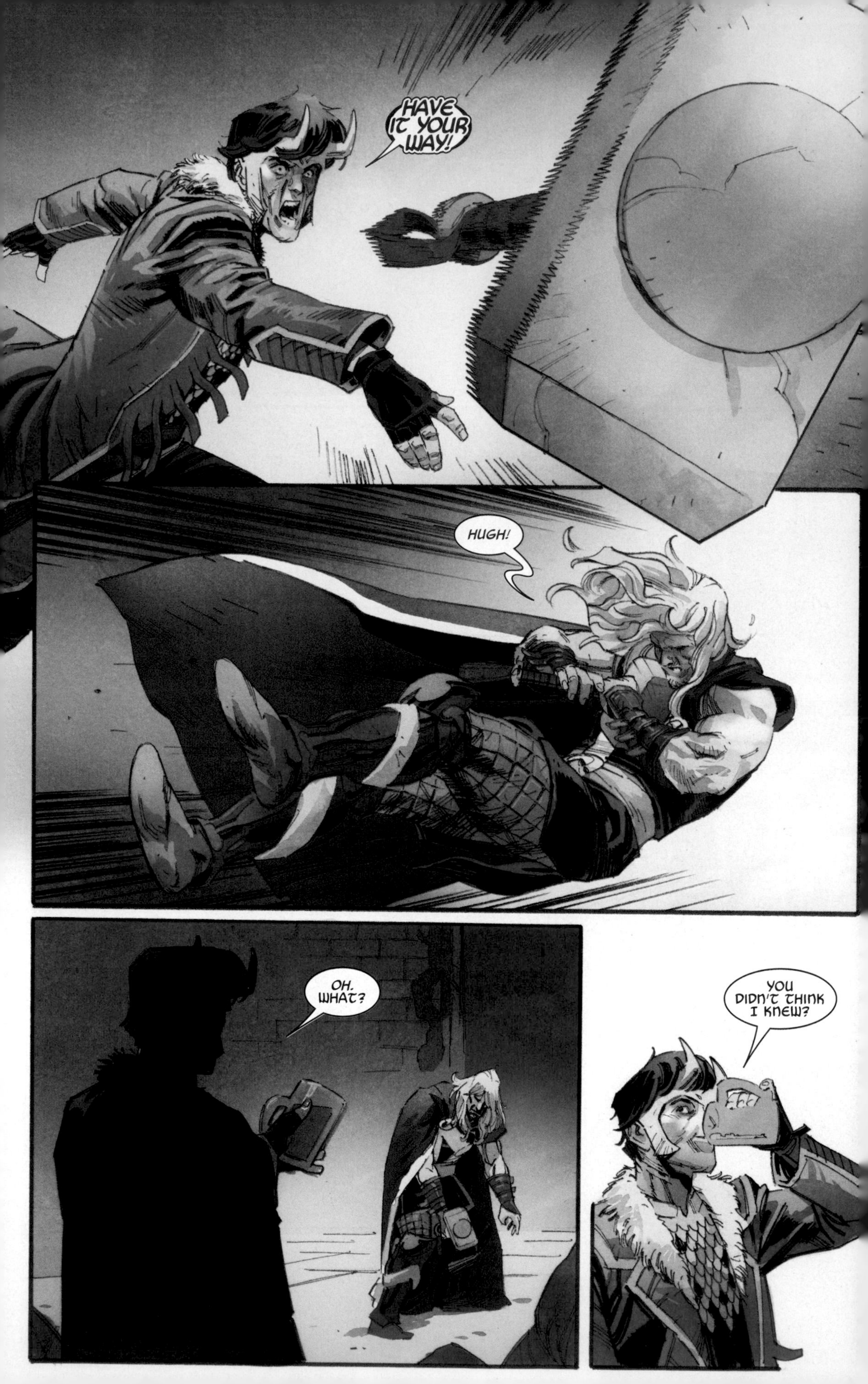
HAVE IT YOUR WAY!
HUGH!
OH. WHAT?
YOU DIDN'T THINK I KNEW?

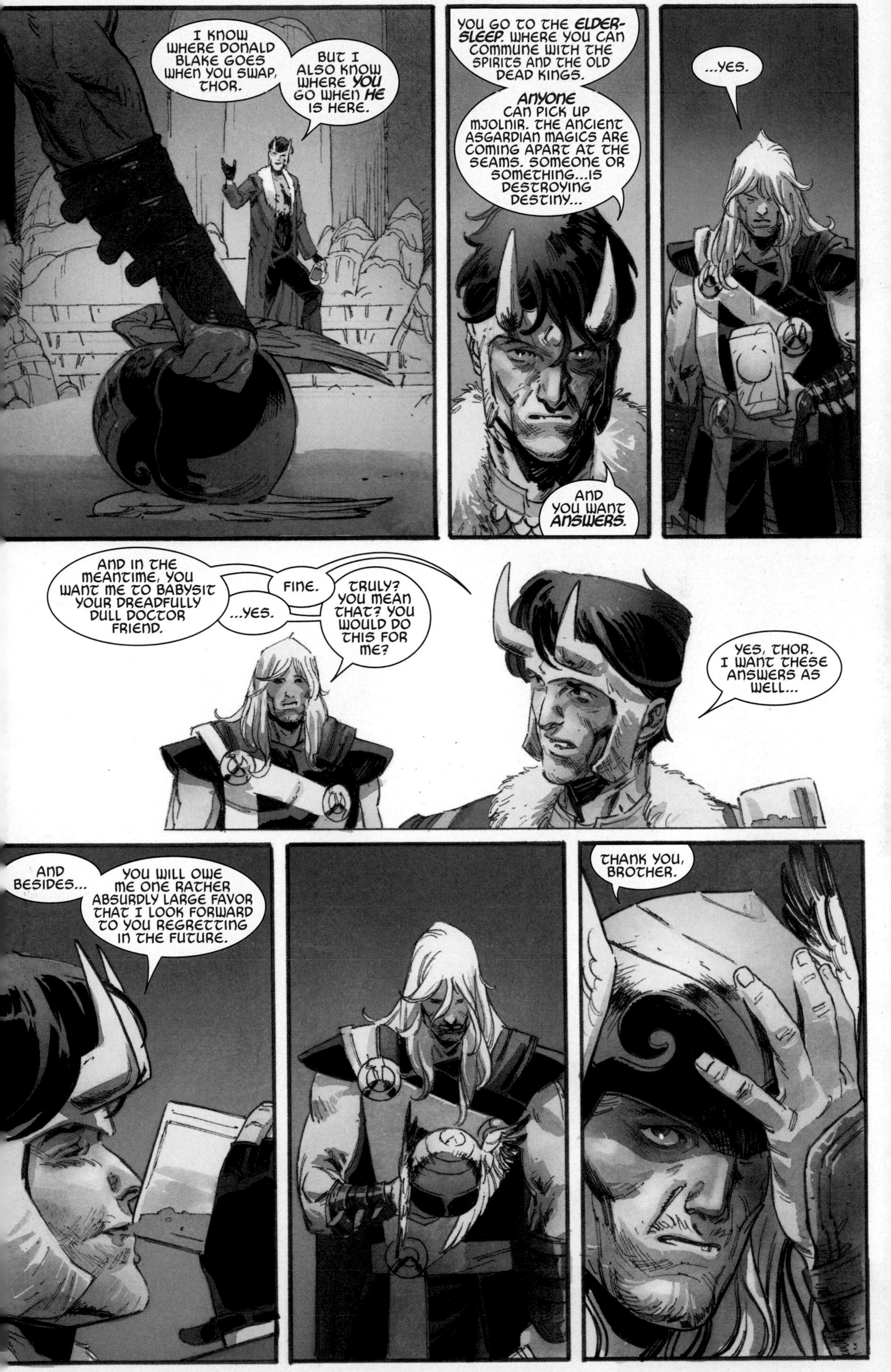
I KNOW WHERE DONALD BLAKE GOES WHEN YOU SWAP, THOR.
BUT I ALSO KNOW WHERE YOU GO WHEN HE IS HERE.
YOU GO TO THE ELDER-SLEEP. WHERE YOU CAN COMMUNE WITH THE SPIRITS AND THE OLD DEAD KINGS.
ANYONE CAN PICK UP MJOLNIR. THE ANCIENT ASGARDIAN MAGICS ARE COMING APART AT THE SEAMS. SOMEONE OR SOMETHING...IS DESTROYING DESTINY...
AND YOU WANT ANSWERS.
...YES.
AND IN THE MEANTIME, YOU WANT ME TO BABYSIT YOUR DREADFULLY DULL DOCTOR FRIEND.
...YES.
FINE.
TRULY? YOU MEAN THAT? YOU WOULD DO THIS FOR ME?
YES, THOR. I WANT THESE ANSWERS AS WELL...
AND BESIDES...
YOU WILL OWE ME ONE RATHER ABSURDLY LARGE FAVOR THAT I LOOK FORWARD TO YOU REGRETTING IN THE FUTURE.
THANK YOU, BROTHER.

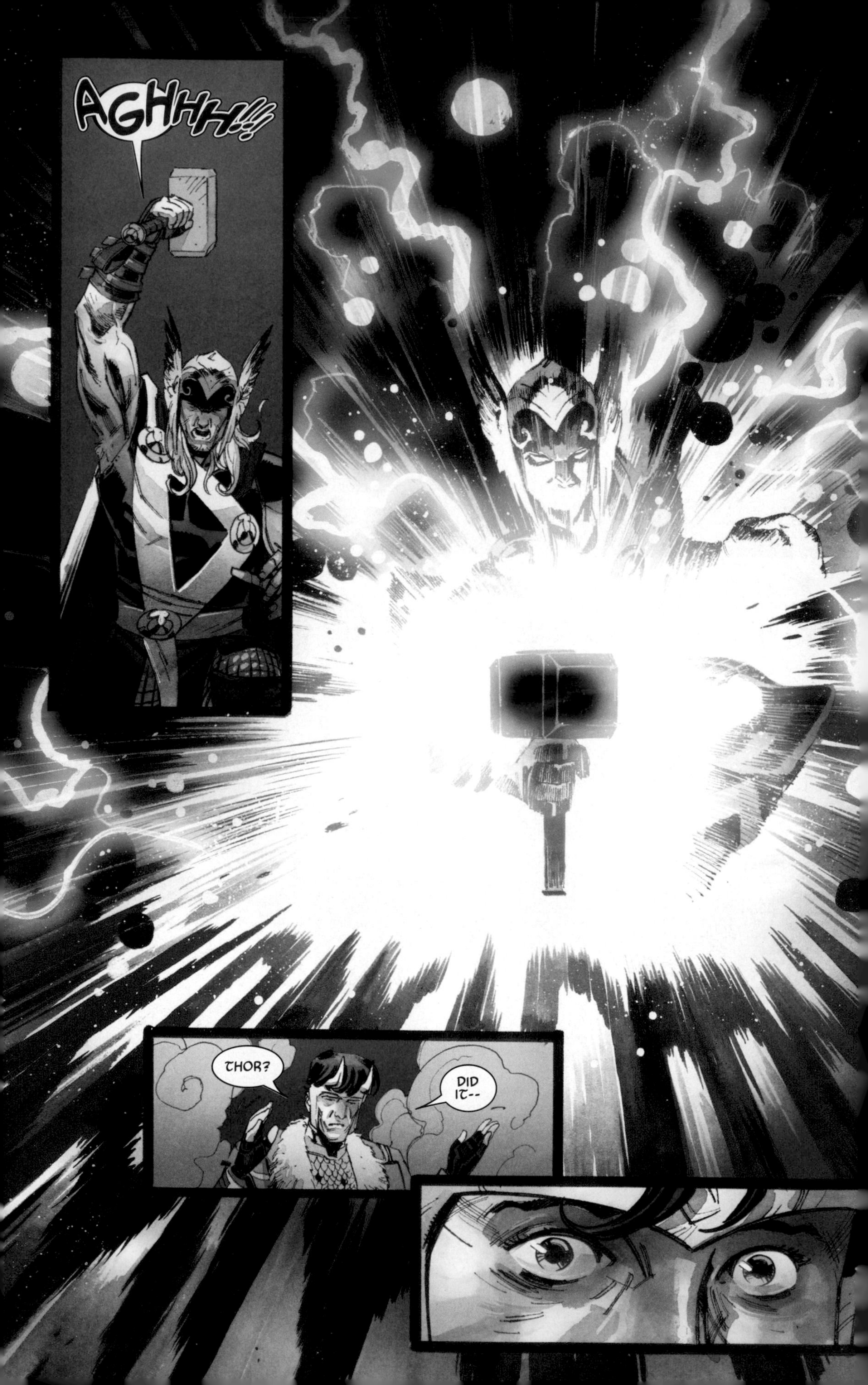
AGHHH!!!
THOR?
DID IT--

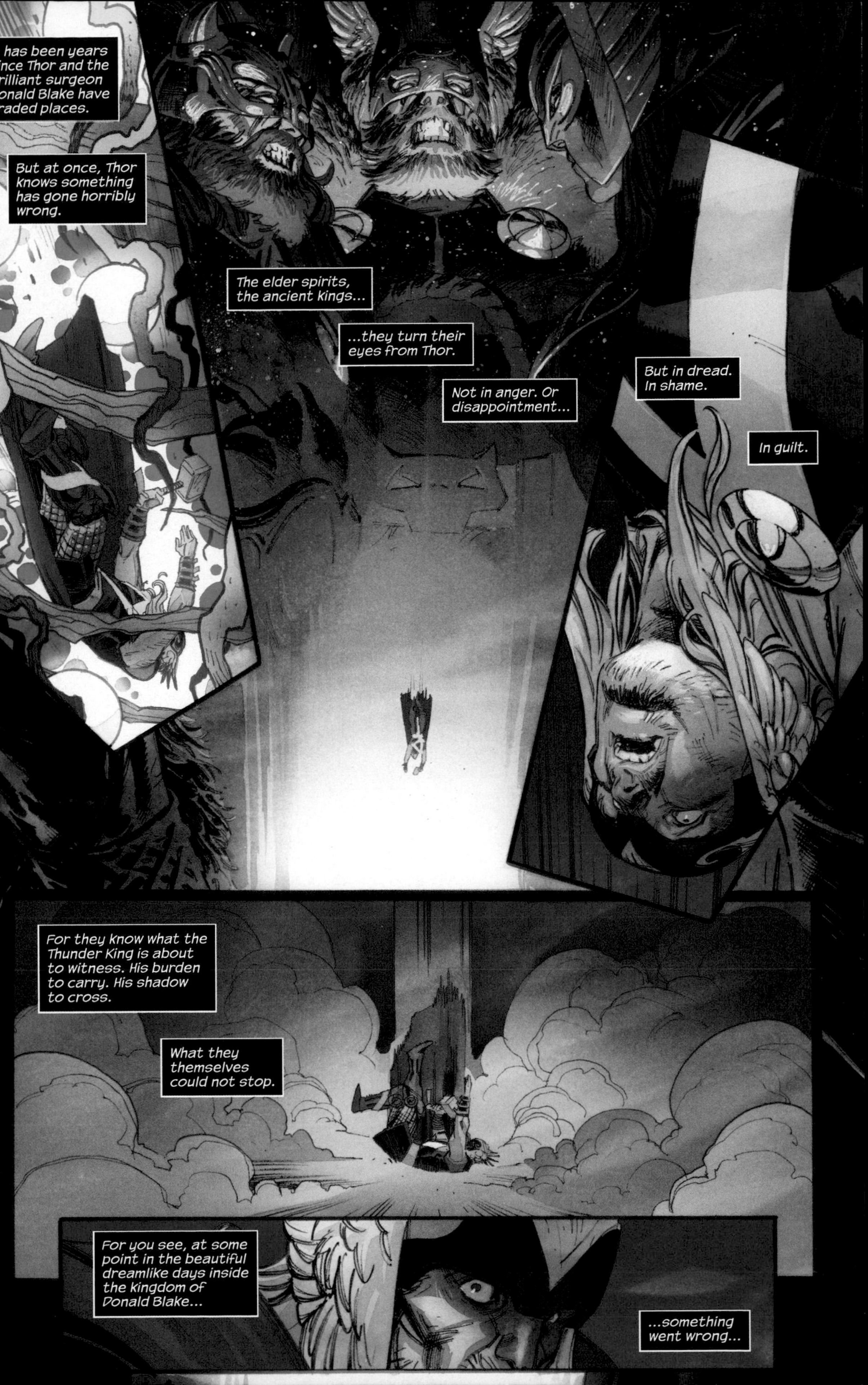
has been years
ince Thor and the
rilliant surgeon
onald Blake have
raded places.
But at once, Thor knows something has gone horribly wrong.
The elder spirits, the ancient kings...
...they turn their eyes from Thor.
Not in anger. Or disappointment...
But in dread. In shame.
In guilt.
For they know what the Thunder King is about to witness. His burden to carry. His shadow to cross.
What they themselves could not stop.
For you see, at some point in the beautiful dreamlike days inside the kingdom of Donald Blake...
...something went wrong...

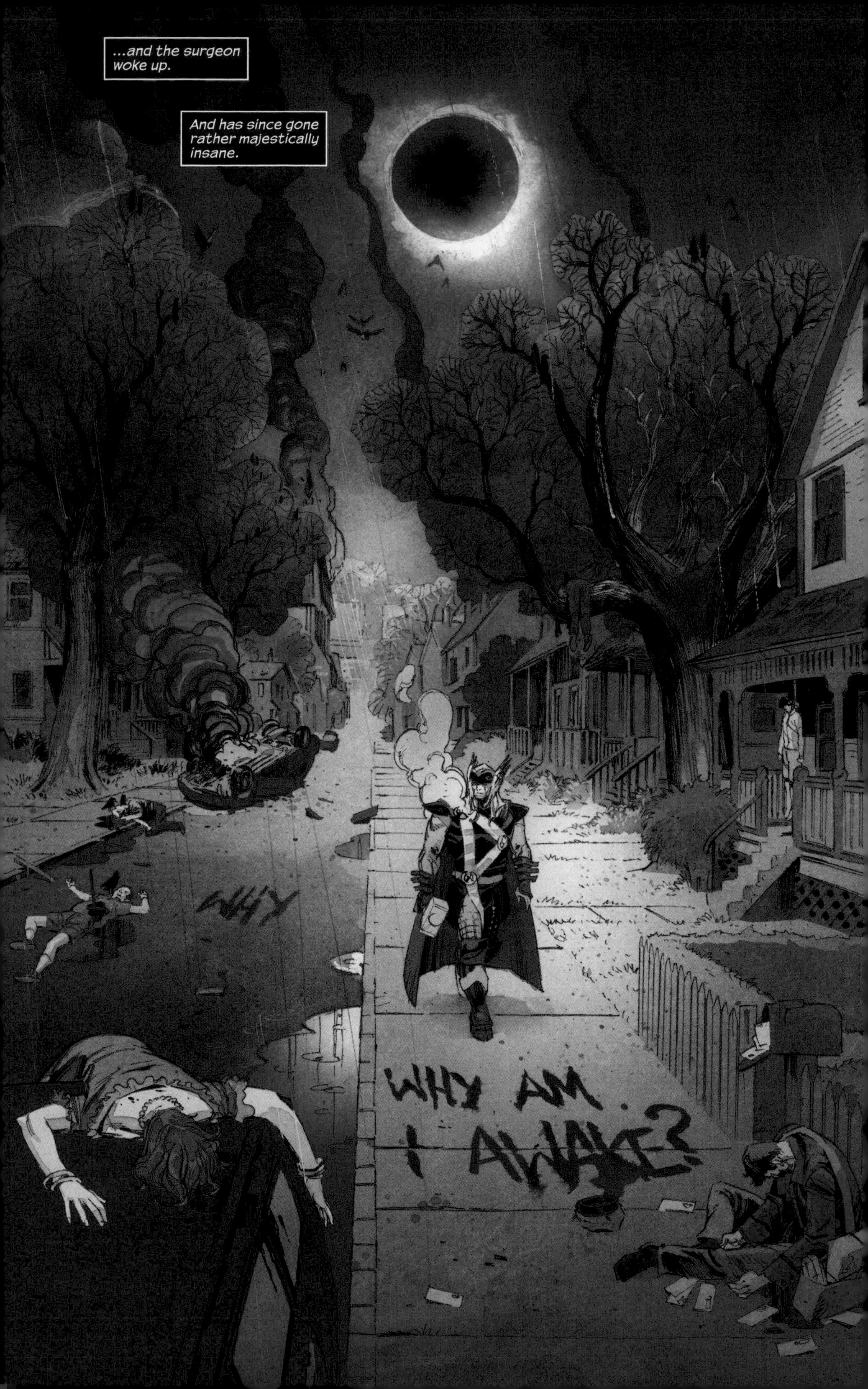
...and the surgeon woke up.
And has since gone rather majestically insane.
WHY
WHY AM I AWAKE?

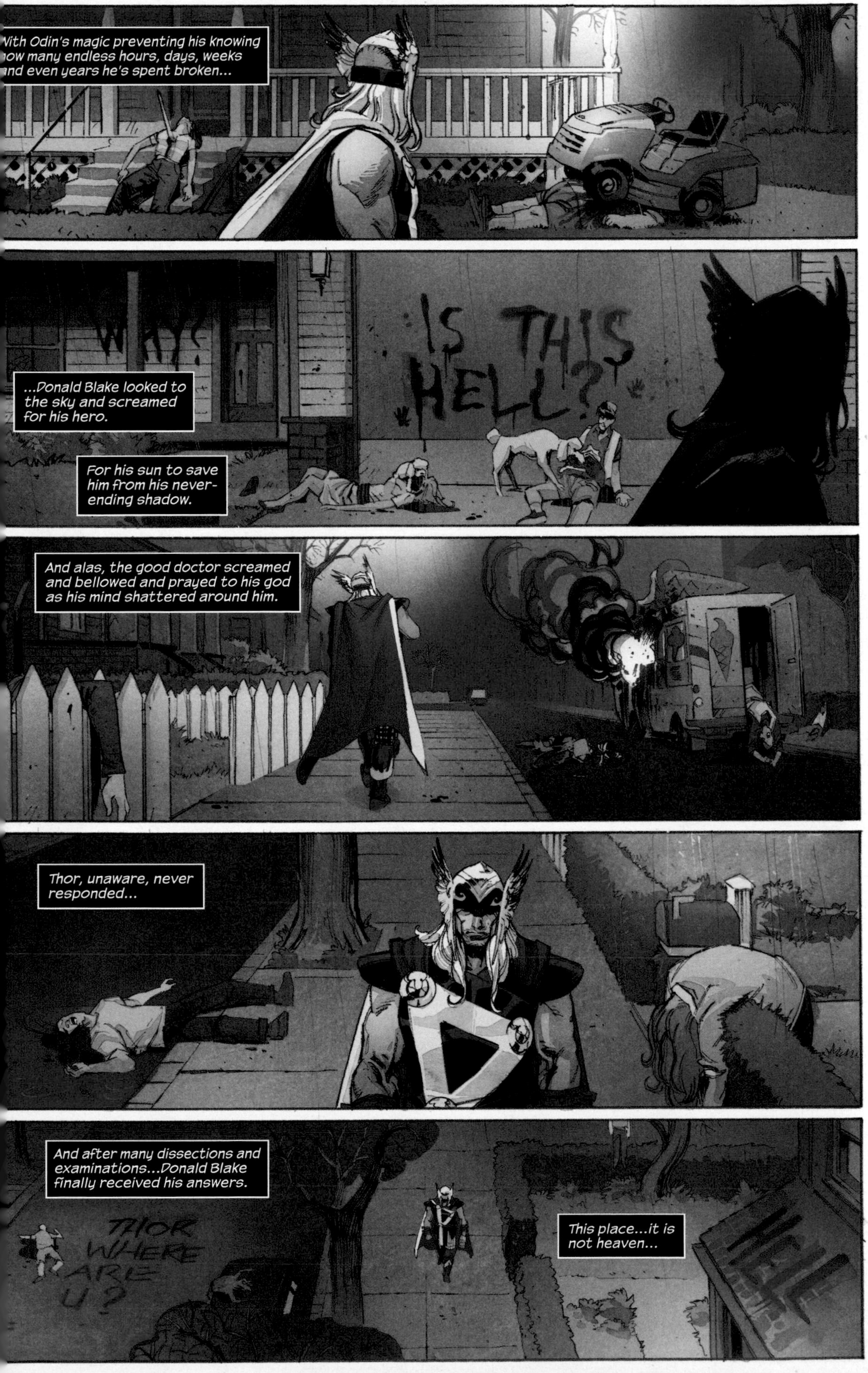
With Odin's magic preventing his knowing how many endless hours, days, weeks and even years he's spent broken...
WHY?
IS THIS HELL?
...Donald Blake looked to the sky and screamed for his hero.
For his sun to save him from his never-ending shadow.
And alas, the good doctor screamed and bellowed and prayed to his god as his mind shattered around him.
Thor, unaware, never responded...
And after many dissections and examinations...Donald Blake finally received his answers.
THOR WHERE ARE U?
This place...it is not heaven...
HELL

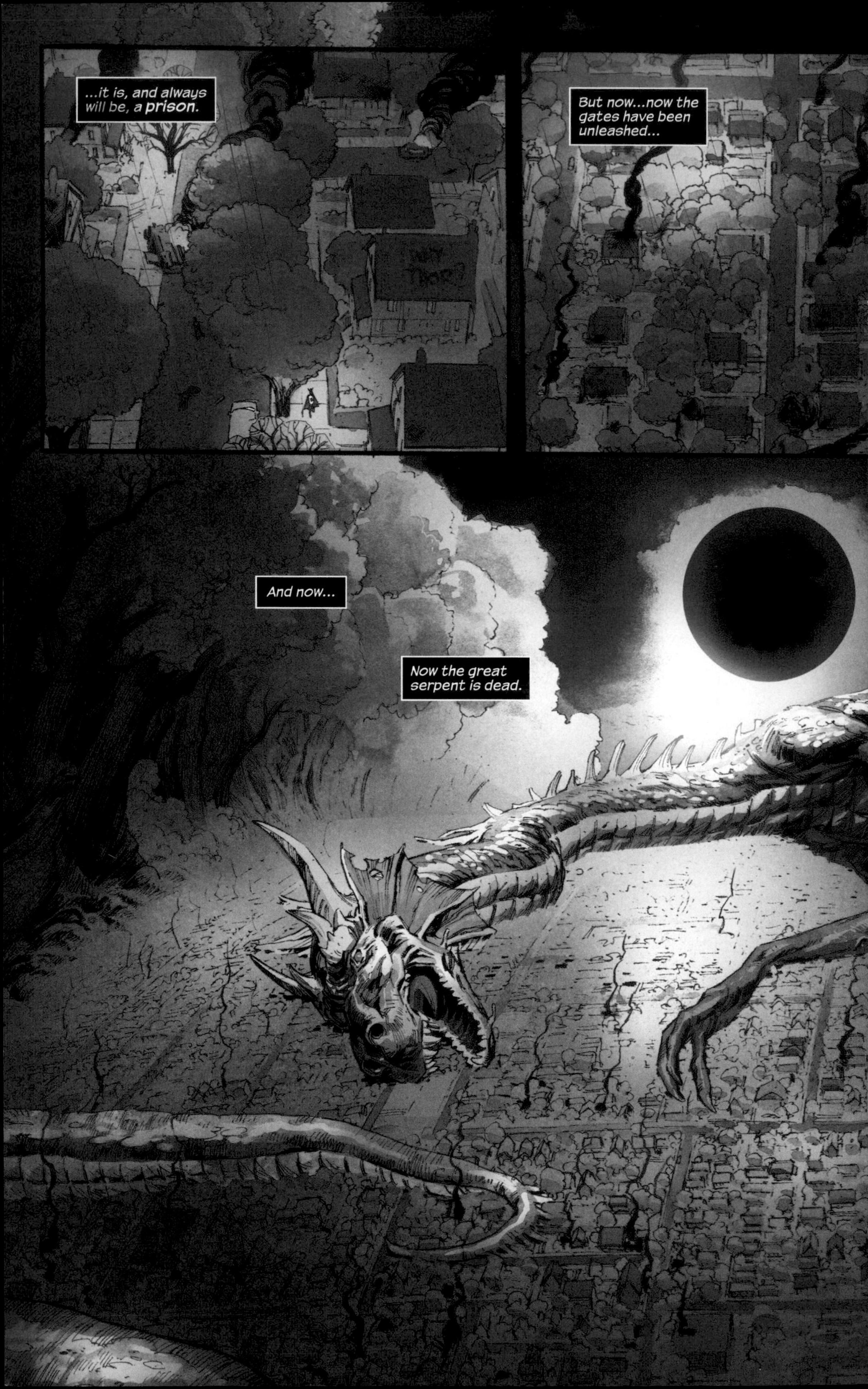
...it is, and always will be, a prison.
But now...now the gates have been unleashed...
And now...
Now the great serpent is dead.

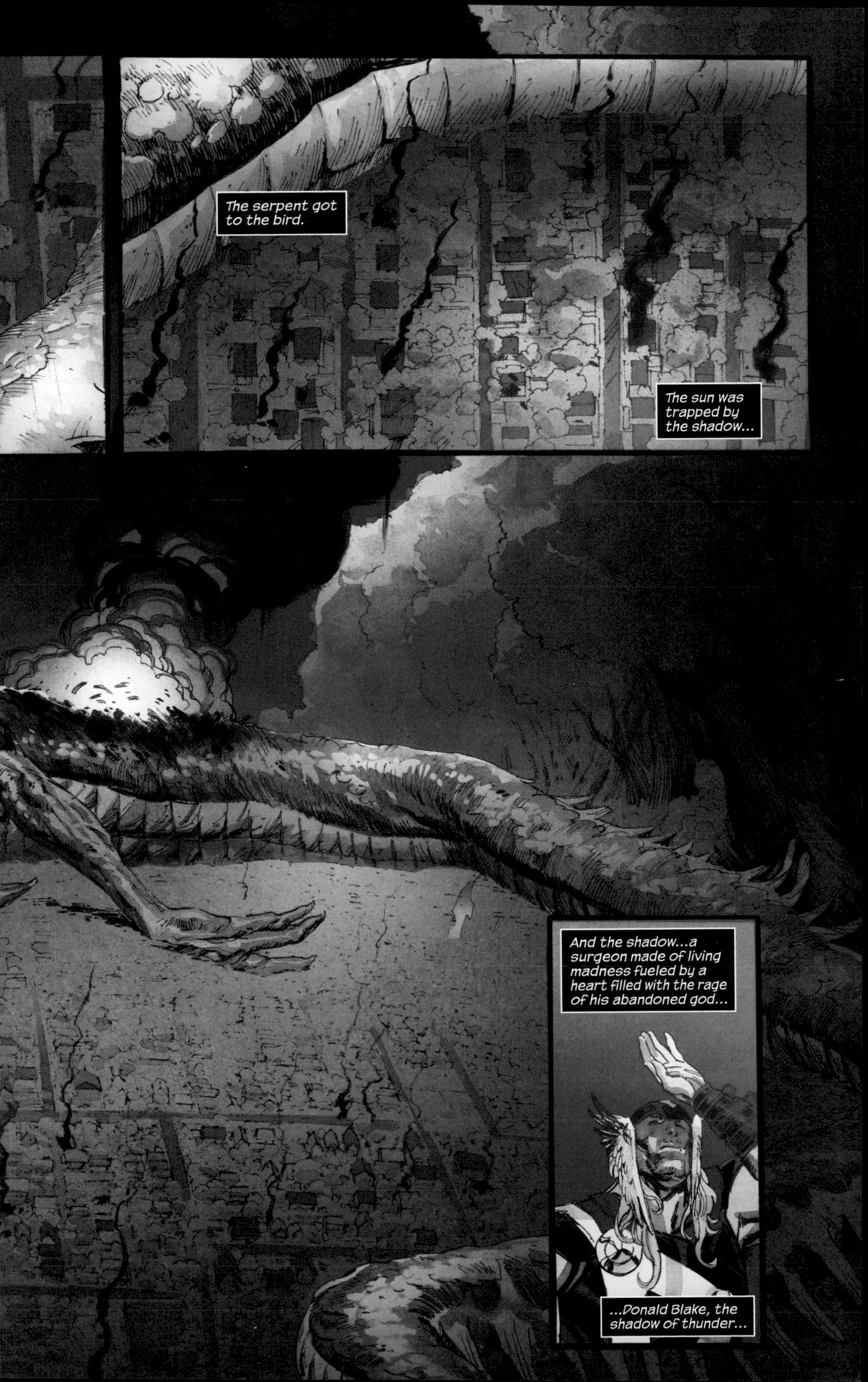
The serpent got to the bird.
The sun was trapped by the shadow...
And the shadow...a surgeon made of living madness fueled by a heart filled with the rage of his abandoned god...
...Donald Blake, the shadow of thunder...

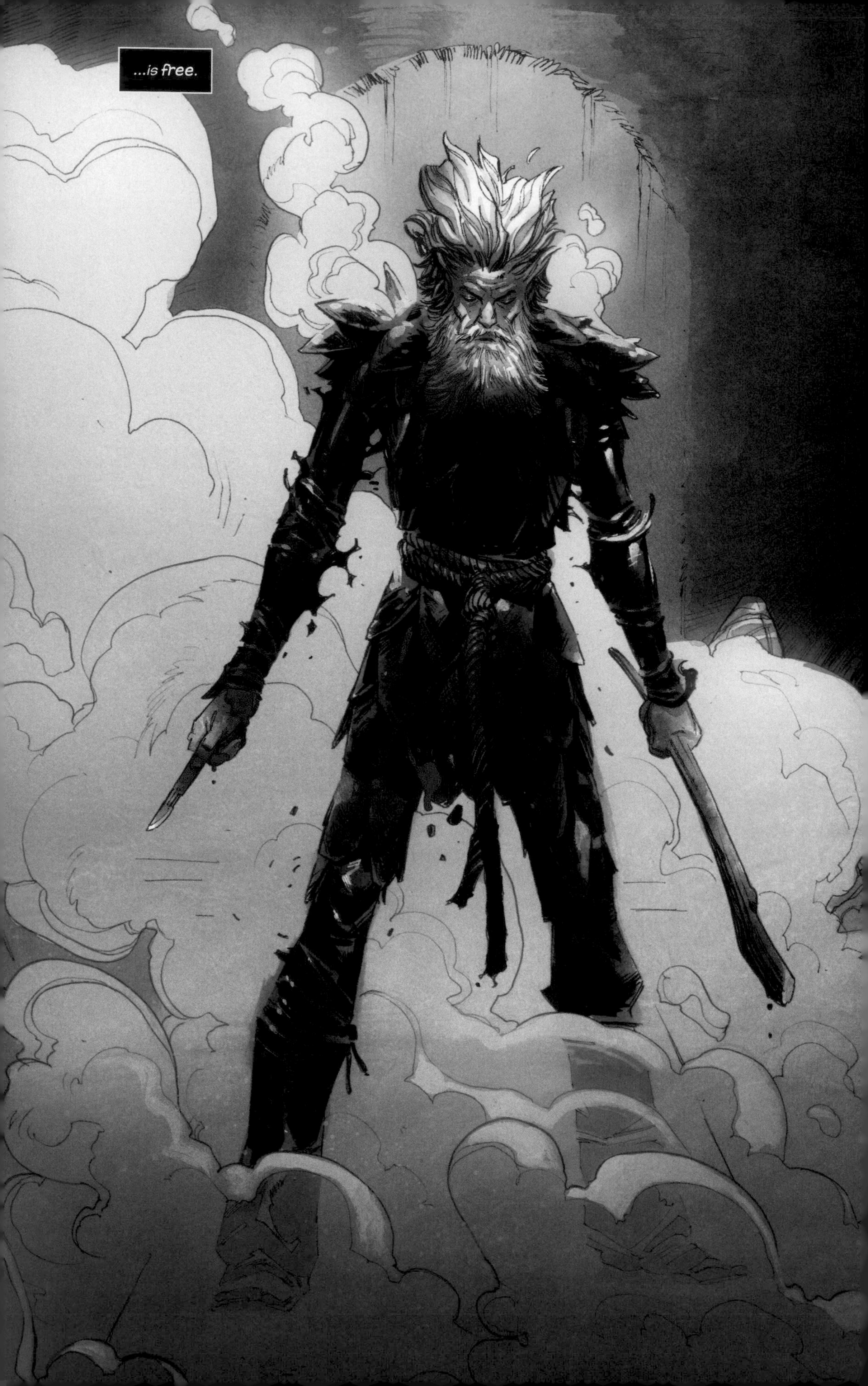
...is free.

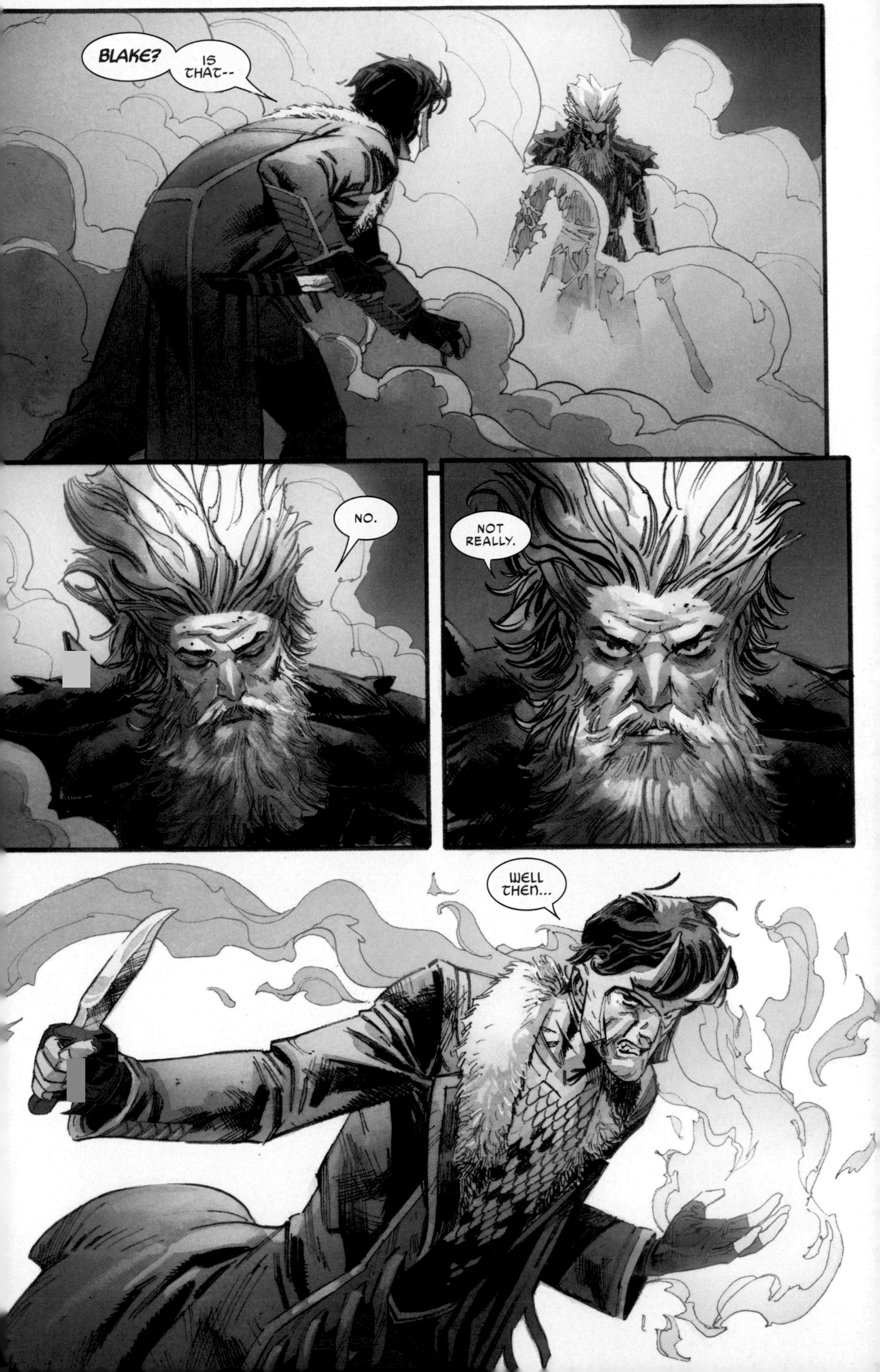
BLAKE?
IS THAT--
NO.
NOT REALLY.
WELL THEN...

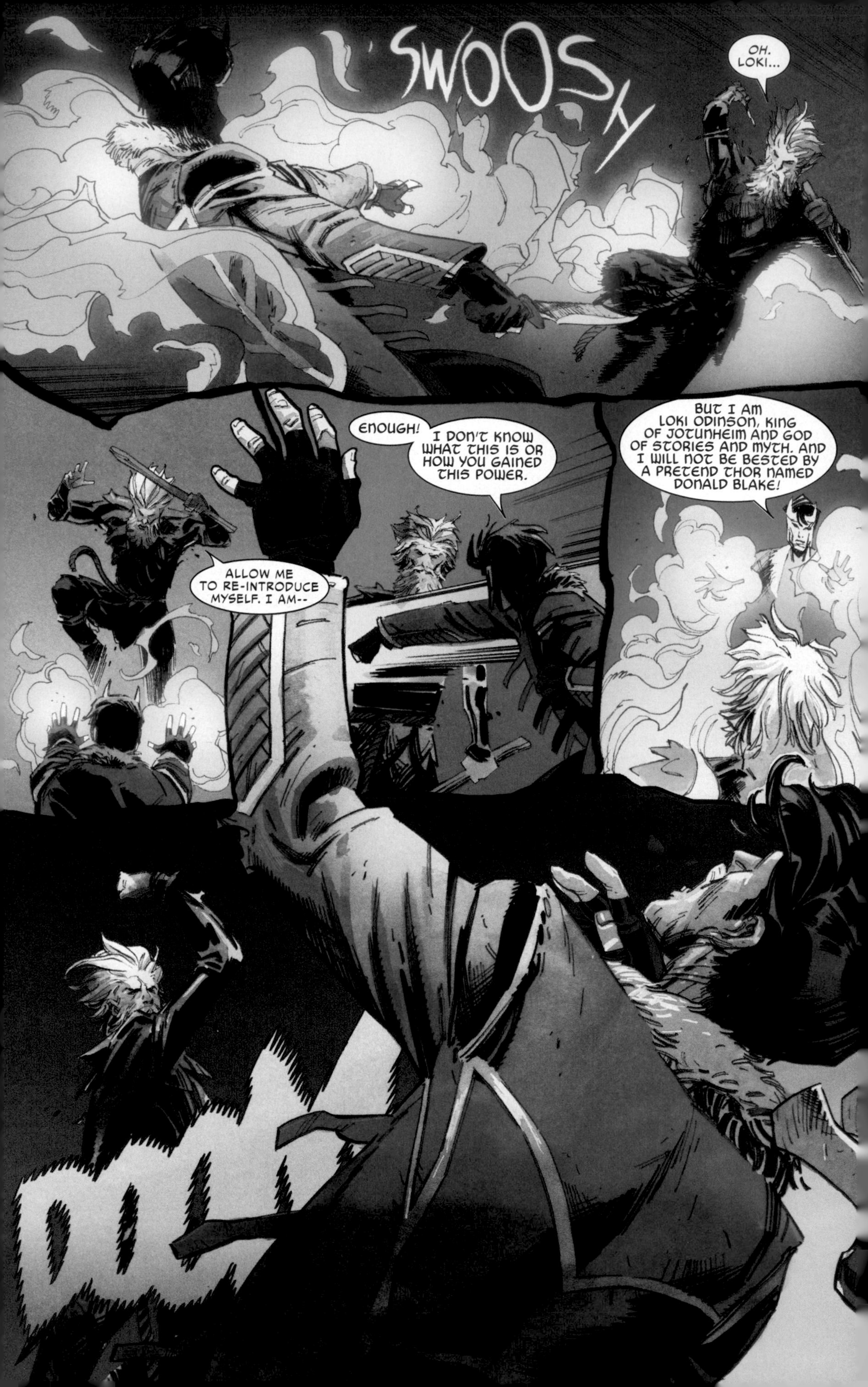
SWOOSH
OH. LOKI...
ALLOW ME TO RE-INTRODUCE MYSELF. I AM--
ENOUGH!
I DON'T KNOW WHAT THIS IS OR HOW YOU GAINED THIS POWER.
BUT I AM LOKI ODINSON, KING OF JOTUNHEIM AND GOD OF STORIES AND MYTH. AND I WILL NOT BE BESTED BY A PRETEND THOR NAMED DONALD BLAKE!

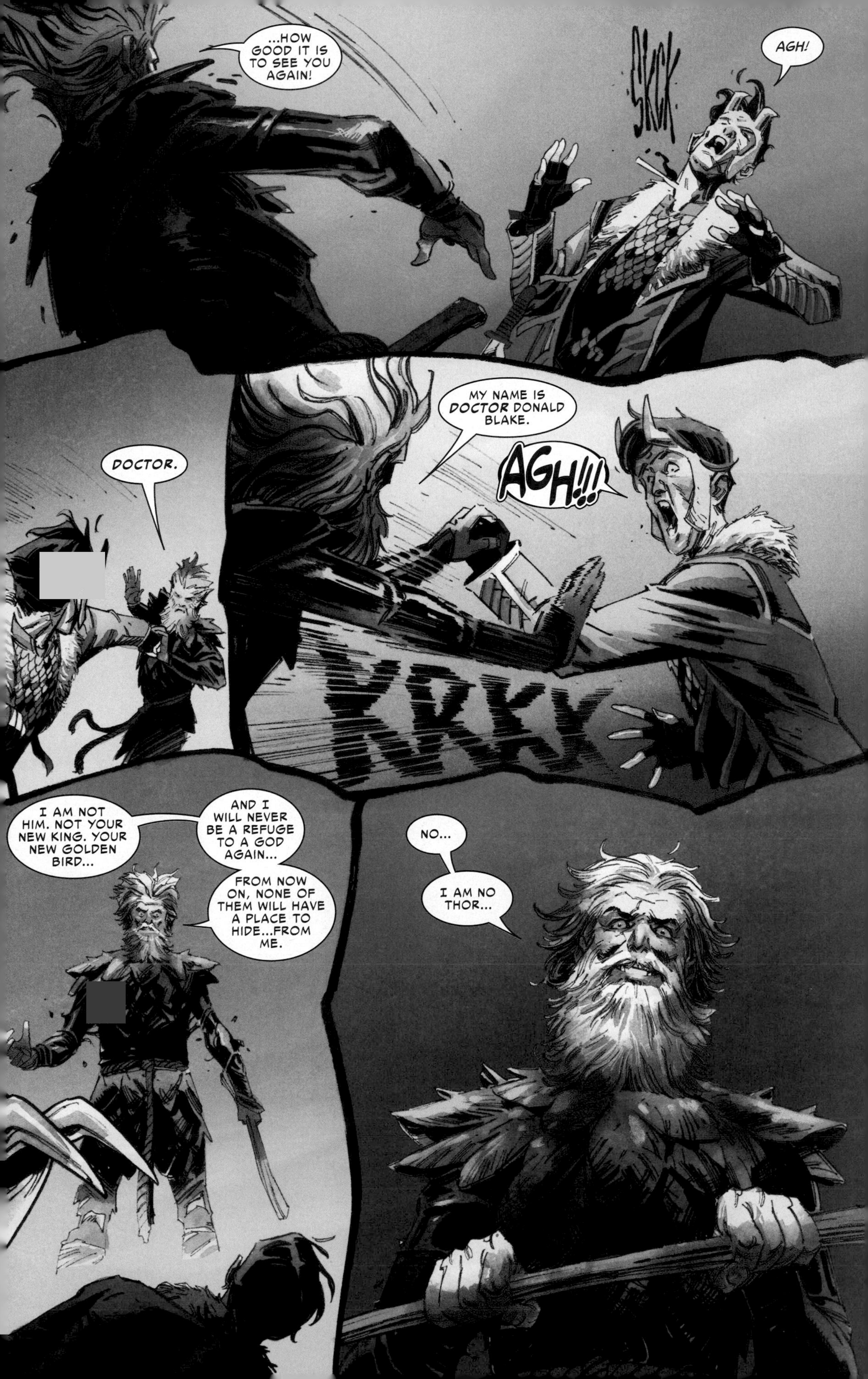
...HOW GOOD IT IS TO SEE YOU AGAIN!
SKCK
AGH!
MY NAME IS DOCTOR DONALD BLAKE.
AGH!!!
KRKX
DOCTOR.
I AM NOT HIM. NOT YOUR NEW KING. YOUR NEW GOLDEN BIRD...
AND I WILL NEVER BE A REFUGE TO A GOD AGAIN...
FROM NOW ON, NONE OF THEM WILL HAVE A PLACE TO HIDE...FROM ME.
NO...
I AM NO THOR...

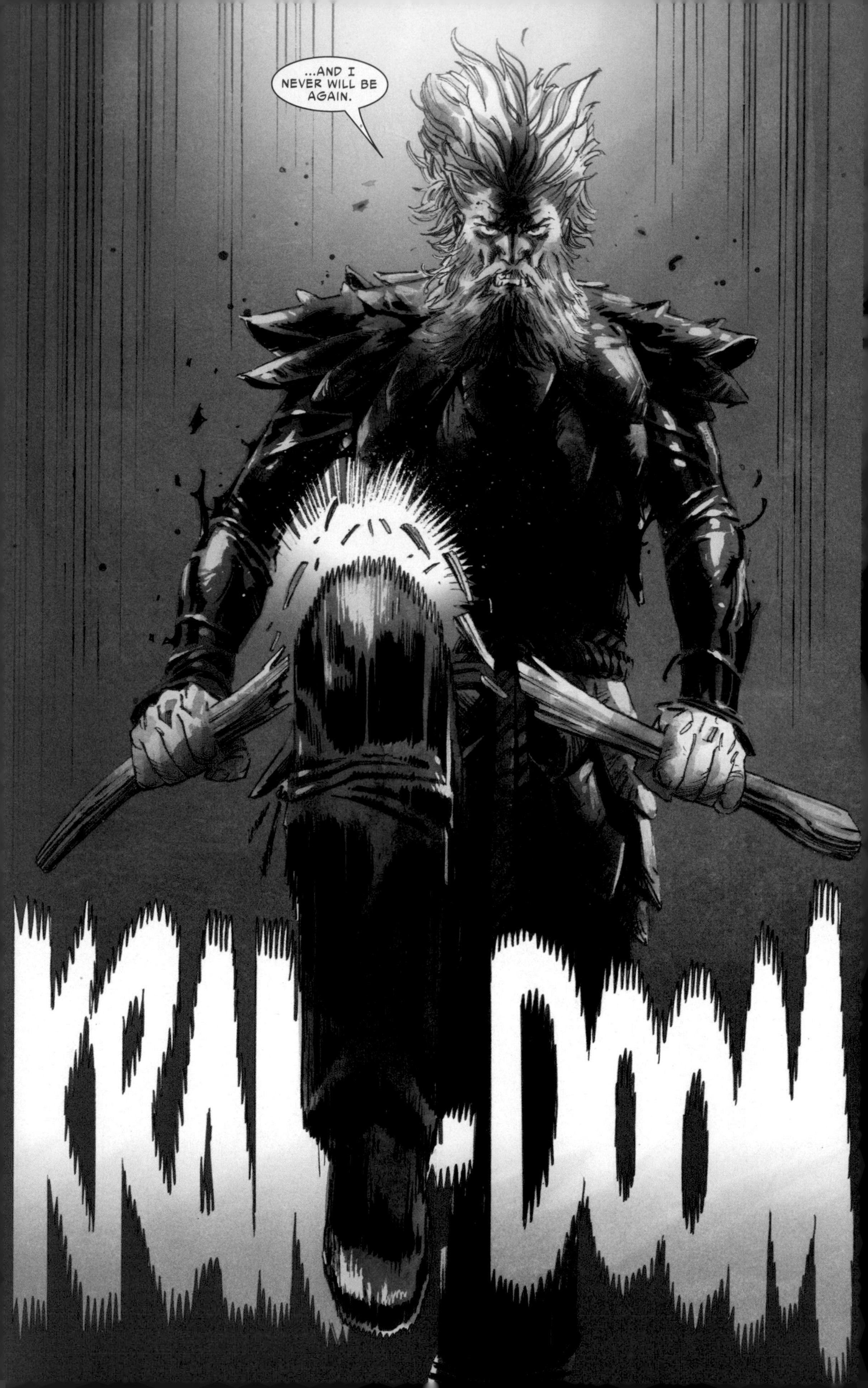
...AND I NEVER WILL BE AGAIN.

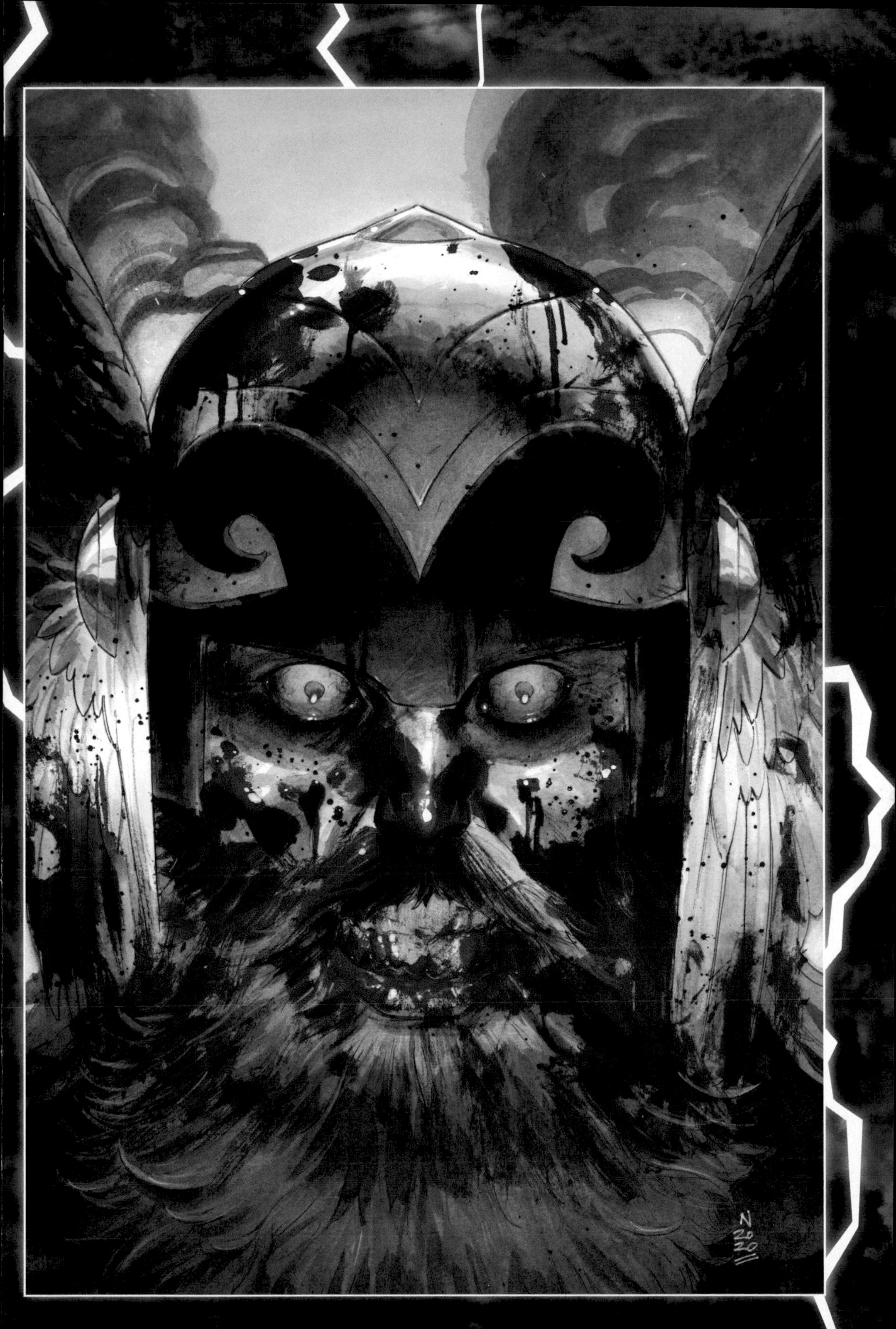

THOR 9 VARIANT BY

Nic Klein

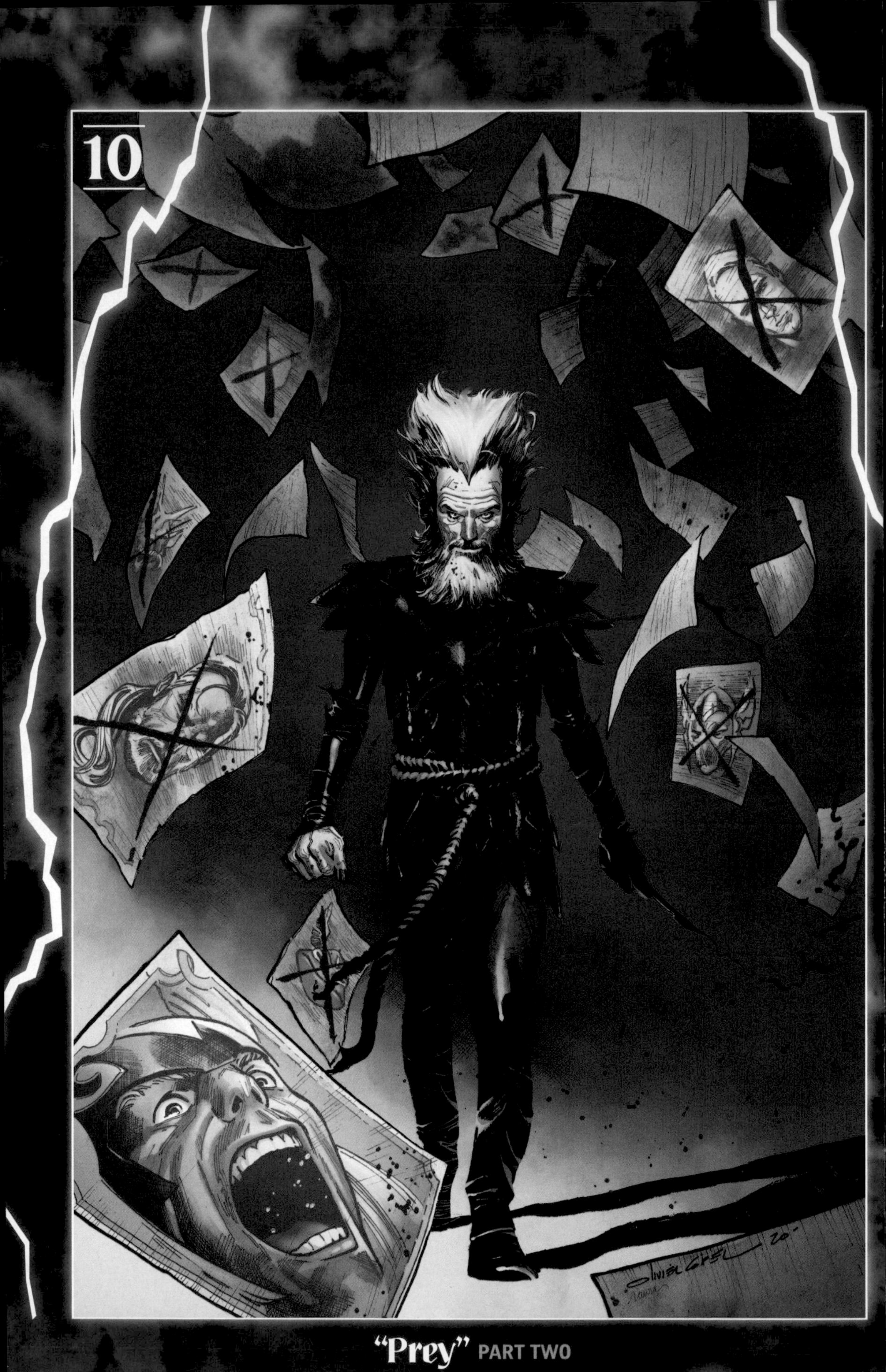
10

“Prey” PART TWO

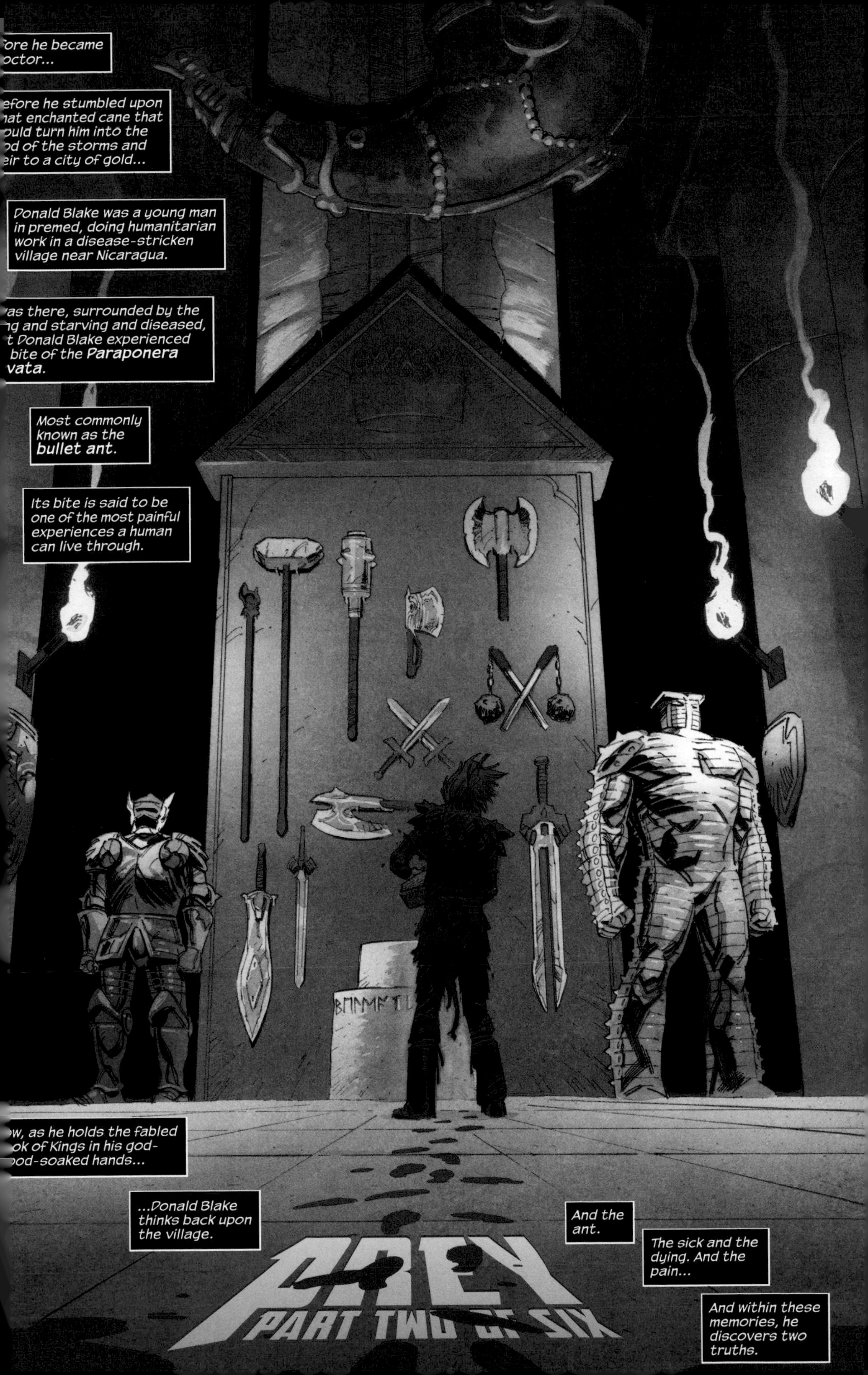

ore he became
octor...
efore he stumbled upon
at enchanted cane that
ould turn him into the
od of the storms and
eir to a city of gold...
Donald Blake was a young man in premed, doing humanitarian work in a disease-stricken village near Nicaragua.
as there, surrounded by the
ng and starving and diseased,
t Donald Blake experienced
bite of the Paraponera
vata.
Most commonly known as the bullet ant.
Its bite is said to be one of the most painful experiences a human can live through.
w, as he holds the fabled
ok of Kings in his god-
ood-soaked hands...
...Donald Blake thinks back upon the village.
And the ant.
The sick and the dying. And the pain...
And within these memories, he discovers two truths.
PART TWO
SIX

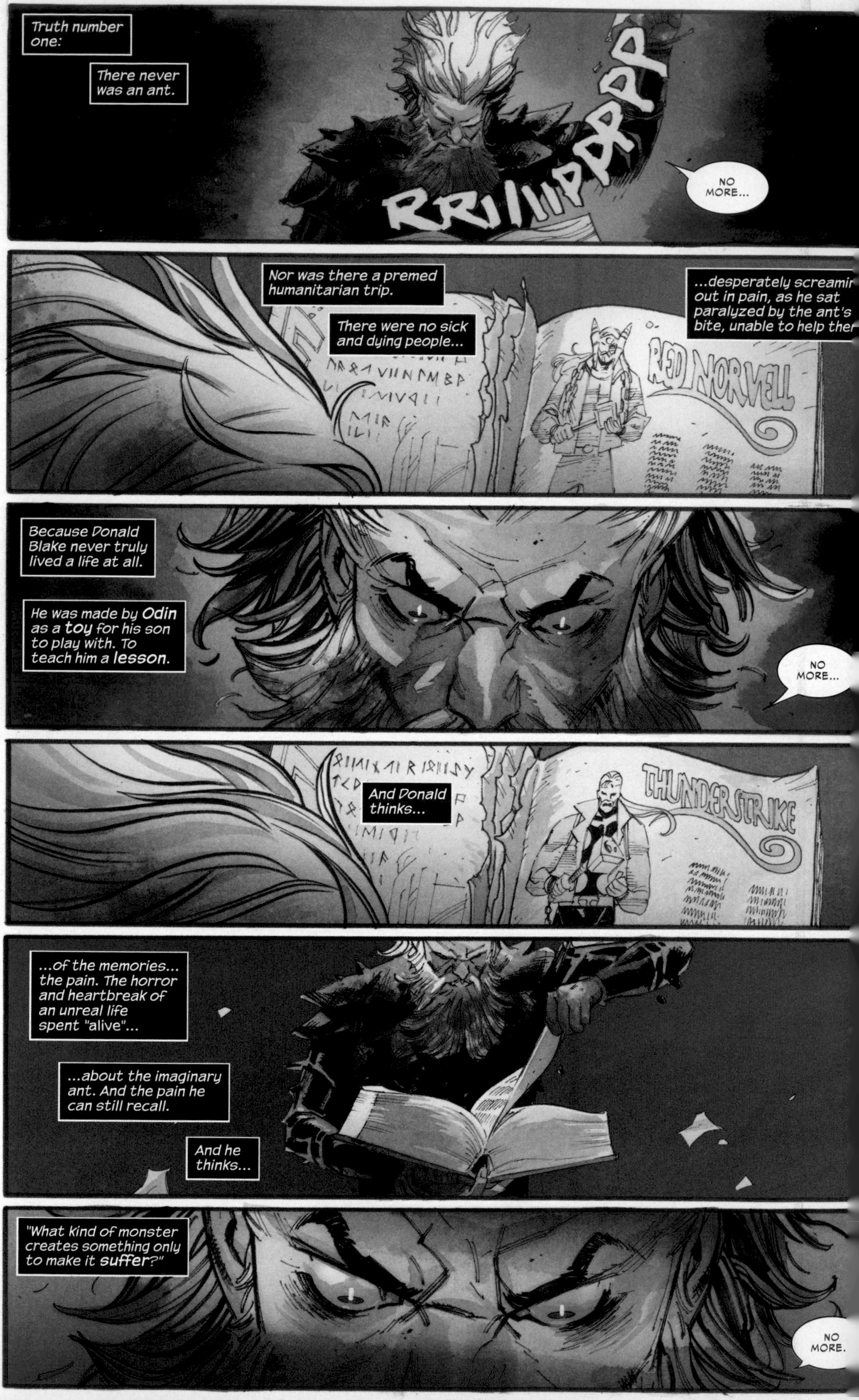

Truth number one:
There never was an ant.
RRIIIIPPPP
NO MORE...
Nor was there a premed humanitarian trip.
There were no sick and dying people...
...desperately screamir out in pain, as he sat paralyzed by the ant's bite, unable to help ther
RED NORVELL
Because Donald Blake never truly lived a life at all.
He was made by **Odin** as a **toy** for his son to play with. To teach him a **lesson**.
NO MORE...
And Donald thinks...
THUNDERSTRIKE
...of the memories... the pain. The horror and heartbreak of an unreal life spent "alive"...
...about the imaginary ant. And the pain he can still recall.
And he thinks...
"What kind of monster creates something only to make it **suffer**?"
NO MORE.

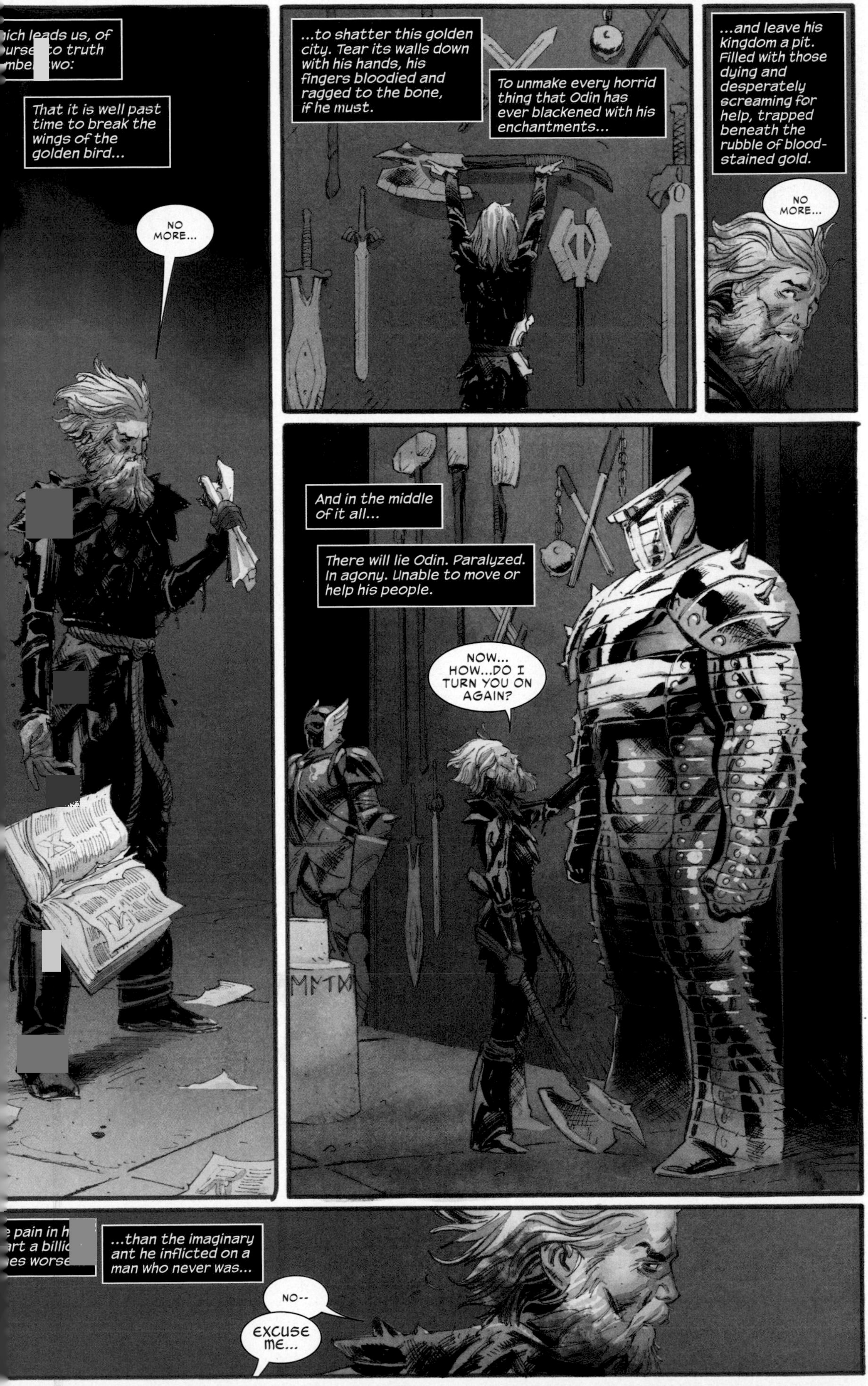

ich leads us, of
urse to truth
mbe wo:
That it is well past time to break the wings of the golden bird...
NO MORE...
...to shatter this golden city. Tear its walls down with his hands, his fingers bloodied and ragged to the bone, if he must.
To unmake every horrid thing that Odin has ever blackened with his enchantments...
...and leave his kingdom a pit. Filled with those dying and desperately screaming for help, trapped beneath the rubble of blood-stained gold.
NO MORE...
And in the middle of it all...
There will lie Odin. Paralyzed. In agony. Unable to move or help his people.
NOW... HOW...DO I TURN YOU ON AGAIN?
e pain in h
art a billi
es worse
...than the imaginary ant he inflicted on a man who never was...
NO--
EXCUSE ME...

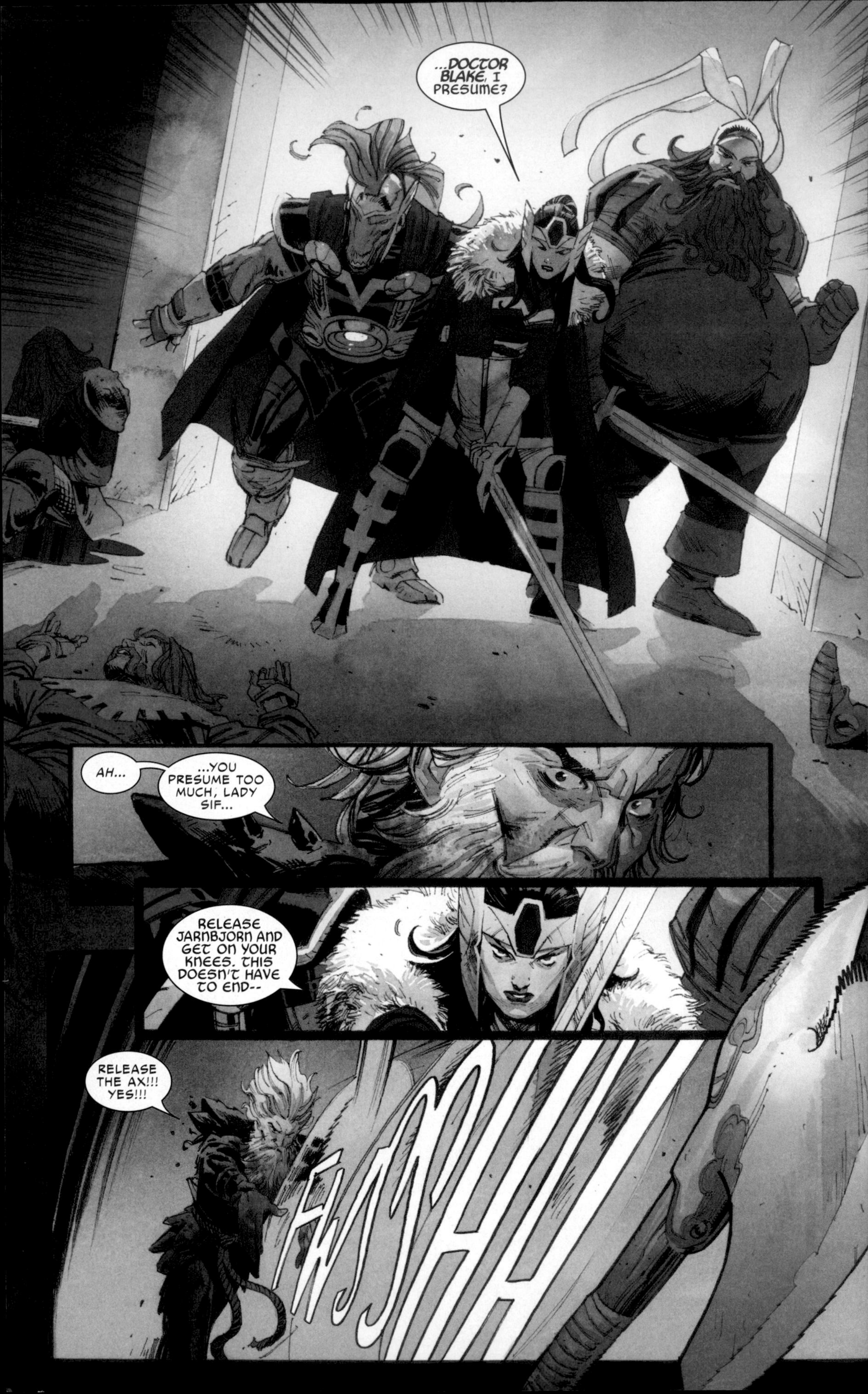
...DOCTOR BLAKE, I PRESUME?
AH...
...YOU PRESUME TOO MUCH, LADY SIF...
RELEASE JARNBJORN AND GET ON YOUR KNEES. THIS DOESN'T HAVE TO END--
RELEASE THE AX!!! YES!!!
FWSHH

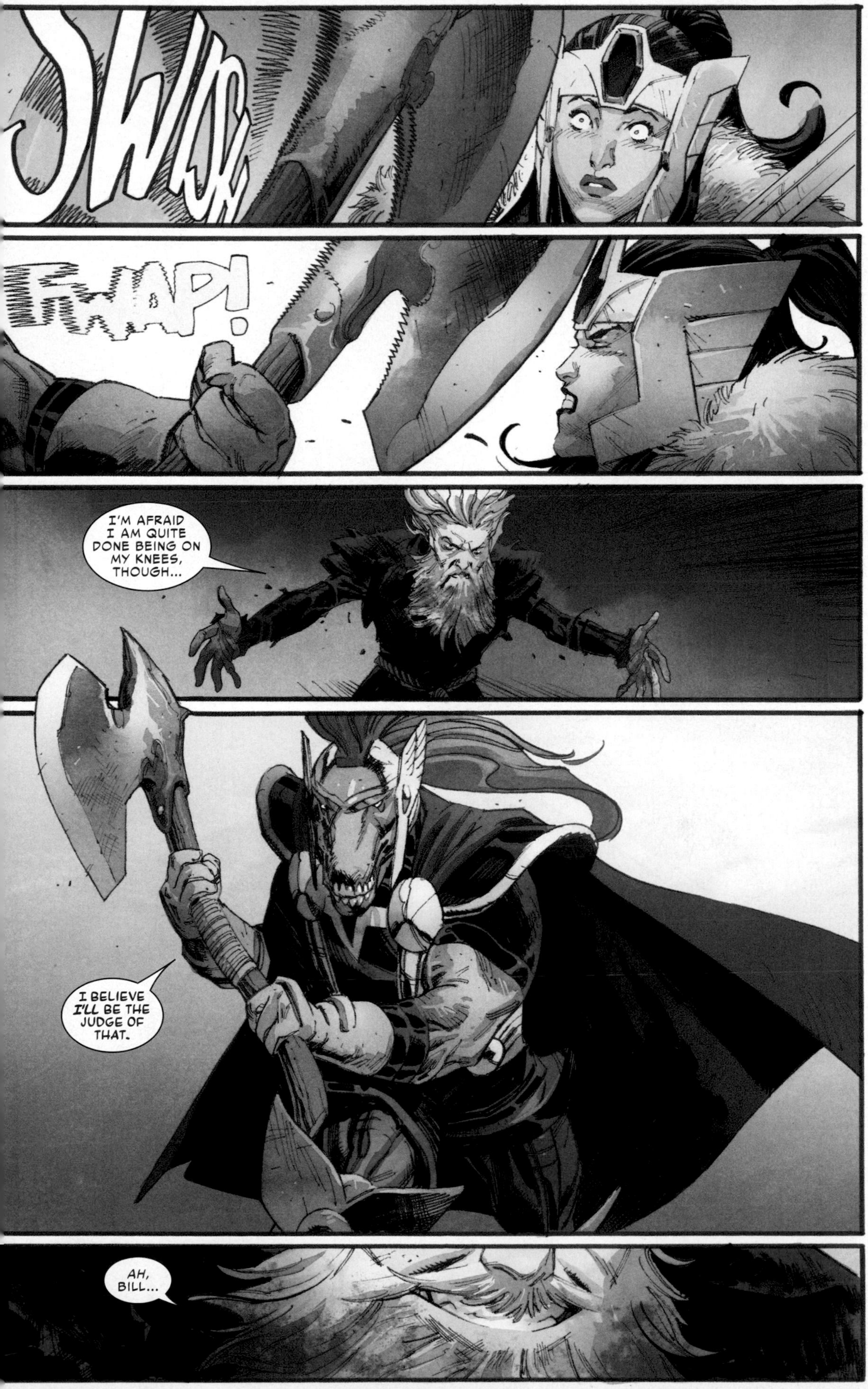
SWISH
FWAP!
I'M AFRAID I AM QUITE DONE BEING ON MY KNEES, THOUGH...
I BELIEVE I'LL BE THE JUDGE OF THAT.
AH, BILL...

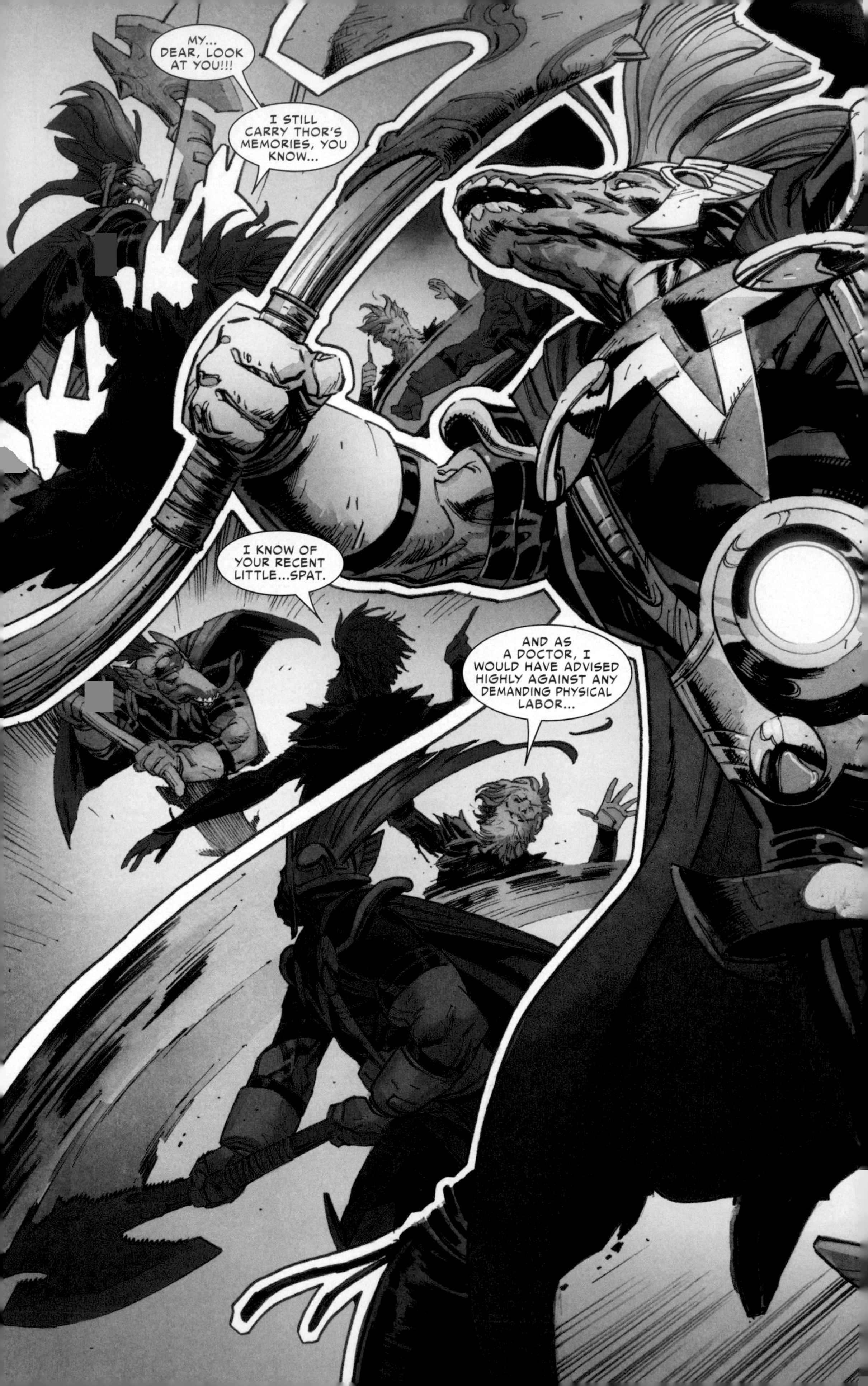
MY... DEAR, LOOK AT YOU!!!
I STILL CARRY THOR'S MEMORIES, YOU KNOW...
I KNOW OF YOUR RECENT LITTLE...SPAT.
AND AS A DOCTOR, I WOULD HAVE ADVISED HIGHLY AGAINST ANY DEMANDING PHYSICAL LABOR...

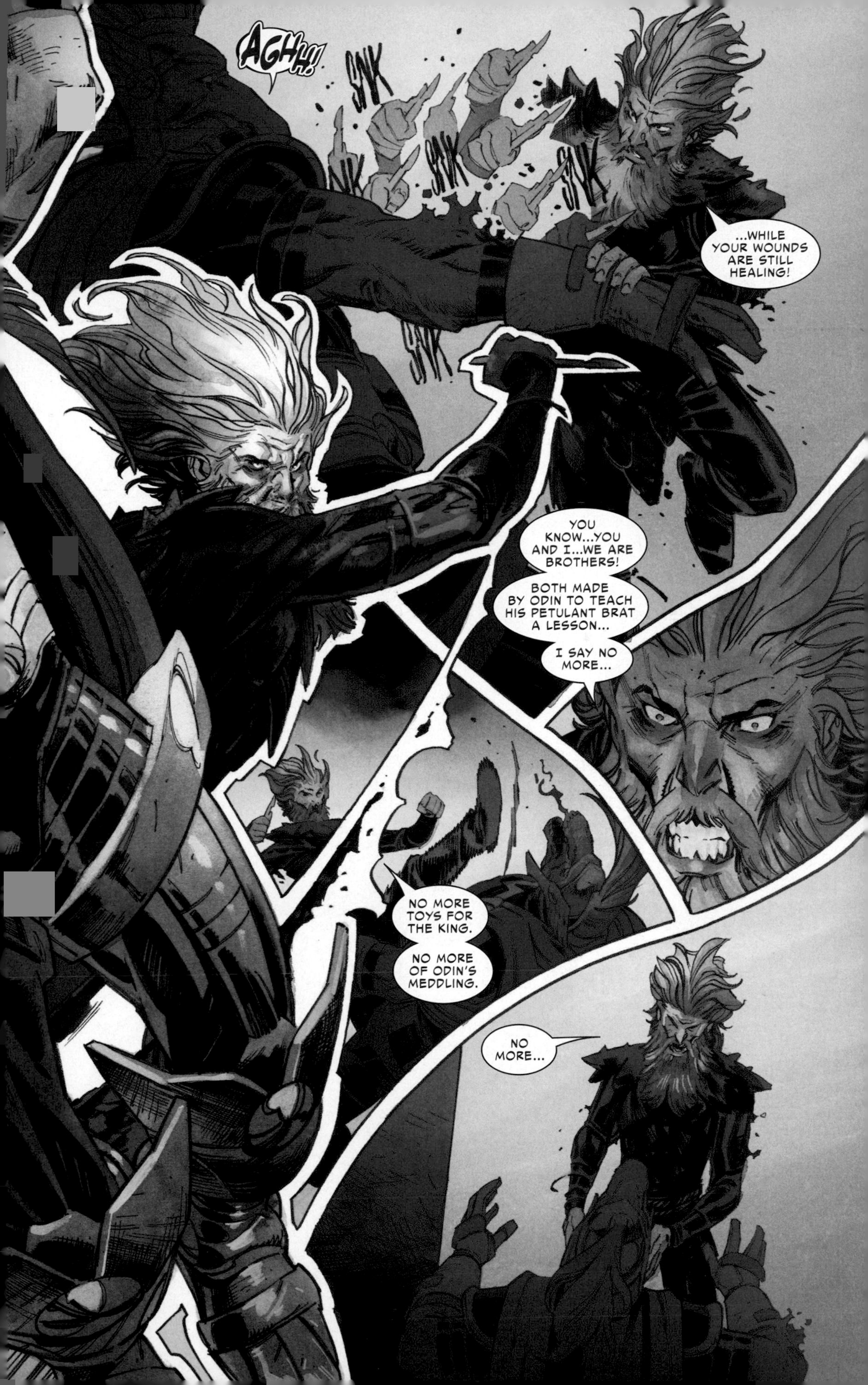
AGHH!!
SNK
SNK
SNK
SNK
...WHILE YOUR WOUNDS ARE STILL HEALING!
SNK
YOU KNOW...YOU AND I...WE ARE BROTHERS!
BOTH MADE BY ODIN TO TEACH HIS PETULANT BRAT A LESSON...
I SAY NO MORE...
NO MORE TOYS FOR THE KING.
NO MORE OF ODIN'S MEDDLING.
NO MORE...

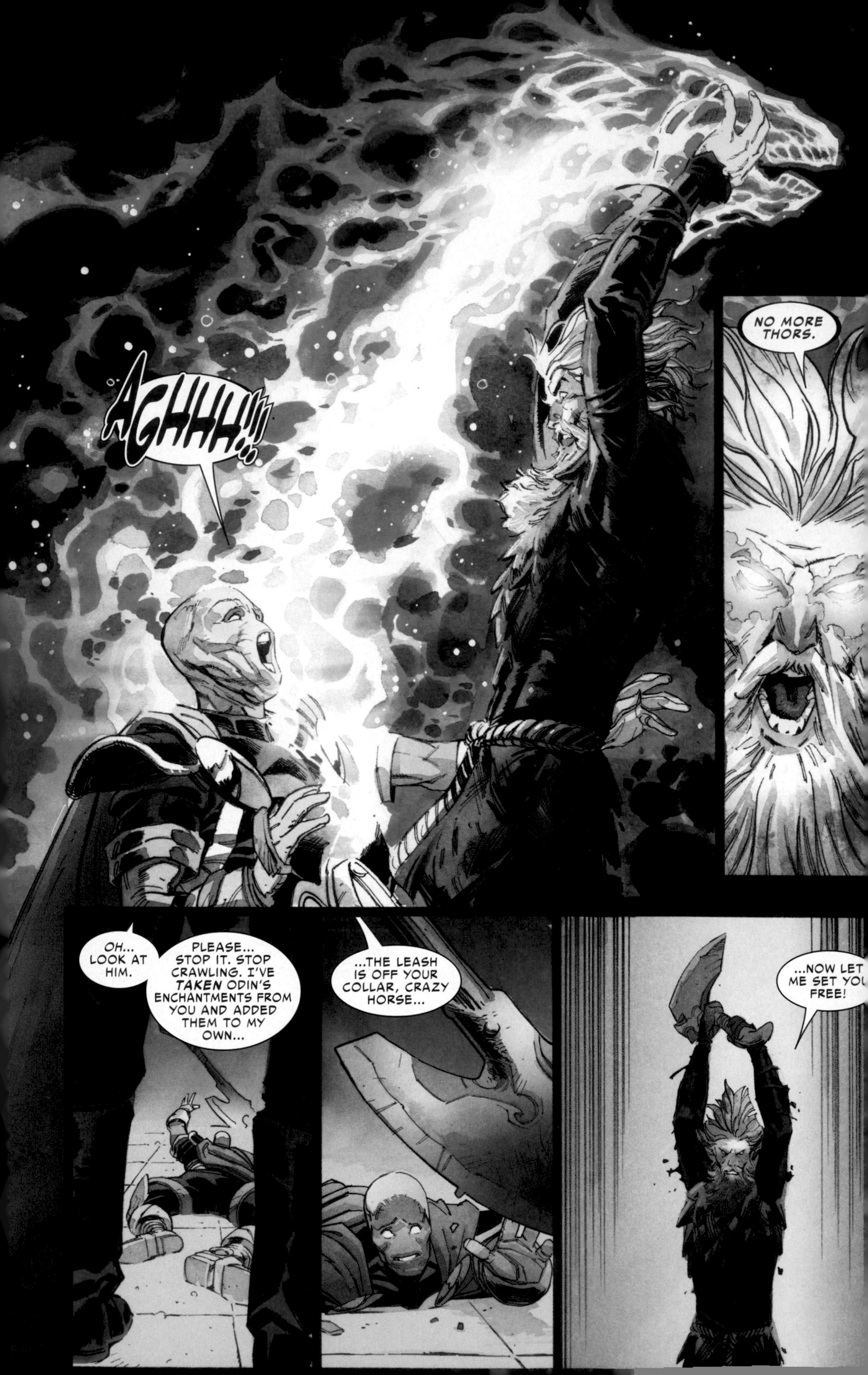
AGHHH!!!
NO MORE THORS.
OH... LOOK AT HIM.
PLEASE... STOP IT. STOP CRAWLING. I'VE TAKEN ODIN'S ENCHANTMENTS FROM YOU AND ADDED THEM TO MY OWN...
...THE LEASH IS OFF YOUR COLLAR, CRAZY HORSE...
...NOW LET ME SET YOU FREE!

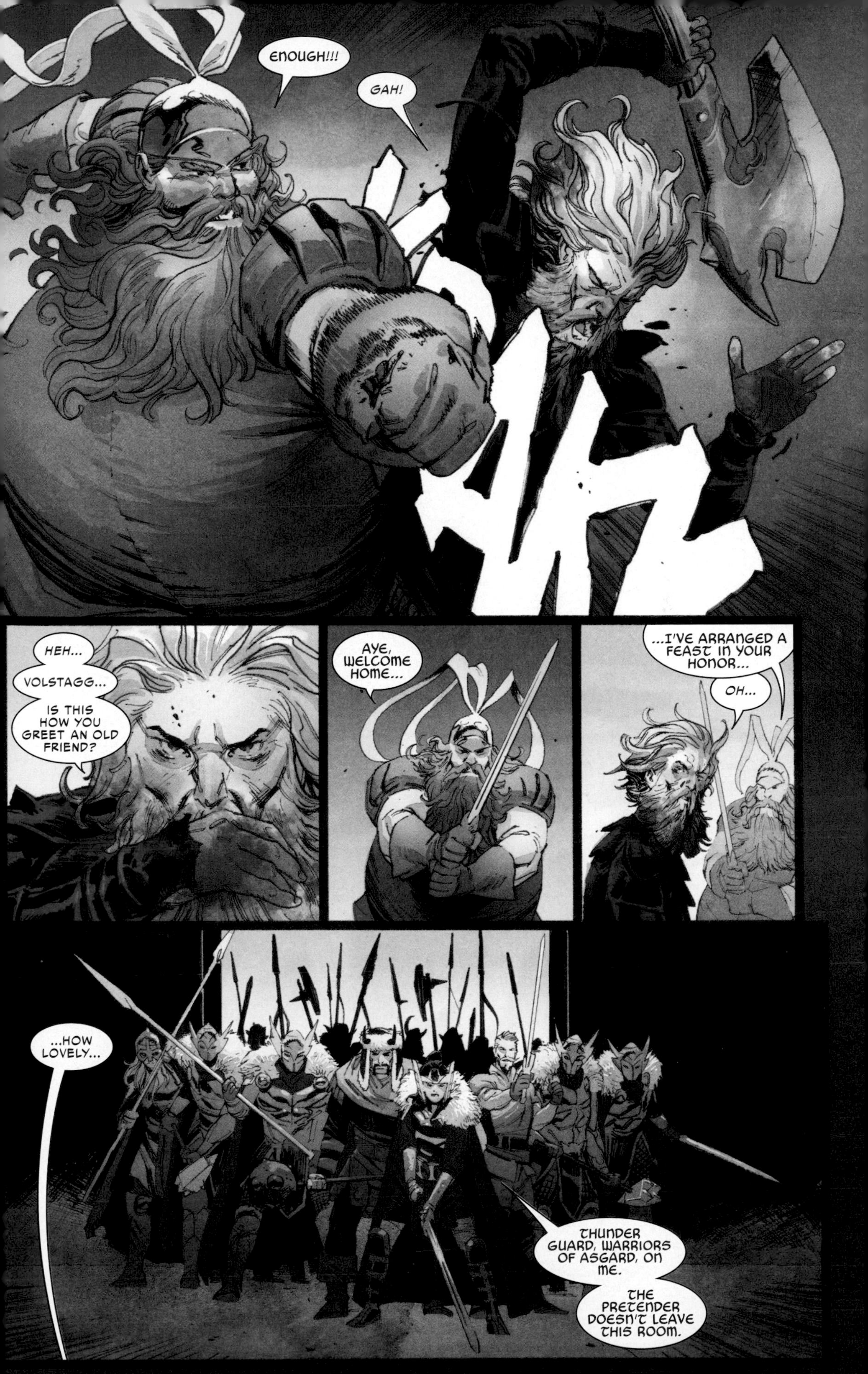
ENOUGH!!!
GAH!
HEH...
VOLSTAGG...
IS THIS HOW YOU GREET AN OLD FRIEND?
AYE, WELCOME HOME...
...I'VE ARRANGED A FEAST IN YOUR HONOR...
OH...
...HOW LOVELY...
THUNDER GUARD, WARRIORS OF ASGARD, ON ME.
THE PRETENDER DOESN'T LEAVE THIS ROOM.

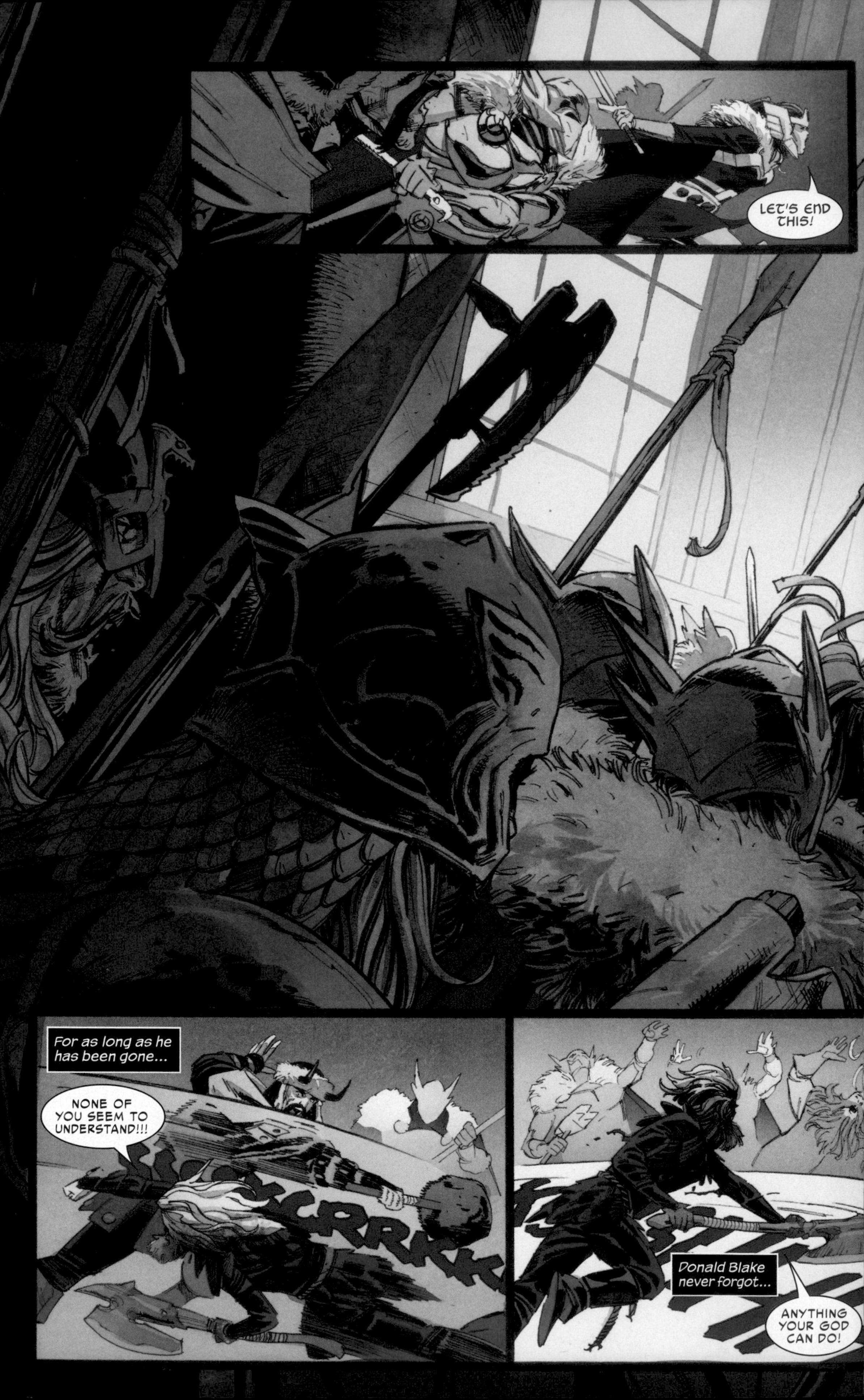
LET'S END THIS!
For as long as he has been gone...
NONE OF YOU SEEM TO UNDERSTAND!!!
KRRKK
Donald Blake never forgot...
ANYTHING YOUR GOD CAN DO!

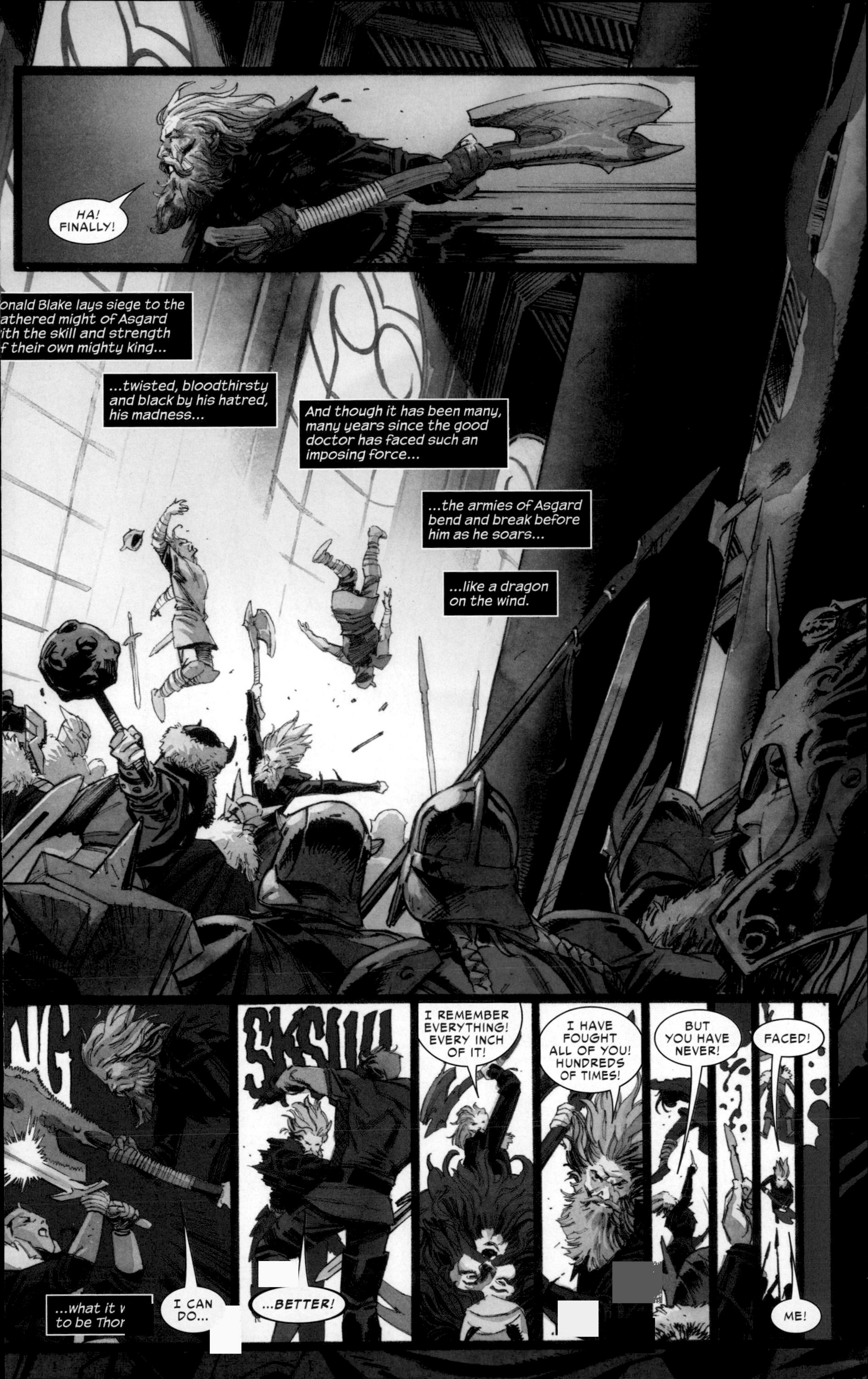

HA! FINALLY!
onald Blake lays siege to the athered might of Asgard ith the skill and strength f their own mighty king...
...twisted, bloodthirsty and black by his hatred, his madness...
And though it has been many, many years since the good doctor has faced such an imposing force...
...the armies of Asgard bend and break before him as he soars...
...like a dragon on the wind.
...what it v to be Thor
I CAN DO...
...BETTER!
I REMEMBER EVERYTHING! EVERY INCH OF IT!
I HAVE FOUGHT ALL OF YOU! HUNDREDS OF TIMES!
BUT YOU HAVE NEVER!
FACED!
ME!

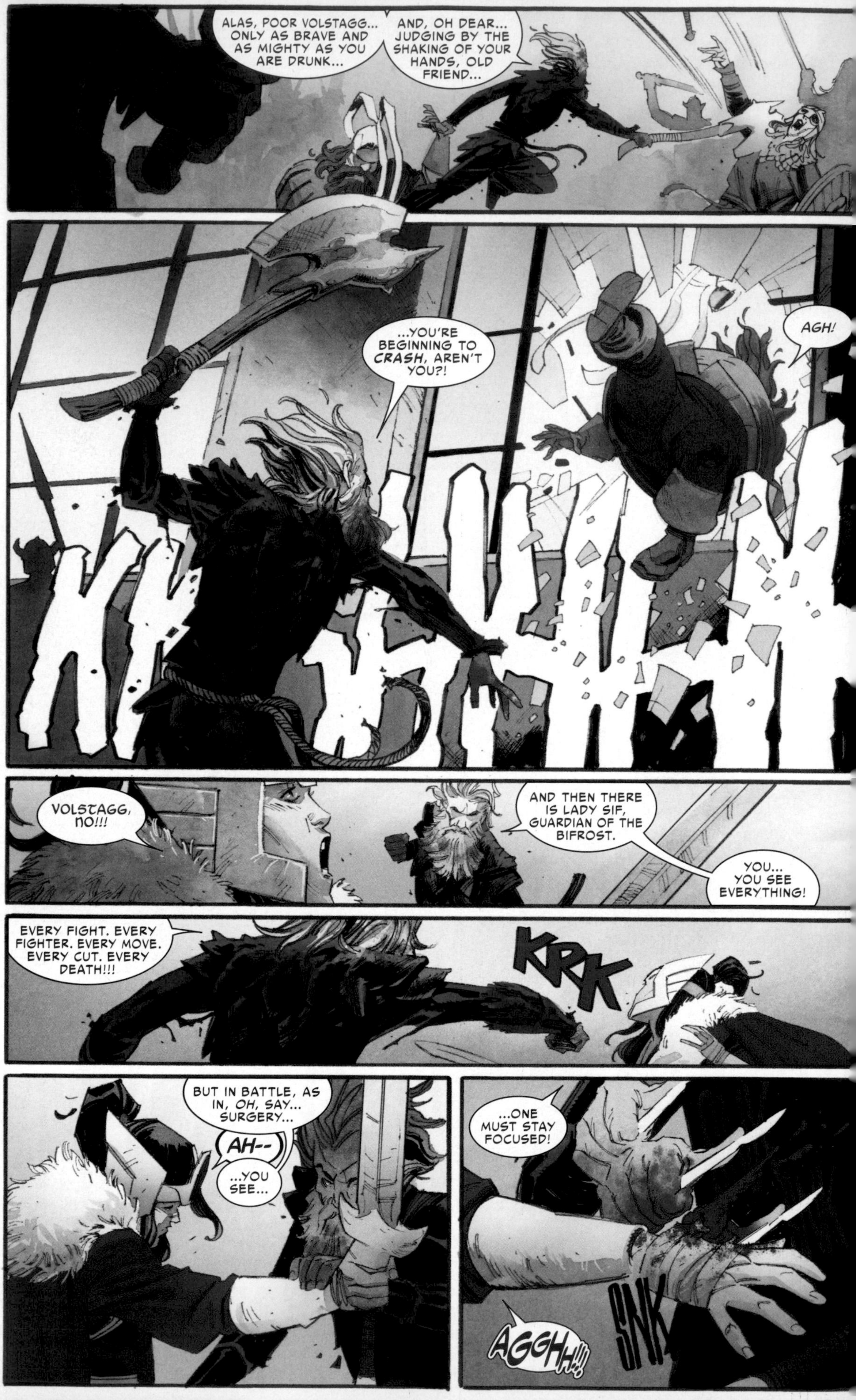
ALAS, POOR VOLSTAGG... ONLY AS BRAVE AND AS MIGHTY AS YOU ARE DRUNK...
AND, OH DEAR... JUDGING BY THE SHAKING OF YOUR HANDS, OLD FRIEND...
...YOU'RE BEGINNING TO CRASH, AREN'T YOU?!
AGH!
VOLSTAGG, NO!!!
AND THEN THERE IS LADY SIF, GUARDIAN OF THE BIFROST.
YOU... YOU SEE EVERYTHING!
EVERY FIGHT. EVERY FIGHTER. EVERY MOVE. EVERY CUT. EVERY DEATH!!!
KRK
BUT IN BATTLE, AS IN, OH, SAY... SURGERY...
AH--
...YOU SEE...
...ONE MUST STAY FOCUSED!
AGGHH!!!
SNK

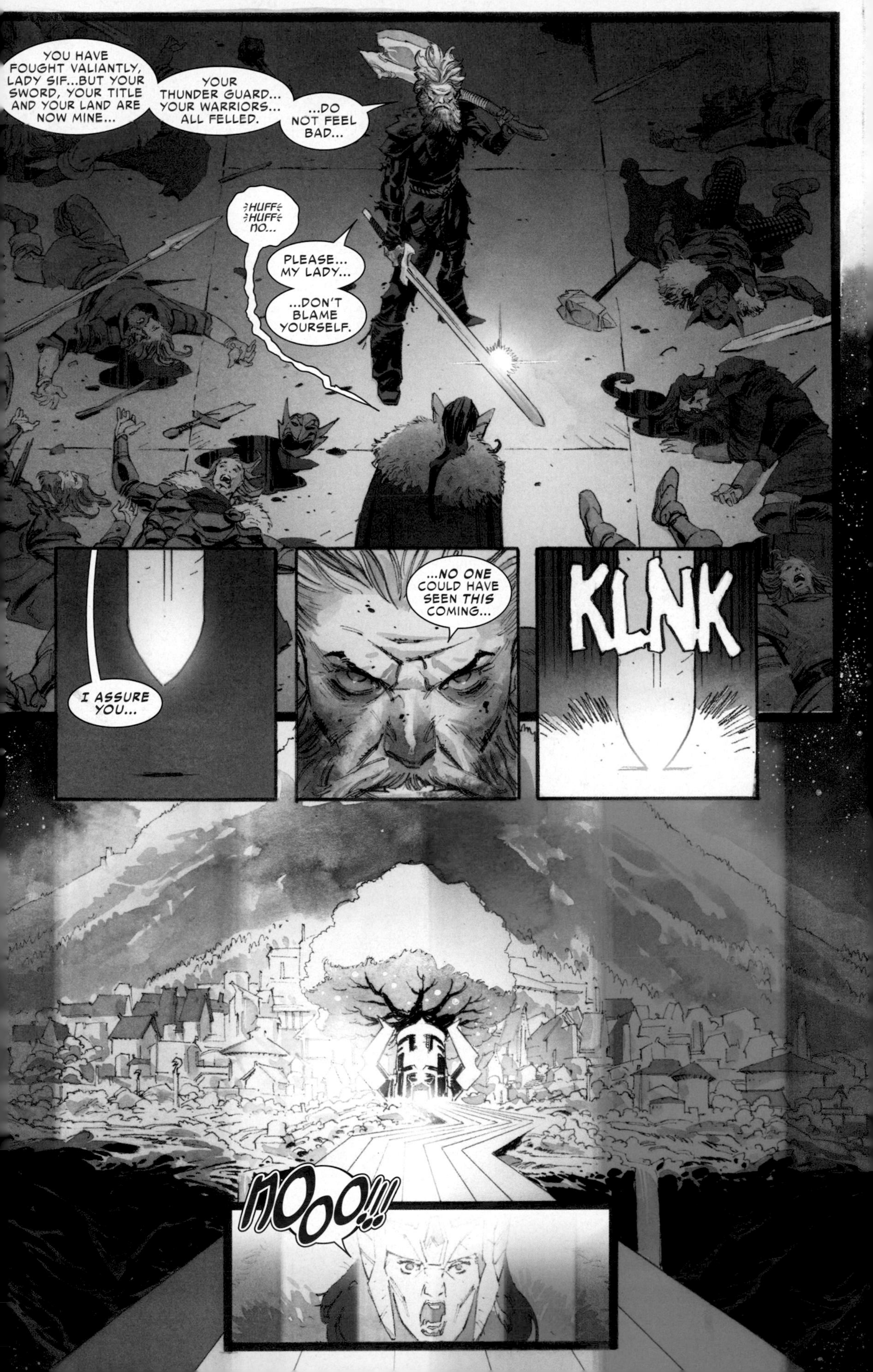
YOU HAVE FOUGHT VALIANTLY, LADY SIF...BUT YOUR SWORD, YOUR TITLE AND YOUR LAND ARE NOW MINE...
YOUR THUNDER GUARD... YOUR WARRIORS... ALL FELLED.
...DO NOT FEEL BAD...
HUFF HUFF NO...
PLEASE... MY LADY...
...DON'T BLAME YOURSELF.
I ASSURE YOU...
...NO ONE COULD HAVE SEEN THIS COMING...
KLNK
NOOO!!!

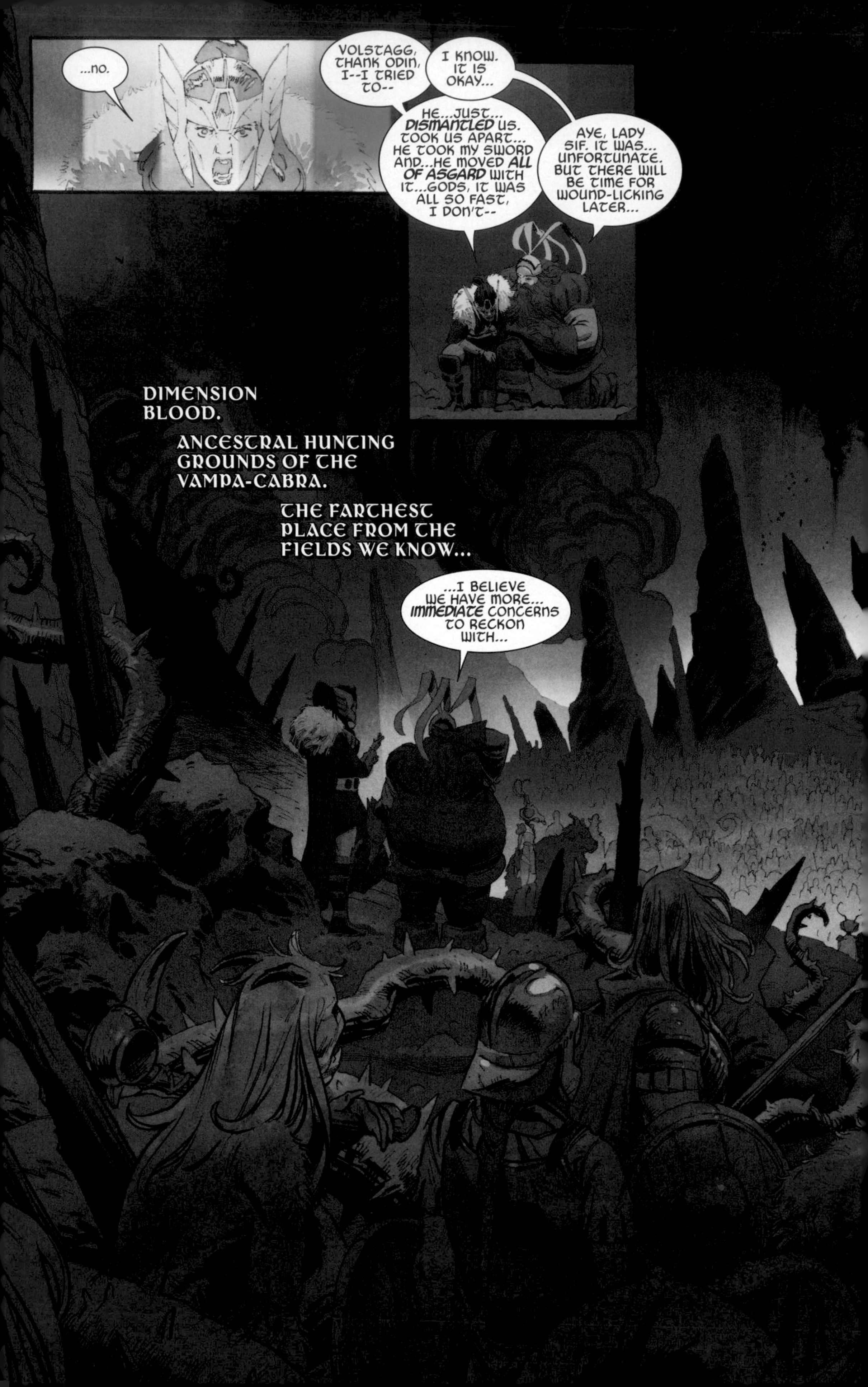
...no.
VOLSTAGG, THANK ODIN, I--I TRIED TO--
I KNOW. IT IS OKAY...
HE...JUST... DISMANTLED US. TOOK US APART... HE TOOK MY SWORD AND...HE MOVED ALL OF ASGARD WITH IT...GODS, IT WAS ALL SO FAST, I DON'T--
AYE, LADY SIF. IT WAS... UNFORTUNATE. BUT THERE WILL BE TIME FOR WOUND-LICKING LATER...
DIMENSION BLOOD.
ANCESTRAL HUNTING GROUNDS OF THE VAMPA-CABRA.
THE FARTHEST PLACE FROM THE FIELDS WE KNOW...
...I BELIEVE WE HAVE MORE... IMMEDIATE CONCERNS TO RECKON WITH...

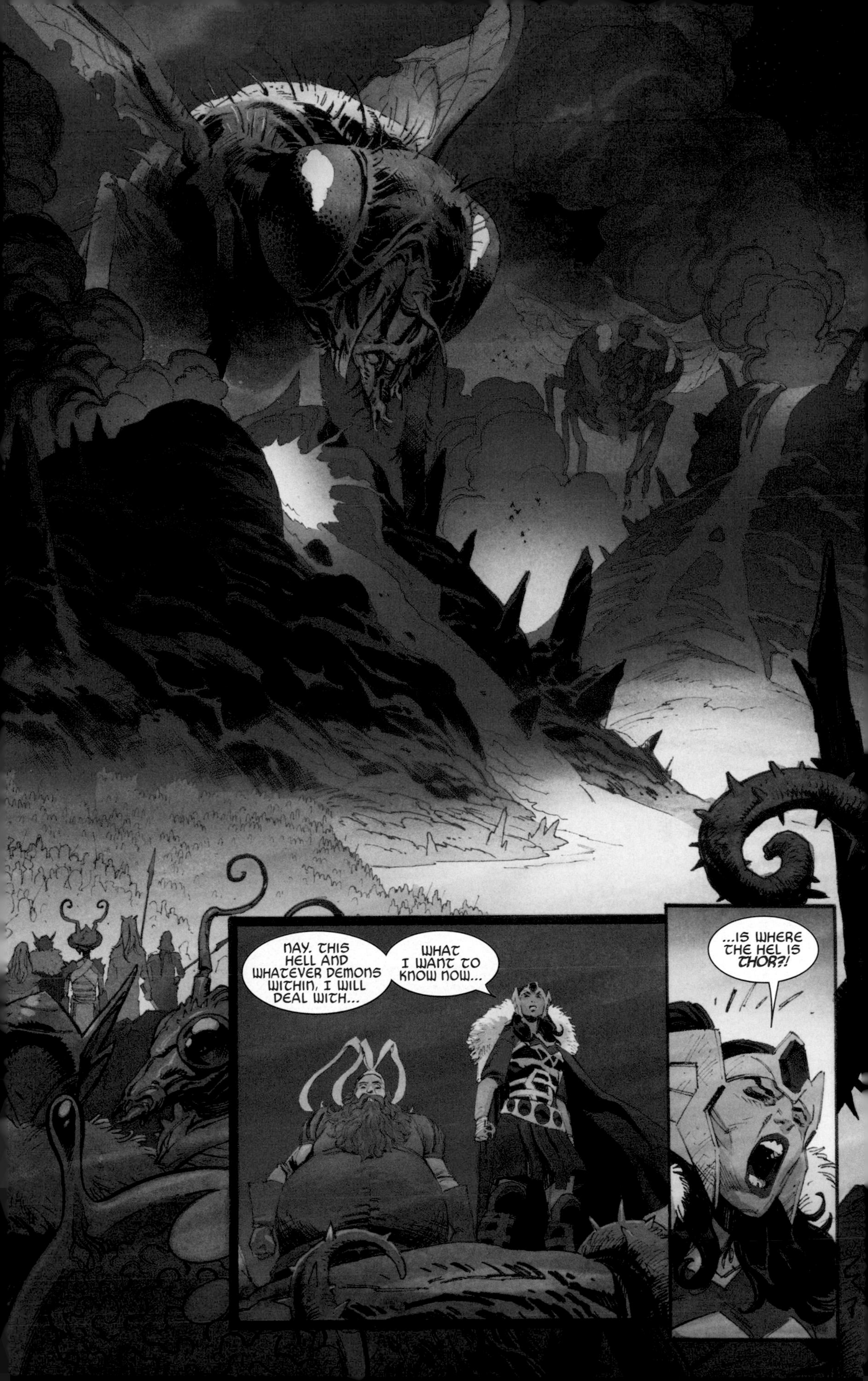
NAY. THIS HELL AND WHATEVER DEMONS WITHIN, I WILL DEAL WITH...
WHAT I WANT TO KNOW NOW...
...IS WHERE THE HEL IS *THOR?!*

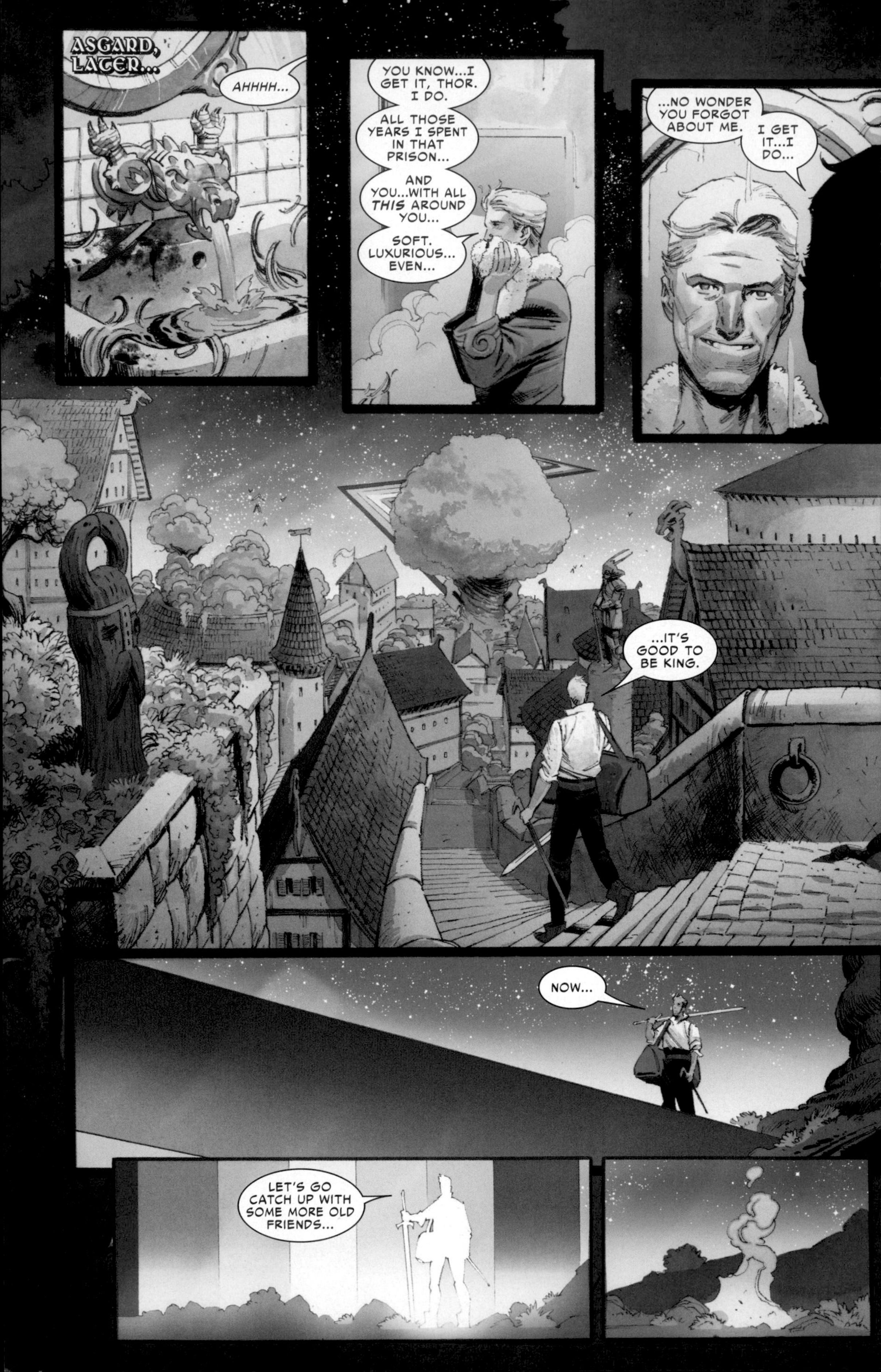
ASGARD, LATER...
AHHHH...
YOU KNOW...I GET IT, THOR. I DO.
ALL THOSE YEARS I SPENT IN THAT PRISON...
AND YOU...WITH ALL THIS AROUND YOU...
SOFT. LUXURIOUS... EVEN...
...NO WONDER YOU FORGOT ABOUT ME.
I GET IT...I DO...
...IT'S GOOD TO BE KING.
NOW...
LET'S GO CATCH UP WITH SOME MORE OLD FRIENDS...

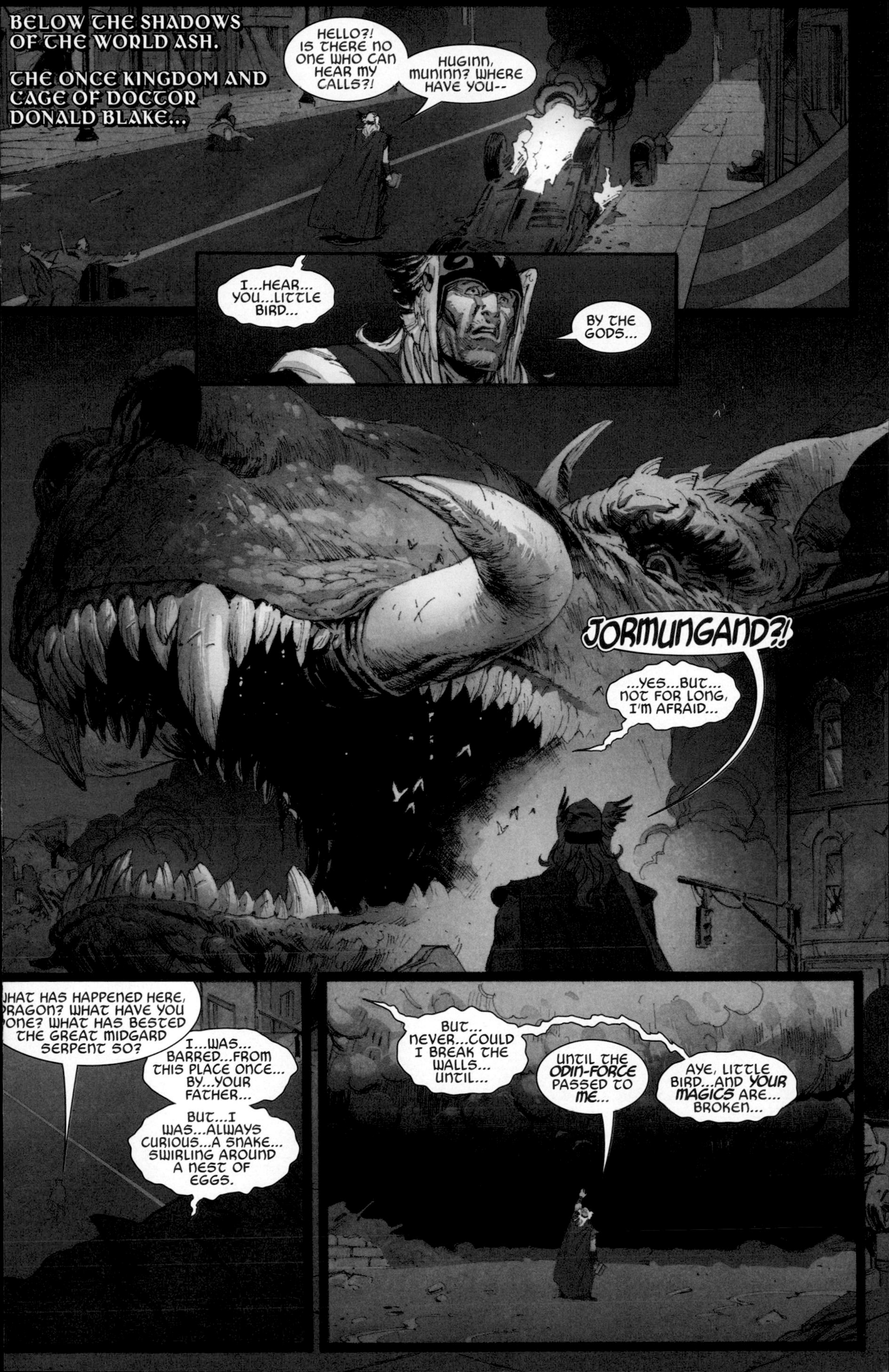
BELOW THE SHADOWS OF THE WORLD ASH.
THE ONCE KINGDOM AND CAGE OF DOCTOR DONALD BLAKE...
HELLO?! IS THERE NO ONE WHO CAN HEAR MY CALLS?!
HUGINN, MUNINN? WHERE HAVE YOU--
I...HEAR... YOU...LITTLE BIRD...
BY THE GODS...
JORMUNGAND?!
...YES...BUT... NOT FOR LONG, I'M AFRAID...
WHAT HAS HAPPENED HERE, DRAGON? WHAT HAVE YOU DONE? WHAT HAS BESTED THE GREAT MIDGARD SERPENT SO?
I...WAS... BARRED...FROM THIS PLACE ONCE... BY...YOUR FATHER...
BUT...I WAS...ALWAYS CURIOUS...A SNAKE... SWIRLING AROUND A NEST OF EGGS.
BUT... NEVER...COULD I BREAK THE WALLS... UNTIL...
UNTIL THE ODIN-FORCE PASSED TO ME...
AYE, LITTLE BIRD...AND YOUR MAGICS ARE... BROKEN...

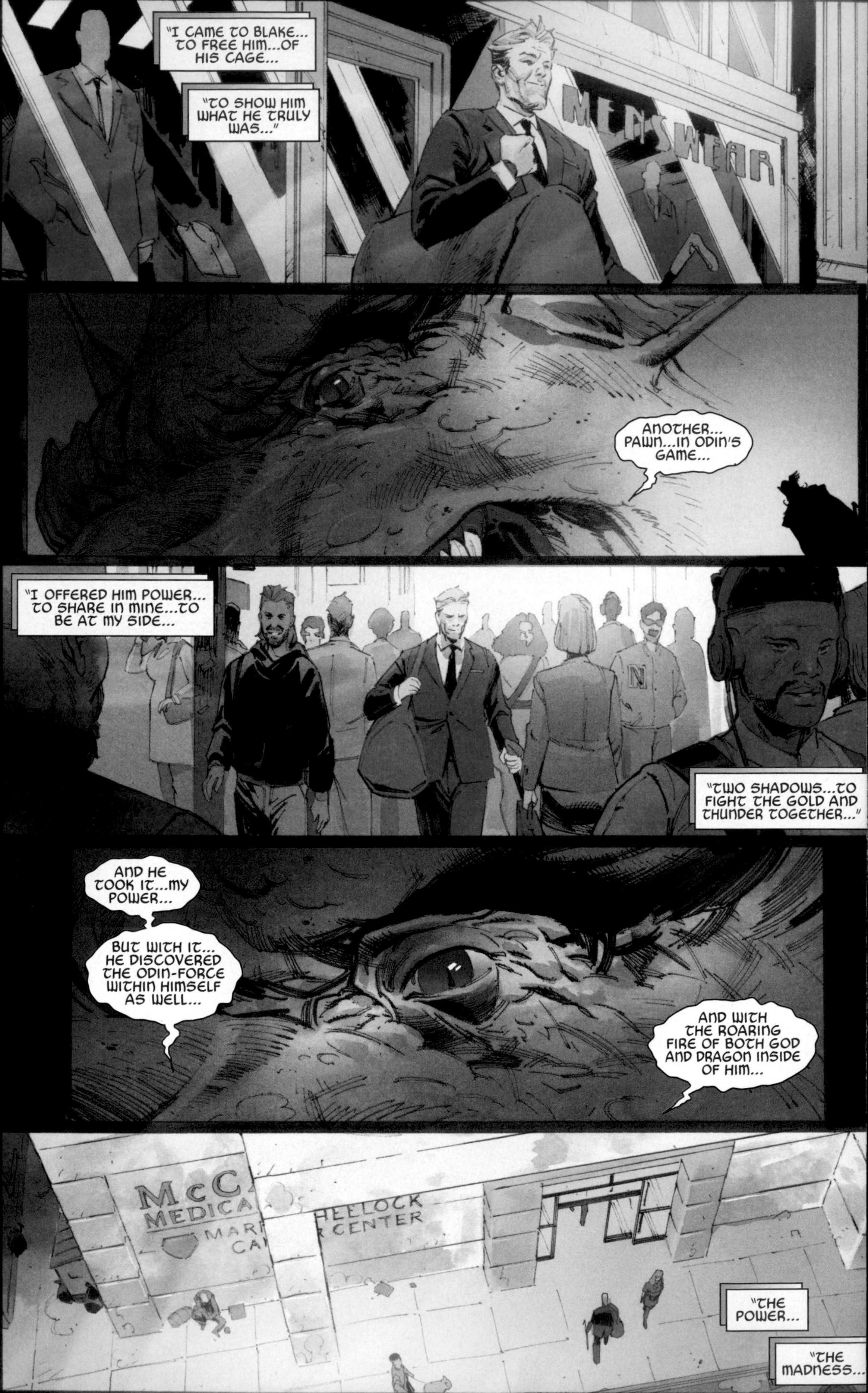

"I CAME TO BLAKE... TO FREE HIM...OF HIS CAGE...
"TO SHOW HIM WHAT HE TRULY WAS..."
MENSWEAR
ANOTHER... PAWN...IN ODIN'S GAME...
"I OFFERED HIM POWER... TO SHARE IN MINE...TO BE AT MY SIDE...
"TWO SHADOWS...TO FIGHT THE GOLD AND THUNDER TOGETHER..."
AND HE TOOK IT...MY POWER...
BUT WITH IT... HE DISCOVERED THE ODIN-FORCE WITHIN HIMSELF AS WELL...
AND WITH THE ROARING FIRE OF BOTH GOD AND DRAGON INSIDE OF HIM...
"THE POWER...
"THE MADNESS...

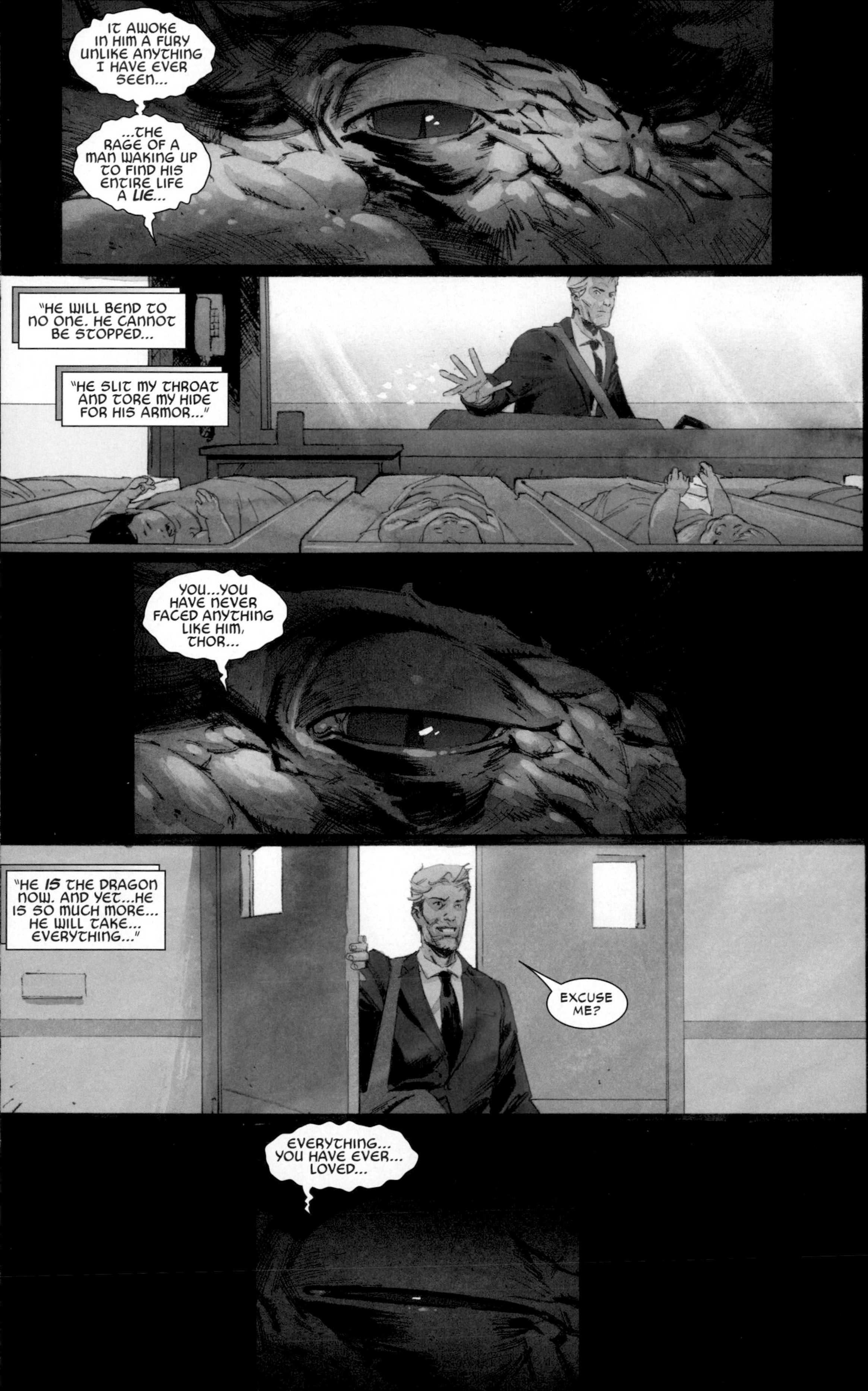
IT AWOKE IN HIM A FURY UNLIKE ANYTHING I HAVE EVER SEEN...
...THE RAGE OF A MAN WAKING UP TO FIND HIS ENTIRE LIFE A LIE...
"HE WILL BEND TO NO ONE. HE CANNOT BE STOPPED...
"HE SLIT MY THROAT AND TORE MY HIDE FOR HIS ARMOR..."
YOU...YOU HAVE NEVER FACED ANYTHING LIKE HIM, THOR...
"HE IS THE DRAGON NOW. AND YET...HE IS SO MUCH MORE... HE WILL TAKE... EVERYTHING..."
EXCUSE ME?
EVERYTHING... YOU HAVE EVER... LOVED...

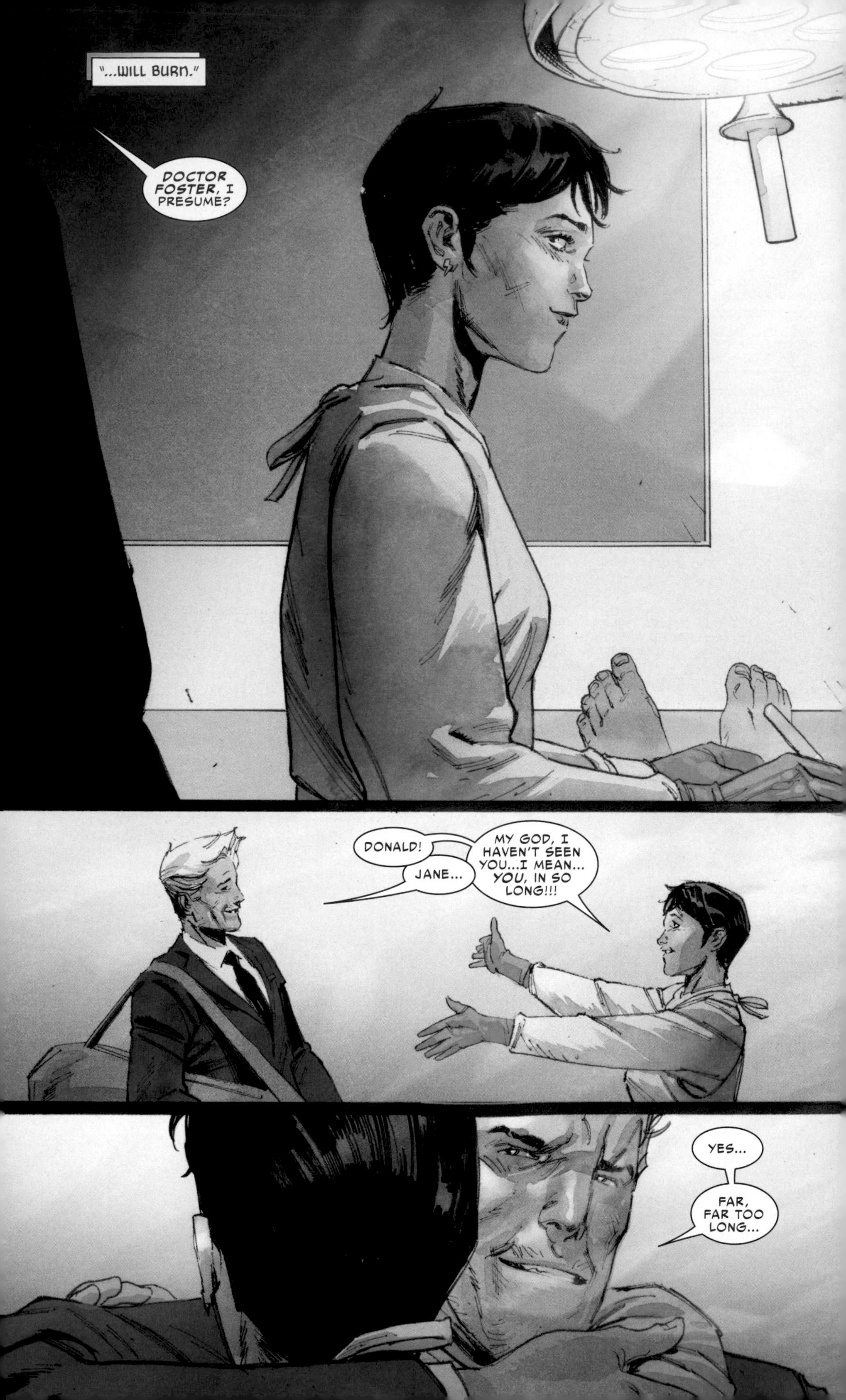
"...WILL BURN."
DOCTOR FOSTER, I PRESUME?
DONALD!
JANE...
MY GOD, I HAVEN'T SEEN YOU...I MEAN... YOU, IN SO LONG!!!
YES...
FAR, FAR TOO LONG...

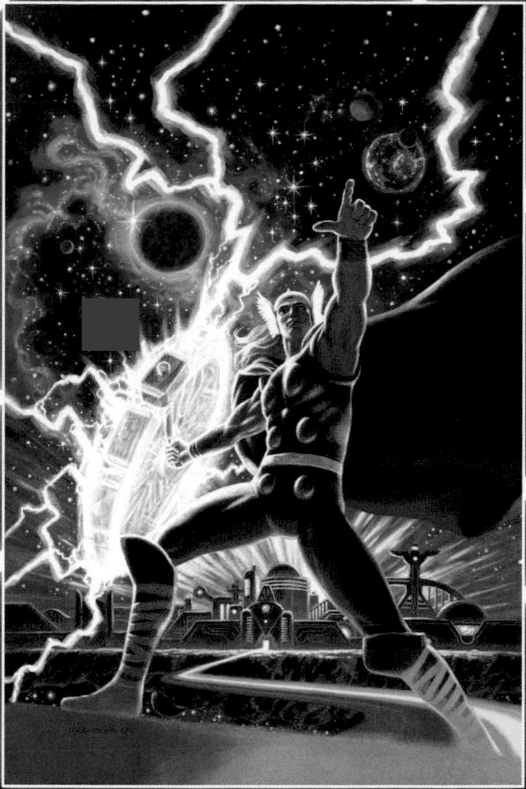

THOR 9 VARIANT BY
Greg Hildebrandt

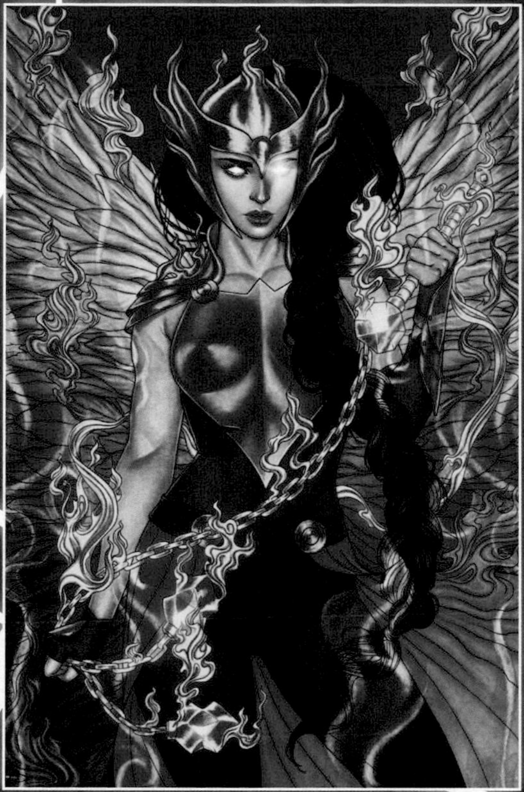

THOR 9 PHOENIX VARIANT BY
Jenny Frison

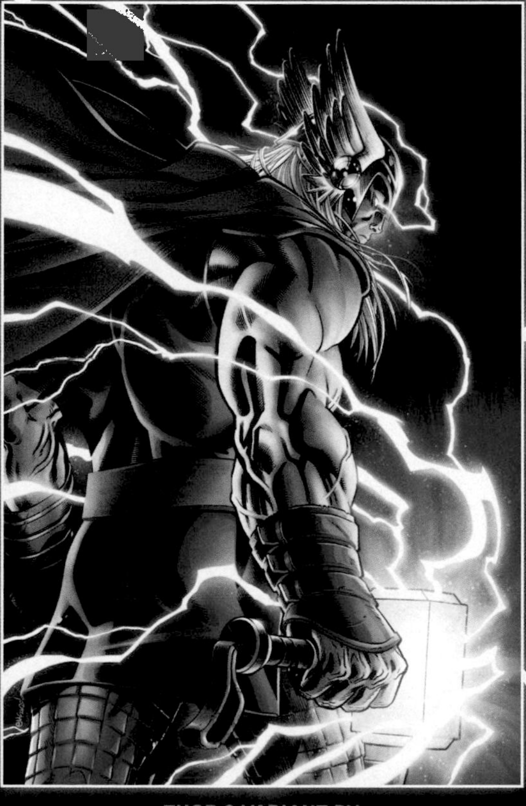

THOR 9 VARIANT BY
Ed McGuiness & Laura Martin

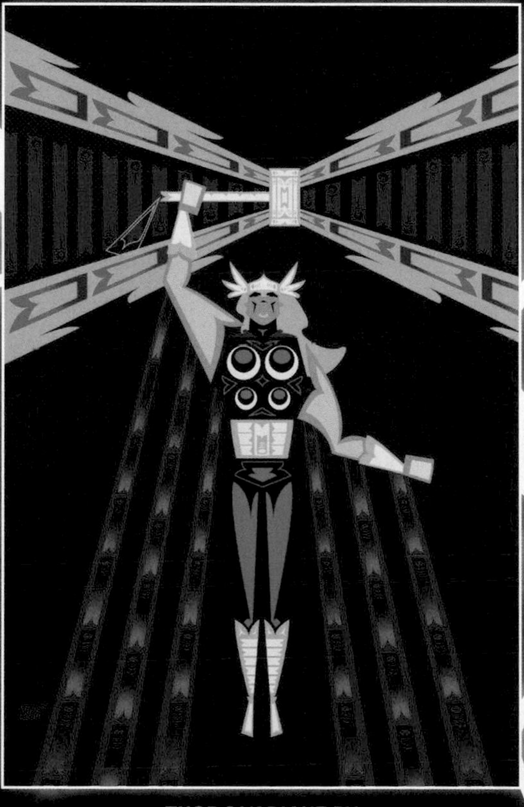

THOR 9 VARIANT BY
Jeffrey Veregge

11

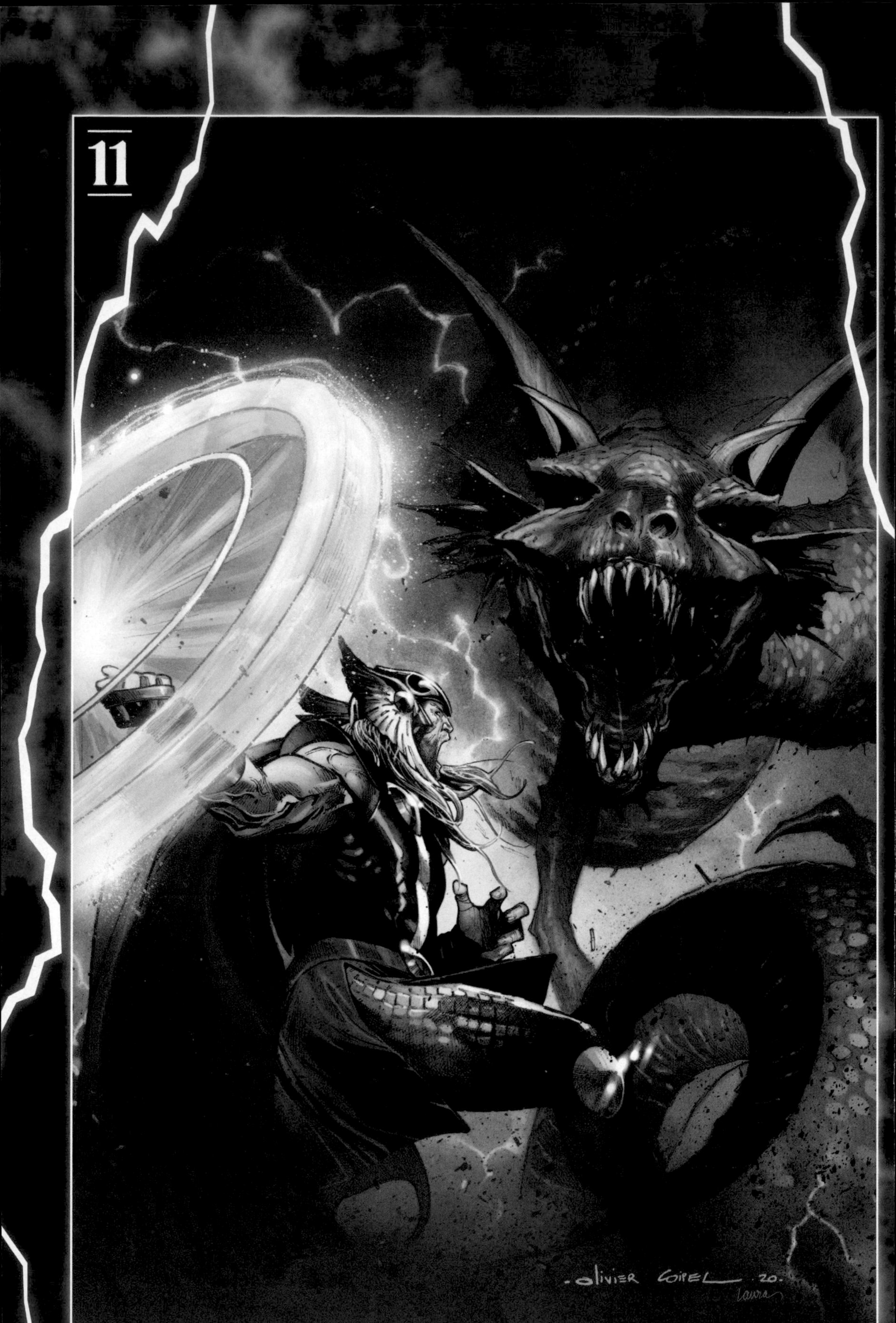
OLIVIER COIPEL 20.
Laura

"Prey" PART THREE

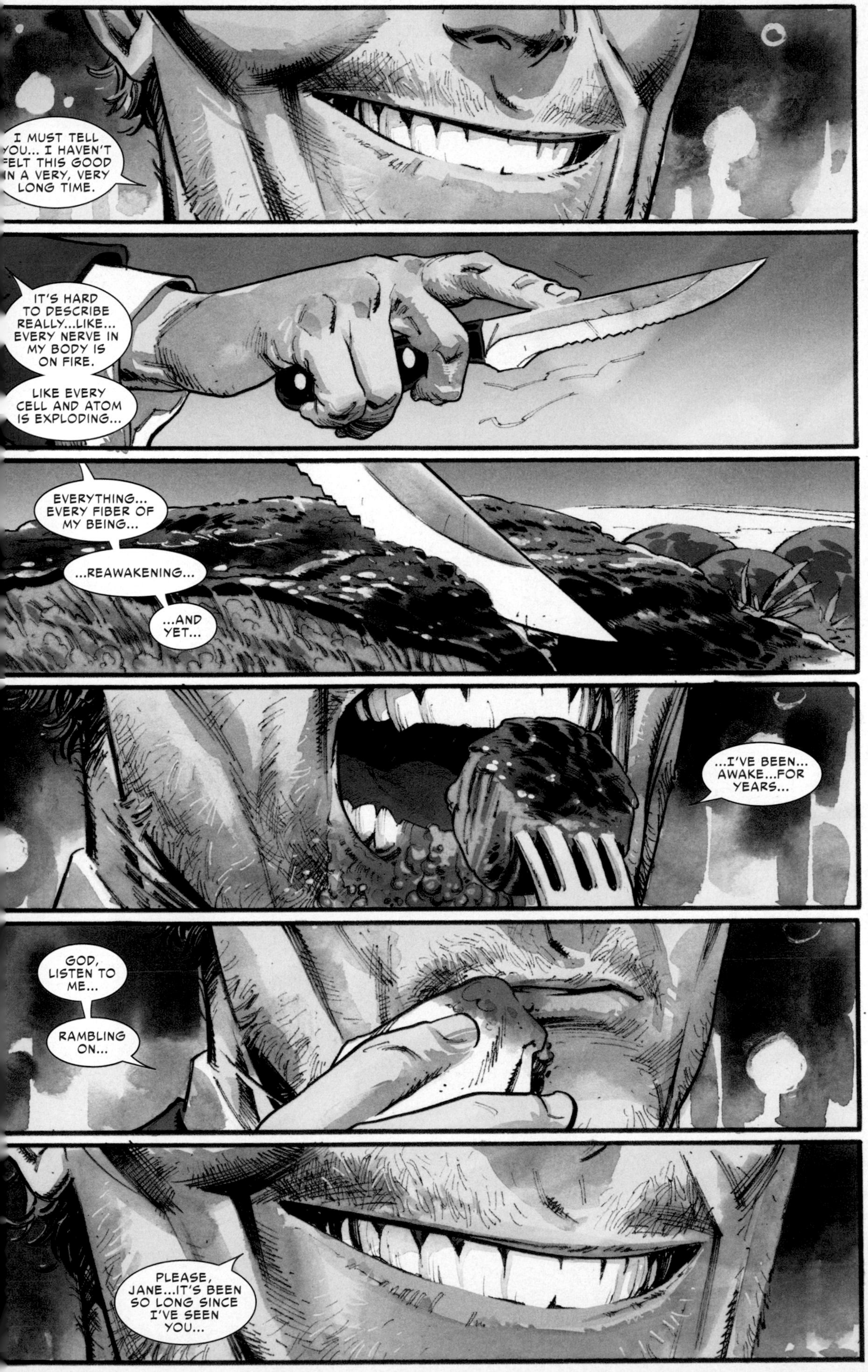
I MUST TELL YOU... I HAVEN'T FELT THIS GOOD IN A VERY, VERY LONG TIME.
IT'S HARD TO DESCRIBE REALLY...LIKE... EVERY NERVE IN MY BODY IS ON FIRE.
LIKE EVERY CELL AND ATOM IS EXPLODING...
EVERYTHING... EVERY FIBER OF MY BEING...
...REAWAKENING...
...AND YET...
...I'VE BEEN... AWAKE...FOR YEARS...
GOD, LISTEN TO ME...
RAMBLING ON...
PLEASE, JANE...IT'S BEEN SO LONG SINCE I'VE SEEN YOU...

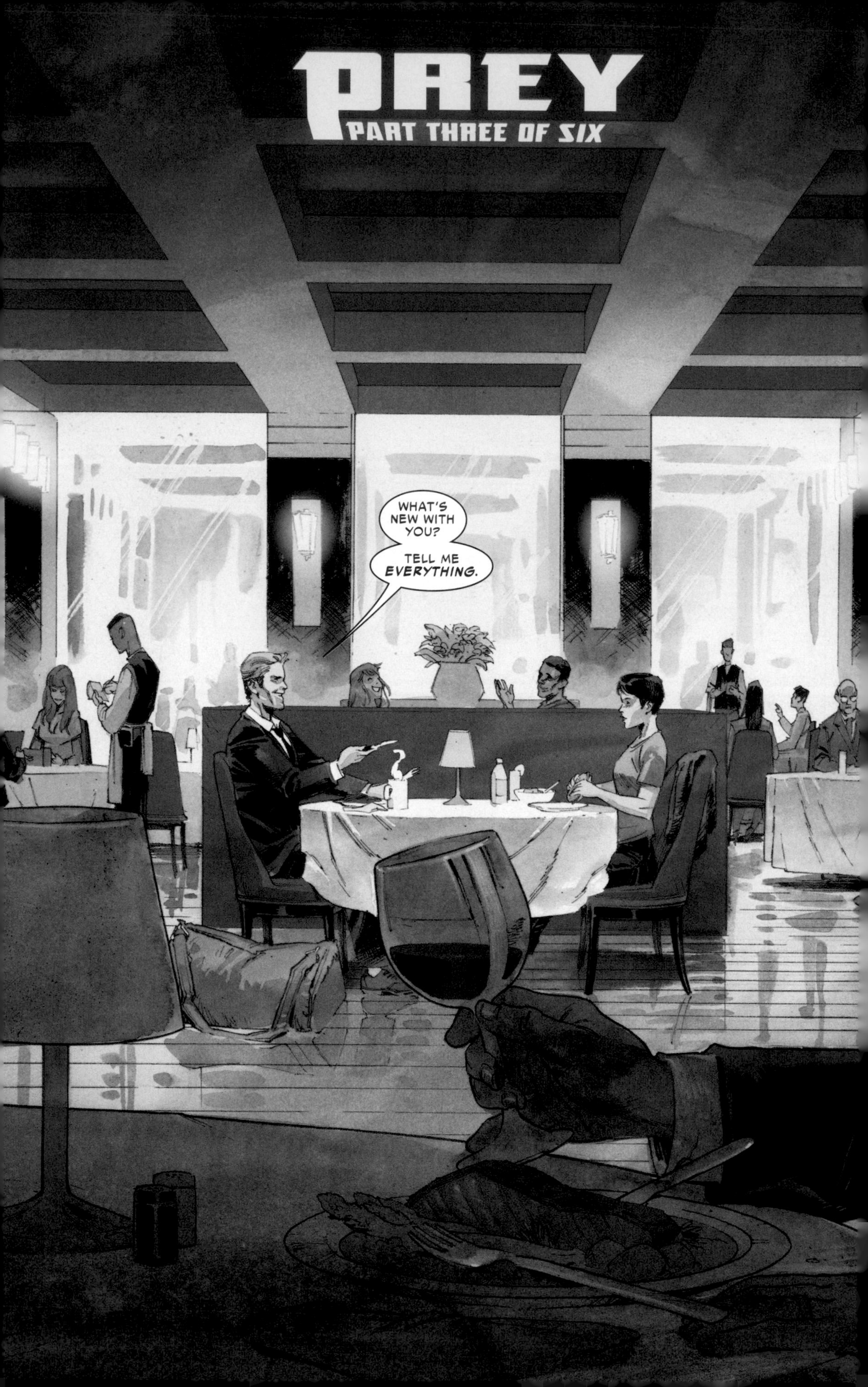
PREY
PART THREE OF SIX
WHAT'S NEW WITH YOU?
TELL ME *EVERYTHING.*

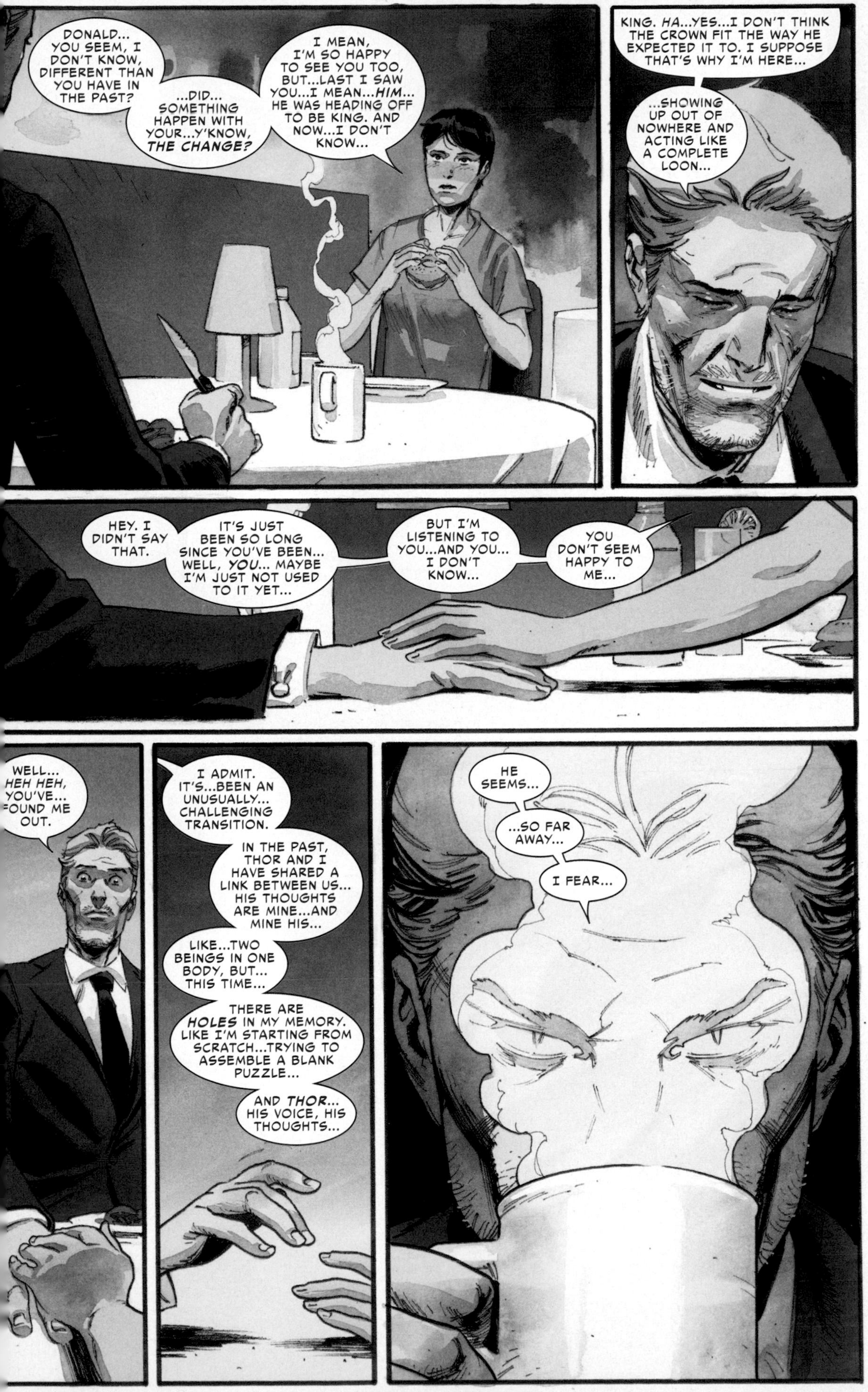
DONALD... YOU SEEM, I DON'T KNOW, DIFFERENT THAN YOU HAVE IN THE PAST?
...DID... SOMETHING HAPPEN WITH YOUR...Y'KNOW, *THE CHANGE?*
I MEAN, I'M SO HAPPY TO SEE YOU TOO, BUT...LAST I SAW YOU...I MEAN...*HIM*... HE WAS HEADING OFF TO BE KING. AND NOW...I DON'T KNOW...
KING. *HA*...YES...I DON'T THINK THE CROWN FIT THE WAY HE EXPECTED IT TO. I SUPPOSE THAT'S WHY I'M HERE...
...SHOWING UP OUT OF NOWHERE AND ACTING LIKE A COMPLETE LOON...
HEY. I DIDN'T SAY THAT.
IT'S JUST BEEN SO LONG SINCE YOU'VE BEEN... WELL, *YOU*... MAYBE I'M JUST NOT USED TO IT YET...
BUT I'M LISTENING TO YOU...AND YOU... I DON'T KNOW...
YOU DON'T SEEM HAPPY TO ME...
WELL... *HEH HEH,* YOU'VE... FOUND ME OUT.
I ADMIT. IT'S...BEEN AN UNUSUALLY... CHALLENGING TRANSITION.
IN THE PAST, THOR AND I HAVE SHARED A LINK BETWEEN US... HIS THOUGHTS ARE MINE...AND MINE HIS...
LIKE...TWO BEINGS IN ONE BODY, BUT... THIS TIME...
THERE ARE *HOLES* IN MY MEMORY. LIKE I'M STARTING FROM SCRATCH...TRYING TO ASSEMBLE A BLANK PUZZLE...
AND *THOR*... HIS VOICE, HIS THOUGHTS...
HE SEEMS...
...SO FAR AWAY...
I FEAR...

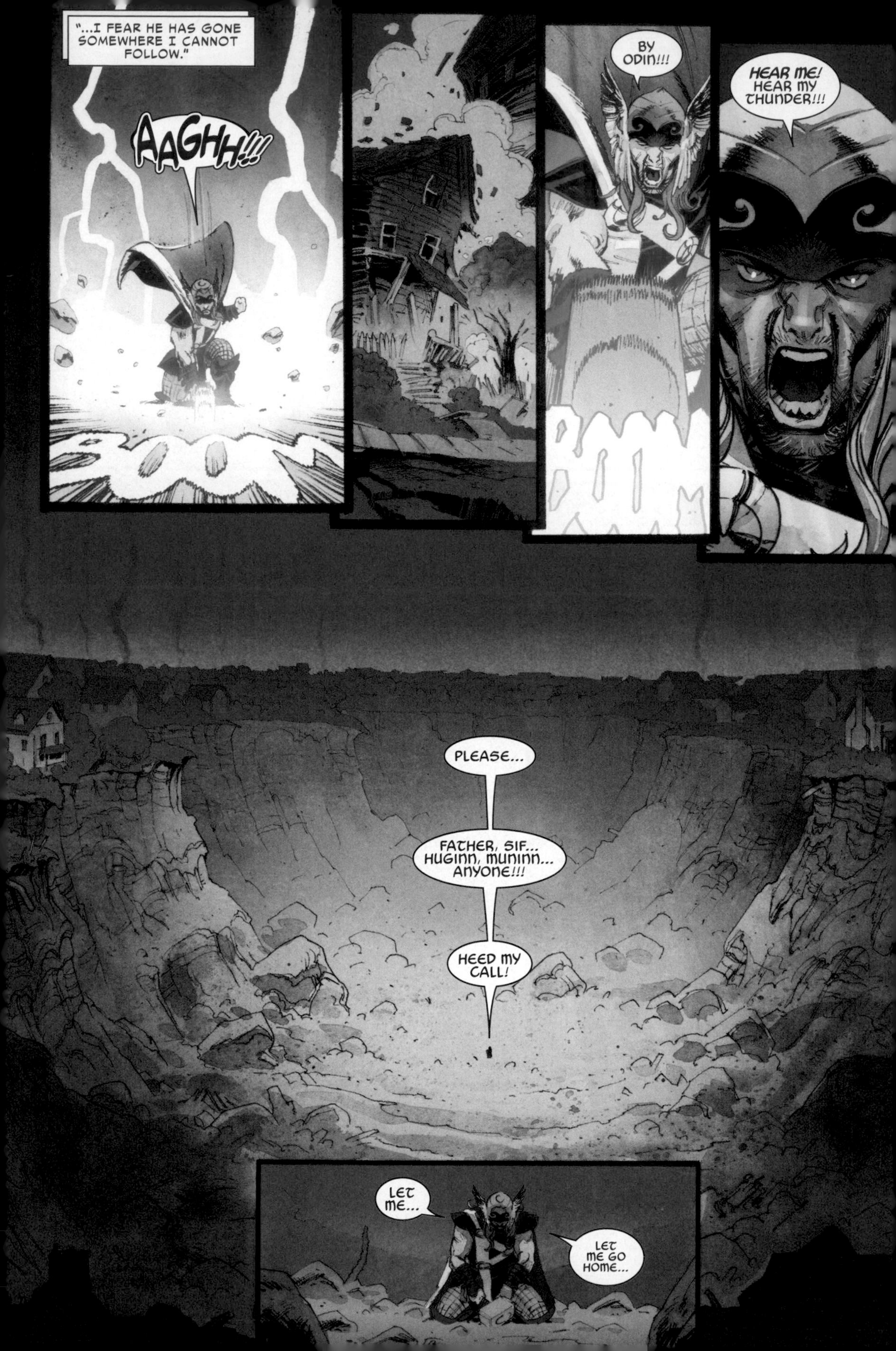
"...I FEAR HE HAS GONE SOMEWHERE I CANNOT FOLLOW."
AAGHH!!!
BOOM
BY ODIN!!!
BRAKA
HEAR ME! HEAR MY THUNDER!!!
PLEASE...
FATHER, SIF... HUGINN, MUNINN... ANYONE!!!
HEED MY CALL!
LET ME...
LET ME GO HOME...

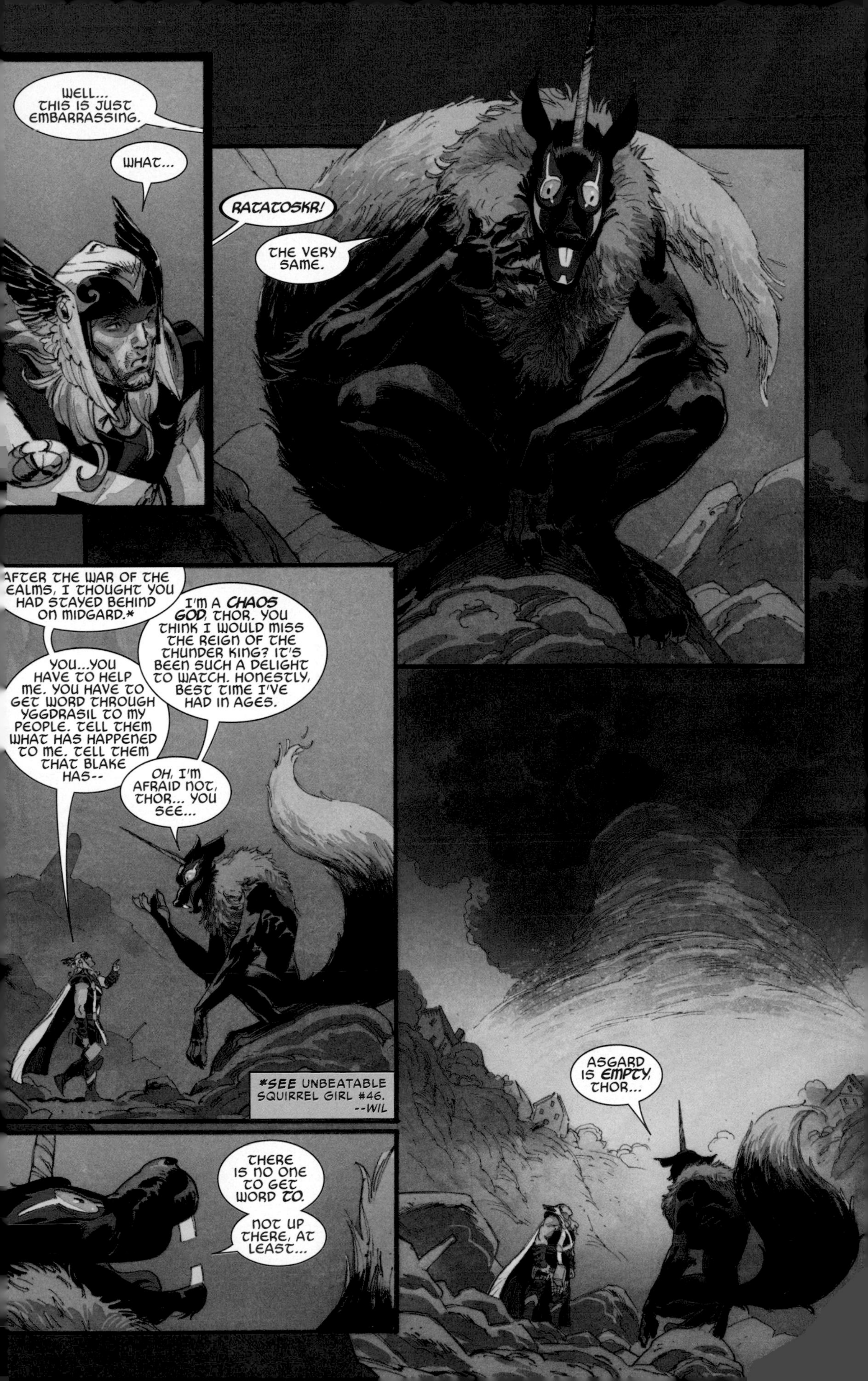

WELL... THIS IS JUST EMBARRASSING.
WHAT...
RATATOSKR!
THE VERY SAME.
AFTER THE WAR OF THE EALMS, I THOUGHT YOU HAD STAYED BEHIND ON MIDGARD.*
I'M A CHAOS GOD, THOR. YOU THINK I WOULD MISS THE REIGN OF THE THUNDER KING? IT'S BEEN SUCH A DELIGHT TO WATCH. HONESTLY, BEST TIME I'VE HAD IN AGES.
YOU...YOU HAVE TO HELP ME. YOU HAVE TO GET WORD THROUGH YGGDRASIL TO MY PEOPLE. TELL THEM WHAT HAS HAPPENED TO ME. TELL THEM THAT BLAKE HAS--
OH, I'M AFRAID NOT, THOR... YOU SEE...
*SEE UNBEATABLE SQUIRREL GIRL #46. --WIL
ASGARD IS EMPTY, THOR...
THERE IS NO ONE TO GET WORD TO.
NOT UP THERE, AT LEAST...

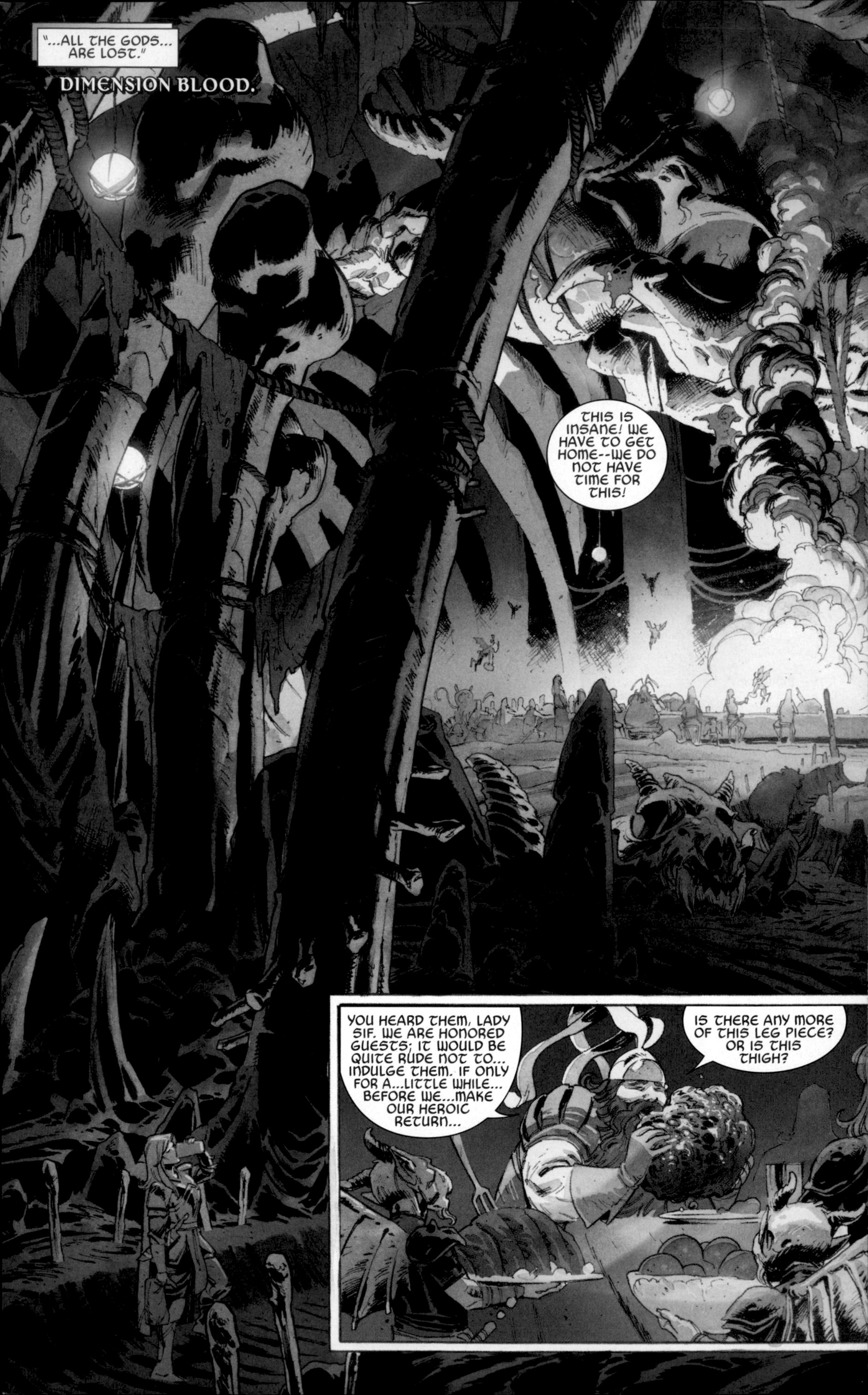
"...ALL THE GODS... ARE LOST."
DIMENSION BLOOD.
THIS IS INSANE! WE HAVE TO GET HOME--WE DO NOT HAVE TIME FOR THIS!
YOU HEARD THEM, LADY SIF. WE ARE HONORED GUESTS; IT WOULD BE QUITE RUDE NOT TO... INDULGE THEM. IF ONLY FOR A...LITTLE WHILE... BEFORE WE...MAKE OUR HEROIC RETURN...
IS THERE ANY MORE OF THIS LEG PIECE? OR IS THIS THIGH?

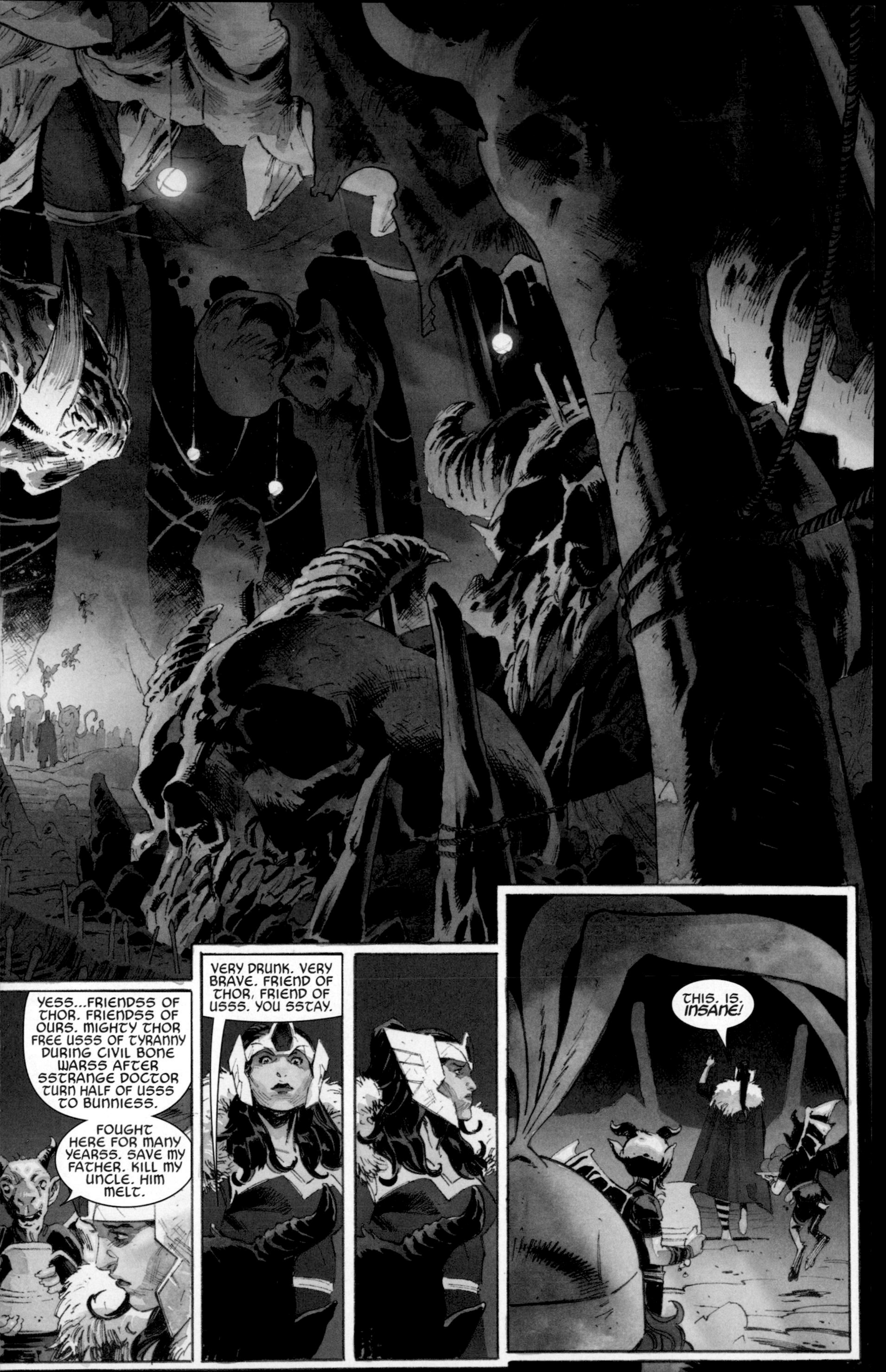
YESS...FRIENDSS OF THOR. FRIENDSS OF OURS. MIGHTY THOR FREE USSS OF TYRANNY DURING CIVIL BONE WARSS AFTER SSTRANGE DOCTOR TURN HALF OF USSS TO BUNNIESS.
FOUGHT HERE FOR MANY YEARSS. SAVE MY FATHER. KILL MY UNCLE. HIM MELT.
VERY DRUNK. VERY BRAVE. FRIEND OF THOR, FRIEND OF USSS. YOU SSTAY.
THIS. IS. INSANE!

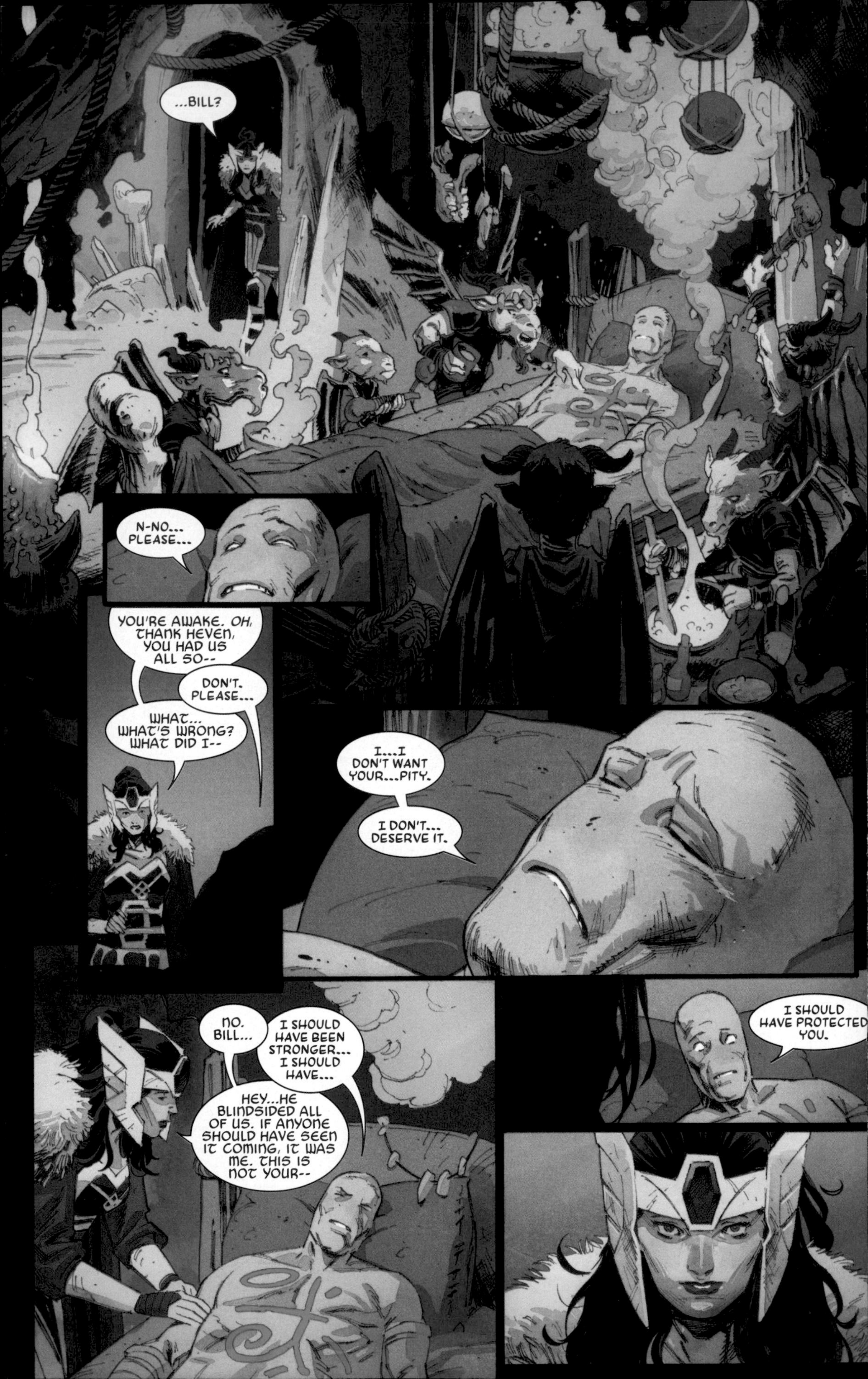
...BILL?
N-NO... PLEASE...
YOU'RE AWAKE. OH, THANK HEVEN, YOU HAD US ALL SO--
DON'T. PLEASE...
WHAT... WHAT'S WRONG? WHAT DID I--
I...I DON'T WANT YOUR...PITY.
I DON'T... DESERVE IT.
NO. BILL...
I SHOULD HAVE BEEN STRONGER... I SHOULD HAVE...
HEY...HE BLINDSIDED ALL OF US. IF ANYONE SHOULD HAVE SEEN IT COMING, IT WAS ME. THIS IS NOT YOUR--
I SHOULD HAVE PROTECTED YOU.

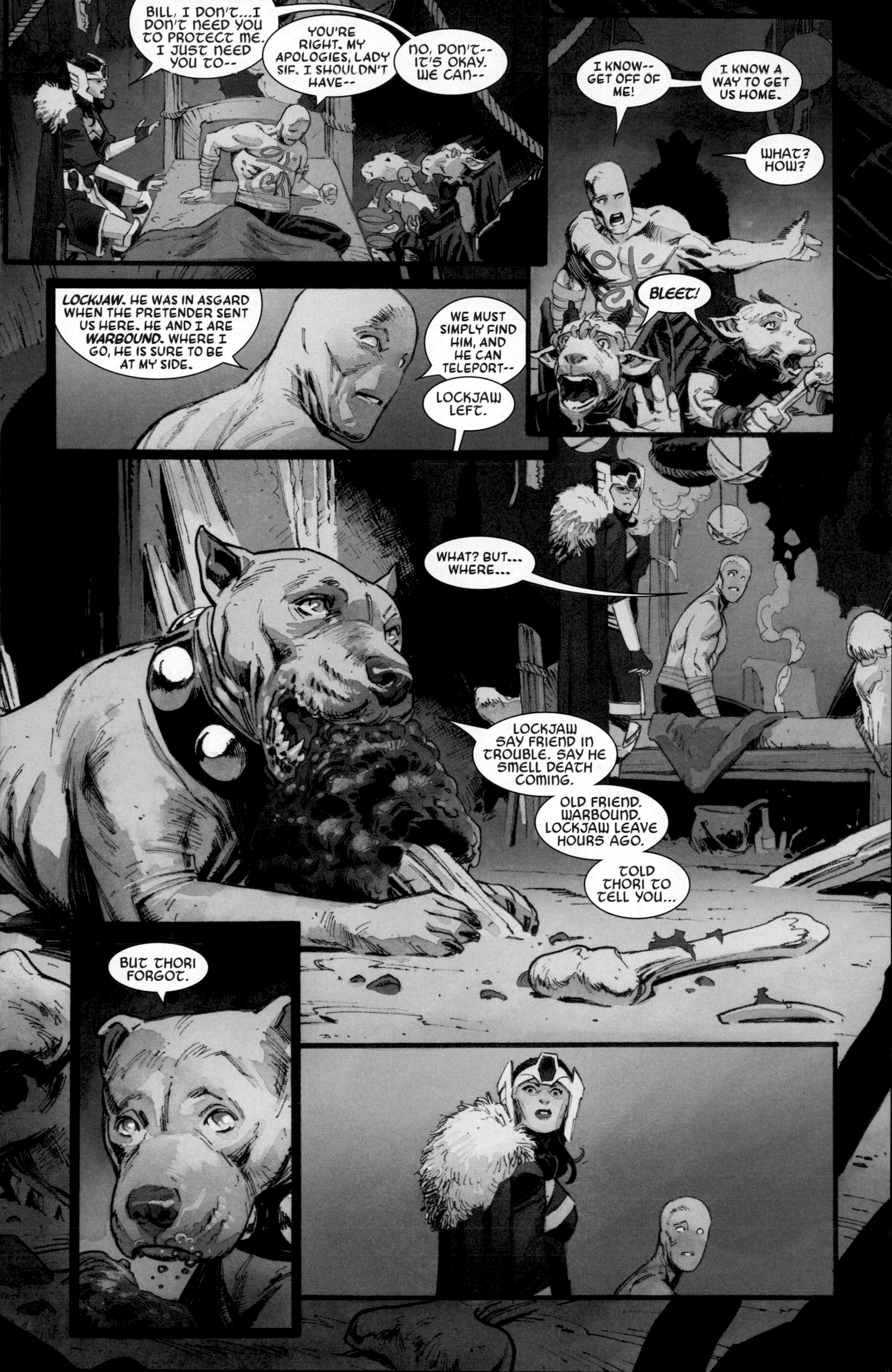

BILL, I DON'T...I DON'T NEED YOU TO PROTECT ME. I JUST NEED YOU TO--
YOU'RE RIGHT. MY APOLOGIES, LADY SIF. I SHOULDN'T HAVE--
NO, DON'T-- IT'S OKAY. WE CAN--
I KNOW-- GET OFF OF ME!
I KNOW A WAY TO GET US HOME.
WHAT? HOW?
BLEET!
LOCKJAW. HE WAS IN ASGARD WHEN THE PRETENDER SENT US HERE. HE AND I ARE WARBOUND. WHERE I GO, HE IS SURE TO BE AT MY SIDE.
WE MUST SIMPLY FIND HIM, AND HE CAN TELEPORT--
LOCKJAW LEFT.
WHAT? BUT... WHERE...
LOCKJAW SAY FRIEND IN TROUBLE. SAY HE SMELL DEATH COMING.
OLD FRIEND. WARBOUND. LOCKJAW LEAVE HOURS AGO.
TOLD THORI TO TELL YOU...
BUT THORI FORGOT.

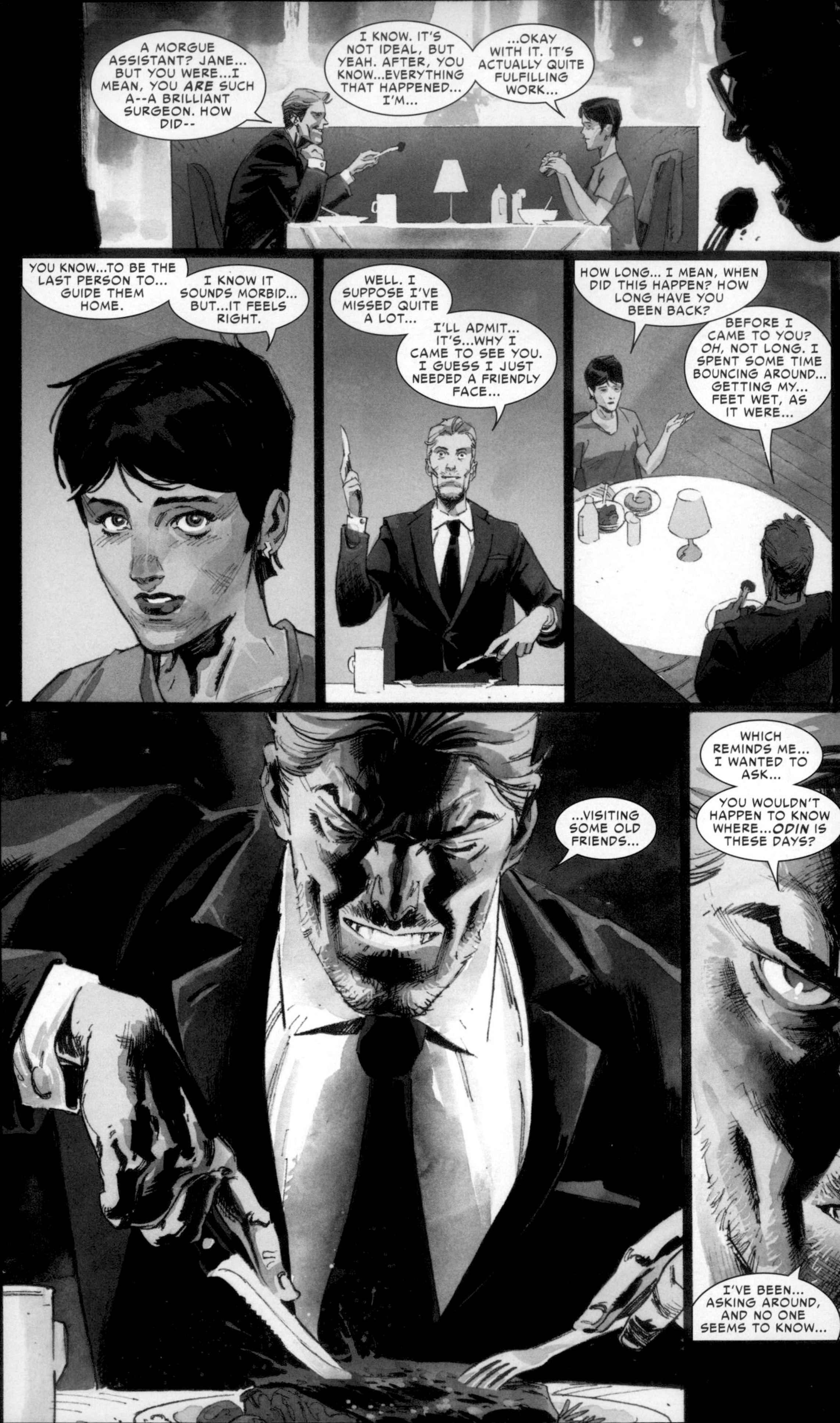
A MORGUE ASSISTANT? JANE... BUT YOU WERE...I MEAN, YOU **ARE** SUCH A--A BRILLIANT SURGEON. HOW DID--
I KNOW. IT'S NOT IDEAL, BUT YEAH. AFTER, YOU KNOW...EVERYTHING THAT HAPPENED... I'M...
...OKAY WITH IT. IT'S ACTUALLY QUITE FULFILLING WORK...
YOU KNOW...TO BE THE LAST PERSON TO... GUIDE THEM HOME.
I KNOW IT SOUNDS MORBID... BUT...IT FEELS RIGHT.
WELL. I SUPPOSE I'VE MISSED QUITE A LOT...
I'LL ADMIT... IT'S...WHY I CAME TO SEE YOU. I GUESS I JUST NEEDED A FRIENDLY FACE...
HOW LONG... I MEAN, WHEN DID THIS HAPPEN? HOW LONG HAVE YOU BEEN BACK?
BEFORE I CAME TO YOU? *OH*, NOT LONG. I SPENT SOME TIME BOUNCING AROUND... GETTING MY... FEET WET, AS IT WERE...
...VISITING SOME OLD FRIENDS...
WHICH REMINDS ME... I WANTED TO ASK...
YOU WOULDN'T HAPPEN TO KNOW WHERE...**ODIN** IS THESE DAYS?
I'VE BEEN... ASKING AROUND, AND NO ONE SEEMS TO KNOW...

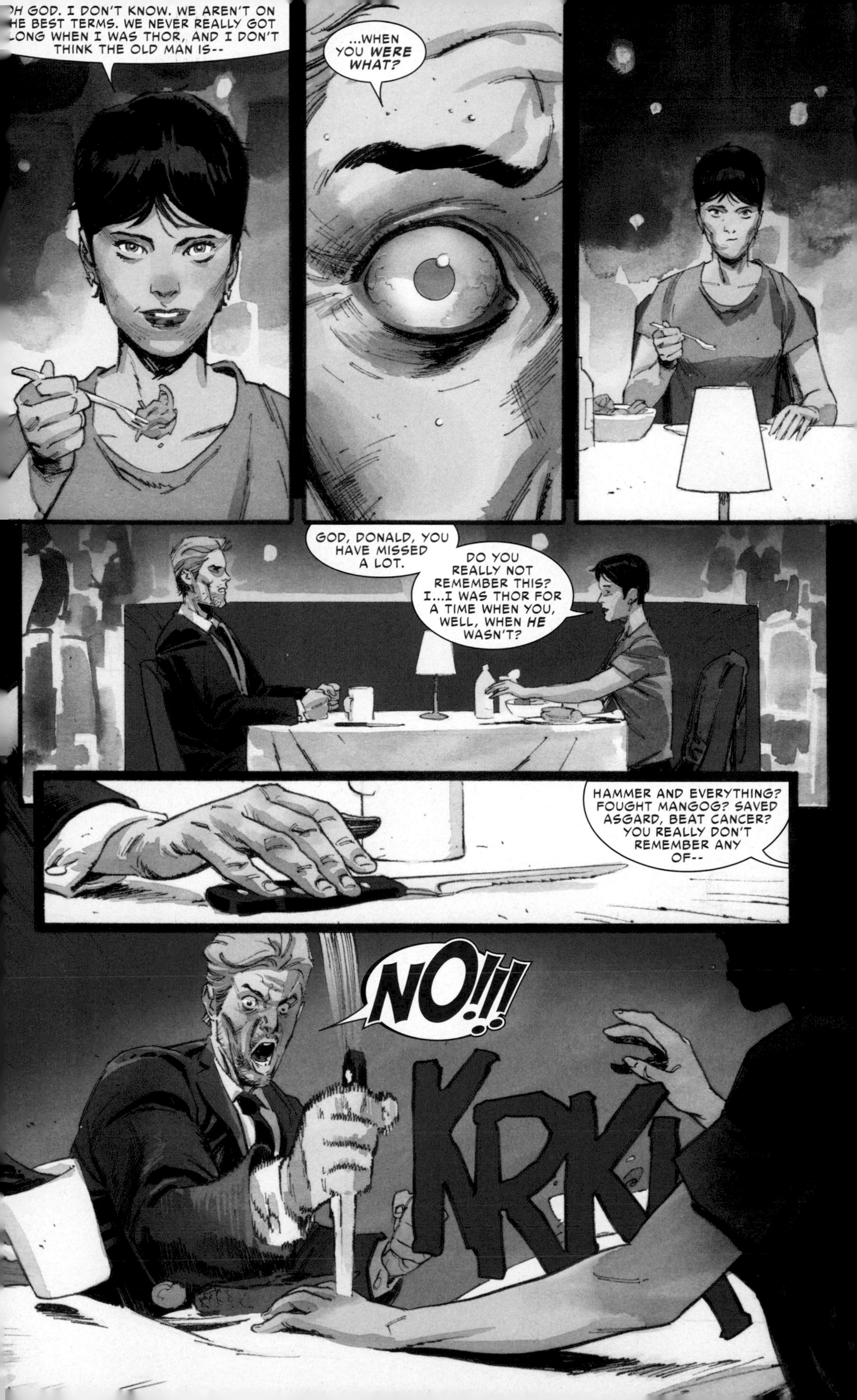
OH GOD. I DON'T KNOW. WE AREN'T ON THE BEST TERMS. WE NEVER REALLY GOT ALONG WHEN I WAS THOR, AND I DON'T THINK THE OLD MAN IS--
...WHEN YOU *WERE* WHAT?
GOD, DONALD, YOU HAVE MISSED A LOT.
DO YOU REALLY NOT REMEMBER THIS? I...I WAS THOR FOR A TIME WHEN YOU, WELL, WHEN *HE* WASN'T?
HAMMER AND EVERYTHING? FOUGHT MANGOG? SAVED ASGARD, BEAT CANCER? YOU REALLY DON'T REMEMBER ANY OF--
NO!!!
KRK

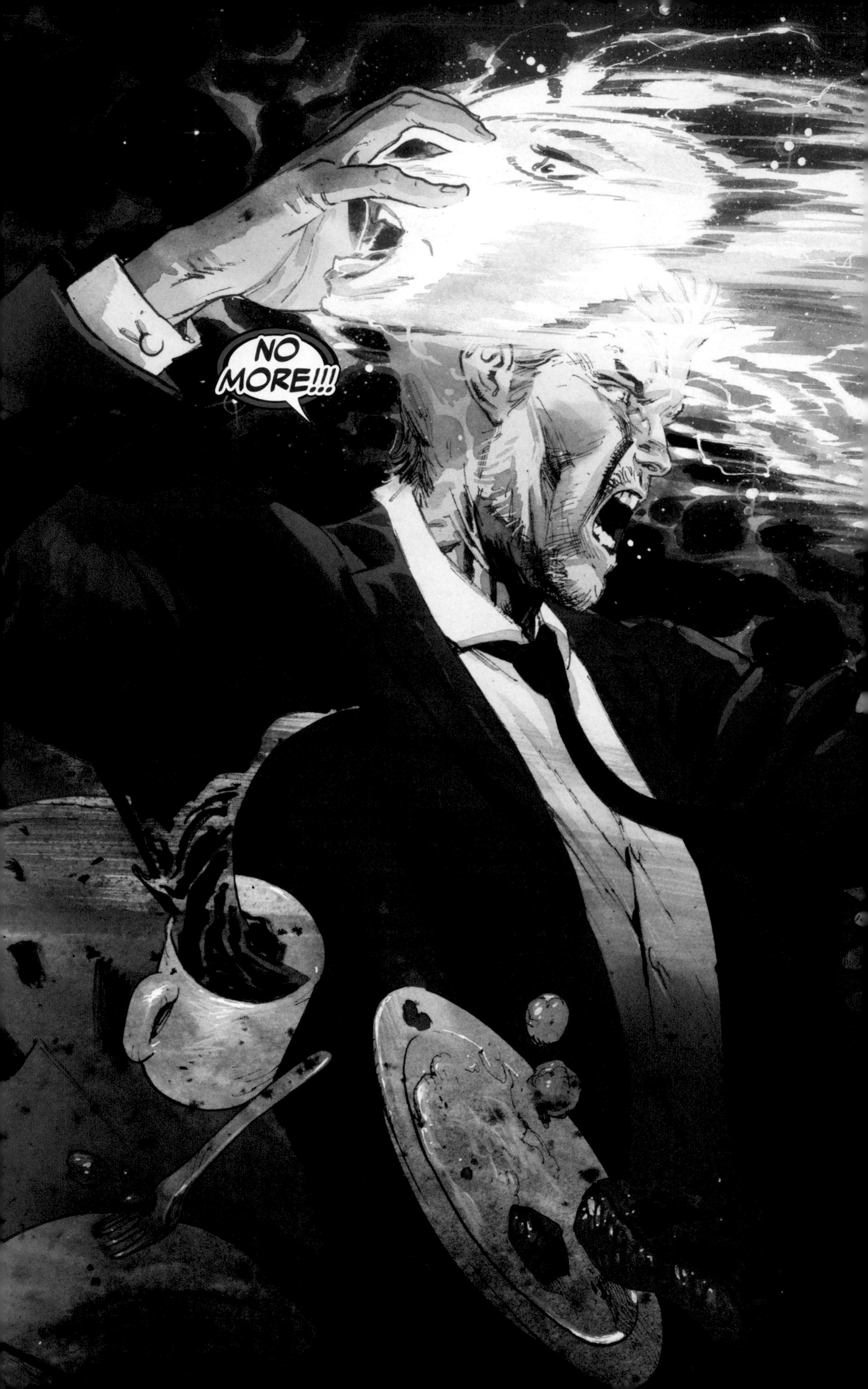
NO MORE!!!

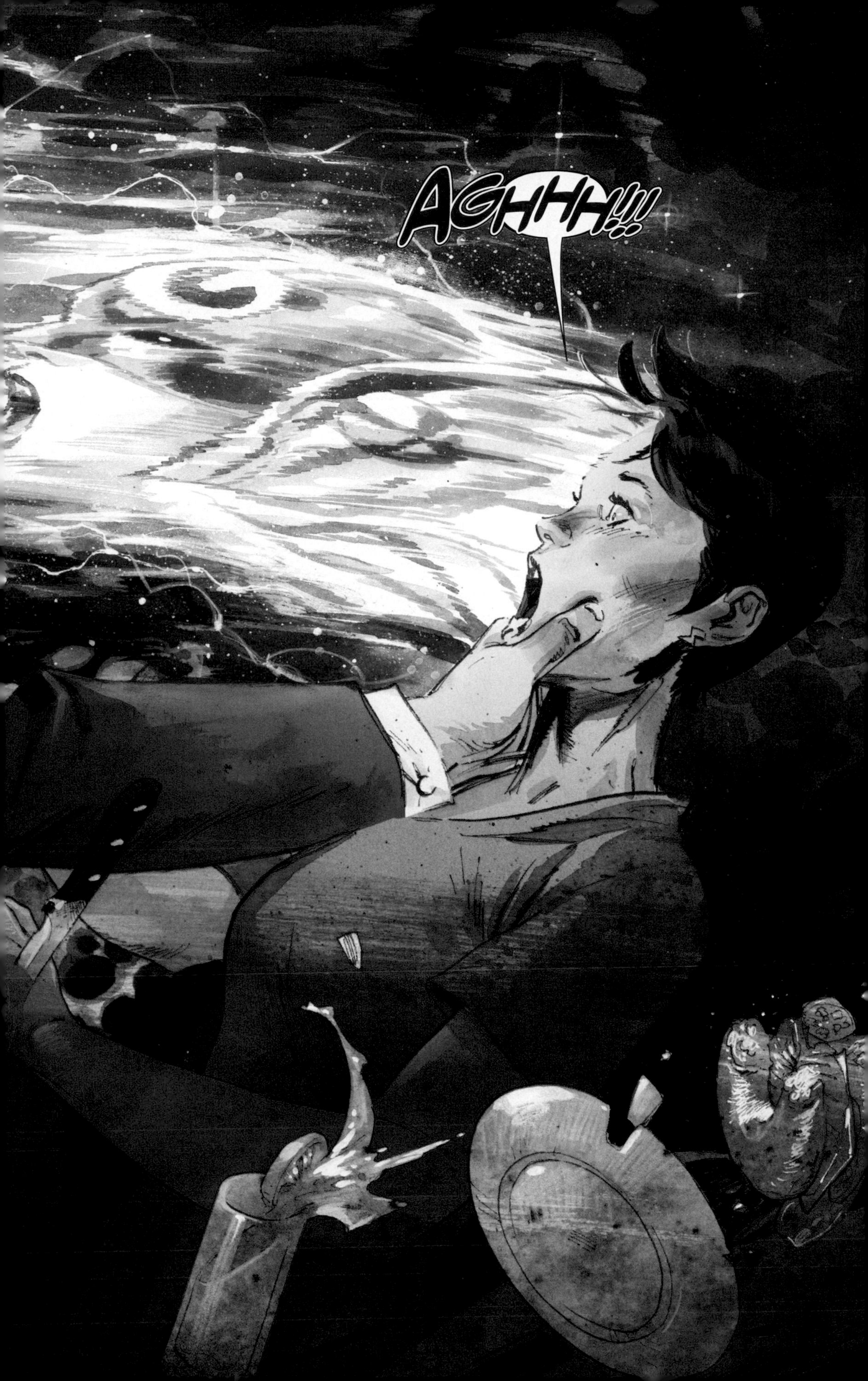
AGHHH!!!

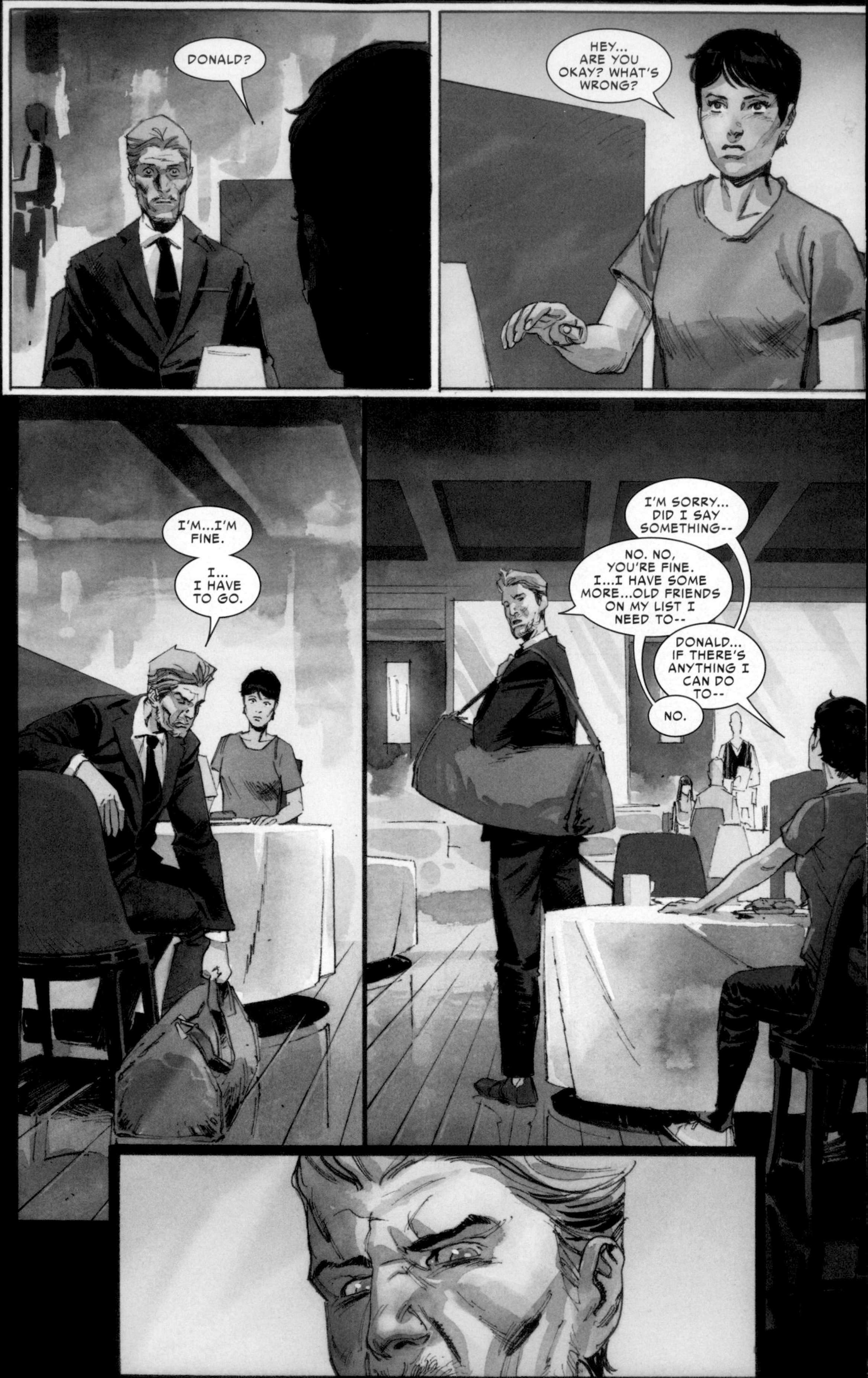
DONALD?
HEY... ARE YOU OKAY? WHAT'S WRONG?
I'M...I'M FINE.
I... I HAVE TO GO.
I'M SORRY... DID I SAY SOMETHING--
NO. NO, YOU'RE FINE. I...I HAVE SOME MORE...OLD FRIENDS ON MY LIST I NEED TO--
DONALD... IF THERE'S ANYTHING I CAN DO TO--
NO.

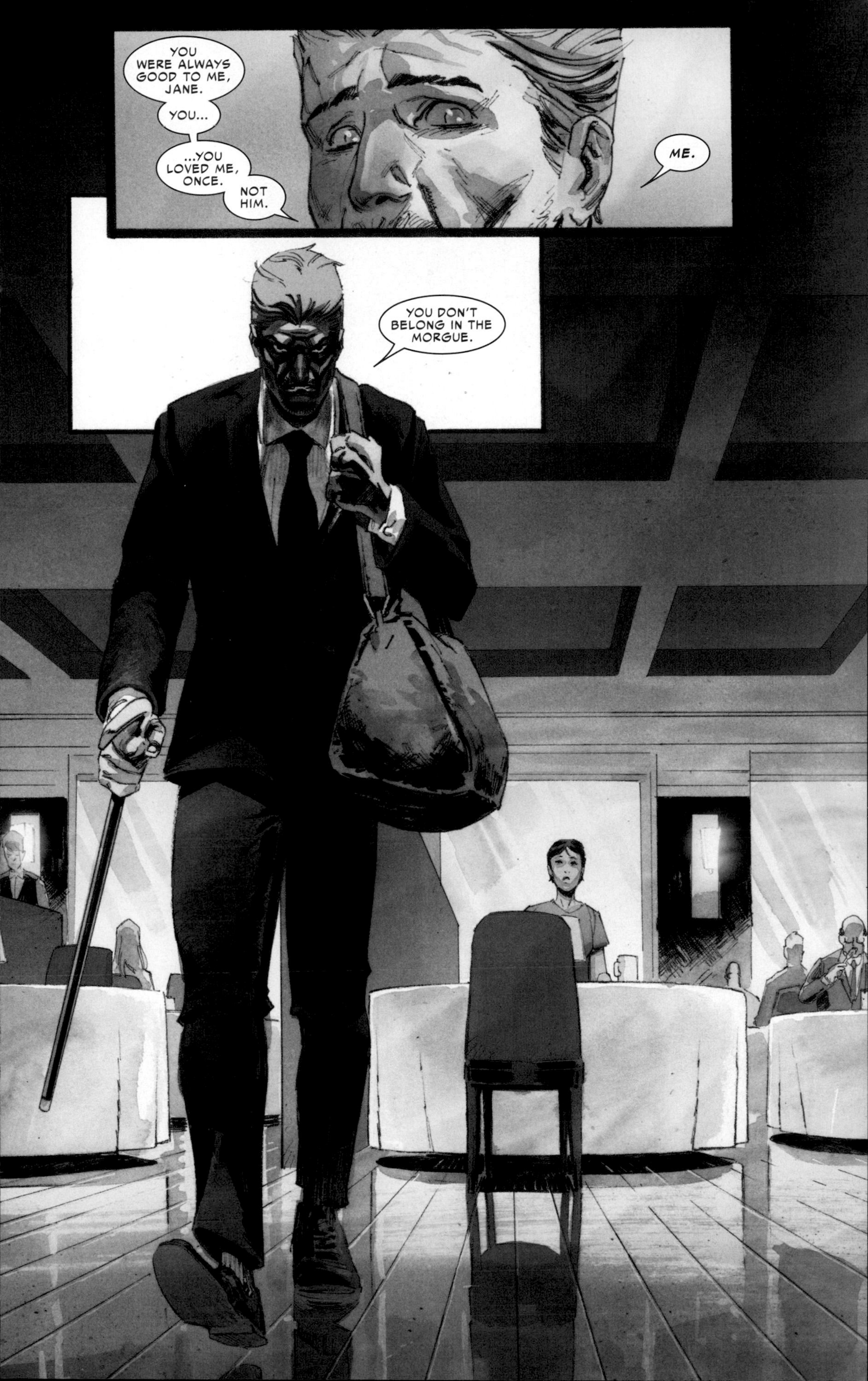
YOU WERE ALWAYS GOOD TO ME, JANE.
YOU...
...YOU LOVED ME, ONCE.
NOT HIM.
ME.
YOU DON'T BELONG IN THE MORGUE.

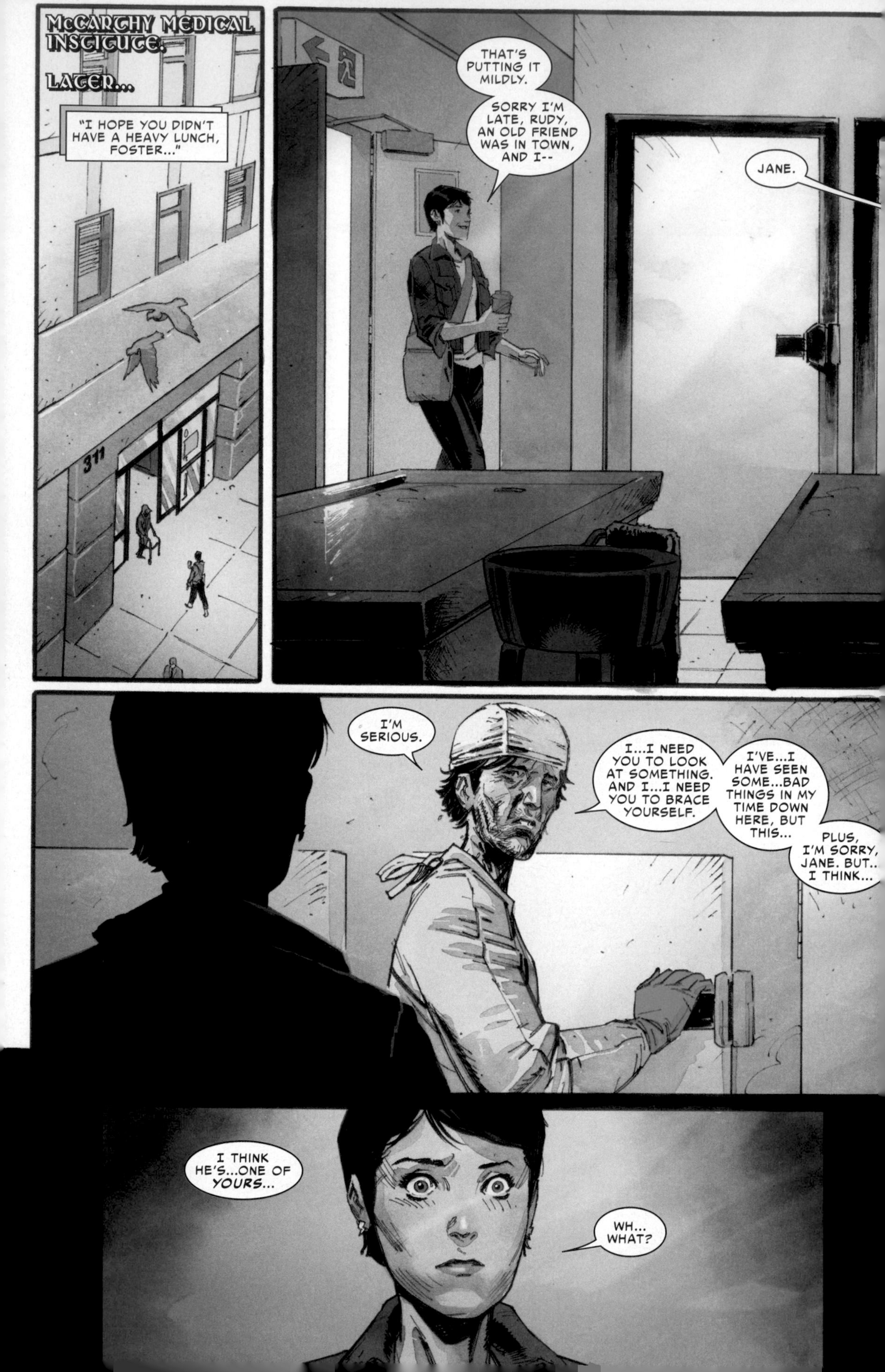
McCARTHY MEDICAL INSTITUTE.
LATER...
"I HOPE YOU DIDN'T HAVE A HEAVY LUNCH, FOSTER..."
311
THAT'S PUTTING IT MILDLY.
SORRY I'M LATE, RUDY, AN OLD FRIEND WAS IN TOWN, AND I--
JANE.
I'M SERIOUS.
I...I NEED YOU TO LOOK AT SOMETHING. AND I...I NEED YOU TO BRACE YOURSELF.
I'VE...I HAVE SEEN SOME...BAD THINGS IN MY TIME DOWN HERE, BUT THIS...
PLUS, I'M SORRY, JANE. BUT... I THINK...
I THINK HE'S...ONE OF YOURS...
WH... WHAT?

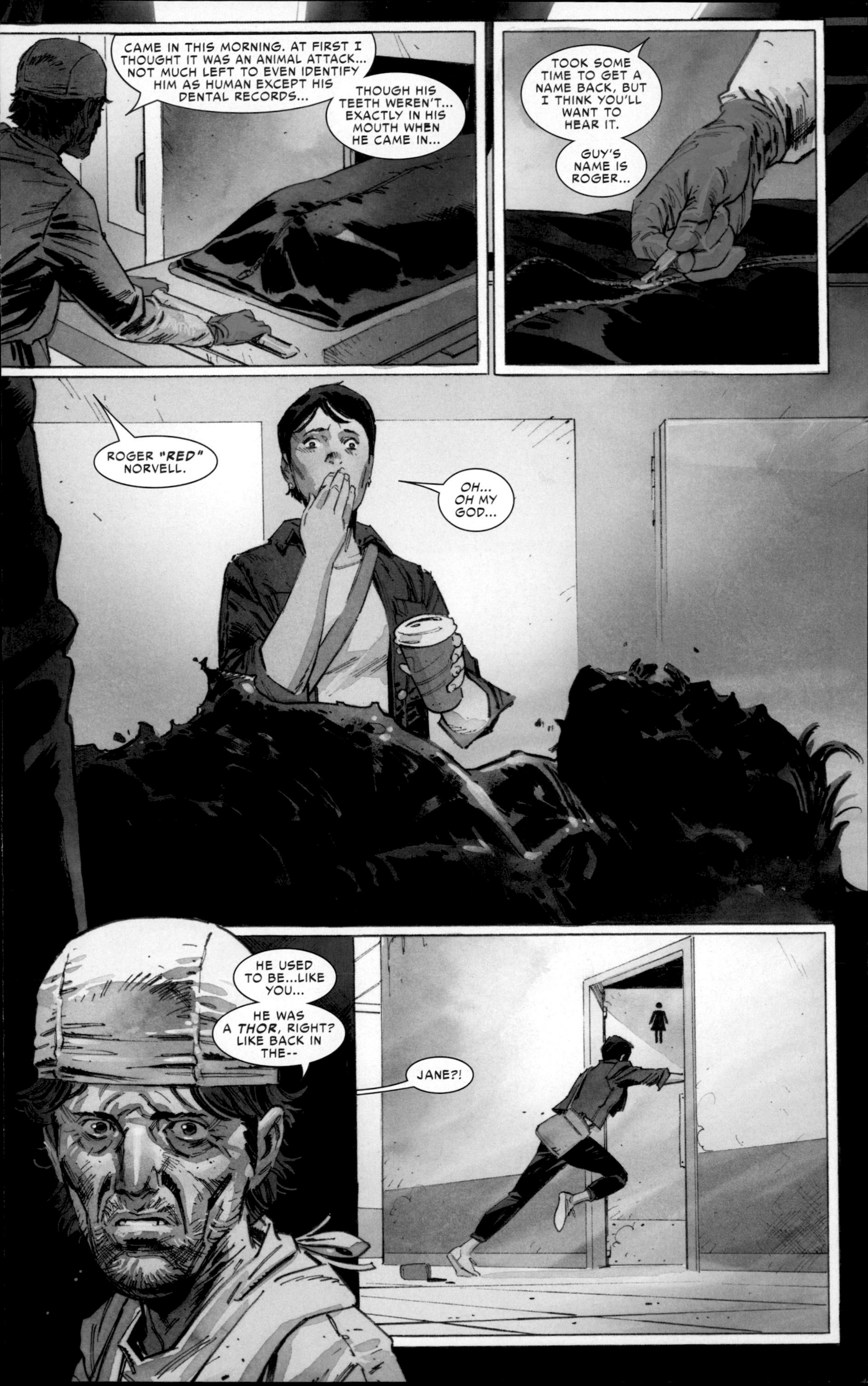
CAME IN THIS MORNING. AT FIRST I THOUGHT IT WAS AN ANIMAL ATTACK... NOT MUCH LEFT TO EVEN IDENTIFY HIM AS HUMAN EXCEPT HIS DENTAL RECORDS...
THOUGH HIS TEETH WEREN'T... EXACTLY IN HIS MOUTH WHEN HE CAME IN...
TOOK SOME TIME TO GET A NAME BACK, BUT I THINK YOU'LL WANT TO HEAR IT.
GUY'S NAME IS ROGER...
ROGER "RED" NORVELL.
OH... OH MY GOD...
HE USED TO BE...LIKE YOU...
HE WAS A THOR, RIGHT? LIKE BACK IN THE--
JANE?!

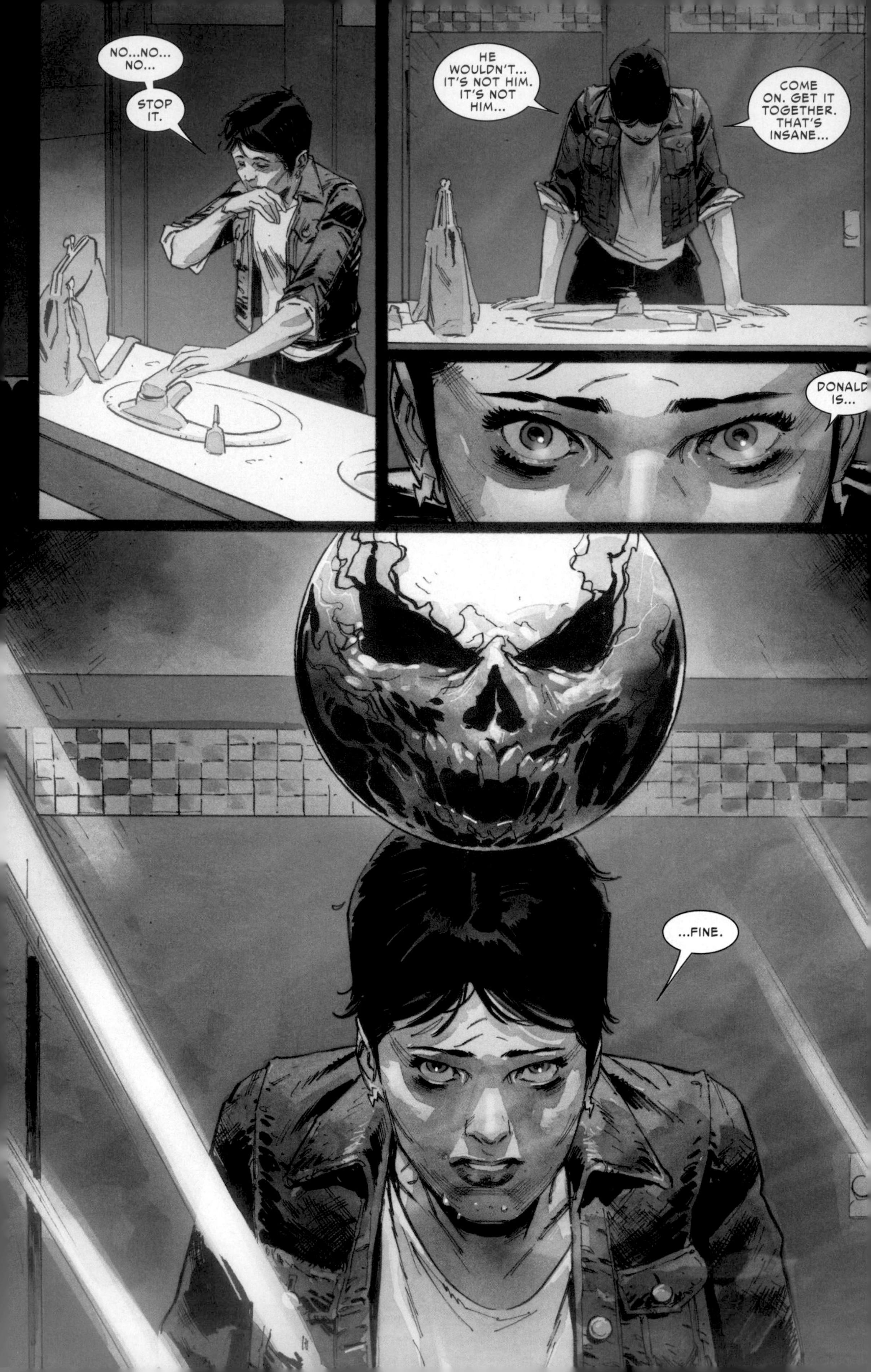
NO...NO... NO...
STOP IT.
HE WOULDN'T... IT'S NOT HIM. IT'S NOT HIM...
COME ON. GET IT TOGETHER. THAT'S INSANE...
DONALD IS...
...FINE.

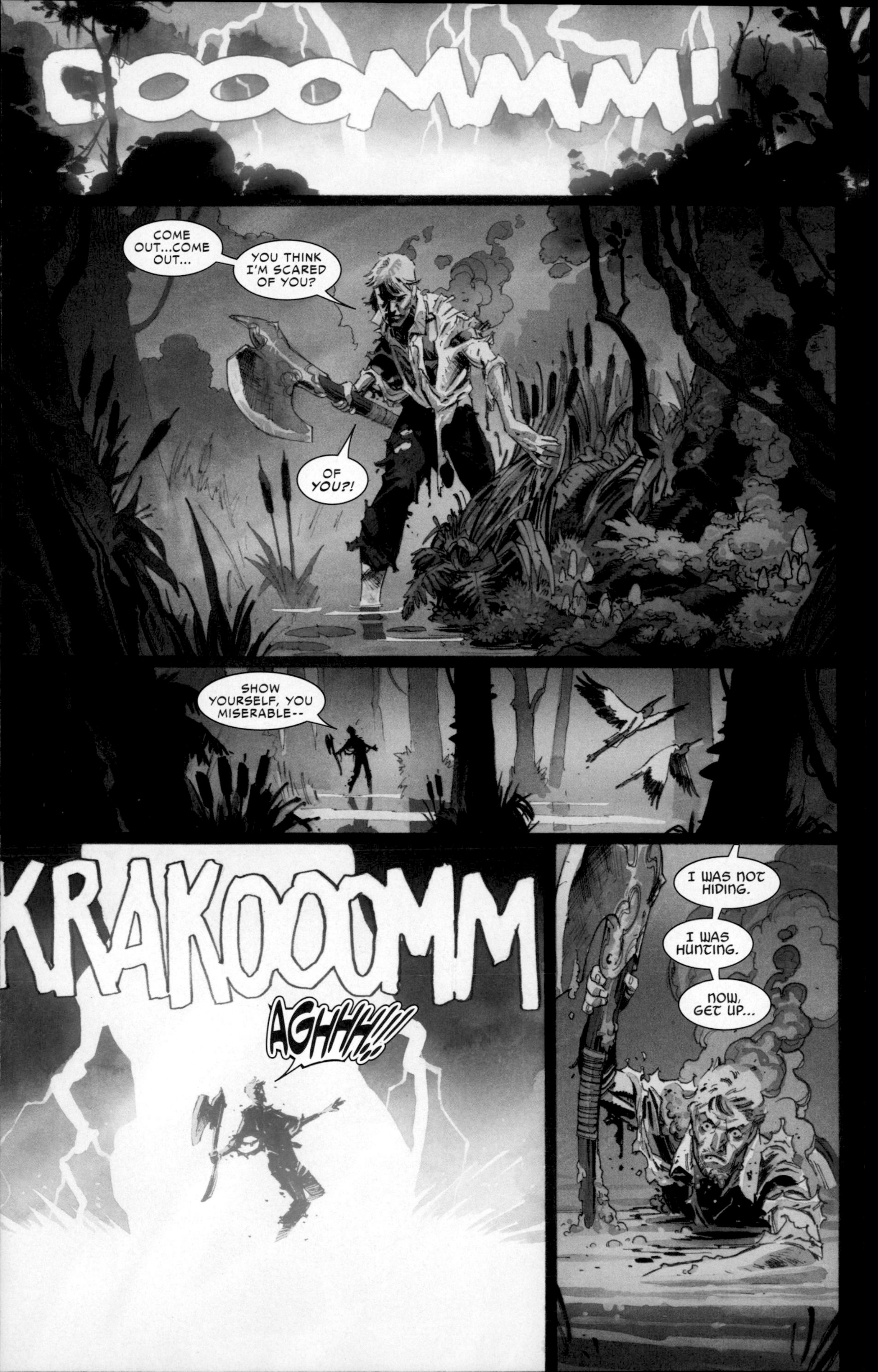

OOOOMMM!
COME OUT...COME OUT...
YOU THINK I'M SCARED OF YOU?
OF YOU?!
SHOW YOURSELF, YOU MISERABLE--
KRAKOOOMM
AGHHH!!!
I WAS NOT HIDING.
I WAS HUNTING.
NOW, GET UP...

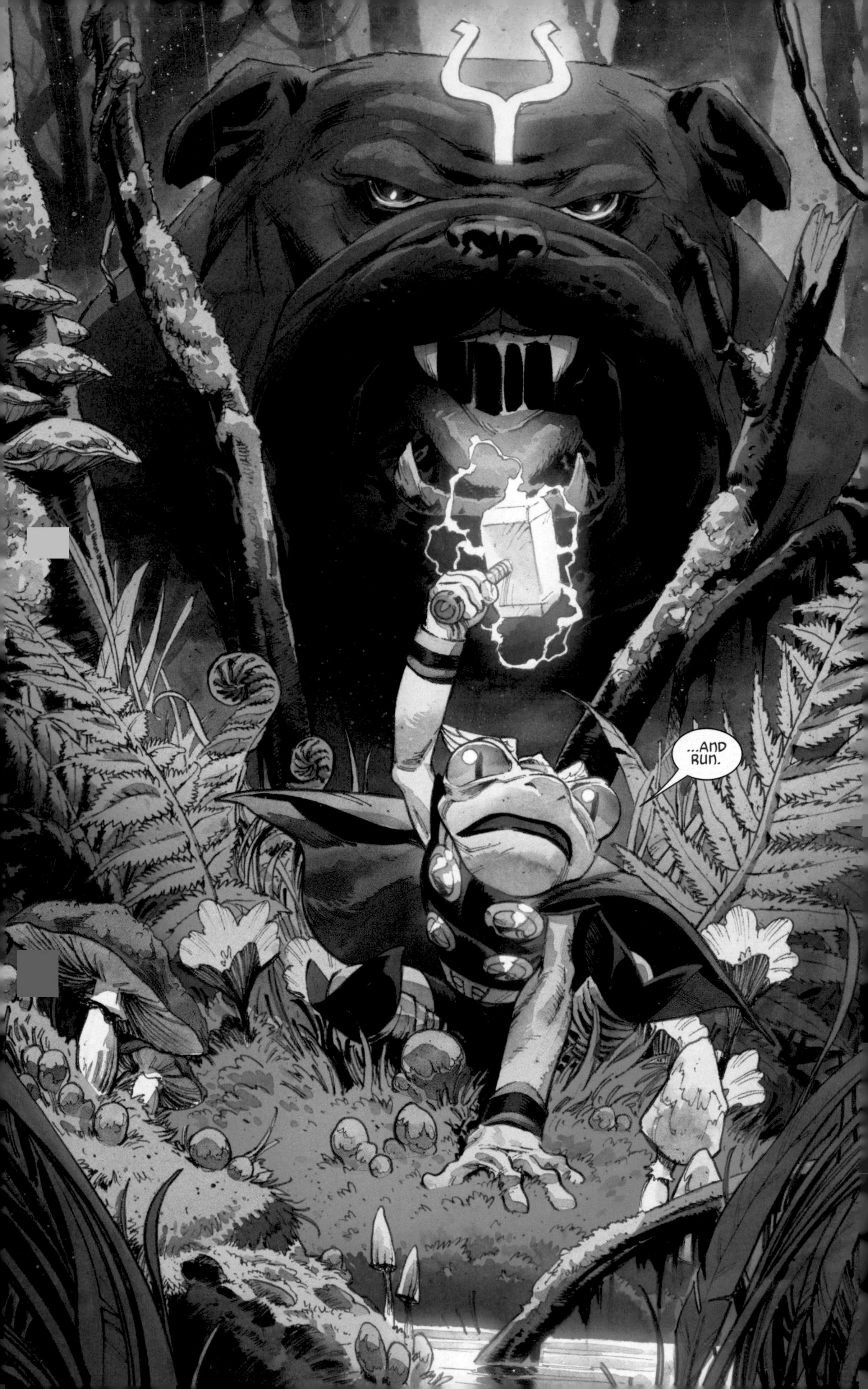
...AND RUN.

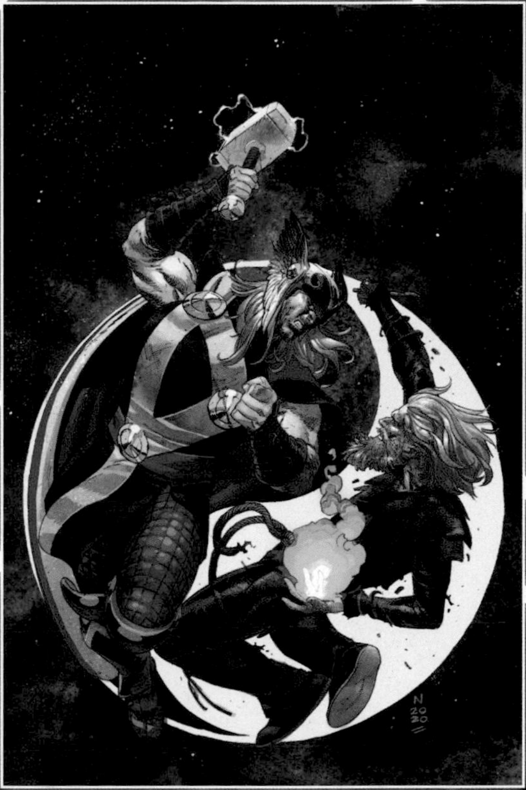

THOR 10 VARIANT BY
Nic Klein

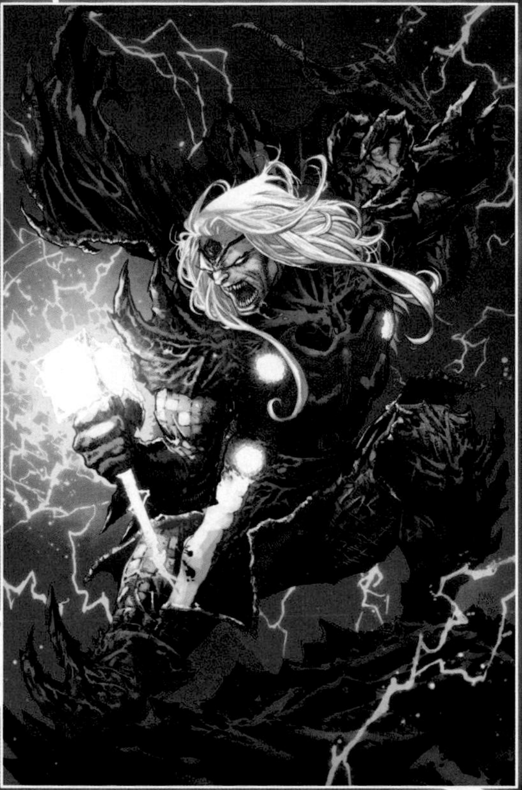

THOR 10 KNULLIFIED VARIANT BY
Ken Lashley & Nolan Woodard

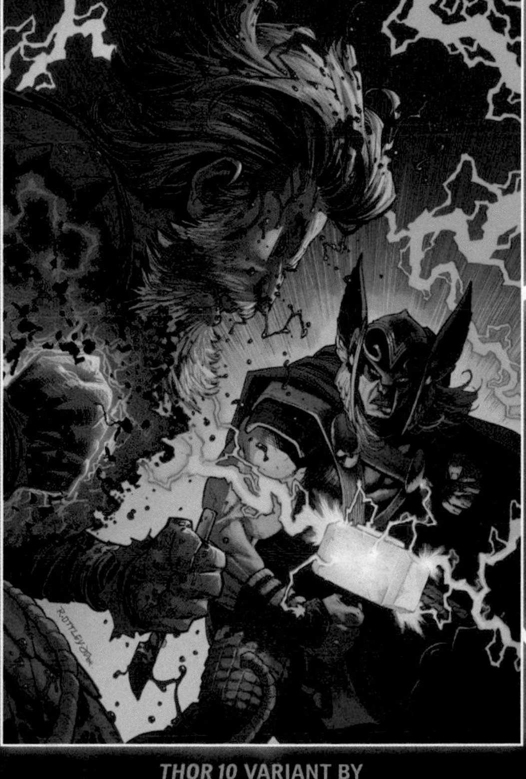

THOR 10 VARIANT BY
Ryan Ottley & Frank Martin

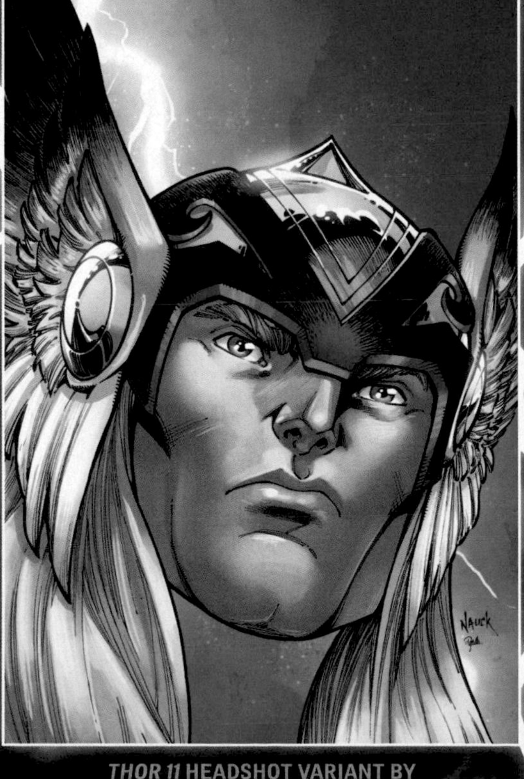

THOR 11 HEADSHOT VARIANT BY
Todd Nauck & Rachelle Rosenberg

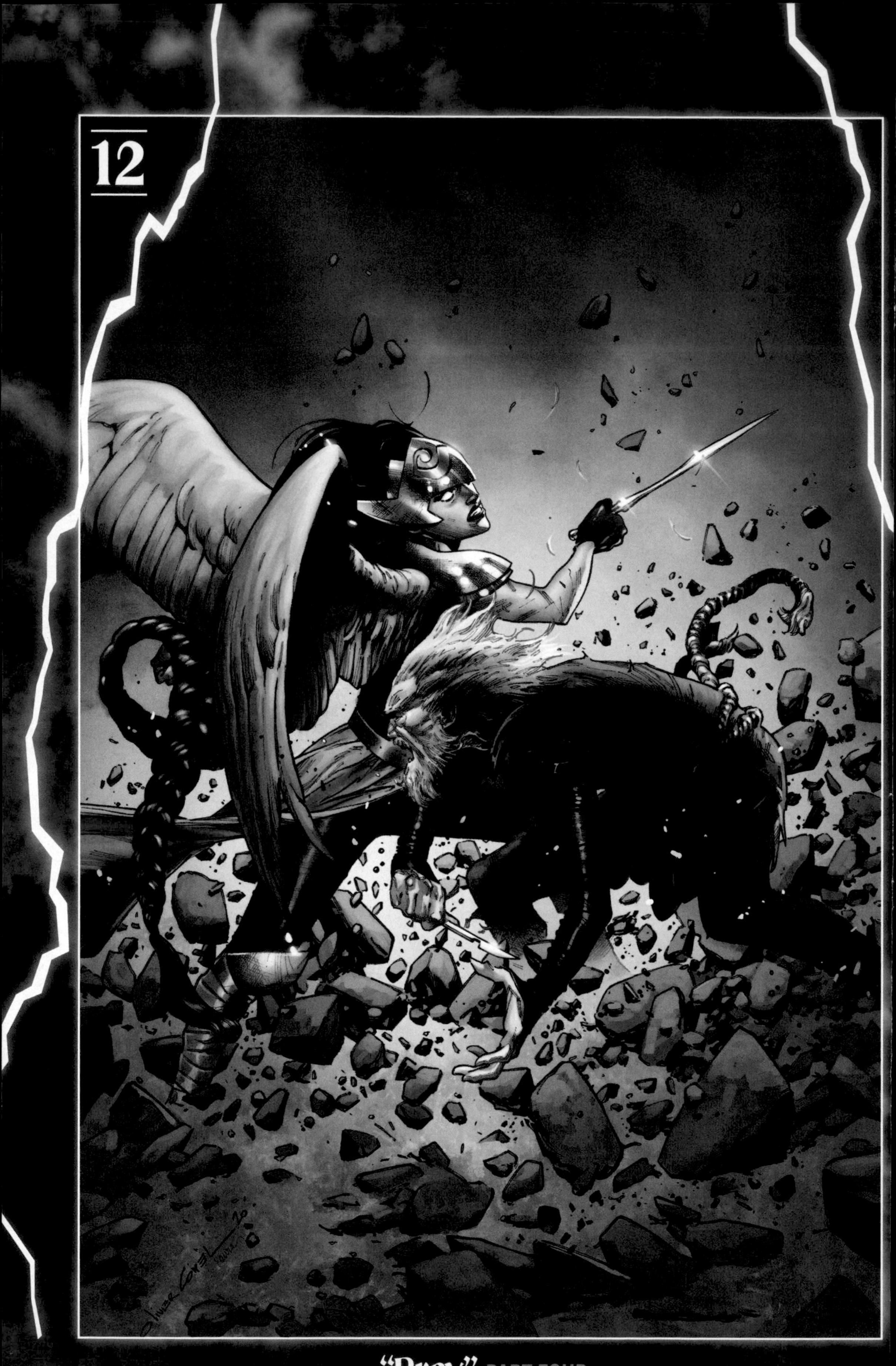
12

"Prey" PART FOUR

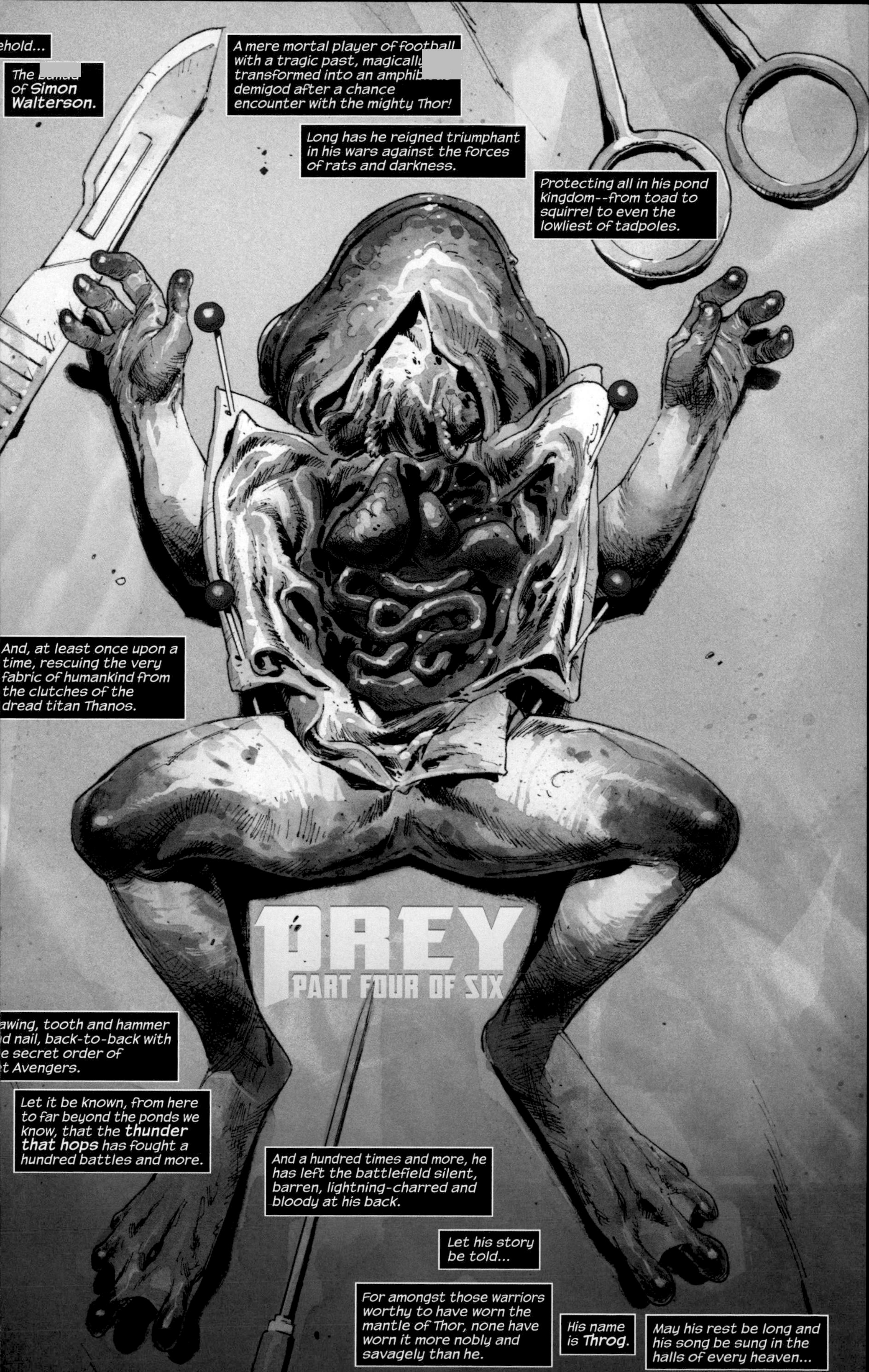
ehold...
The
of Simon Walterson.
A mere mortal player of football with a tragic past, magically transformed into an amphib demigod after a chance encounter with the mighty Thor!
Long has he reigned triumphant in his wars against the forces of rats and darkness.
Protecting all in his pond kingdom--from toad to squirrel to even the lowliest of tadpoles.
And, at least once upon a time, rescuing the very fabric of humankind from the clutches of the dread titan Thanos.
PREY
PART FOUR OF SIX
awing, tooth and hammer d nail, back-to-back with e secret order of t Avengers.
Let it be known, from here to far beyond the ponds we know, that the thunder that hops has fought a hundred battles and more.
And a hundred times and more, he has left the battlefield silent, barren, lightning-charred and bloody at his back.
Let his story be told...
For amongst those warriors worthy to have worn the mantle of Thor, none have worn it more nobly and savagely than he.
His name is Throg.
May his rest be long and his song be sung in the halls of every heaven...

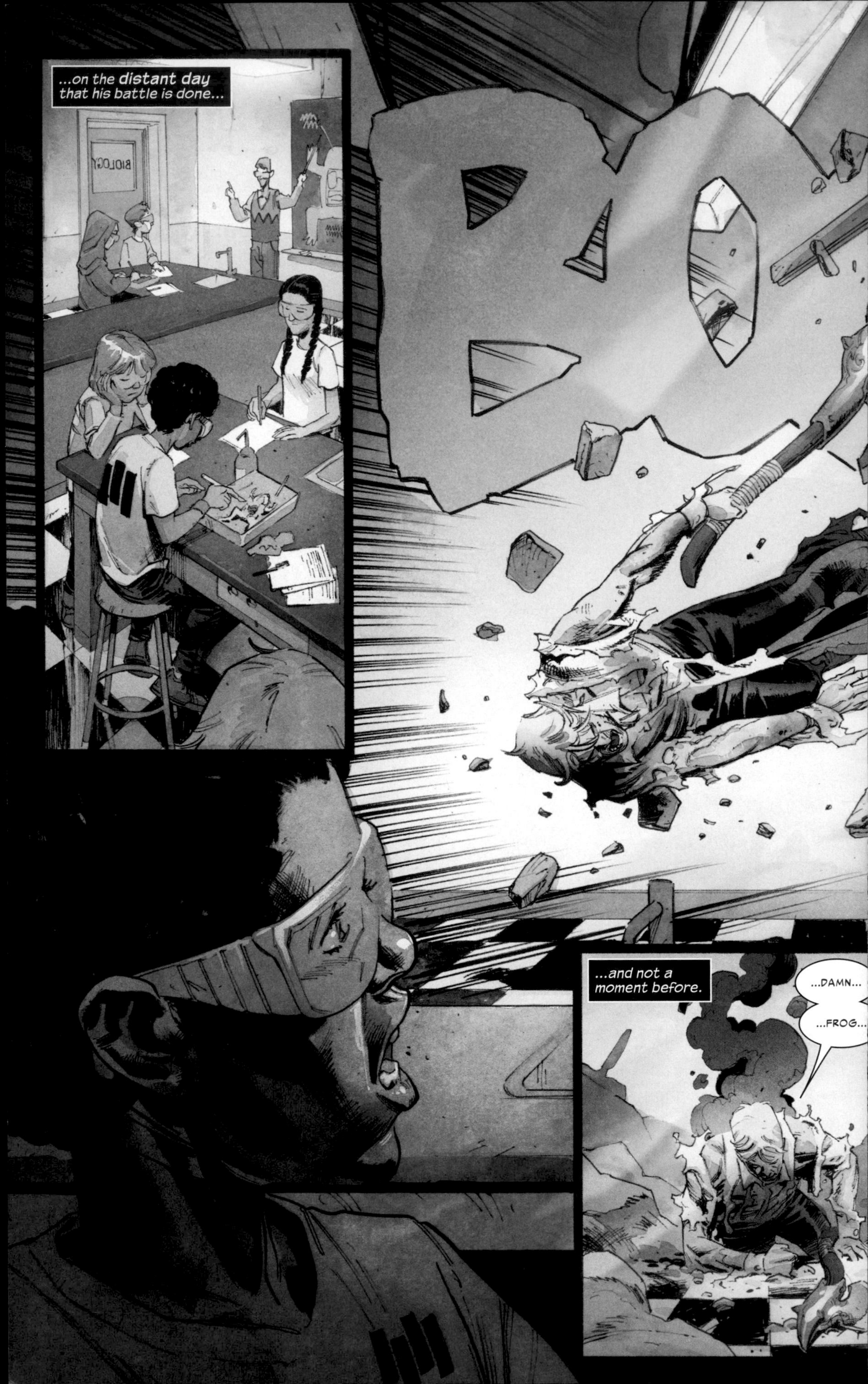

...on the distant day that his battle is done...
BIOLOGY
...and not a moment before.
...DAMN...
...FROG...

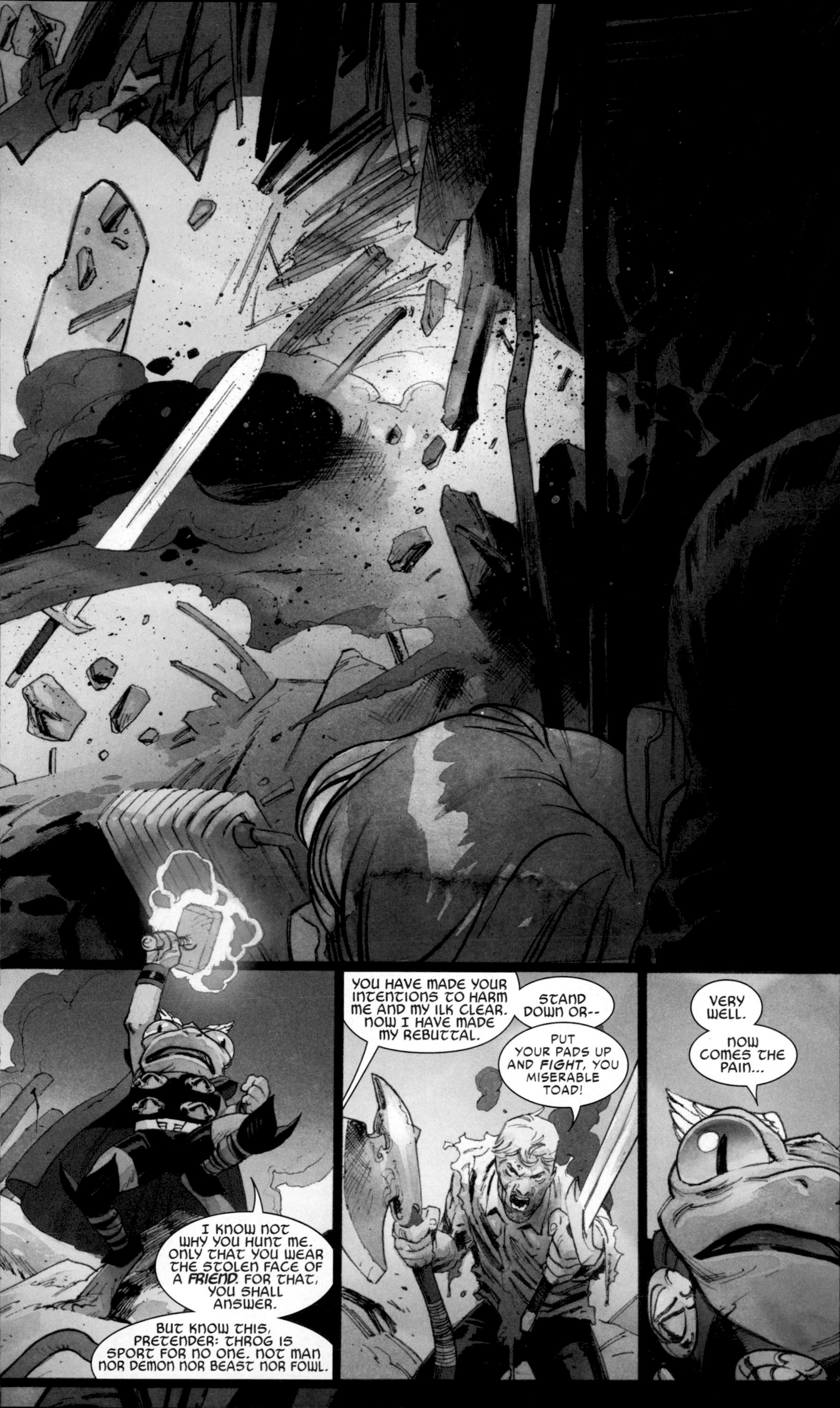
I KNOW NOT WHY YOU HUNT ME. ONLY THAT YOU WEAR THE STOLEN FACE OF A FRIEND. FOR THAT, YOU SHALL ANSWER.
BUT KNOW THIS, PRETENDER: THROG IS SPORT FOR NO ONE. NOT MAN NOR DEMON NOR BEAST NOR FOWL.
YOU HAVE MADE YOUR INTENTIONS TO HARM ME AND MY ILK CLEAR. NOW I HAVE MADE MY REBUTTAL.
STAND DOWN OR--
PUT YOUR PADS UP AND FIGHT, YOU MISERABLE TOAD!
VERY WELL.
NOW COMES THE PAIN...

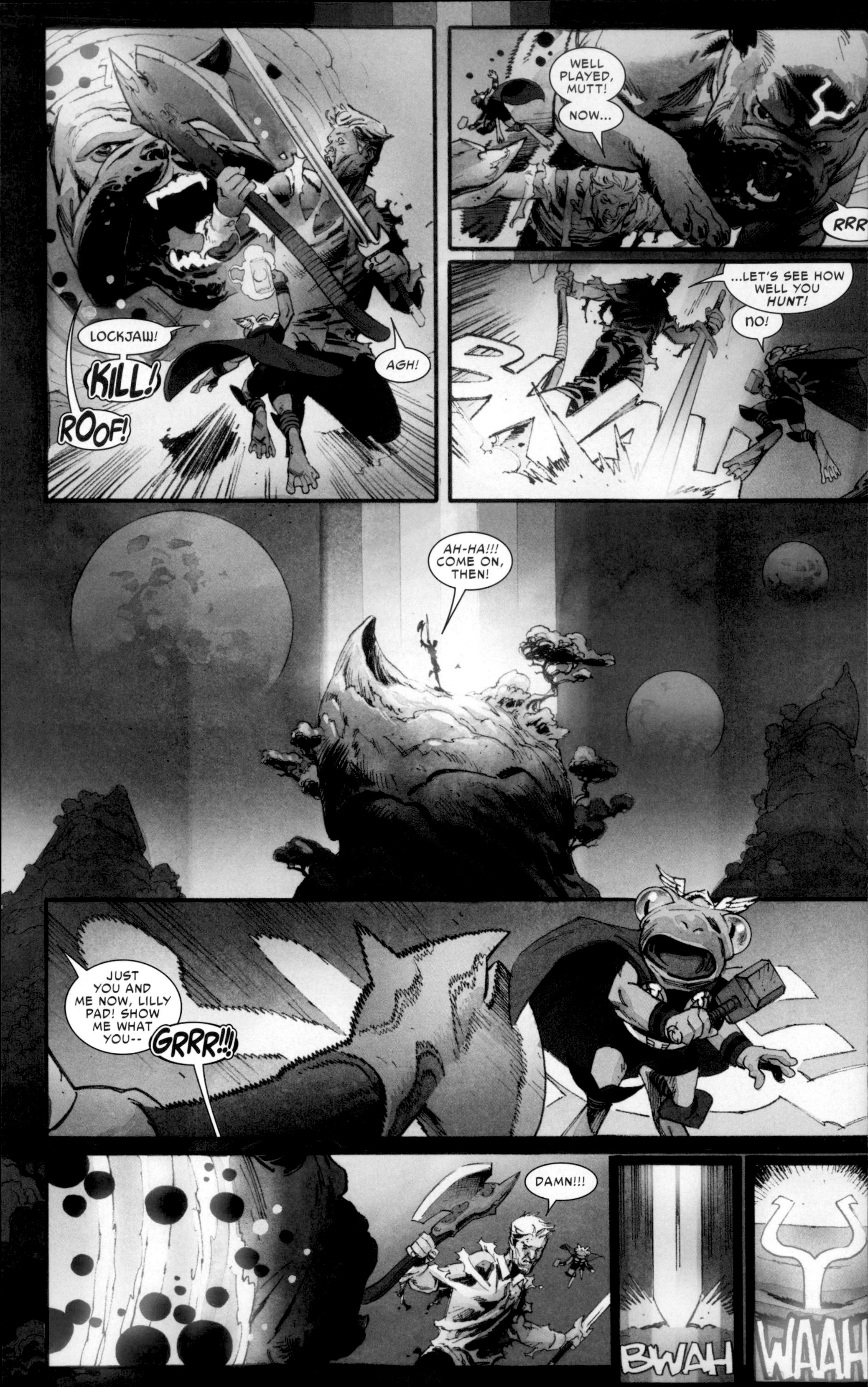
LOCKJAW!
KILL!
ROOF!
AGH!
WELL PLAYED, MUTT!
NOW...
RRR
...LET'S SEE HOW WELL YOU HUNT!
NO!
AH-HA!!! COME ON, THEN!
JUST YOU AND ME NOW, LILLY PAD! SHOW ME WHAT YOU--
GRRR!!!
DAMN!!!
BWAH
WAAH

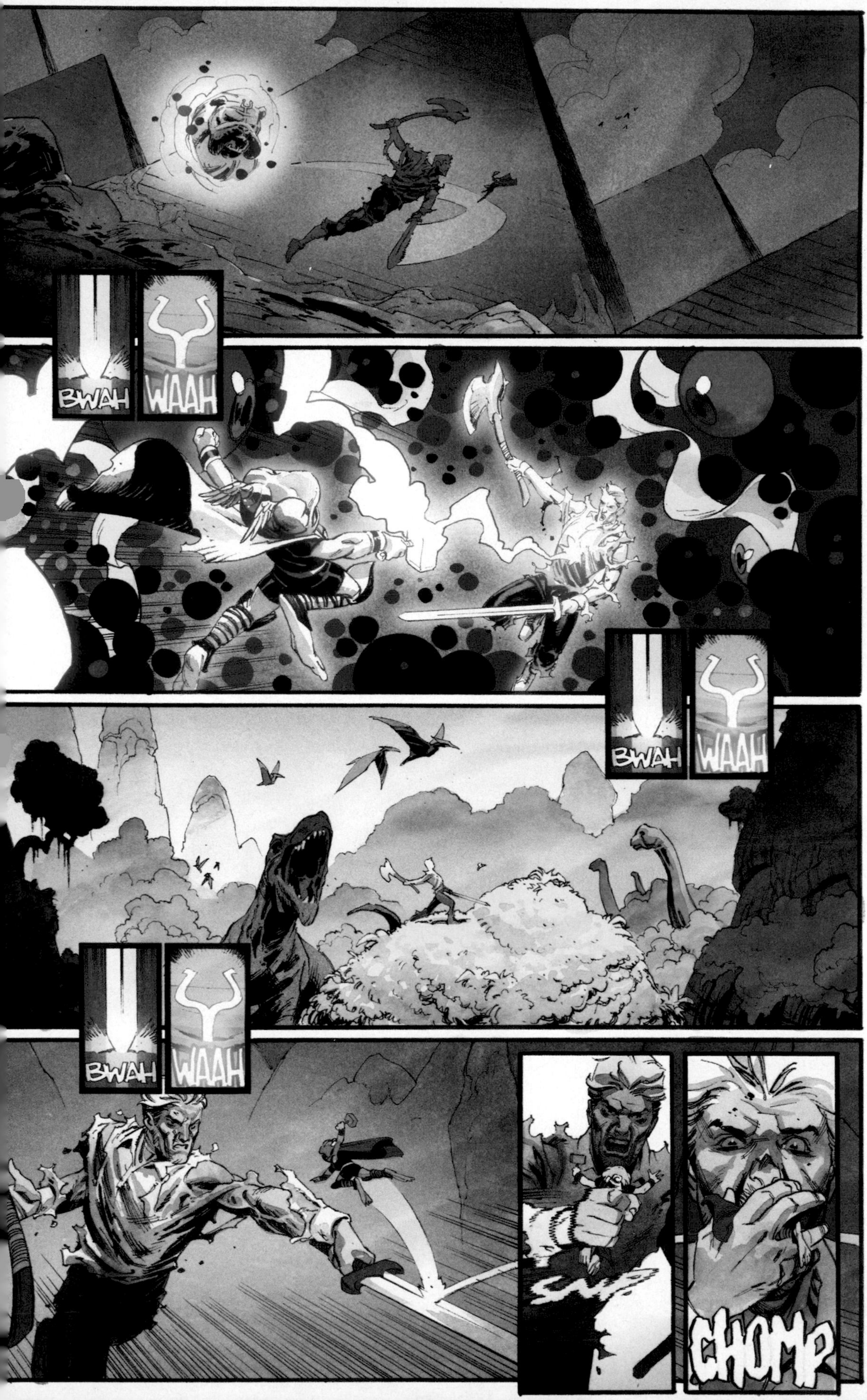
BWAH
WAAH
BWAH
WAAH
BWAH
WAAH
CHOMP

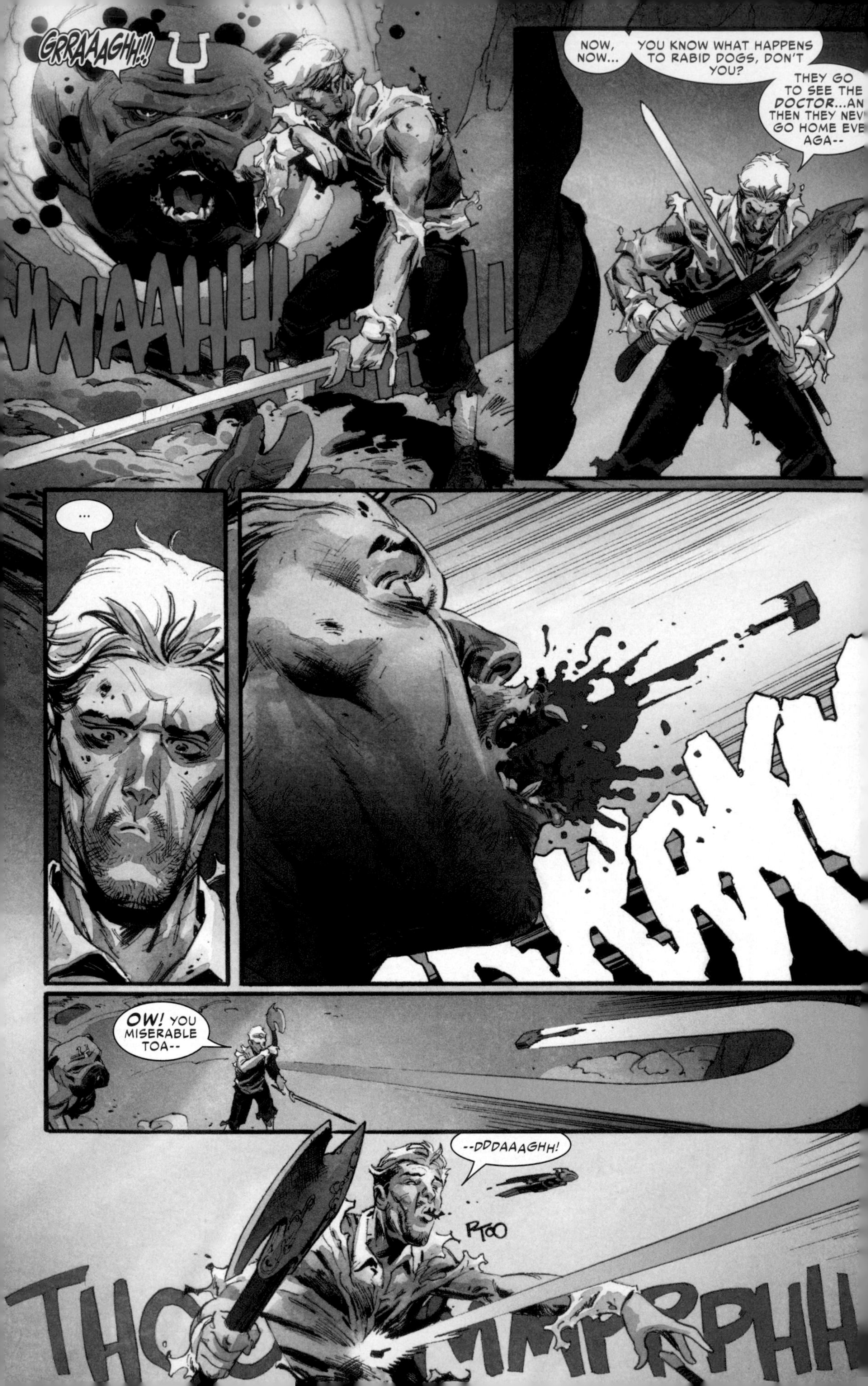
GRRAAAGHH!!!
JWAAHH
NOW, NOW...
YOU KNOW WHAT HAPPENS TO RABID DOGS, DON'T YOU?
THEY GO TO SEE THE DOCTOR...AN THEN THEY NEV GO HOME EVE AGA--
...
OW! YOU MISERABLE TOA--
--DDDAAAGHH!
THOOMMPRPHH

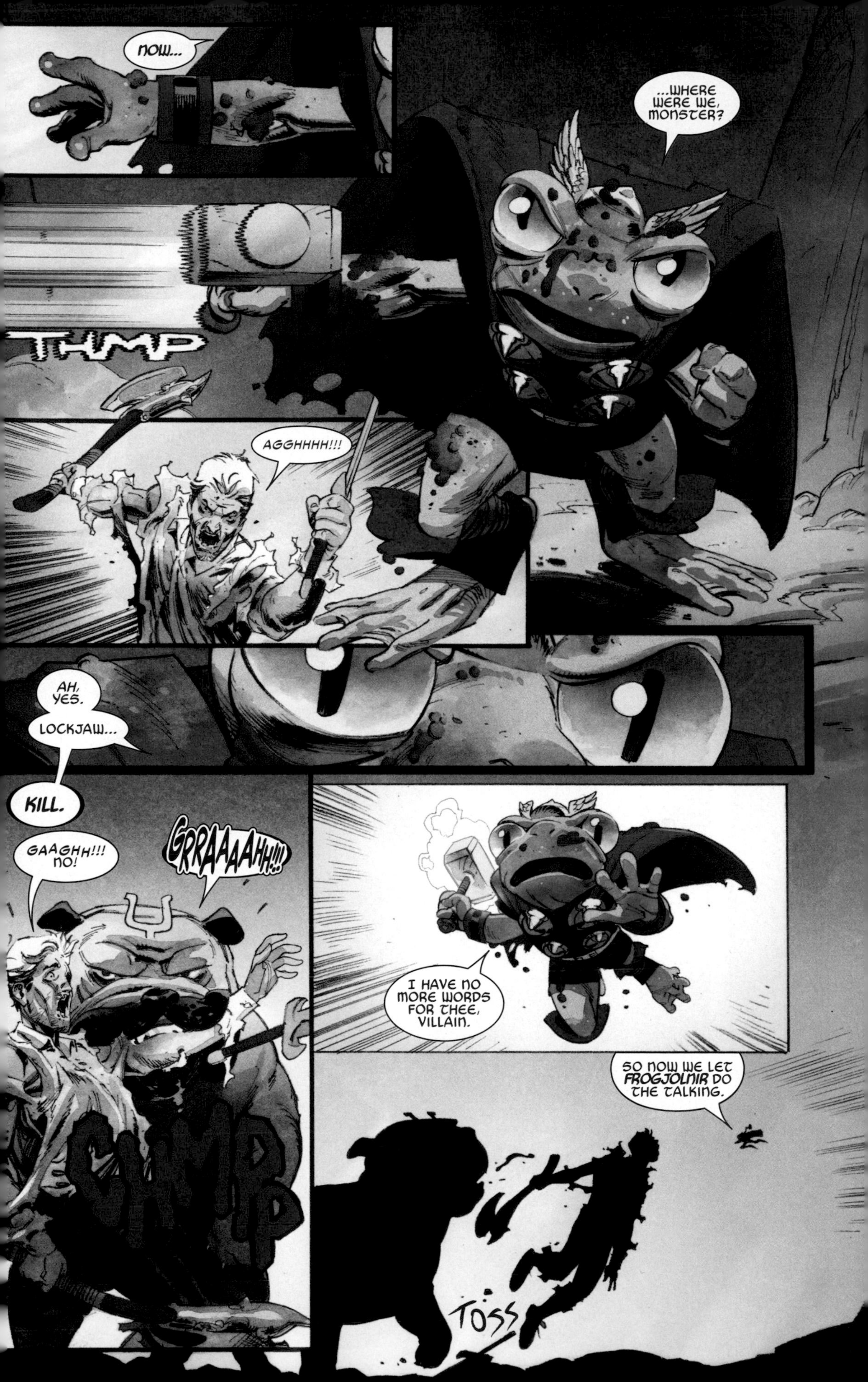
NOW...
...WHERE WERE WE, MONSTER?
THMP
AGGHHHH!!!
AH, YES.
LOCKJAW...
KILL.
GAAGHH!!! NO!
GRRAAAAHH!!!
I HAVE NO MORE WORDS FOR THEE, VILLAIN.
SO NOW WE LET FROGJOLNIR DO THE TALKING.
TOSS

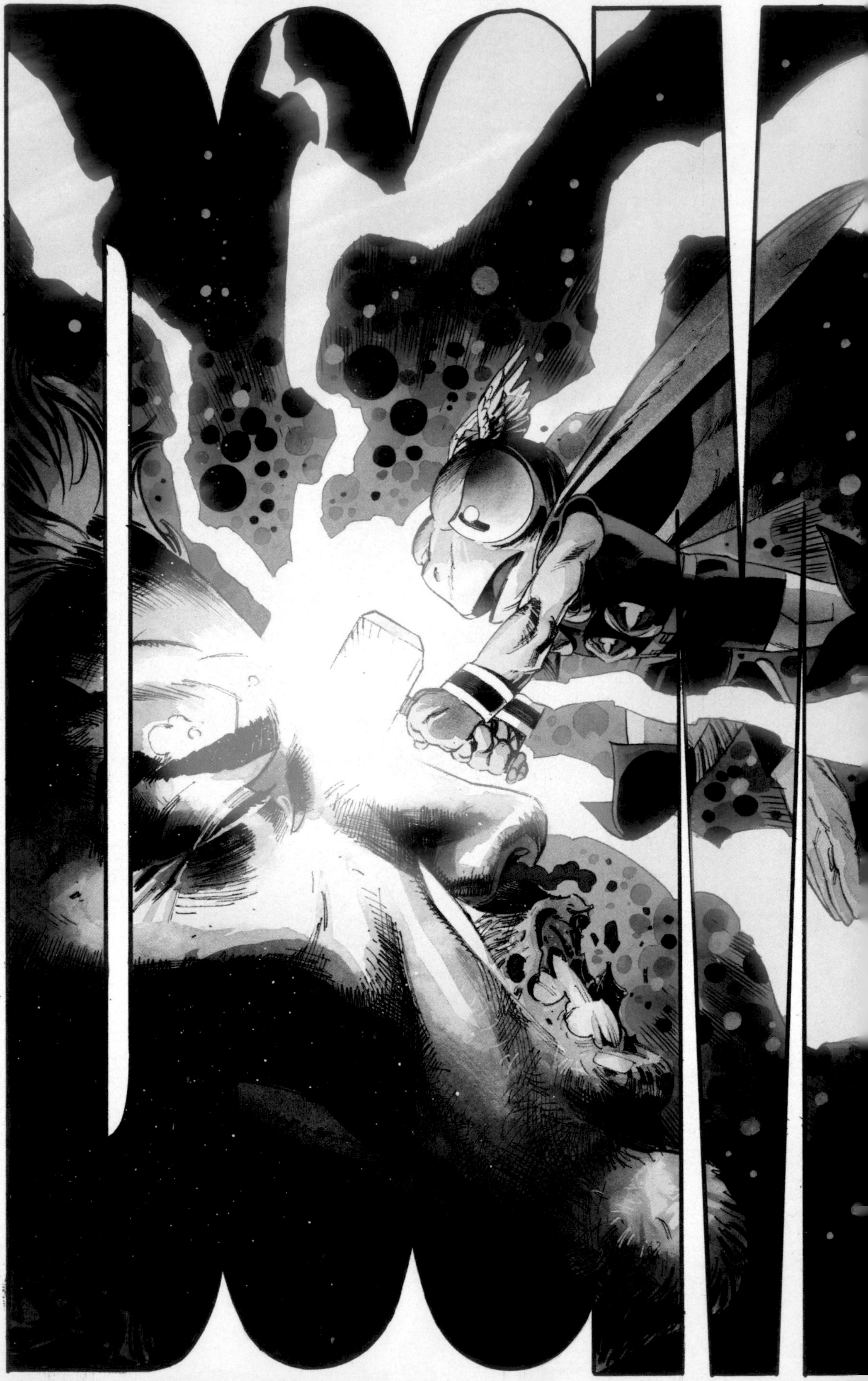

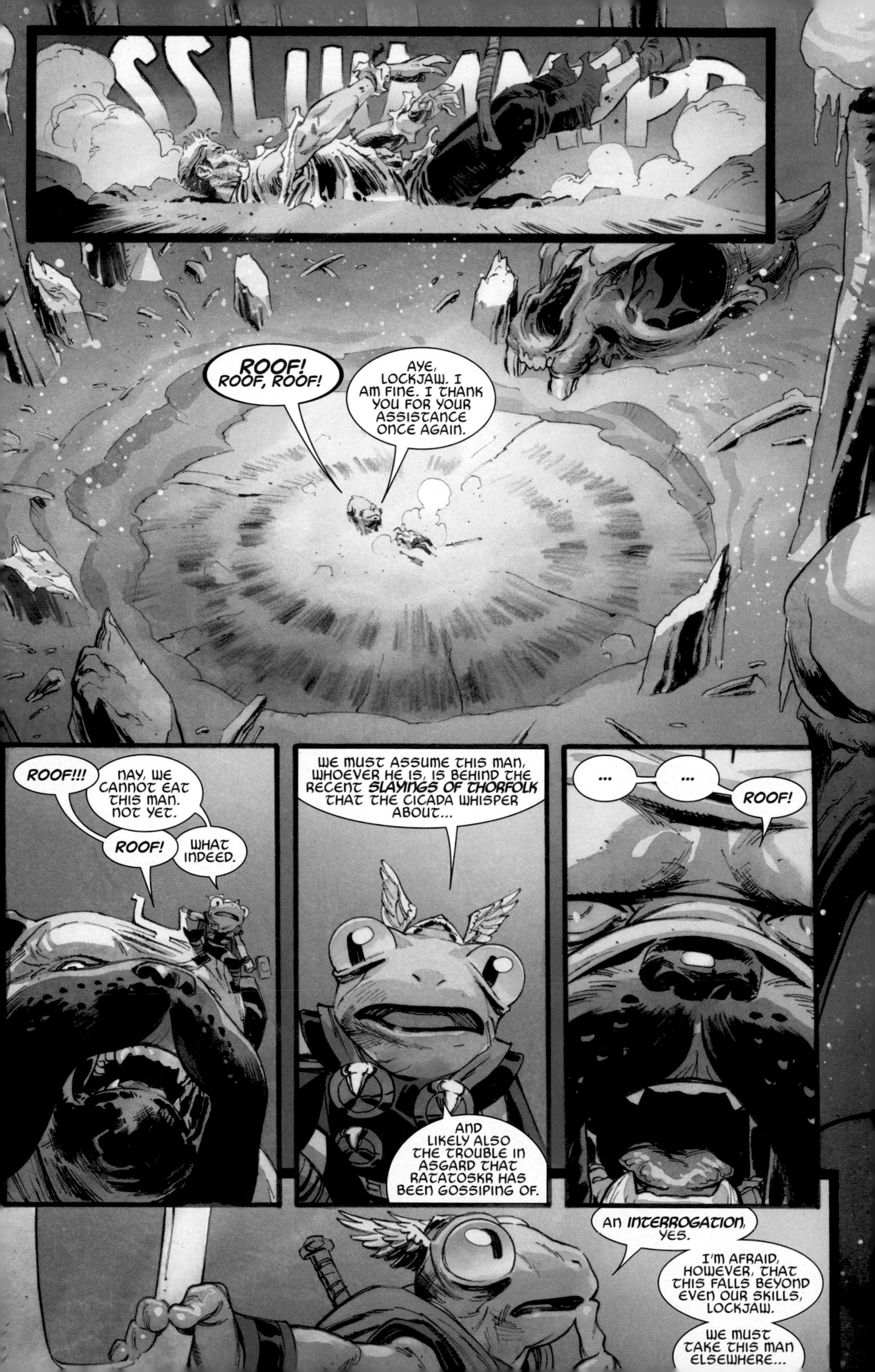
SSLUMMP
ROOF! ROOF, ROOF!
AYE, LOCKJAW. I AM FINE. I THANK YOU FOR YOUR ASSISTANCE ONCE AGAIN.
ROOF!!!
NAY, WE CANNOT EAT THIS MAN. NOT YET.
ROOF!
WHAT INDEED.
WE MUST ASSUME THIS MAN, WHOEVER HE IS, IS BEHIND THE RECENT SLAYINGS OF THORFOLK THAT THE CICADA WHISPER ABOUT...
AND LIKELY ALSO THE TROUBLE IN ASGARD THAT RATATOSKR HAS BEEN GOSSIPING OF.
...
...
ROOF!
AN INTERROGATION, YES.
I'M AFRAID, HOWEVER, THAT THIS FALLS BEYOND EVEN OUR SKILLS, LOCKJAW.
WE MUST TAKE THIS MAN ELSEWHERE...

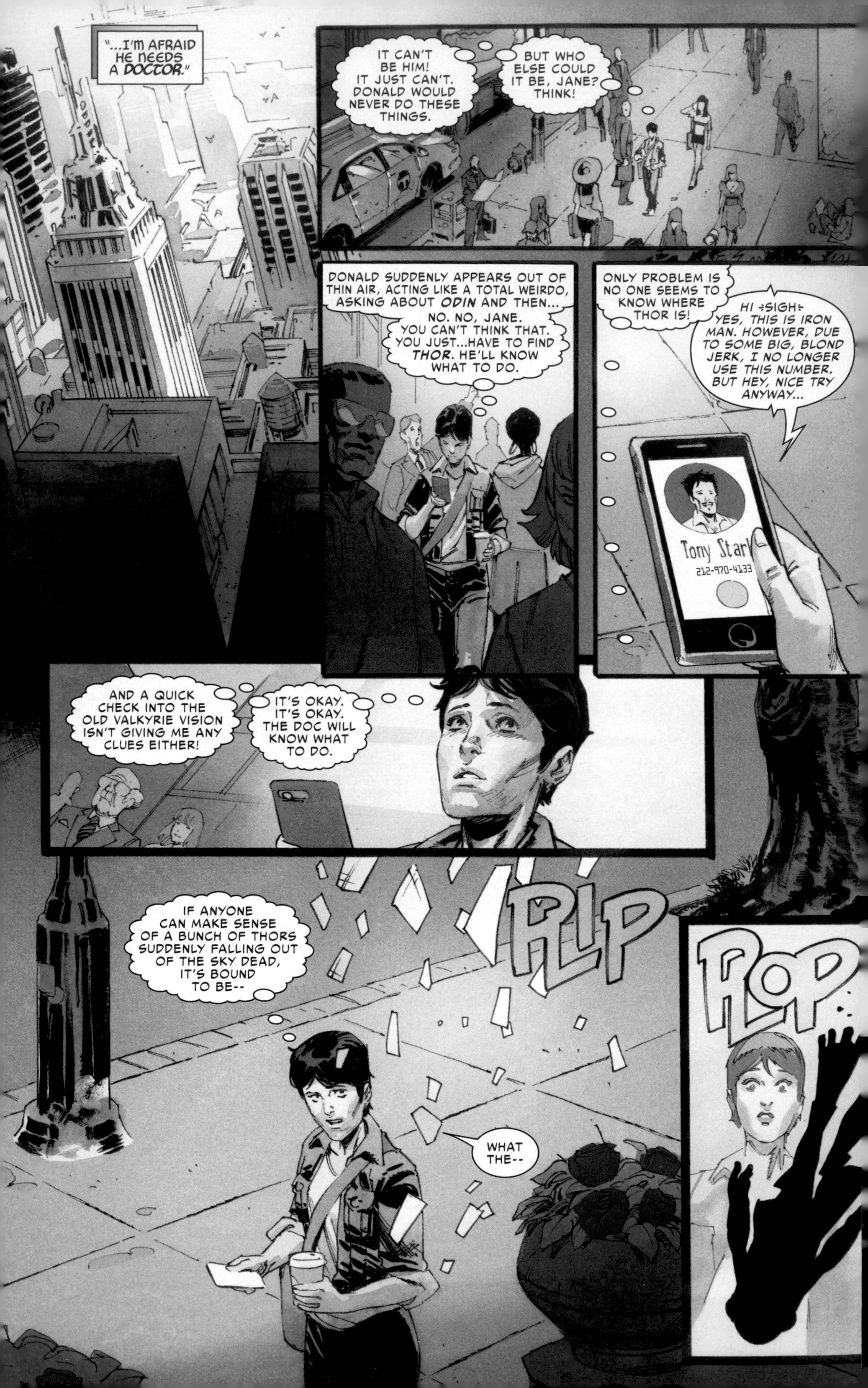
"...I'M AFRAID HE NEEDS A DOCTOR."
IT CAN'T BE HIM! IT JUST CAN'T. DONALD WOULD NEVER DO THESE THINGS.
BUT WHO ELSE COULD IT BE, JANE? THINK!
DONALD SUDDENLY APPEARS OUT OF THIN AIR, ACTING LIKE A TOTAL WEIRDO, ASKING ABOUT ODIN AND THEN...
NO. NO, JANE. YOU CAN'T THINK THAT. YOU JUST...HAVE TO FIND THOR. HE'LL KNOW WHAT TO DO.
ONLY PROBLEM IS NO ONE SEEMS TO KNOW WHERE THOR IS!
HI *SIGH* YES, THIS IS IRON MAN. HOWEVER, DUE TO SOME BIG, BLOND JERK, I NO LONGER USE THIS NUMBER. BUT HEY, NICE TRY ANYWAY...
Tony Stark
212-970-4133
AND A QUICK CHECK INTO THE OLD VALKYRIE VISION ISN'T GIVING ME ANY CLUES EITHER!
IT'S OKAY. IT'S OKAY. THE DOC WILL KNOW WHAT TO DO.
IF ANYONE CAN MAKE SENSE OF A BUNCH OF THORS SUDDENLY FALLING OUT OF THE SKY DEAD, IT'S BOUND TO BE--
RIP
WHAT THE--
POP

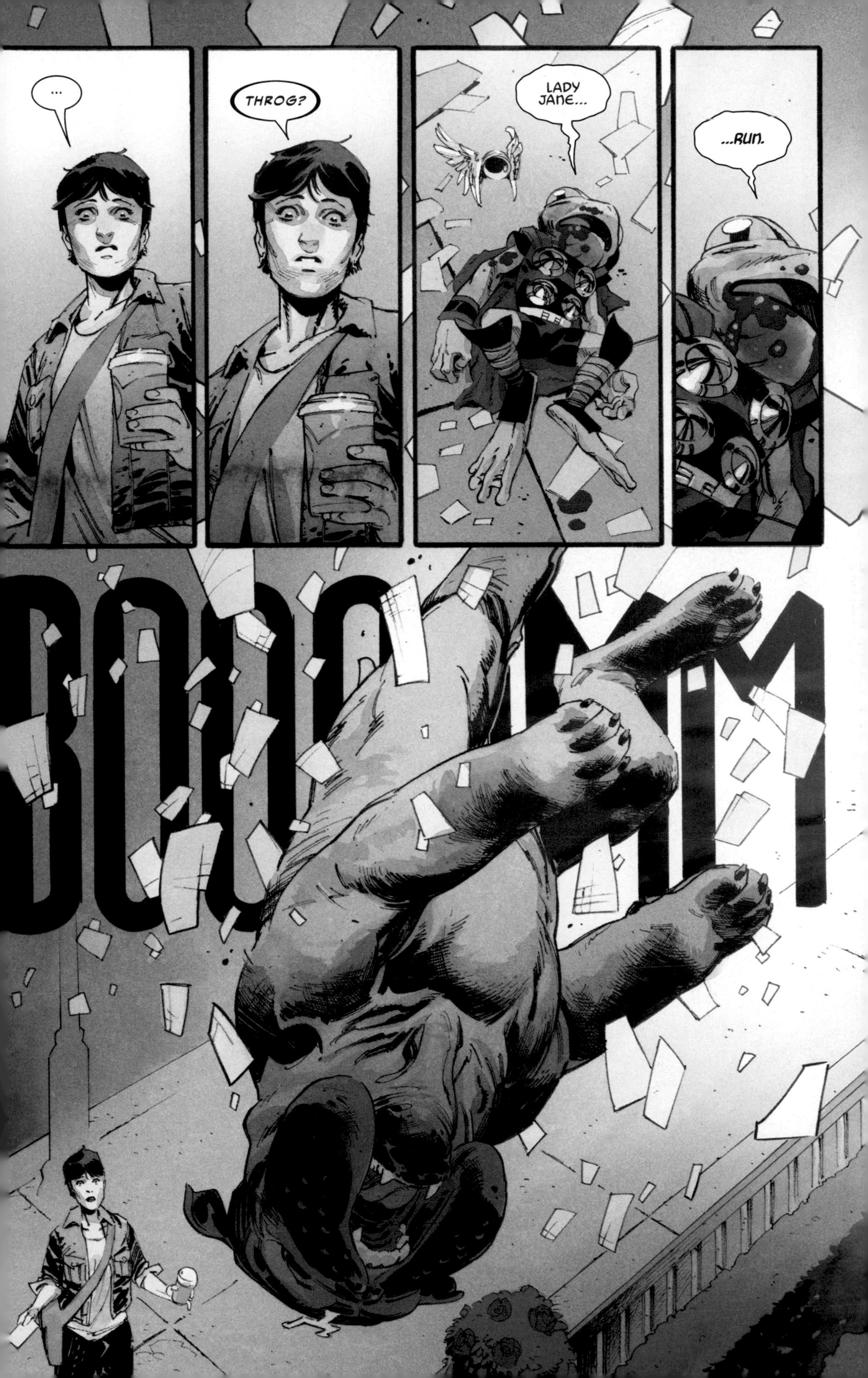
...
THROG?
LADY JANE...
...RUN.
BOOOOM

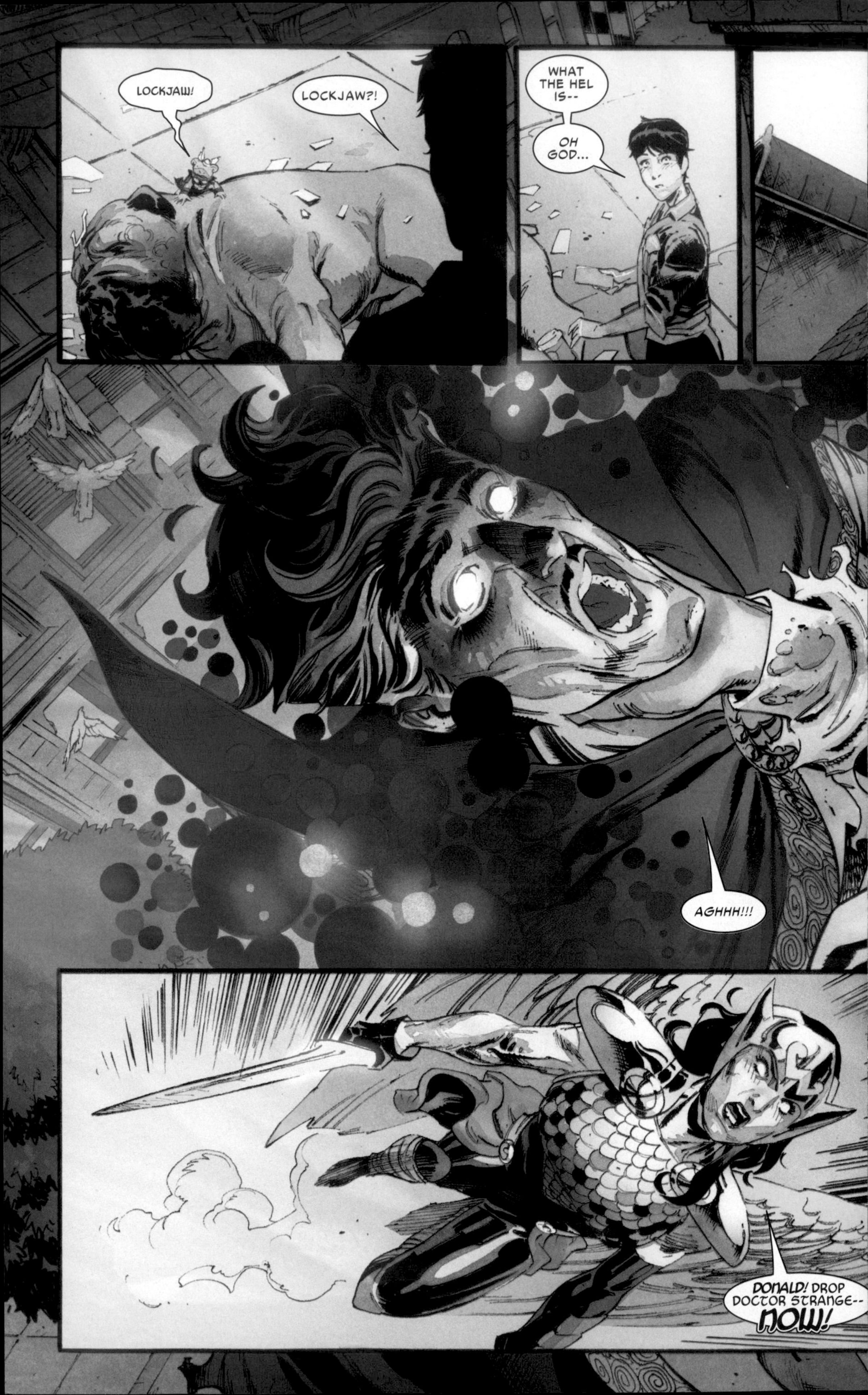
LOCKJAW!
LOCKJAW?!
WHAT THE HEL IS--
OH GOD...
AGHHH!!!
DONALD! DROP DOCTOR STRANGE--
NOW!

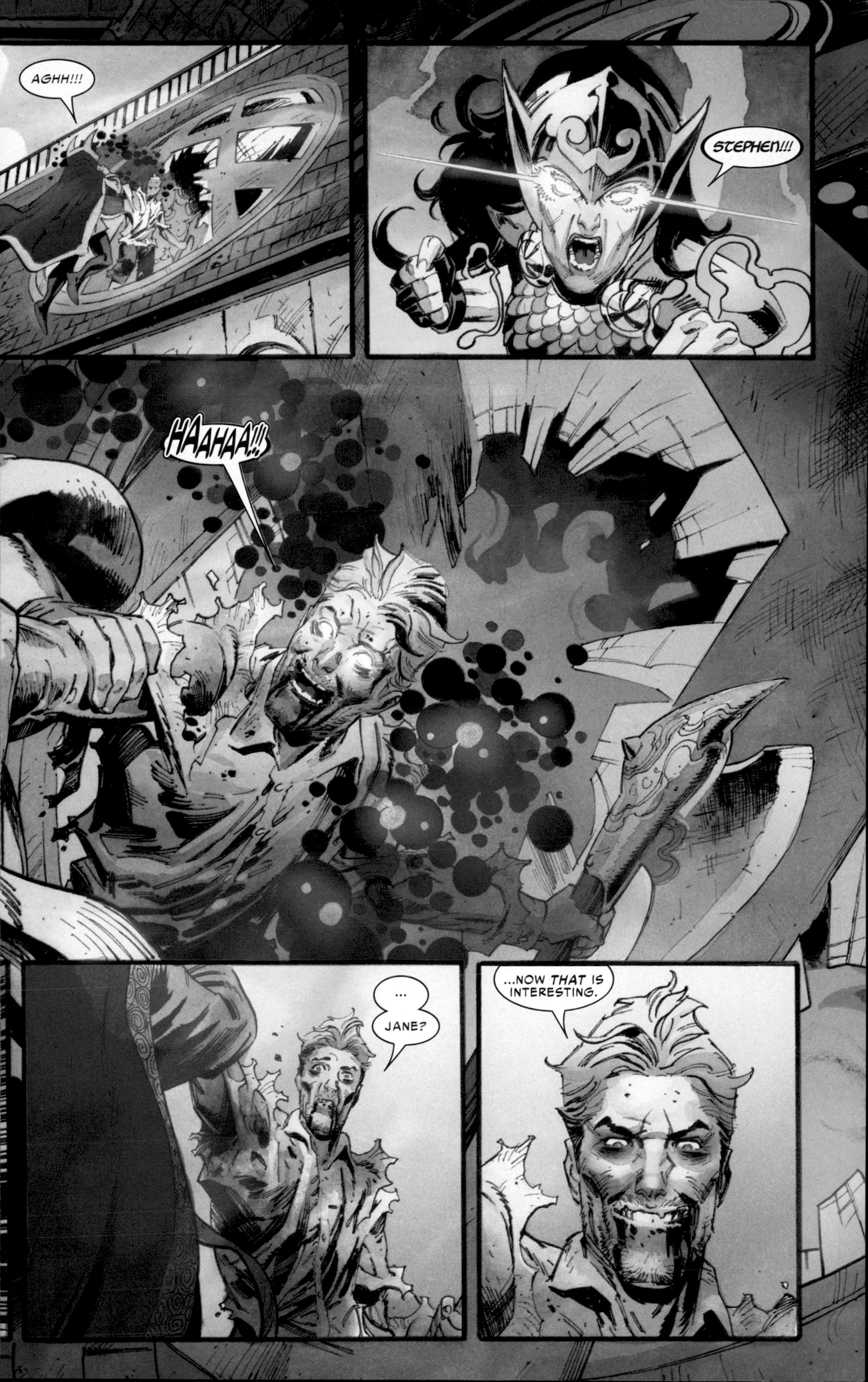
AGHH!!!
STEPHEN!!!
HAAHAA!!!
...
JANE?
...NOW THAT IS INTERESTING.

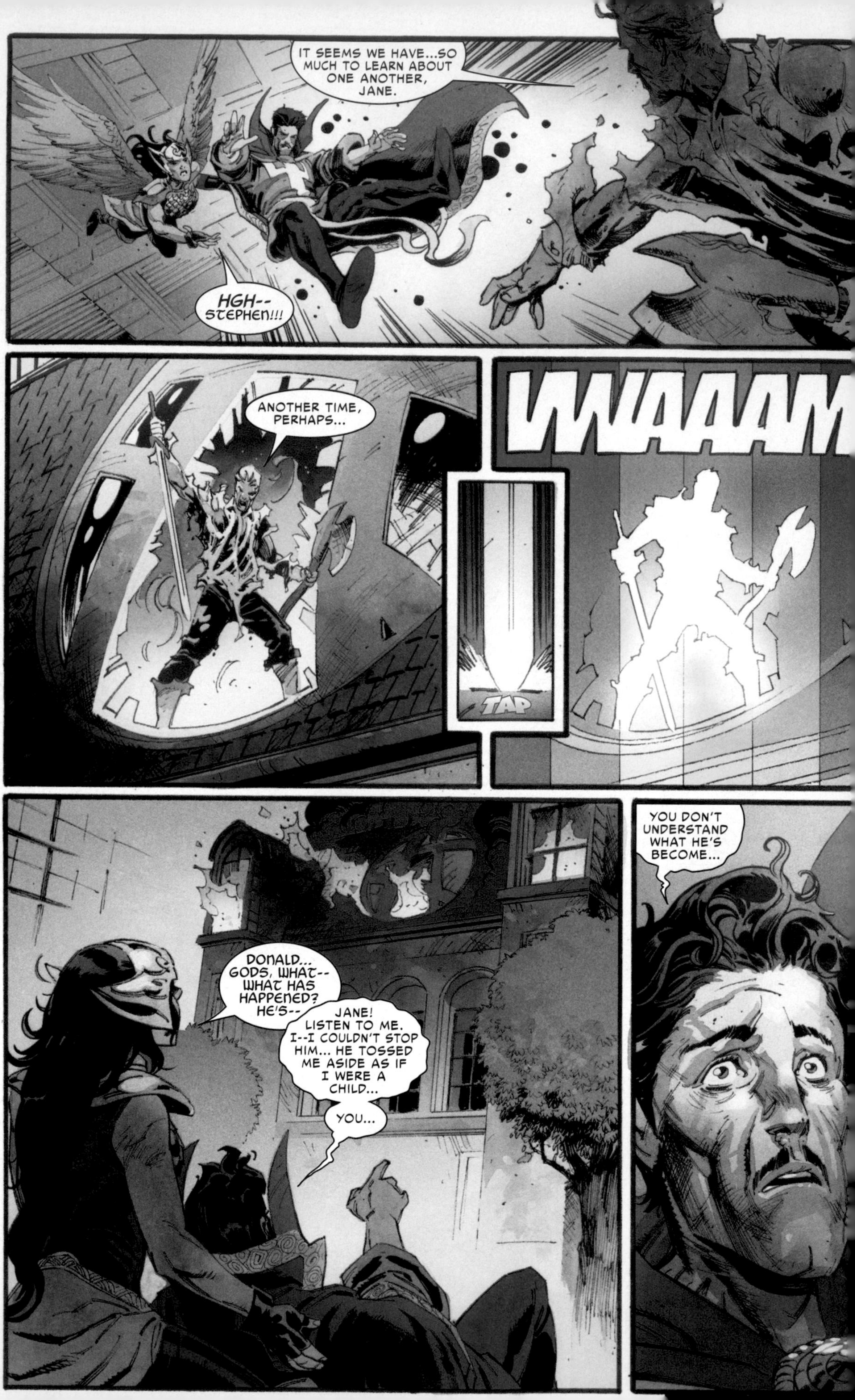
IT SEEMS WE HAVE...SO MUCH TO LEARN ABOUT ONE ANOTHER, JANE.
HGH-- STEPHEN!!!
ANOTHER TIME, PERHAPS...
WAAAAM
TAP
DONALD... GODS, WHAT-- WHAT HAS HAPPENED? HE'S--
JANE! LISTEN TO ME. I--I COULDN'T STOP HIM... HE TOSSED ME ASIDE AS IF I WERE A CHILD...
YOU...
YOU DON'T UNDERSTAND WHAT HE'S BECOME...

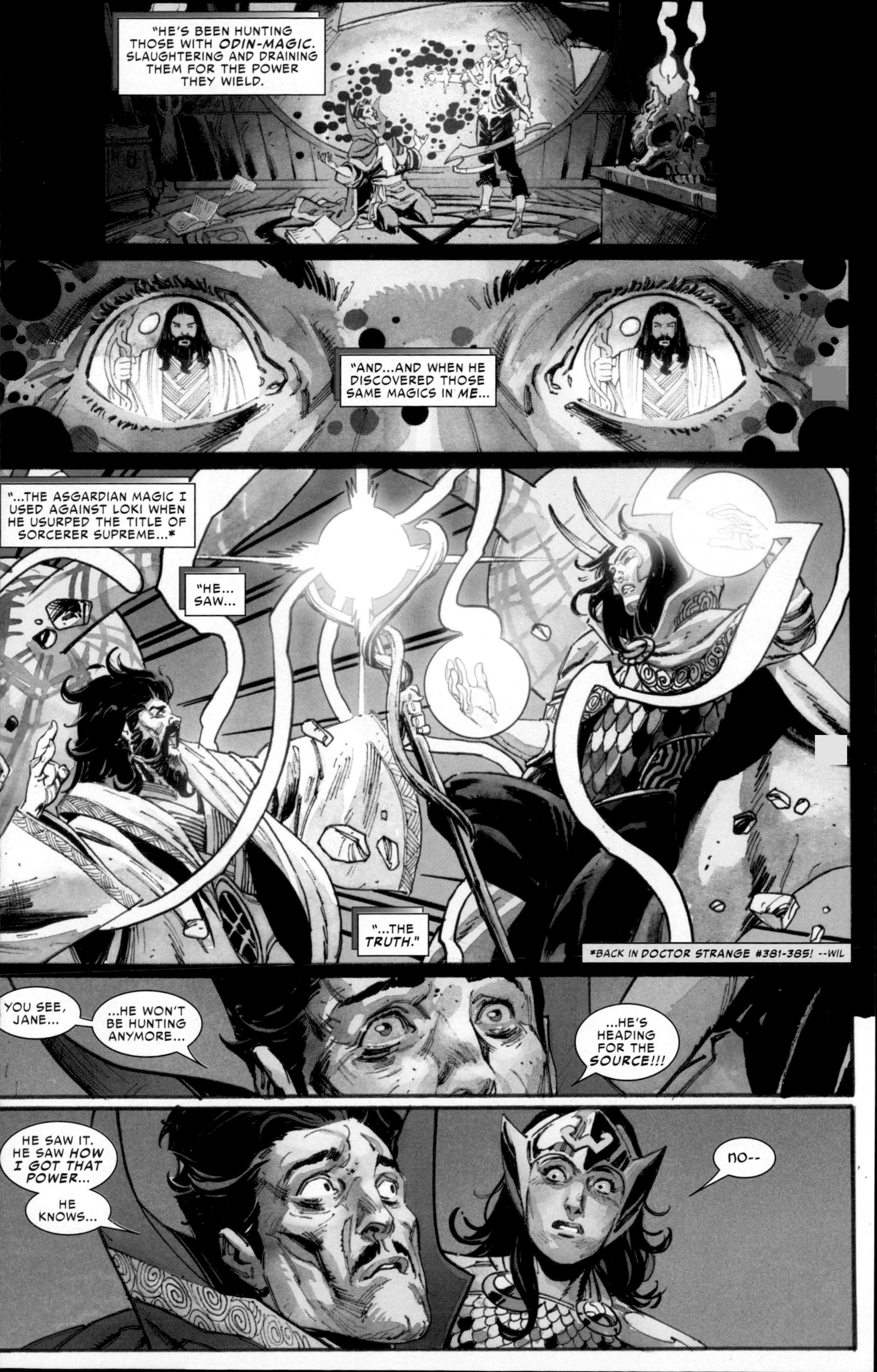
"HE'S BEEN HUNTING THOSE WITH ODIN-MAGIC. SLAUGHTERING AND DRAINING THEM FOR THE POWER THEY WIELD.
"AND...AND WHEN HE DISCOVERED THOSE SAME MAGICS IN ME...
"...THE ASGARDIAN MAGIC I USED AGAINST LOKI WHEN HE USURPED THE TITLE OF SORCERER SUPREME...*
"HE... SAW...
"...THE TRUTH."
*BACK IN DOCTOR STRANGE #381-385! --WIL
YOU SEE, JANE...
...HE WON'T BE HUNTING ANYMORE...
...HE'S HEADING FOR THE SOURCE!!!
HE SAW IT. HE SAW HOW I GOT THAT POWER...
HE KNOWS...
no--

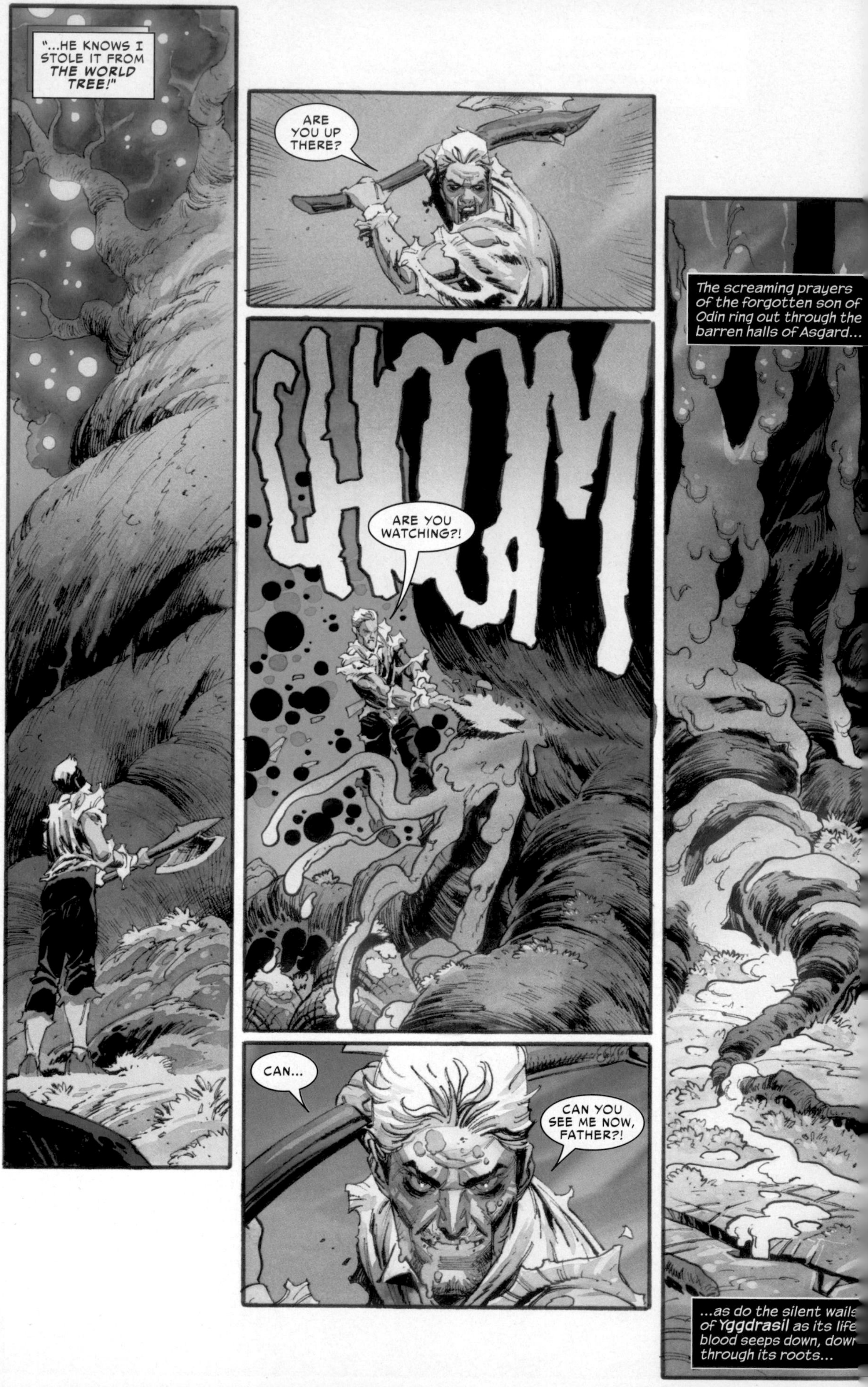
"...HE KNOWS I STOLE IT FROM THE WORLD TREE!"
ARE YOU UP THERE?
CHOM
ARE YOU WATCHING?!
CAN...
CAN YOU SEE ME NOW, FATHER?!
The screaming prayers of the forgotten son of Odin ring out through the barren halls of Asgard...
...as do the silent wails of Yggdrasil as its life blood seeps down, down through its roots...

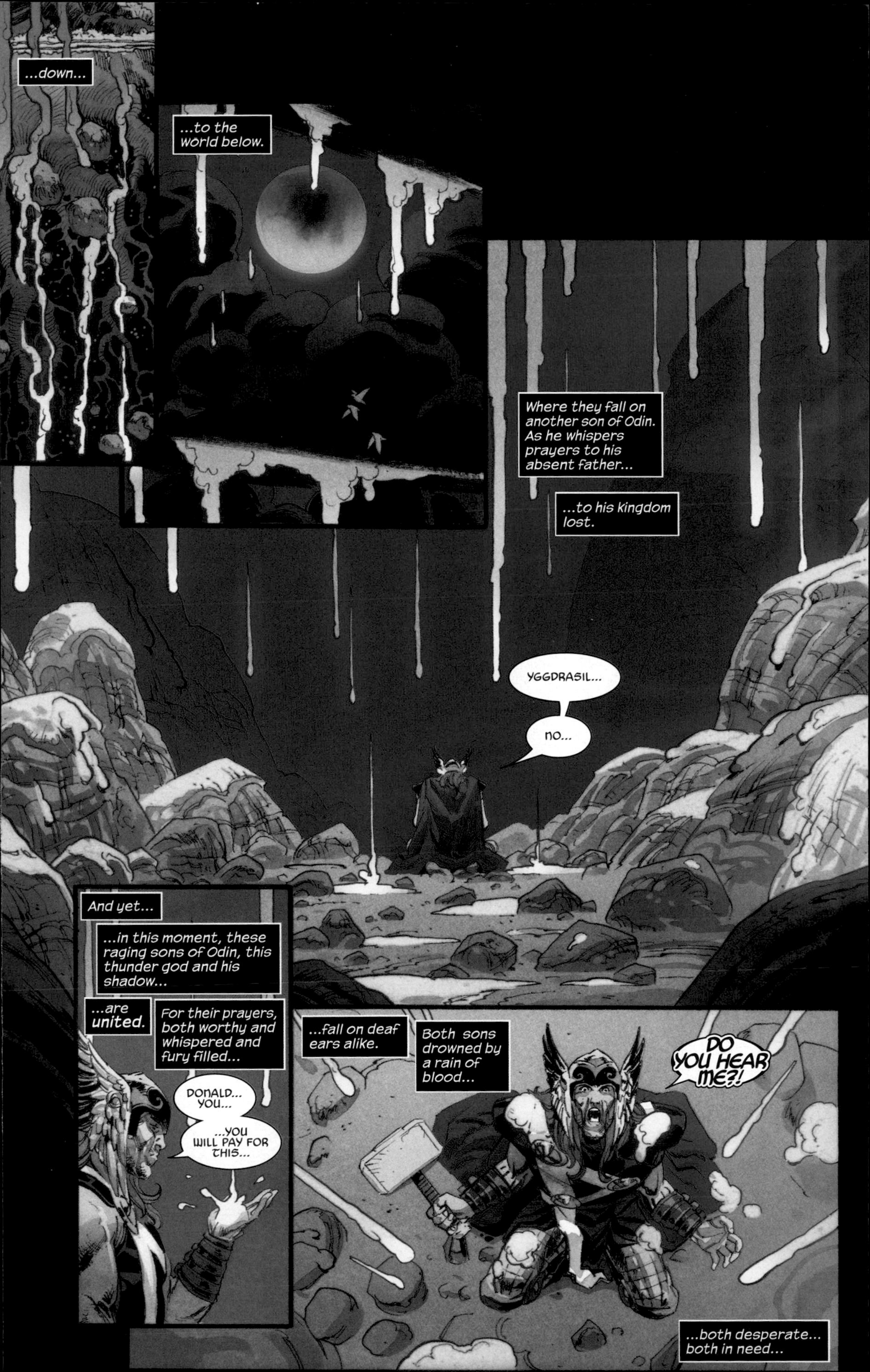

...down...
...to the world below.
Where they fall on another son of Odin. As he whispers prayers to his absent father...
...to his kingdom lost.
YGGDRASIL...
NO...
And yet...
...in this moment, these raging sons of Odin, this thunder god and his shadow...
...are **united**.
For their prayers, both worthy and whispered and fury filled...
DONALD... YOU...
...YOU WILL PAY FOR THIS...
...fall on deaf ears alike.
Both sons drowned by a rain of blood...
DO YOU HEAR ME?!
...both desperate... both in need...

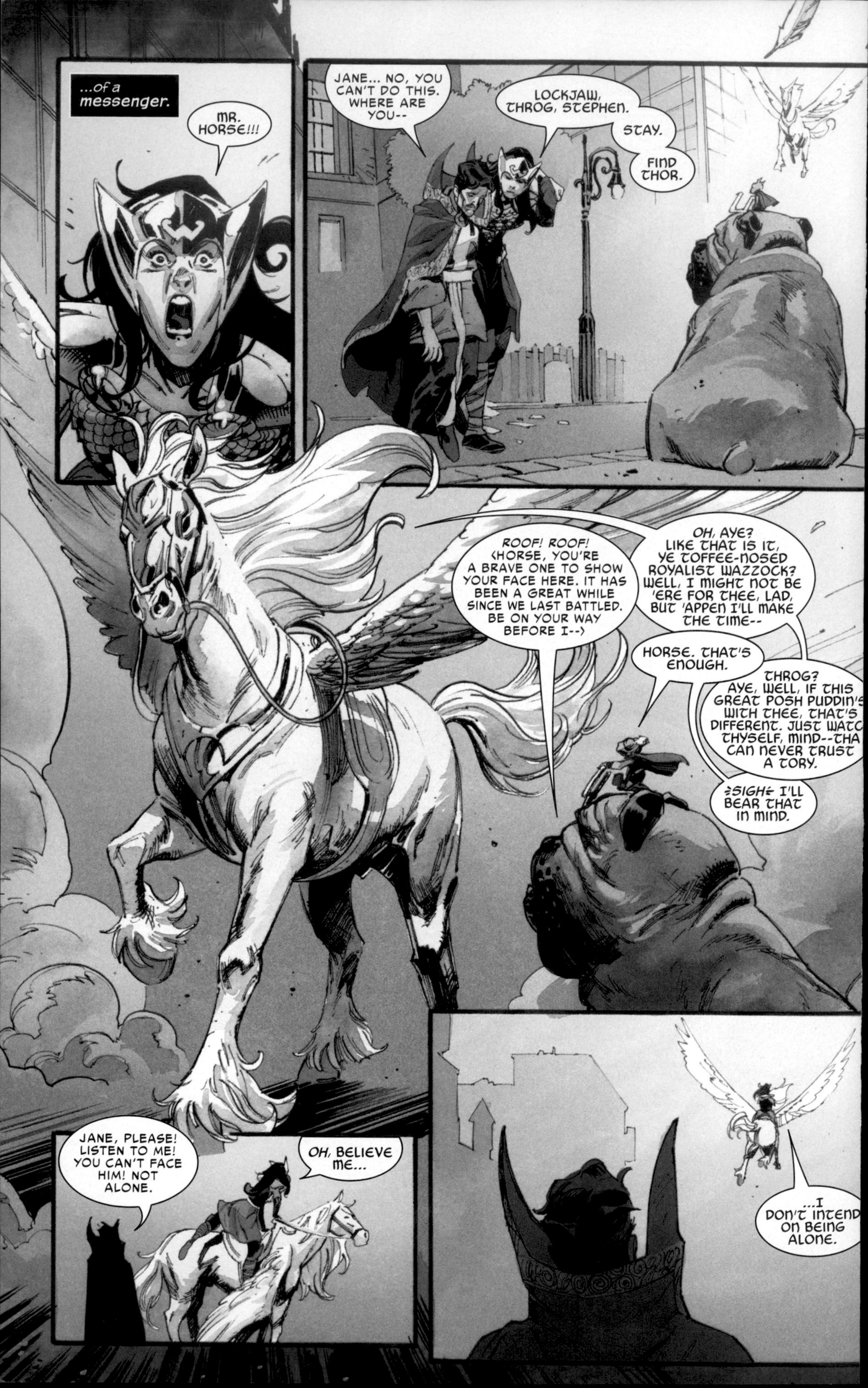
...of a messenger.
MR. HORSE!!!
JANE... NO, YOU CAN'T DO THIS. WHERE ARE YOU--
LOCKJAW, THROG, STEPHEN.
STAY.
FIND THOR.
ROOF! ROOF! ‹HORSE, YOU'RE A BRAVE ONE TO SHOW YOUR FACE HERE. IT HAS BEEN A GREAT WHILE SINCE WE LAST BATTLED. BE ON YOUR WAY BEFORE I--›
OH, AYE? LIKE THAT IS IT, YE TOFFEE-NOSED ROYALIST WAZZOCK? WELL, I MIGHT NOT BE 'ERE FOR THEE, LAD, BUT 'APPEN I'LL MAKE THE TIME--
HORSE. THAT'S ENOUGH.
THROG? AYE, WELL, IF THIS GREAT POSH PUDDIN'S WITH THEE, THAT'S DIFFERENT. JUST WATC THYSELF, MIND--THA CAN NEVER TRUST A TORY.
≈SIGH≈ I'LL BEAR THAT IN MIND.
JANE, PLEASE! LISTEN TO ME! YOU CAN'T FACE HIM! NOT ALONE.
OH, BELIEVE ME...
...I DON'T INTEND ON BEING ALONE.

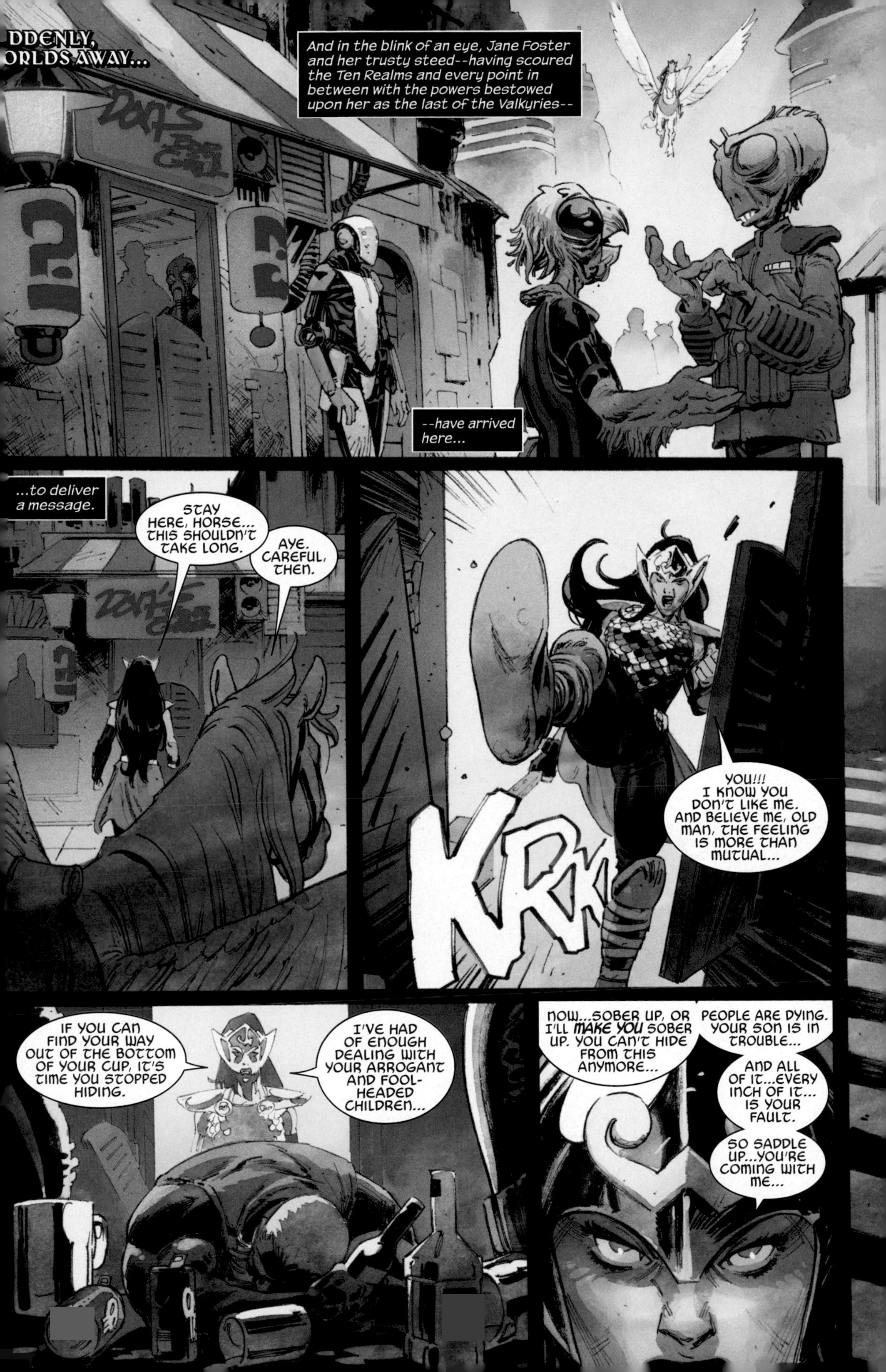
DDENLY, ORLDS AWAY...
And in the blink of an eye, Jane Foster and her trusty steed--having scoured the Ten Realms and every point in between with the powers bestowed upon her as the last of the Valkyries--
--have arrived here...
...to deliver a message.
STAY HERE, HORSE... THIS SHOULDN'T TAKE LONG.
AYE. CAREFUL, THEN.
KRA
YOU!!! I KNOW YOU DON'T LIKE ME. AND BELIEVE ME, OLD MAN, THE FEELING IS MORE THAN MUTUAL...
IF YOU CAN FIND YOUR WAY OUT OF THE BOTTOM OF YOUR CUP, IT'S TIME YOU STOPPED HIDING.
I'VE HAD OF ENOUGH DEALING WITH YOUR ARROGANT AND FOOL-HEADED CHILDREN...
NOW...SOBER UP, OR I'LL MAKE YOU SOBER UP. YOU CAN'T HIDE FROM THIS ANYMORE...
PEOPLE ARE DYING. YOUR SON IS IN TROUBLE...
AND ALL OF IT...EVERY INCH OF IT... IS YOUR FAULT.
SO SADDLE UP...YOU'RE COMING WITH ME...

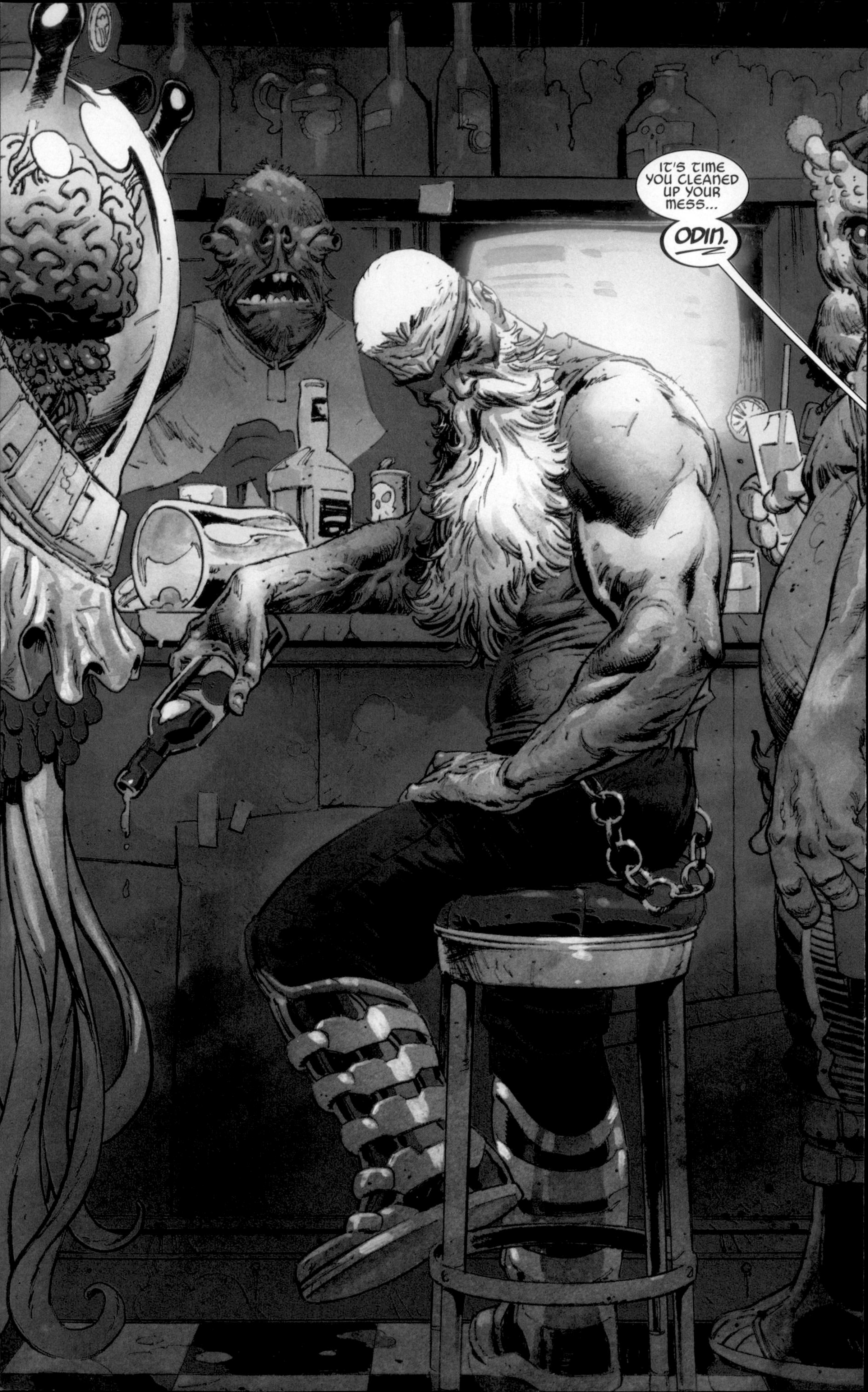
IT'S TIME YOU CLEANED UP YOUR MESS...
ODIN.

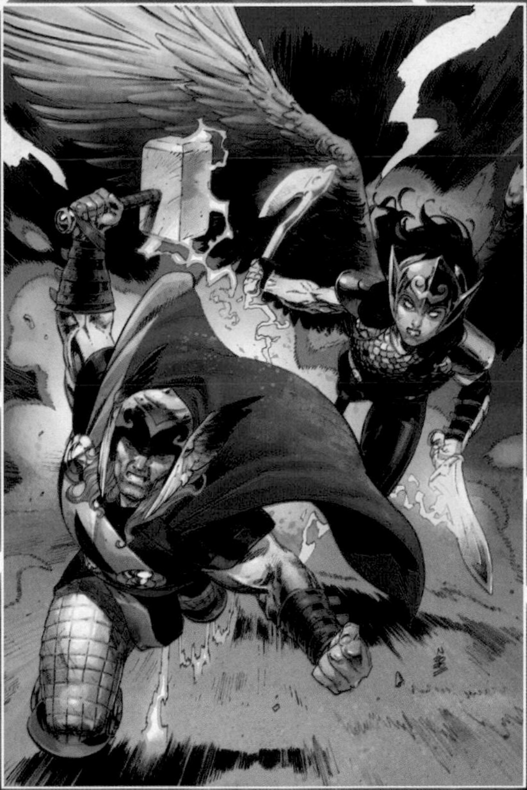

THOR 11 VARIANT BY
Nic Klein

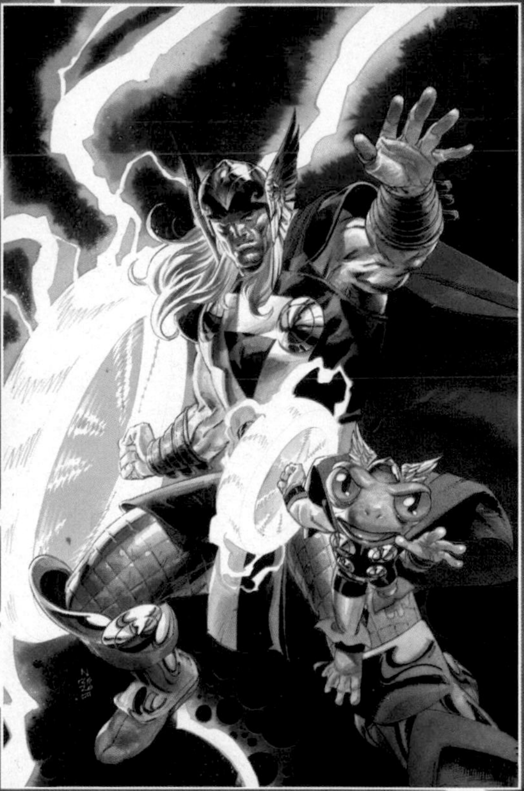

THOR 12 VARIANT BY
Nic Klein

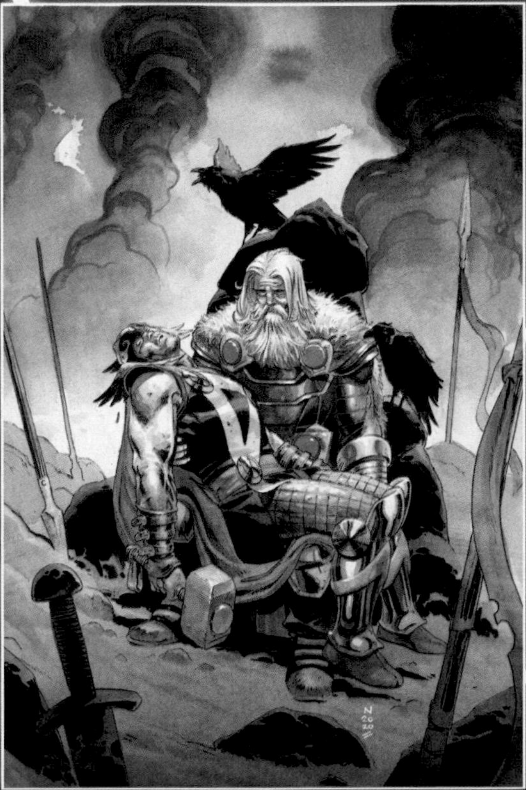

THOR 13 VARIANT BY
Nic Klein

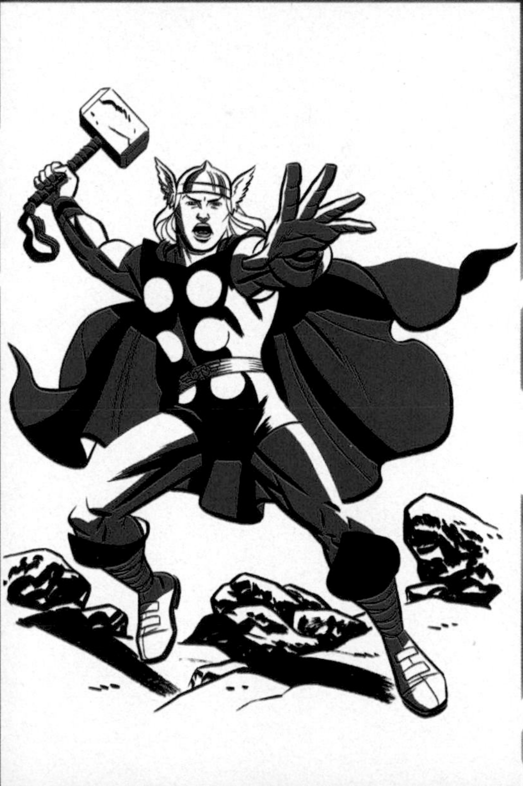

THOR 13 VARIANT BY
Michael Cho

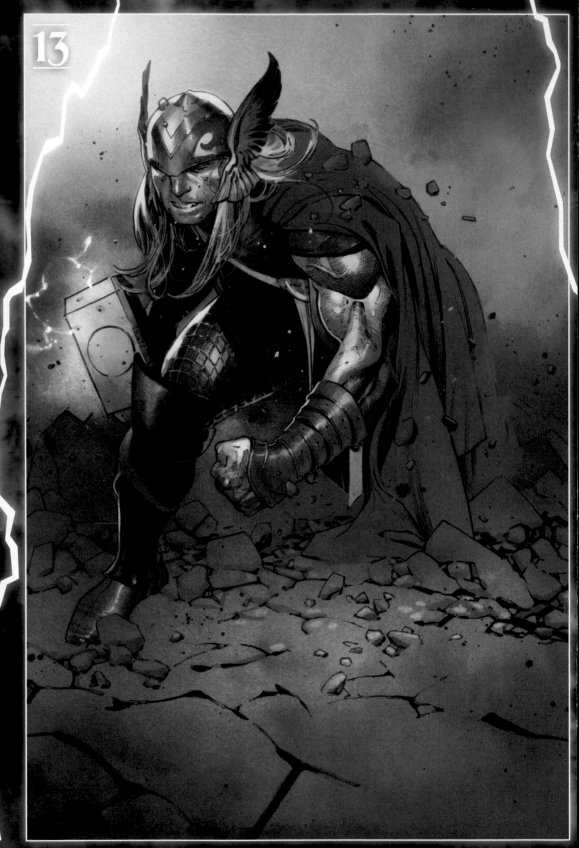

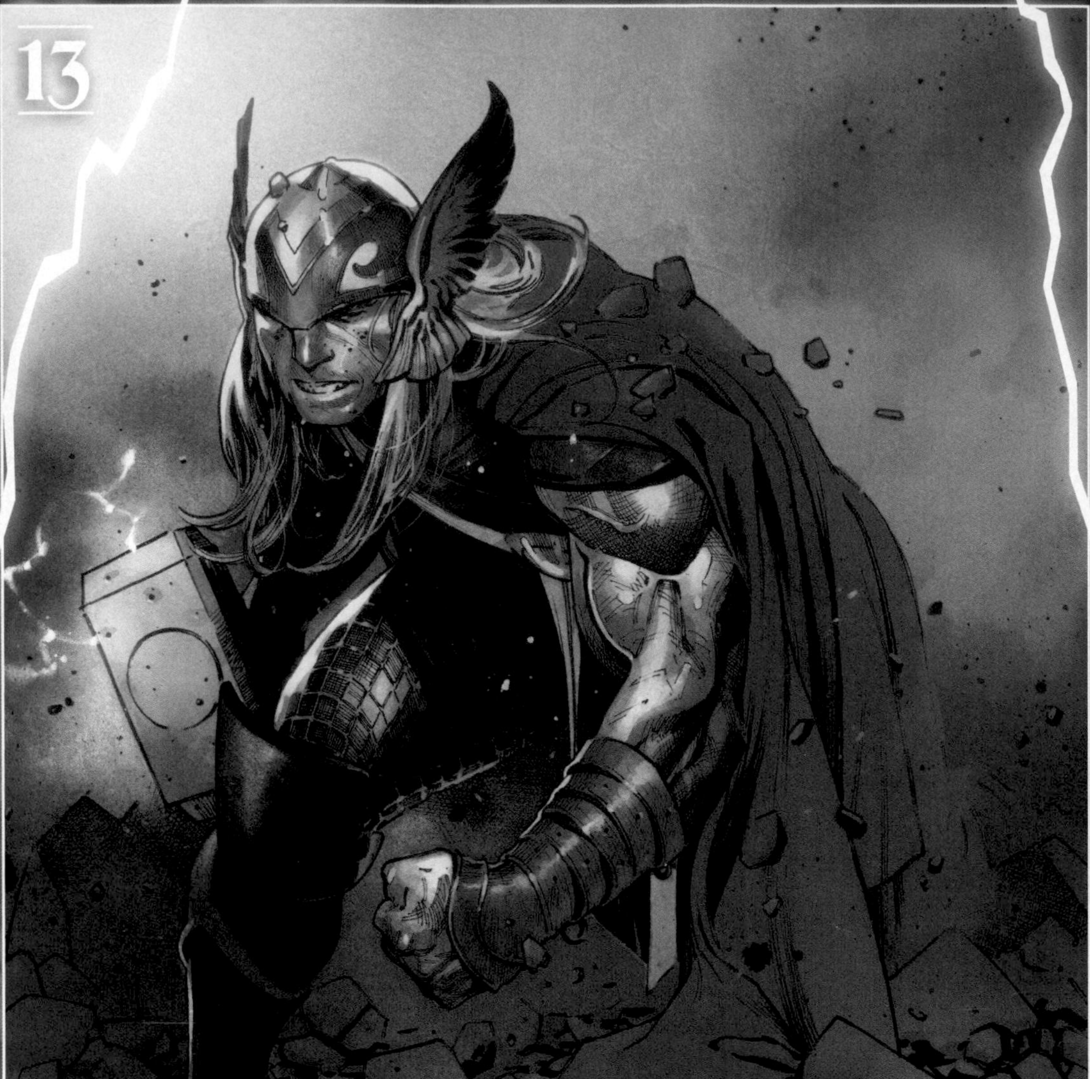
13

"Prey" PART FIVE

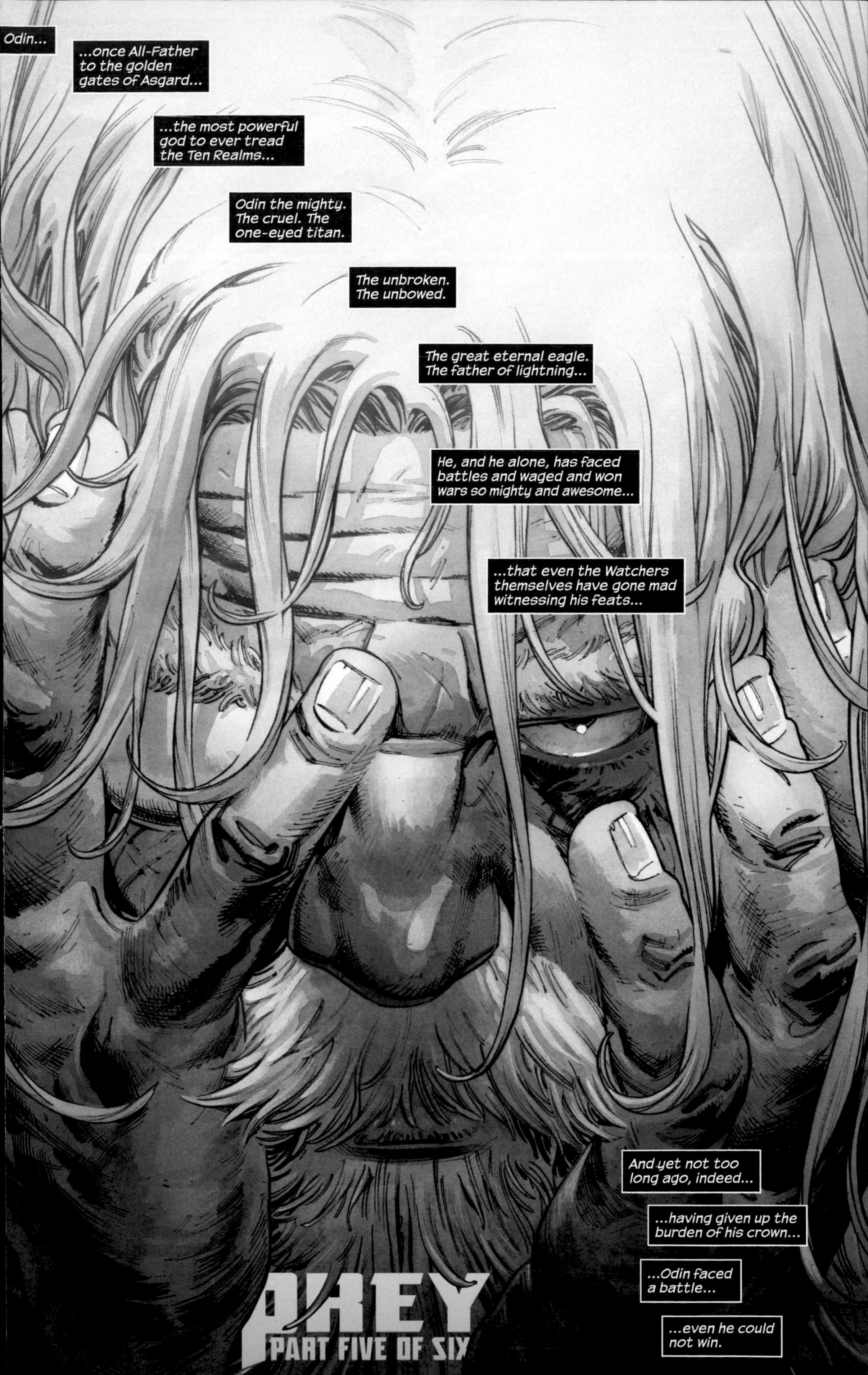
Odin...
...once All-Father to the golden gates of Asgard...
...the most powerful god to ever tread the Ten Realms...
Odin the mighty. The cruel. The one-eyed titan.
The unbroken. The unbowed.
The great eternal eagle. The father of lightning...
He, and he alone, has faced battles and waged and won wars so mighty and awesome...
...that even the Watchers themselves have gone mad witnessing his feats...
And yet not too long ago, indeed...
...having given up the burden of his crown...
...Odin faced a battle...
...even he could not win.
PREY
PART FIVE OF SIX

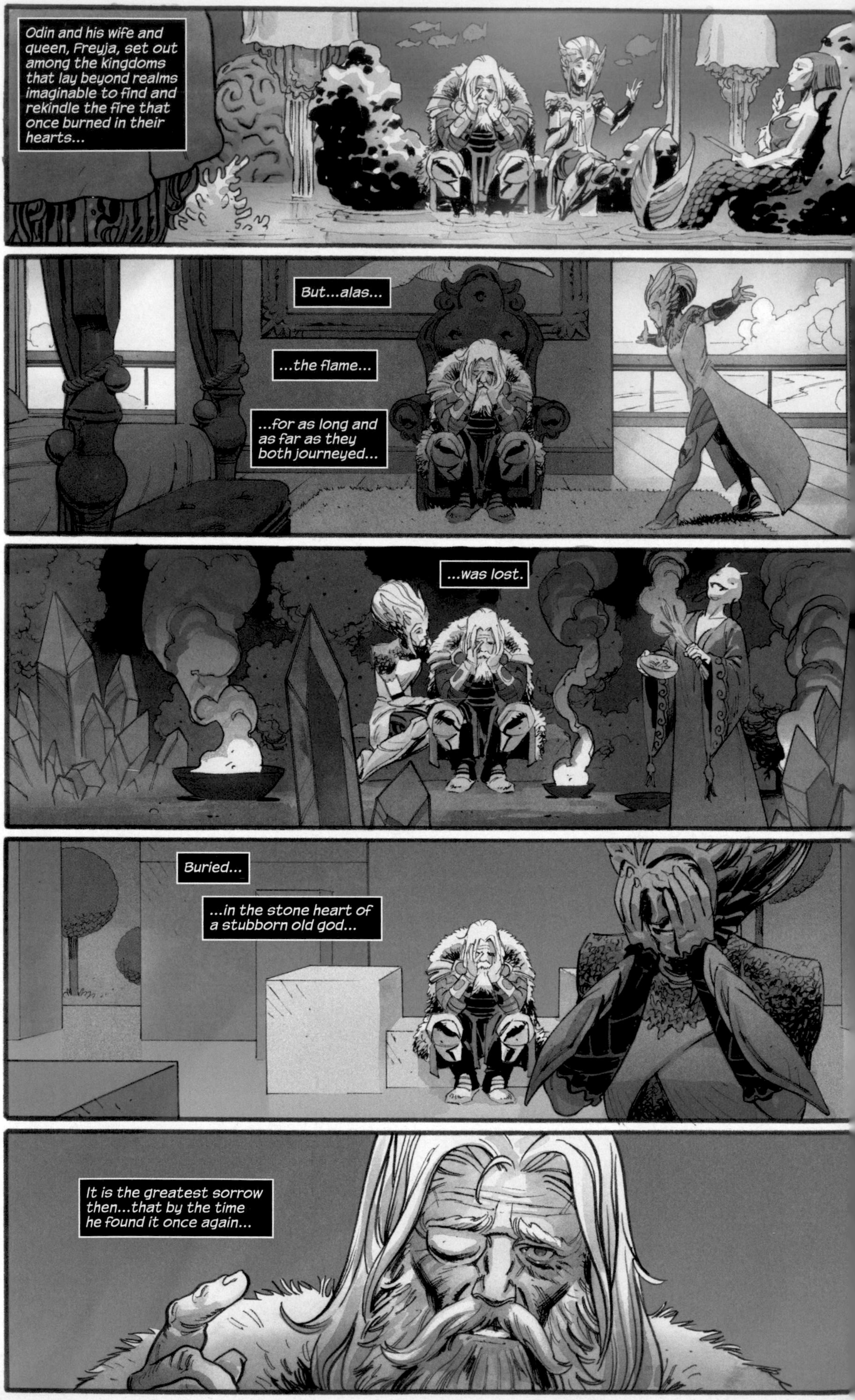
Odin and his wife and queen, Freyja, set out among the kingdoms that lay beyond realms imaginable to find and rekindle the fire that once burned in their hearts...
But...alas...
...the flame...
...for as long and as far as they both journeyed...
...was lost.
Buried...
...in the stone heart of a stubborn old god...
It is the greatest sorrow then...that by the time he found it once again...

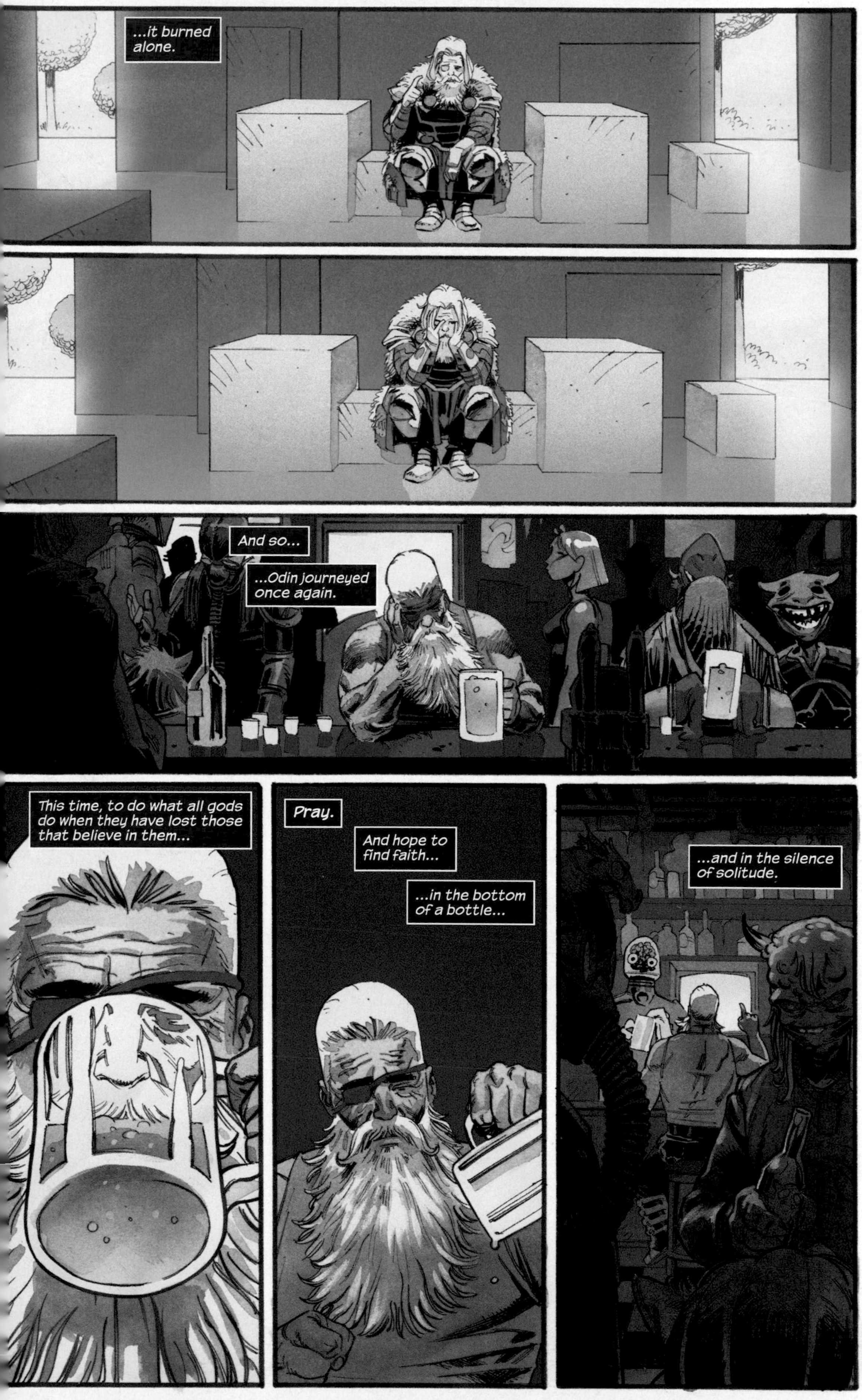

...it burned alone.
And so...
...Odin journeyed once again.
This time, to do what all gods do when they have lost those that believe in them...
Pray.
And hope to find faith...
...in the bottom of a bottle...
...and in the silence of solitude.

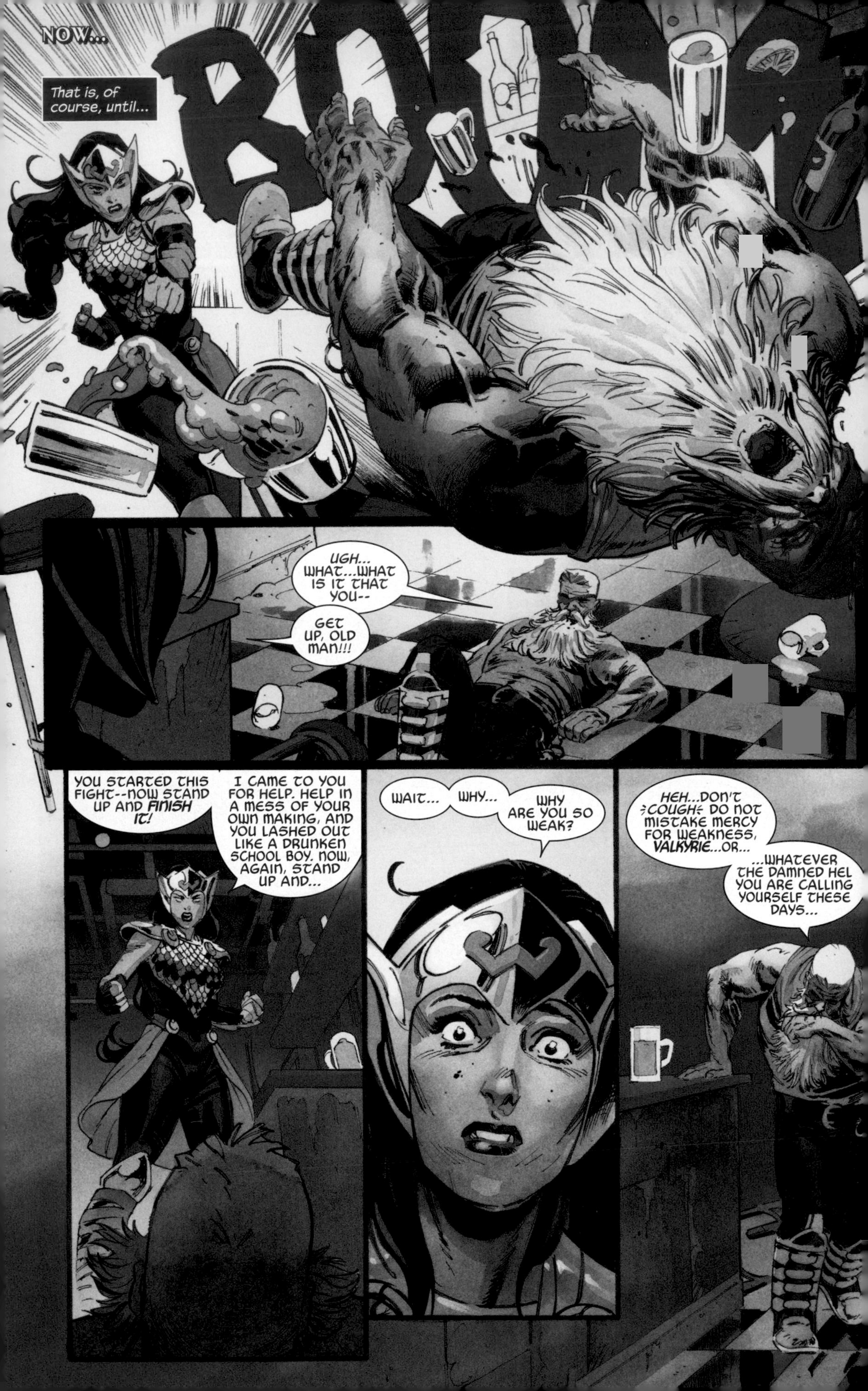
NOW...
That is, of course, until...
BOOM
UGH... WHAT...WHAT IS IT THAT YOU--
GET UP, OLD MAN!!!
YOU STARTED THIS FIGHT--NOW STAND UP AND FINISH IT!
I CAME TO YOU FOR HELP. HELP IN A MESS OF YOUR OWN MAKING, AND YOU LASHED OUT LIKE A DRUNKEN SCHOOL BOY. NOW, AGAIN, STAND UP AND...
WAIT...
WHY...
WHY ARE YOU SO WEAK?
HEH...DON'T *COUGH* DO NOT MISTAKE MERCY FOR WEAKNESS, VALKYRIE...OR...
...WHATEVER THE DAMNED HEL YOU ARE CALLING YOURSELF THESE DAYS...

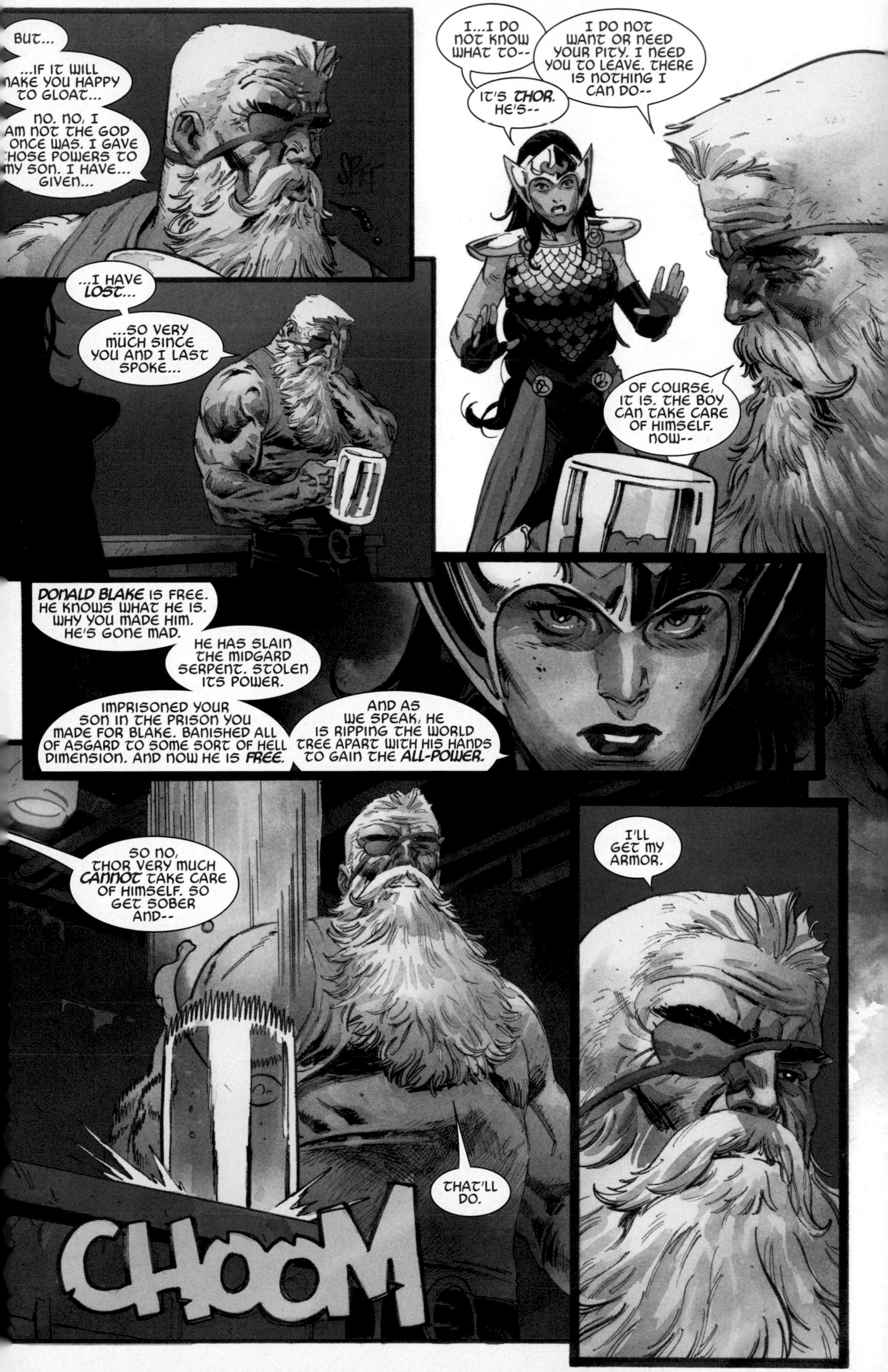
BUT...
...IF IT WILL MAKE YOU HAPPY TO GLOAT...
NO. NO, I AM NOT THE GOD I ONCE WAS. I GAVE THOSE POWERS TO MY SON. I HAVE... GIVEN...
SPFFT
...I HAVE LOST...
...SO VERY MUCH SINCE YOU AND I LAST SPOKE...
I...I DO NOT KNOW WHAT TO--
IT'S THOR. HE'S--
I DO NOT WANT OR NEED YOUR PITY. I NEED YOU TO LEAVE. THERE IS NOTHING I CAN DO--
OF COURSE, IT IS. THE BOY CAN TAKE CARE OF HIMSELF. NOW--
DONALD BLAKE IS FREE. HE KNOWS WHAT HE IS. WHY YOU MADE HIM. HE'S GONE MAD.
HE HAS SLAIN THE MIDGARD SERPENT. STOLEN ITS POWER.
IMPRISONED YOUR SON IN THE PRISON YOU MADE FOR BLAKE. BANISHED ALL OF ASGARD TO SOME SORT OF HELL DIMENSION. AND NOW HE IS FREE.
AND AS WE SPEAK, HE IS RIPPING THE WORLD TREE APART WITH HIS HANDS TO GAIN THE ALL-POWER.
SO NO, THOR VERY MUCH CANNOT TAKE CARE OF HIMSELF. SO GET SOBER AND--
CHOOM
THAT'LL DO.
I'LL GET MY ARMOR.

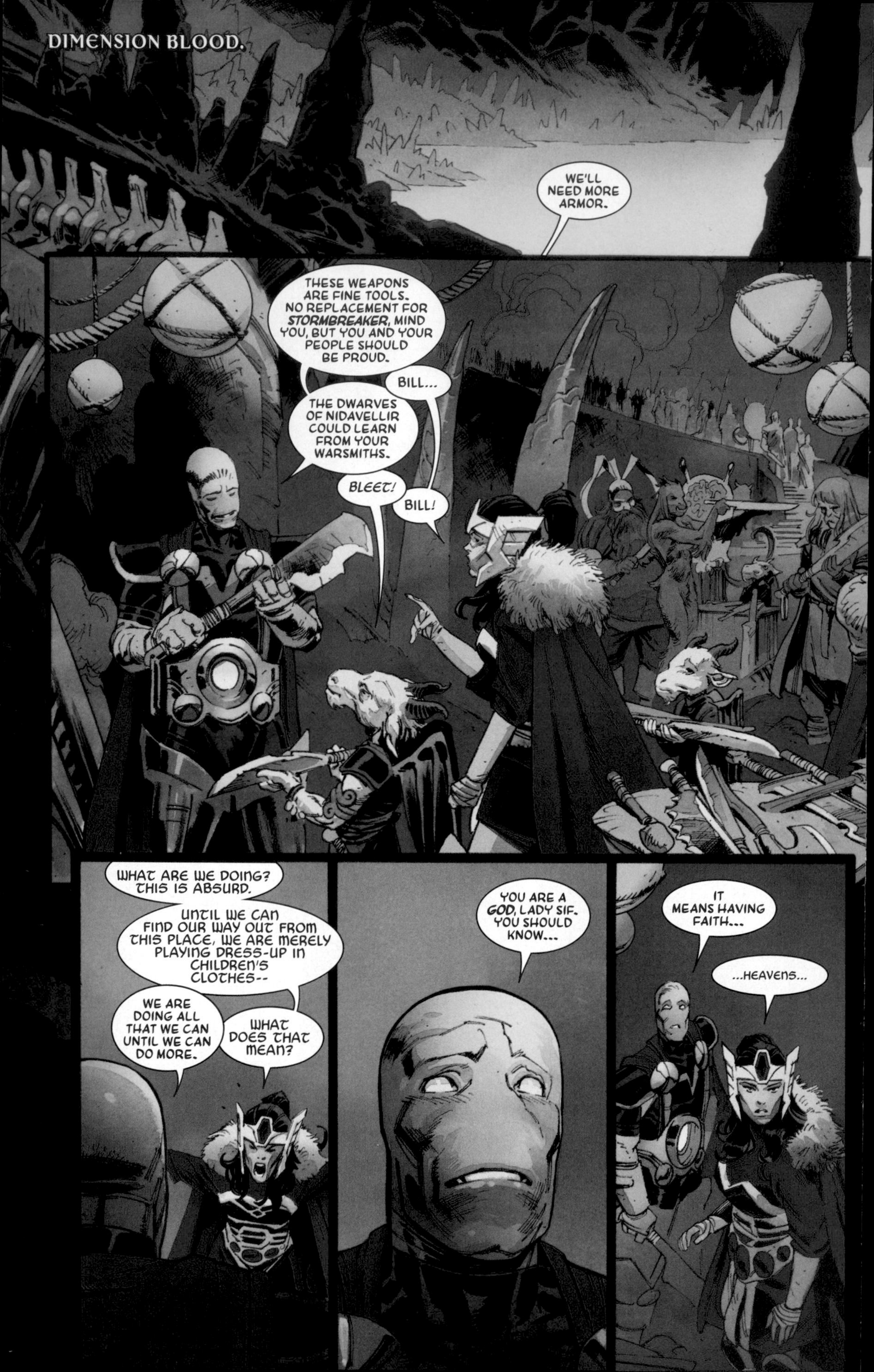
DIMENSION BLOOD.
WE'LL NEED MORE ARMOR.
THESE WEAPONS ARE FINE TOOLS. NO REPLACEMENT FOR STORMBREAKER, MIND YOU, BUT YOU AND YOUR PEOPLE SHOULD BE PROUD.
BILL...
THE DWARVES OF NIDAVELLIR COULD LEARN FROM YOUR WARSMITHS.
BLEET!
BILL!
WHAT ARE WE DOING? THIS IS ABSURD.
UNTIL WE CAN FIND OUR WAY OUT FROM THIS PLACE, WE ARE MERELY PLAYING DRESS-UP IN CHILDREN'S CLOTHES--
WE ARE DOING ALL THAT WE CAN UNTIL WE CAN DO MORE.
WHAT DOES THAT MEAN?
YOU ARE A GOD, LADY SIF. YOU SHOULD KNOW...
IT MEANS HAVING FAITH...
...HEAVENS...

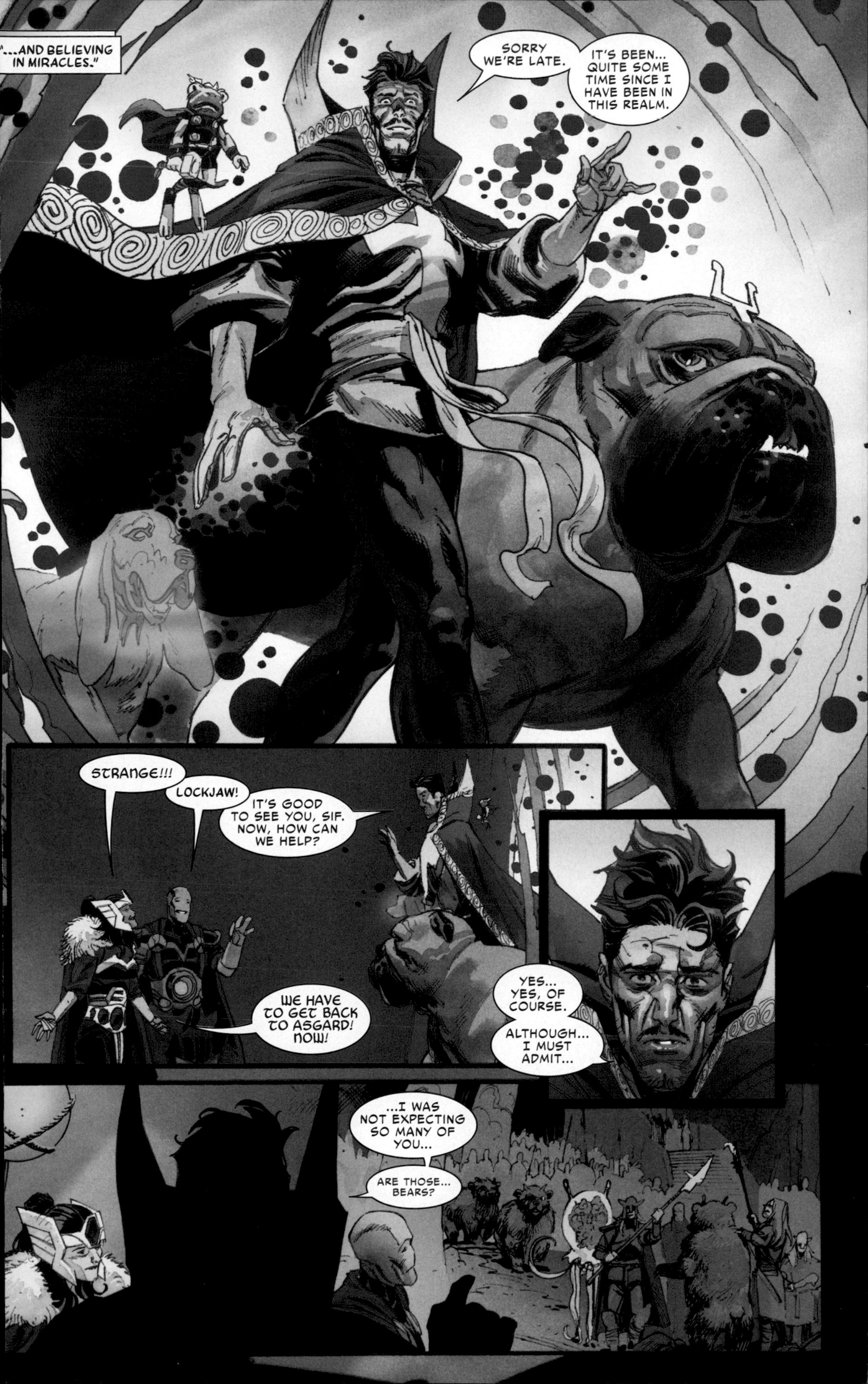
"...AND BELIEVING IN MIRACLES."
SORRY WE'RE LATE.
IT'S BEEN... QUITE SOME TIME SINCE I HAVE BEEN IN THIS REALM.
STRANGE!!!
LOCKJAW!
IT'S GOOD TO SEE YOU, SIF. NOW, HOW CAN WE HELP?
WE HAVE TO GET BACK TO ASGARD! NOW!
YES... YES, OF COURSE.
ALTHOUGH... I MUST ADMIT...
...I WAS NOT EXPECTING SO MANY OF YOU...
ARE THOSE... BEARS?

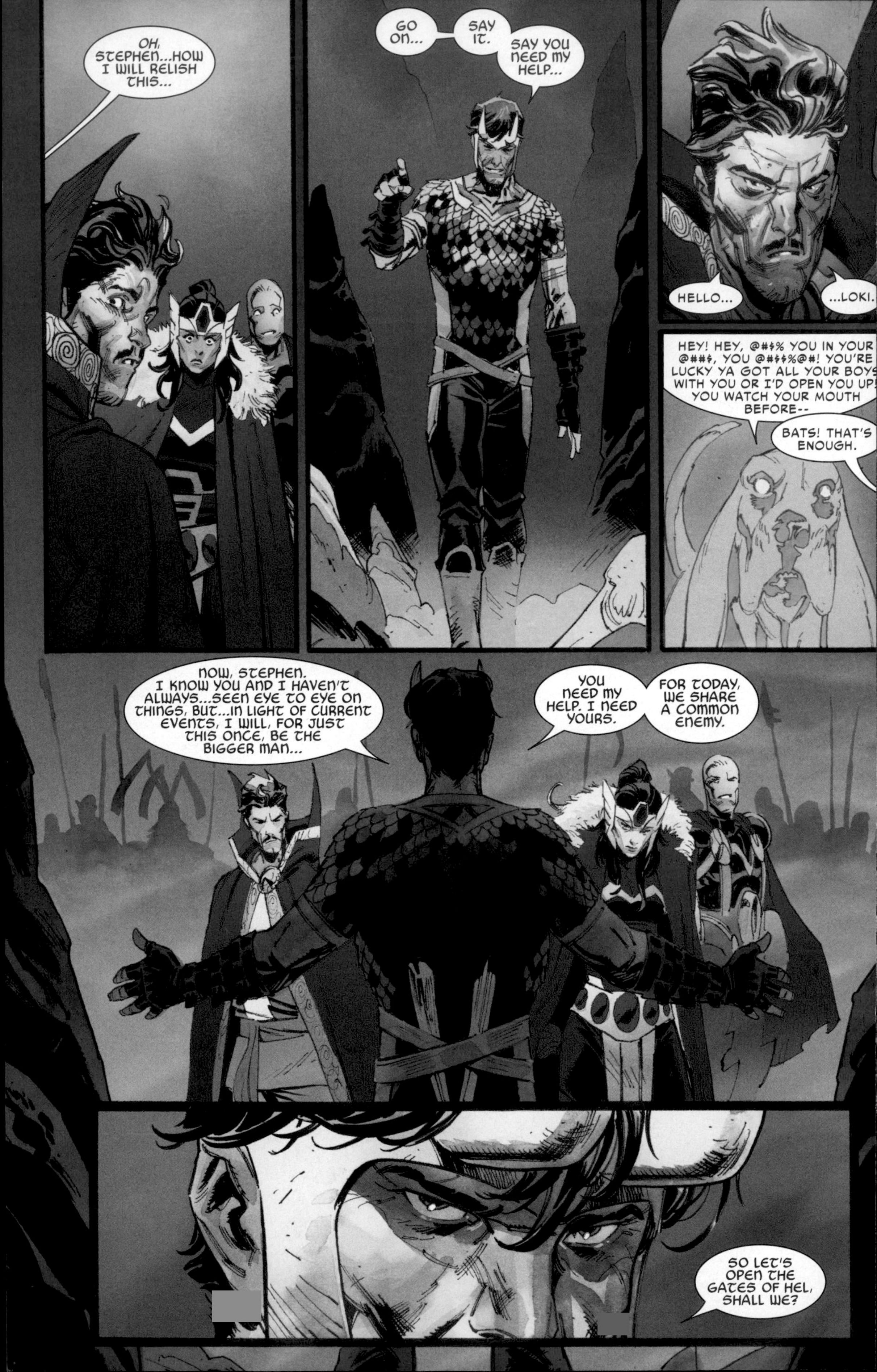
OH, STEPHEN...HOW I WILL RELISH THIS...
GO ON...
SAY IT.
SAY YOU NEED MY HELP...
HELLO...
...LOKI.
HEY! HEY, @#$% YOU IN YOUR @##$, YOU @#$$%@#! YOU'RE LUCKY YA GOT ALL YOUR BOYS WITH YOU OR I'D OPEN YOU UP! YOU WATCH YOUR MOUTH BEFORE--
BATS! THAT'S ENOUGH.
NOW, STEPHEN. I KNOW YOU AND I HAVEN'T ALWAYS...SEEN EYE TO EYE ON THINGS, BUT...IN LIGHT OF CURRENT EVENTS, I WILL, FOR JUST THIS ONCE, BE THE BIGGER MAN...
YOU NEED MY HELP. I NEED YOURS.
FOR TODAY, WE SHARE A COMMON ENEMY.
SO LET'S OPEN THE GATES OF HEL, SHALL WE?

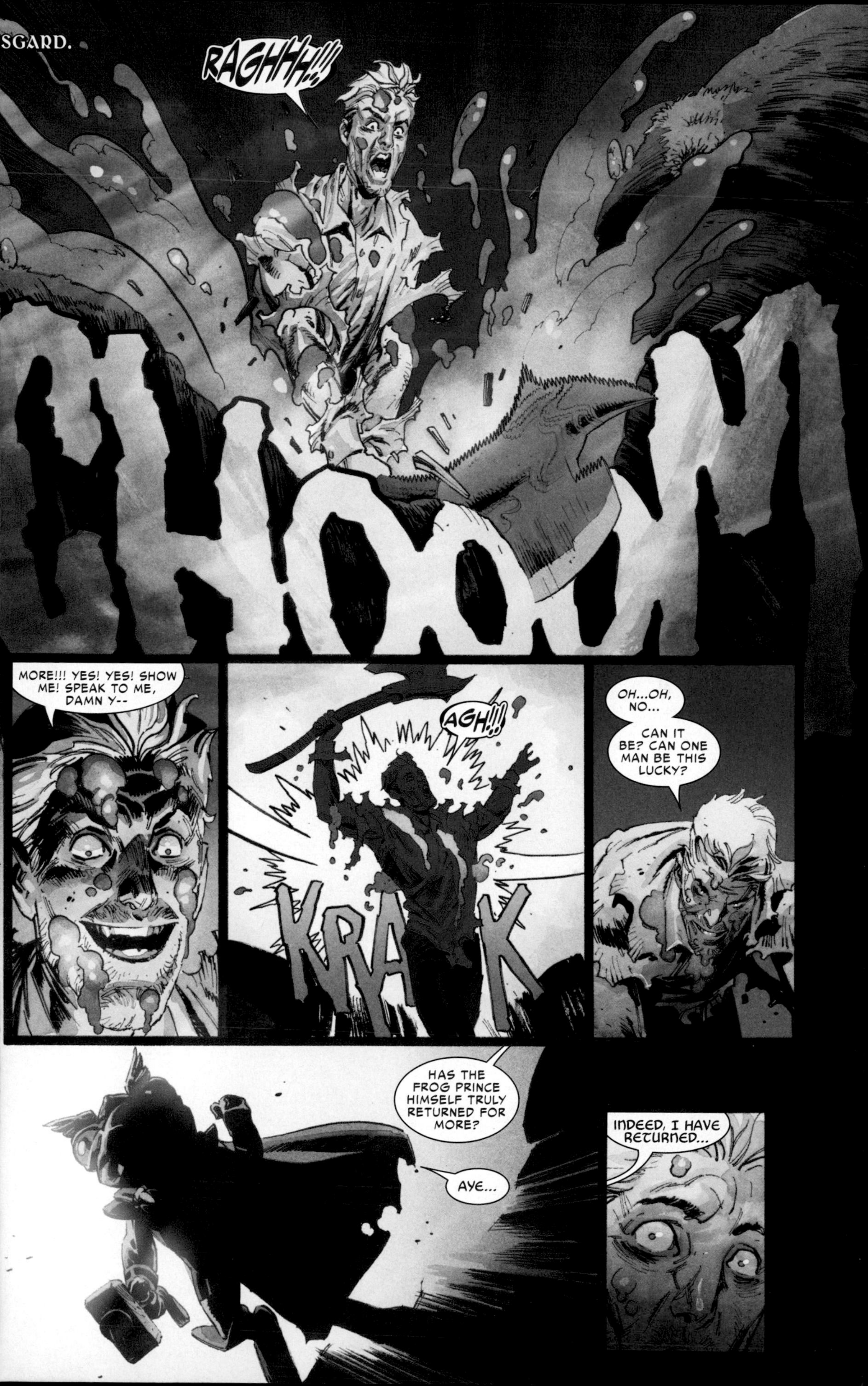
SGARD.
RAGHHH!!!
MORE!!! YES! YES! SHOW ME! SPEAK TO ME, DAMN Y--
AGH!!!
KRAK
OH...OH, NO...
CAN IT BE? CAN ONE MAN BE THIS LUCKY?
HAS THE FROG PRINCE HIMSELF TRULY RETURNED FOR MORE?
AYE...
INDEED, I HAVE RETURNED...

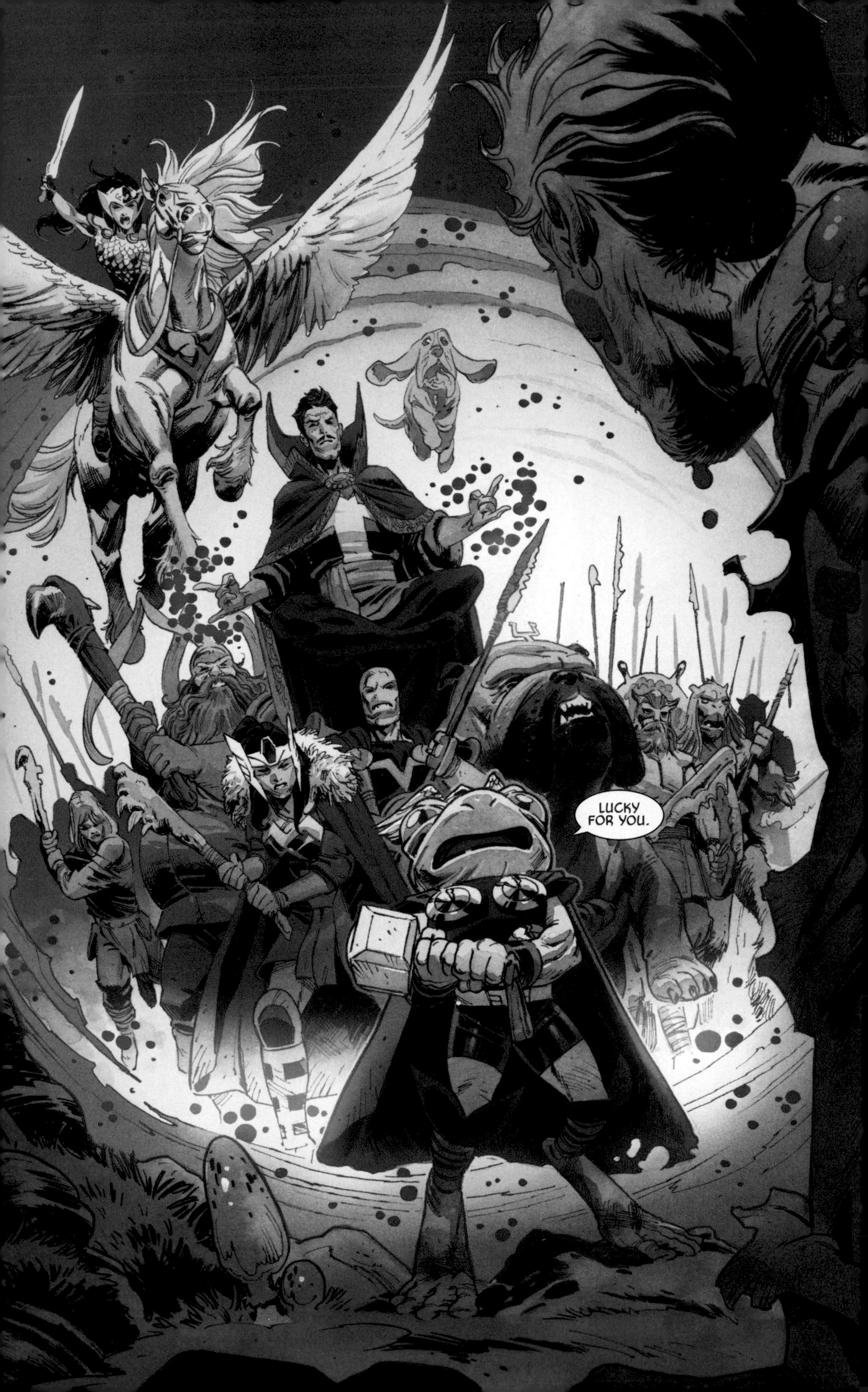
LUCKY FOR YOU.

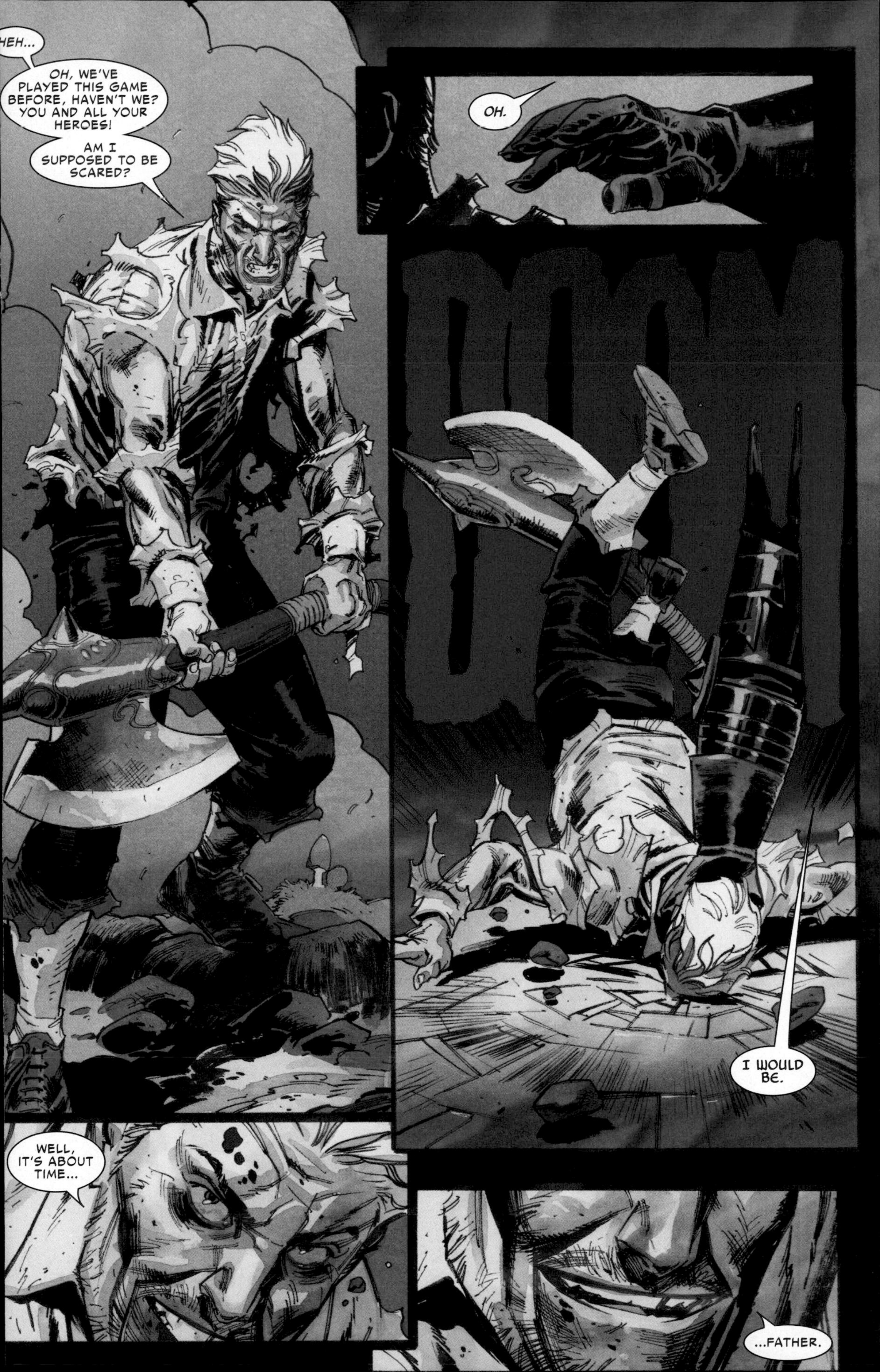
HEH...
OH, WE'VE PLAYED THIS GAME BEFORE, HAVEN'T WE? YOU AND ALL YOUR HEROES!
AM I SUPPOSED TO BE SCARED?
OH.
DOOM
I WOULD BE.
WELL, IT'S ABOUT TIME...
...FATHER.

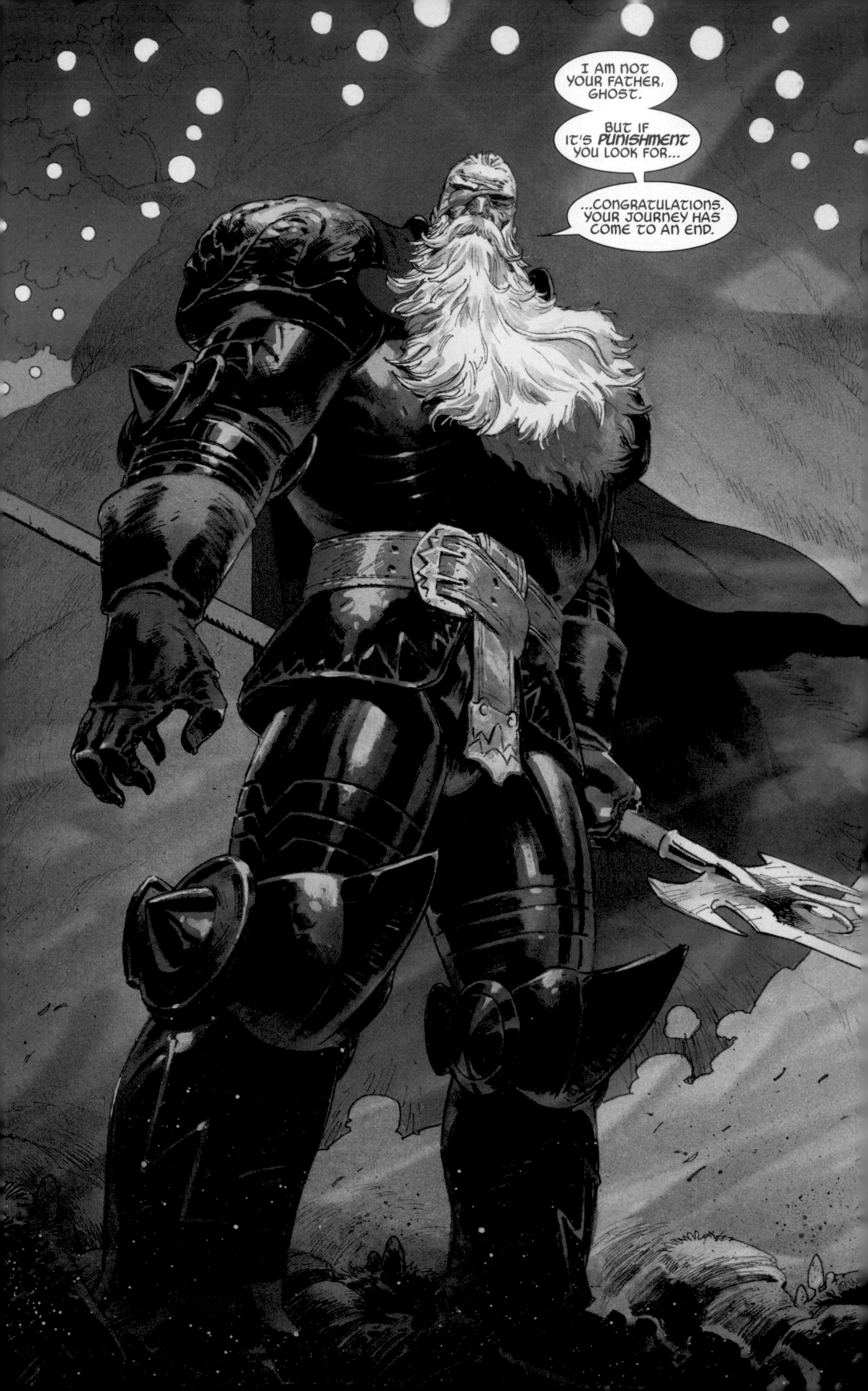
I AM NOT YOUR FATHER, GHOST.
BUT IF IT'S *PUNISHMENT* YOU LOOK FOR...
...CONGRATULATIONS. YOUR JOURNEY HAS COME TO AN END.

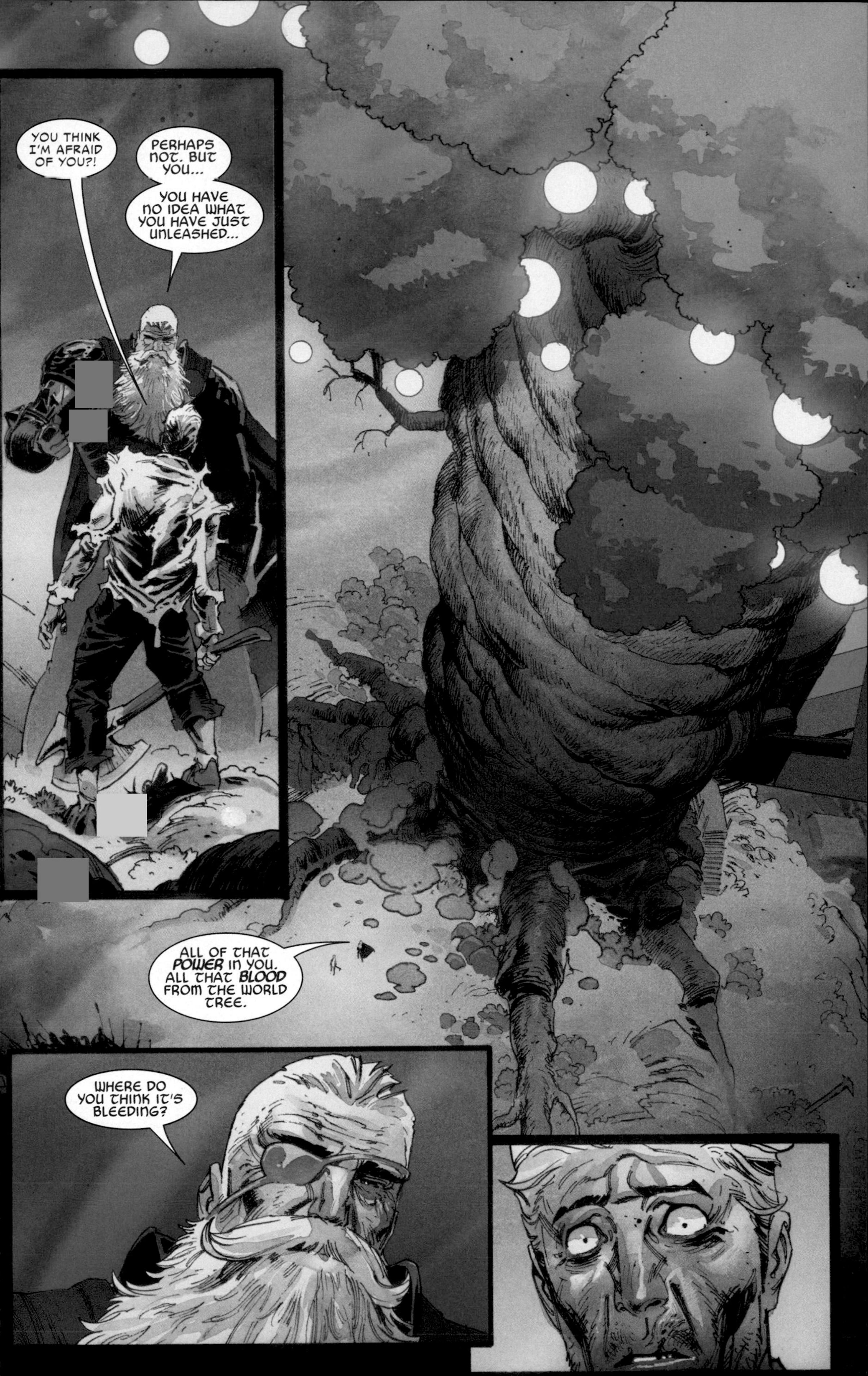
YOU THINK I'M AFRAID OF YOU?!
PERHAPS NOT. BUT YOU...
YOU HAVE NO IDEA WHAT YOU HAVE JUST UNLEASHED...
ALL OF THAT POWER IN YOU. ALL THAT BLOOD FROM THE WORLD TREE.
WHERE DO YOU THINK IT'S BLEEDING?

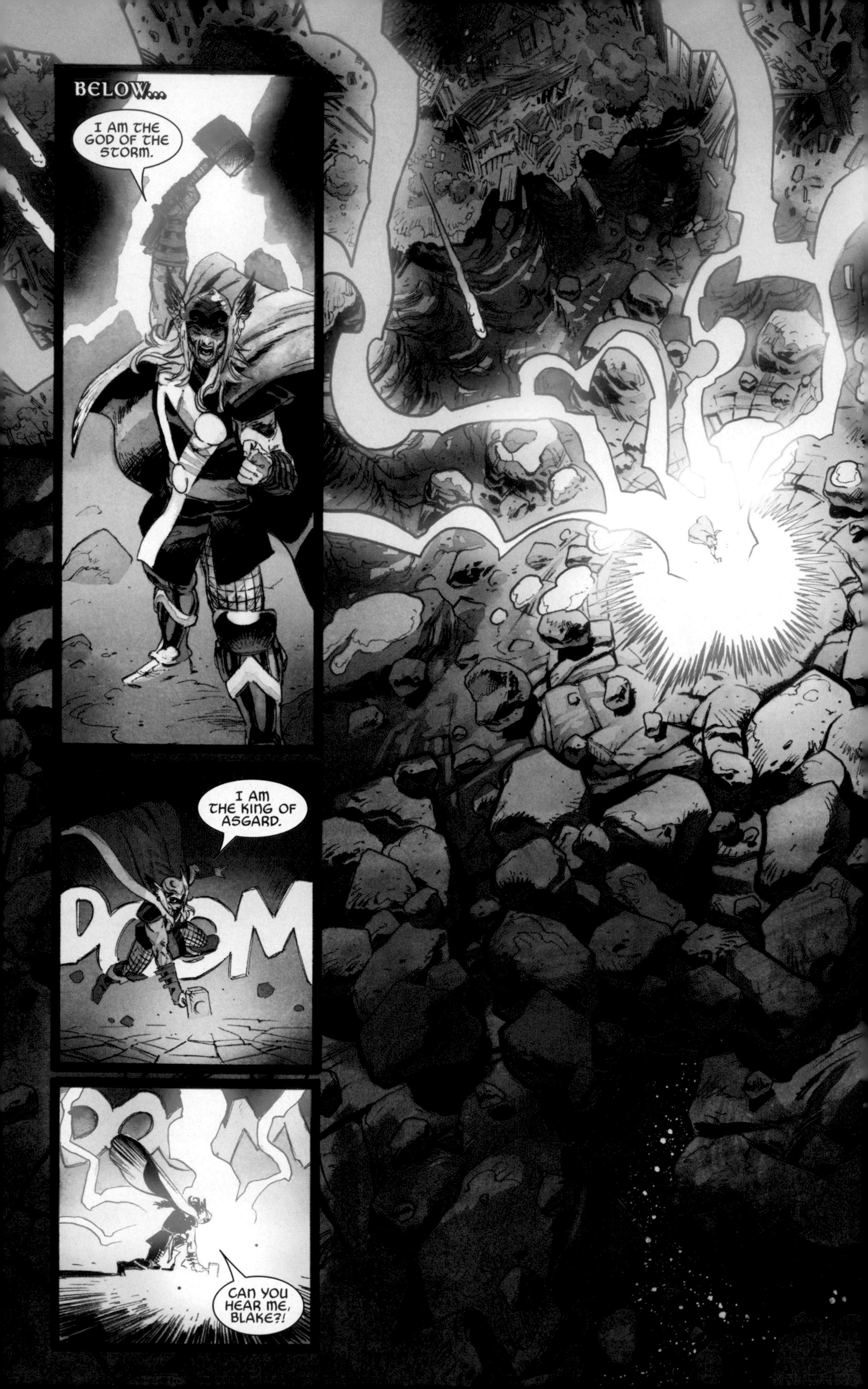
BELOW...
I AM THE GOD OF THE STORM.
I AM THE KING OF ASGARD.
DOOM
CAN YOU HEAR ME, BLAKE?!

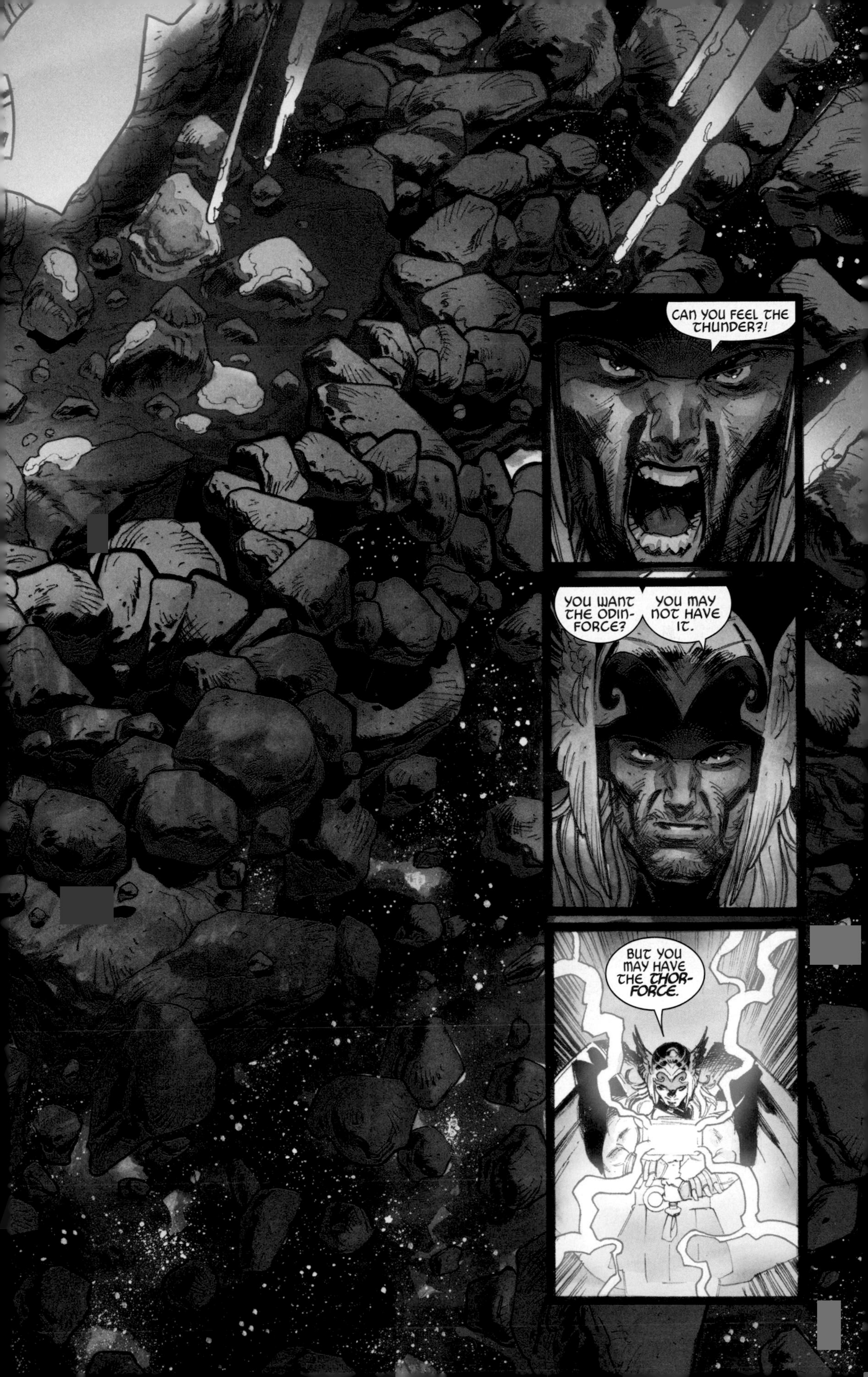
CAN YOU FEEL THE THUNDER?!
YOU WANT THE ODIN-FORCE?
YOU MAY NOT HAVE IT.
BUT YOU MAY HAVE THE *THOR-FORCE*.

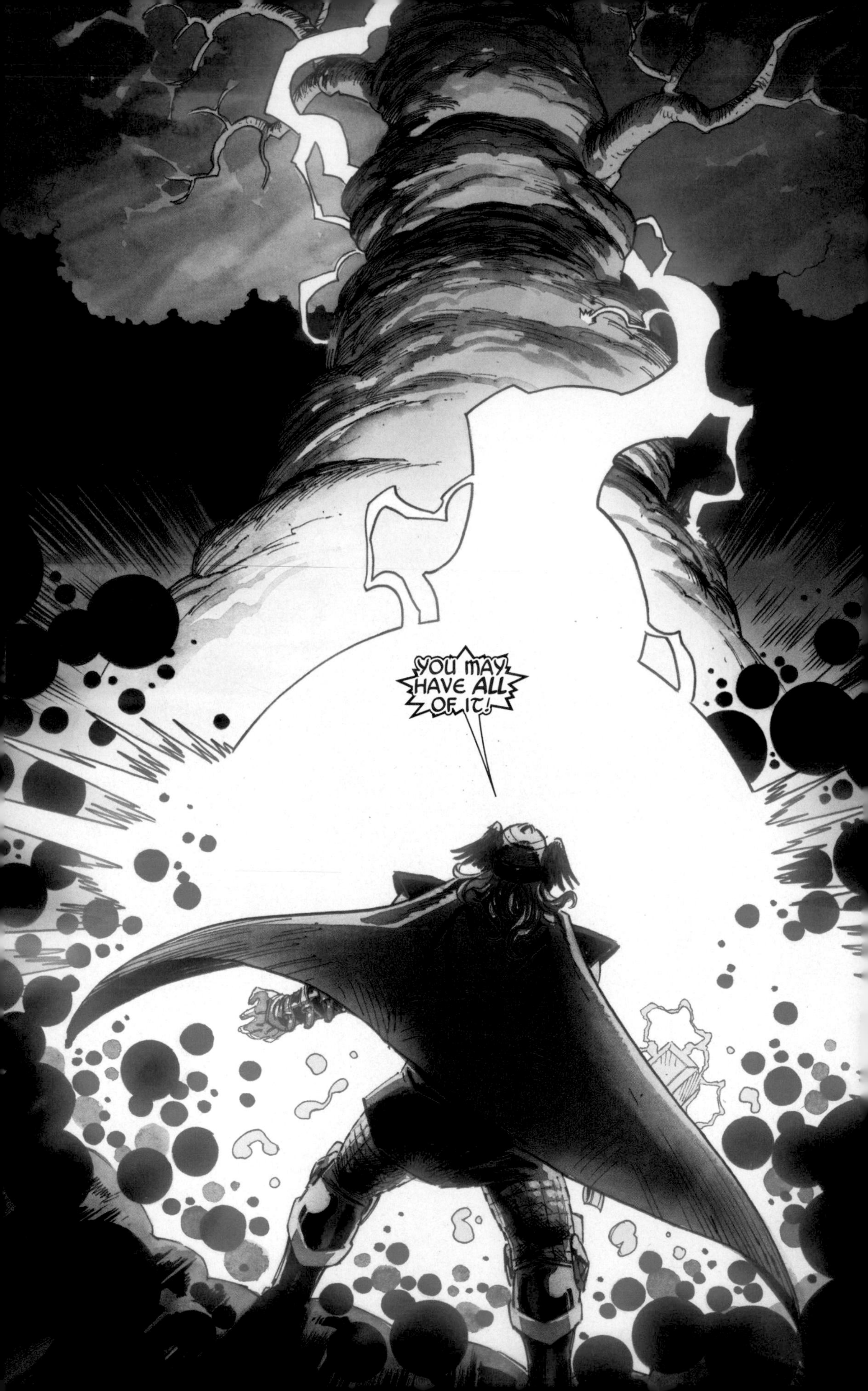
YOU MAY HAVE ALL OF IT!

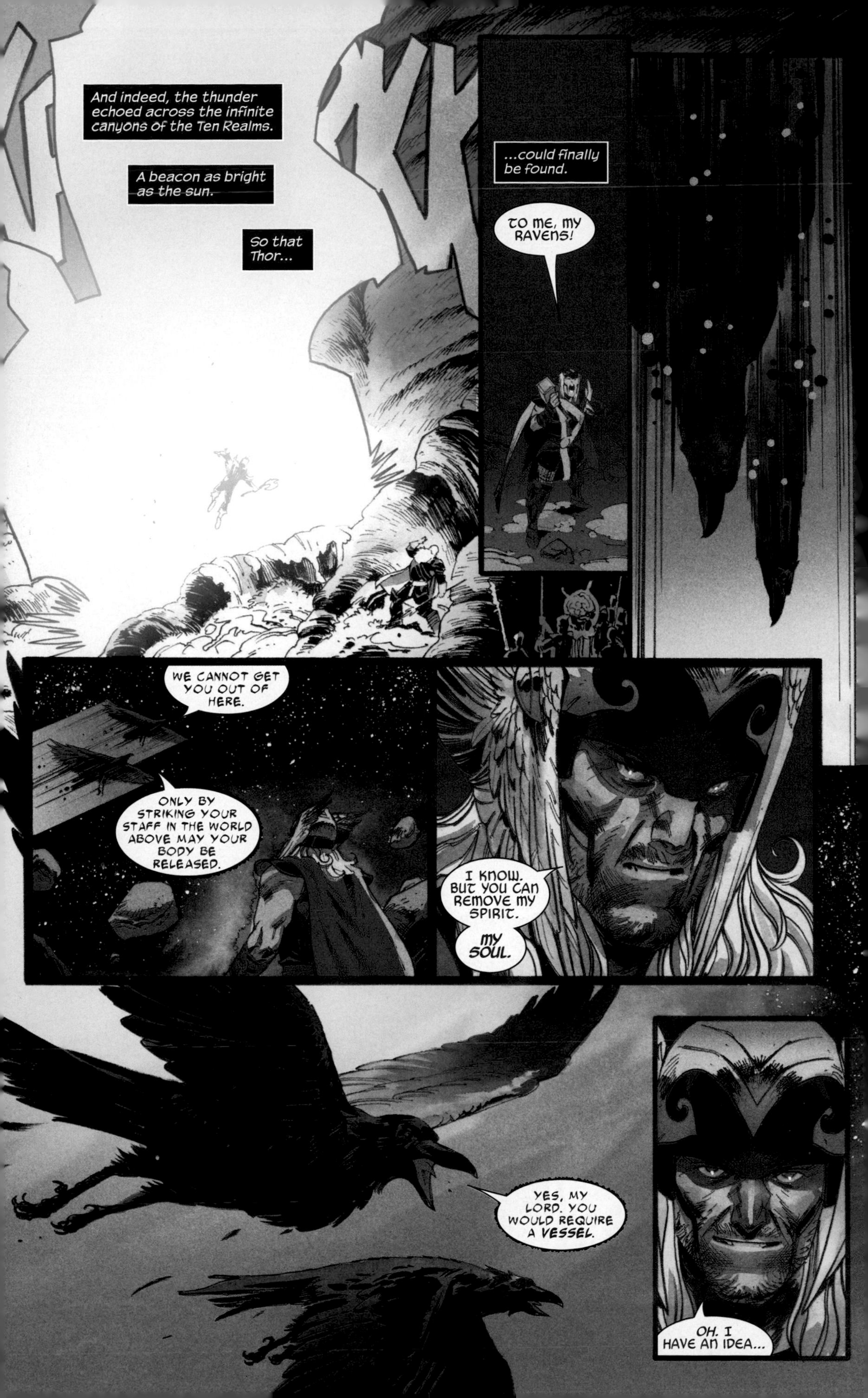
And indeed, the thunder echoed across the infinite canyons of the Ten Realms.
A beacon as bright as the sun.
So that Thor...
...could finally be found.
TO ME, MY RAVENS!
WE CANNOT GET YOU OUT OF HERE.
ONLY BY STRIKING YOUR STAFF IN THE WORLD ABOVE MAY YOUR BODY BE RELEASED.
I KNOW. BUT YOU CAN REMOVE MY SPIRIT.
MY SOUL.
YES, MY LORD. YOU WOULD REQUIRE A VESSEL.
OH. I HAVE AN IDEA...

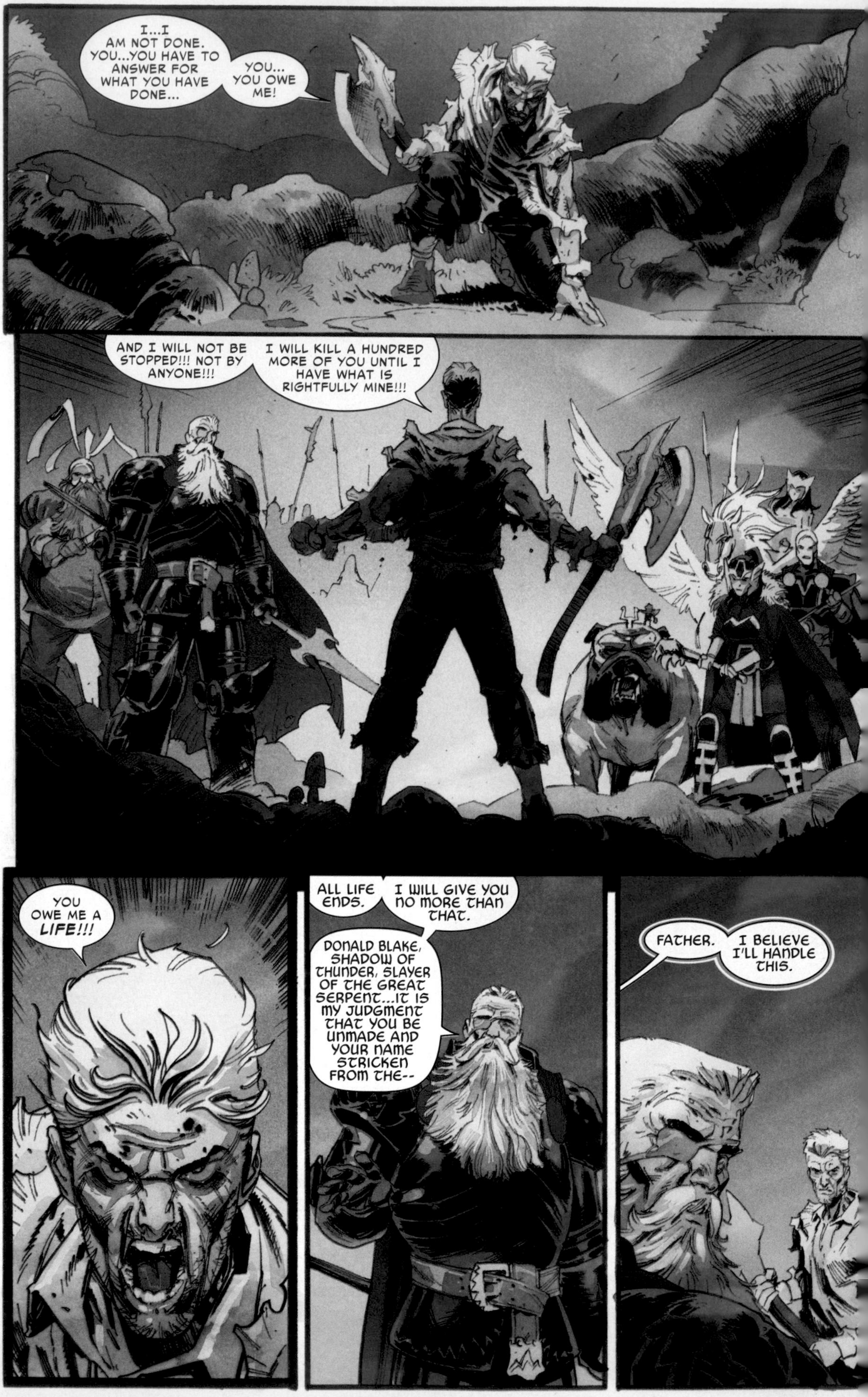
I...I AM NOT DONE. YOU...YOU HAVE TO ANSWER FOR WHAT YOU HAVE DONE...
YOU... YOU OWE ME!
AND I WILL NOT BE STOPPED!!! NOT BY ANYONE!!!
I WILL KILL A HUNDRED MORE OF YOU UNTIL I HAVE WHAT IS RIGHTFULLY MINE!!!
YOU OWE ME A LIFE!!!
ALL LIFE ENDS.
I WILL GIVE YOU NO MORE THAN THAT.
DONALD BLAKE, SHADOW OF THUNDER, SLAYER OF THE GREAT SERPENT...IT IS MY JUDGMENT THAT YOU BE UNMADE AND YOUR NAME STRICKEN FROM THE--
FATHER.
I BELIEVE I'LL HANDLE THIS.

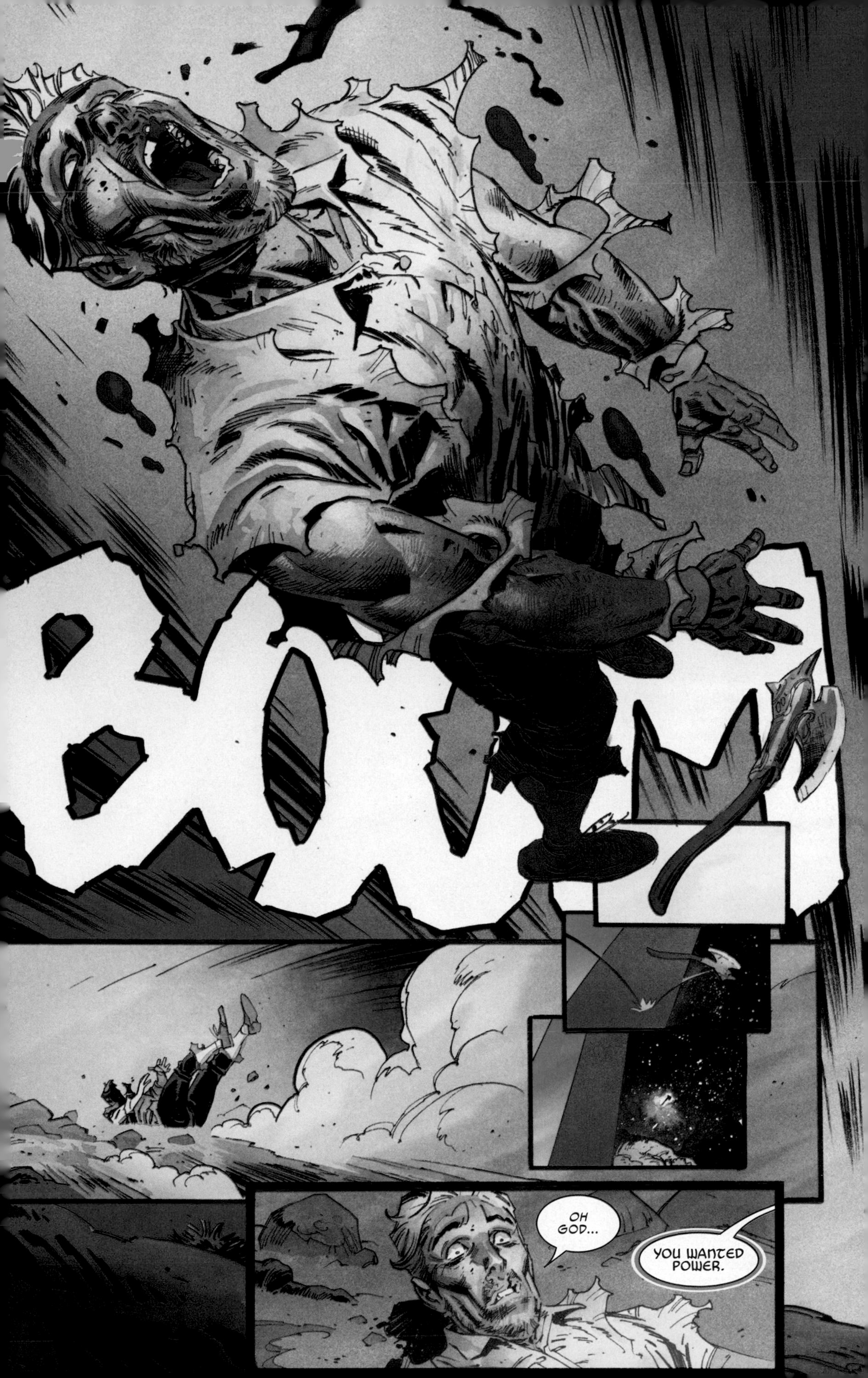
BOOM
OH GOD...
YOU WANTED POWER.

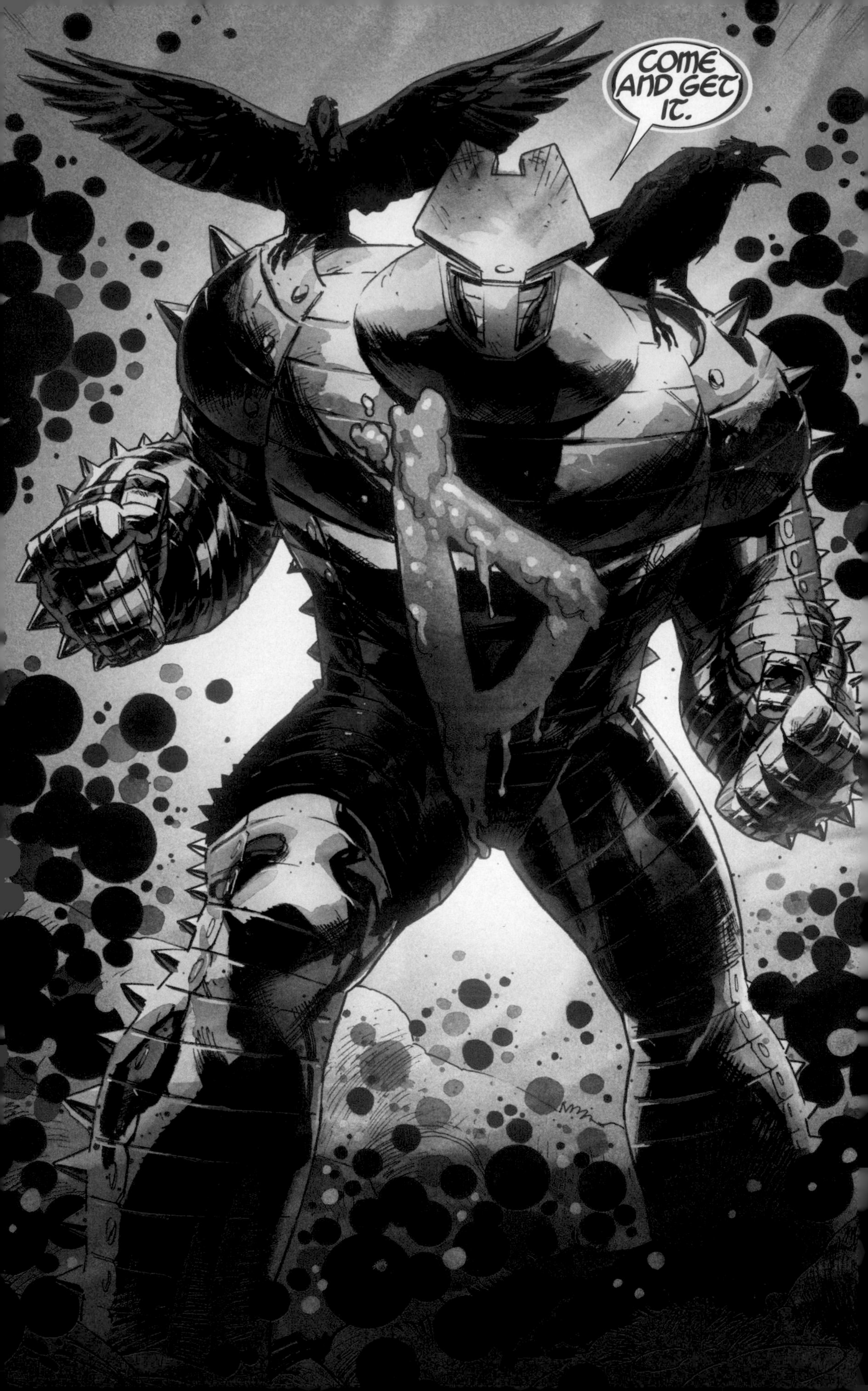
COME AND GET IT.

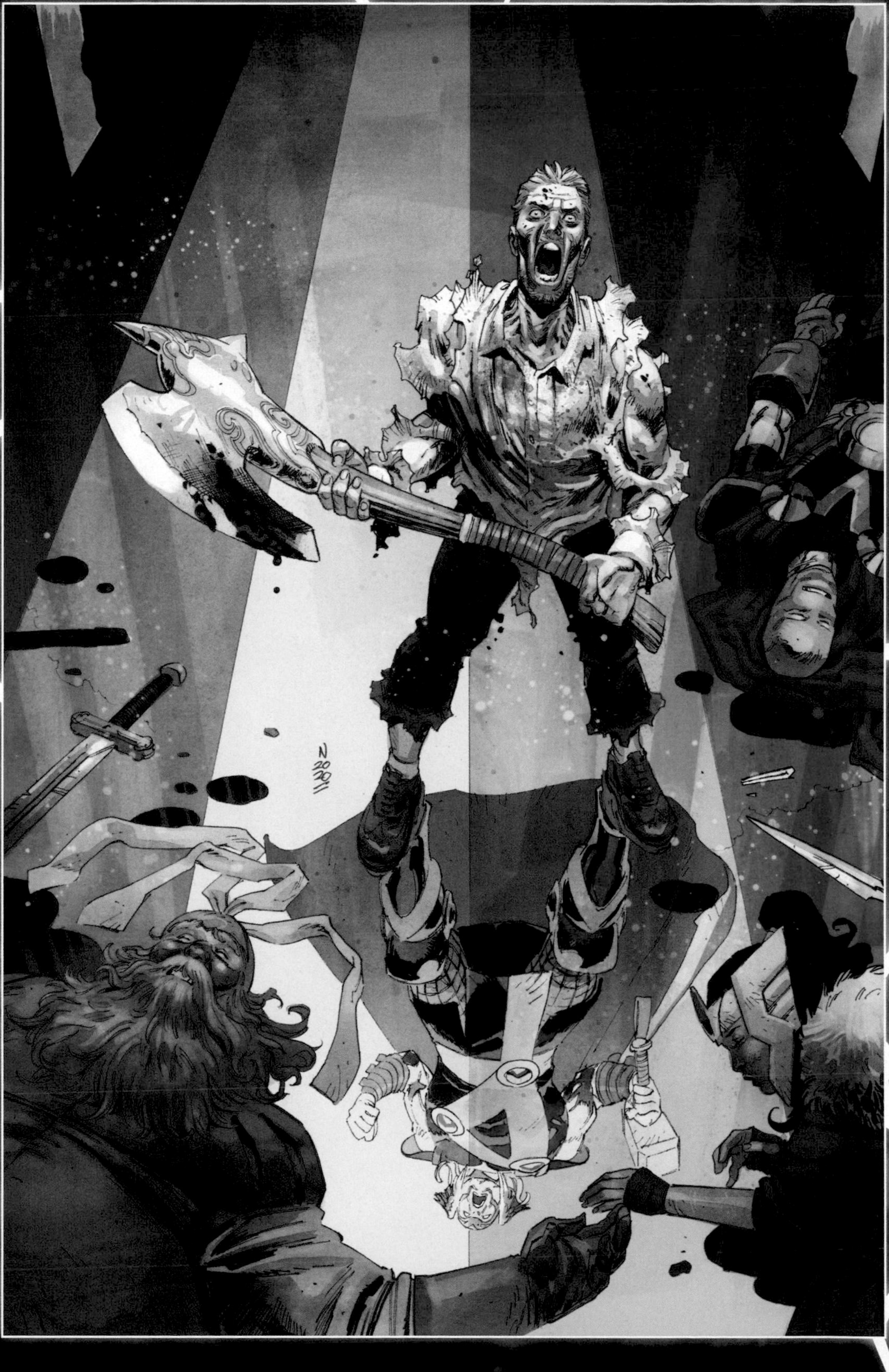

THOR 14 VARIANT BY
Nic Klein

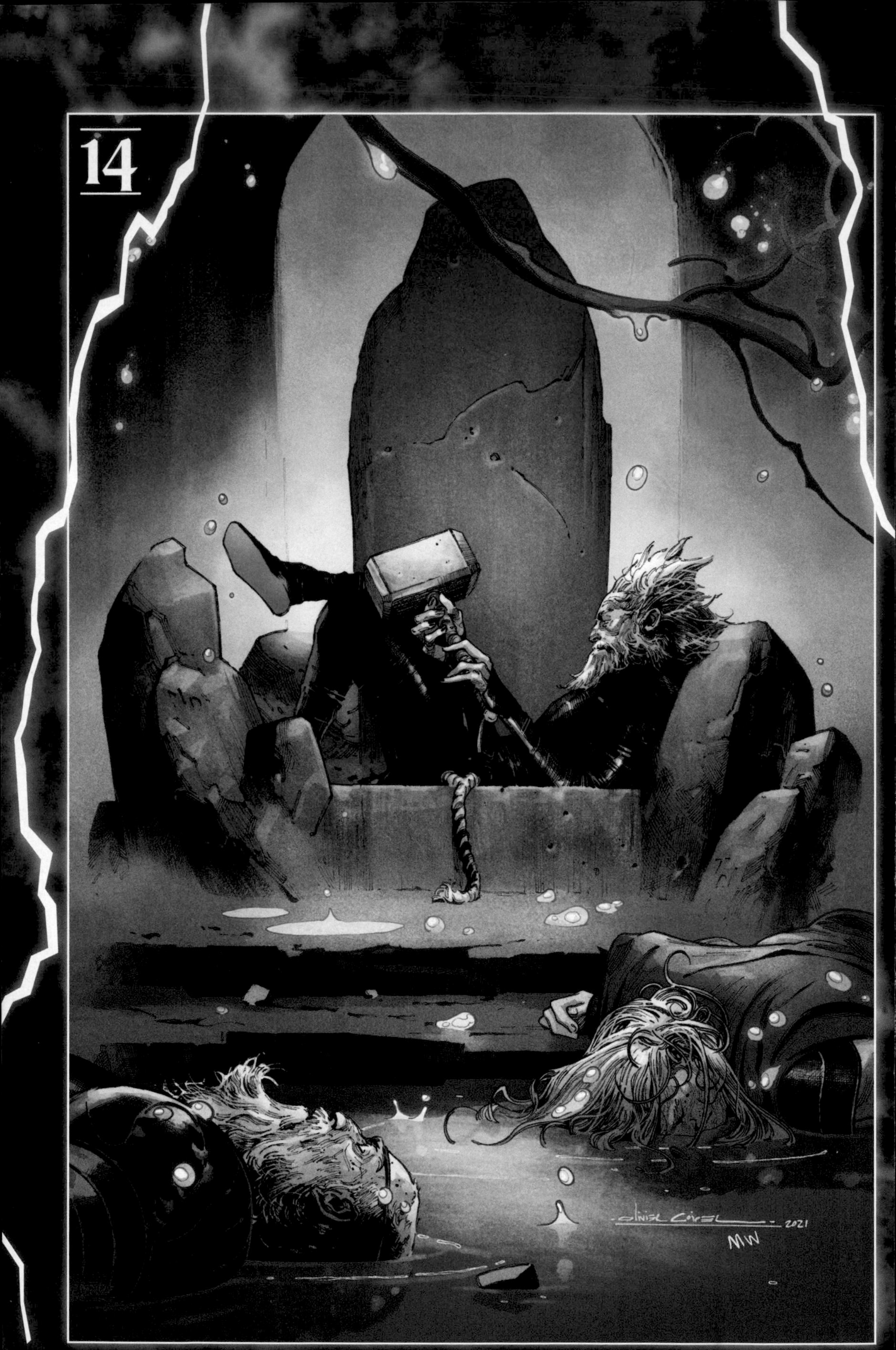
14

"Prey" PART SIX

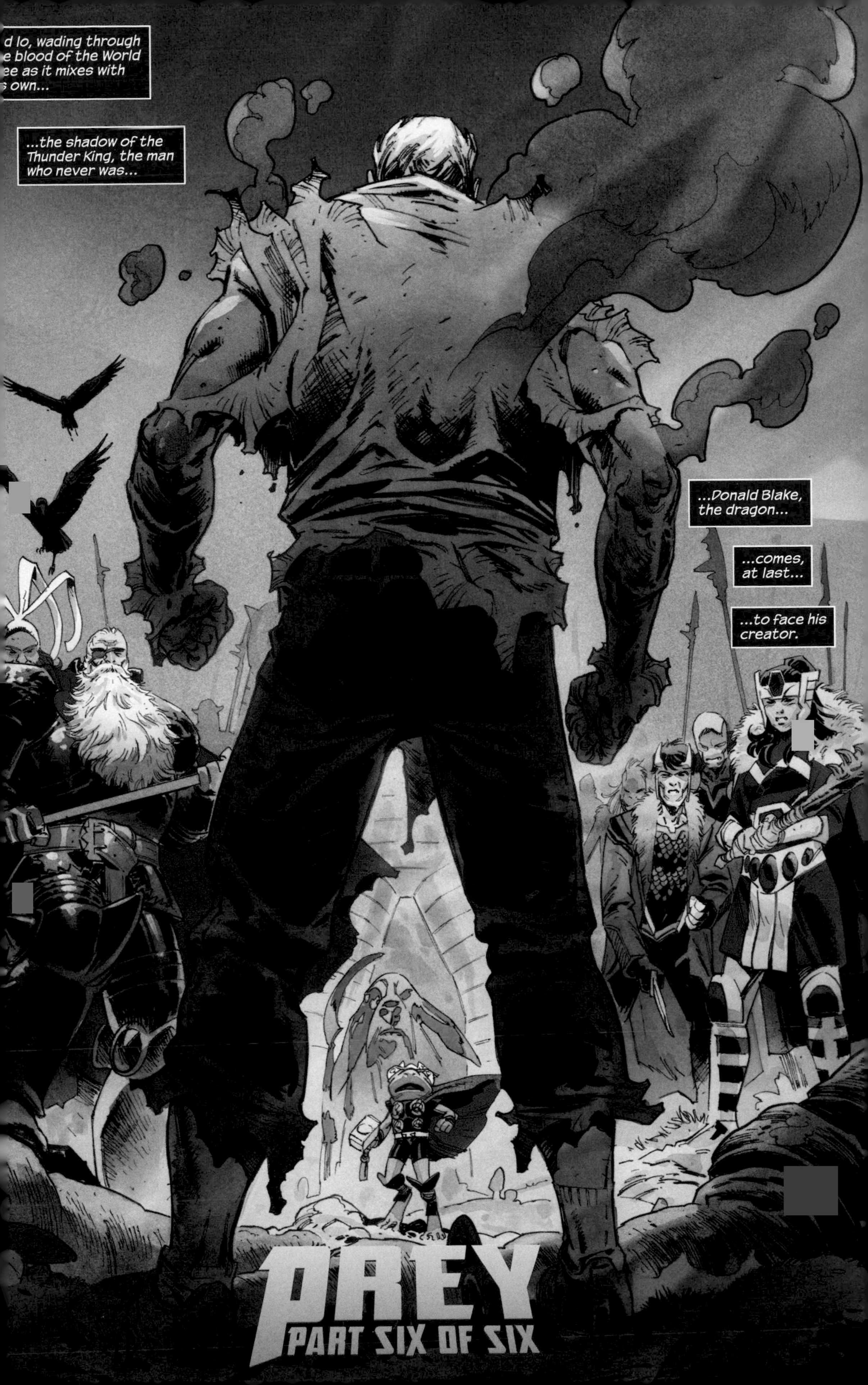
d lo, wading through
e blood of the World
ee as it mixes with
s own...
...the shadow of the
Thunder King, the man
who never was...
...Donald Blake,
the dragon...
...comes,
at last...
...to face his
creator.
PREY
PART SIX OF SIX

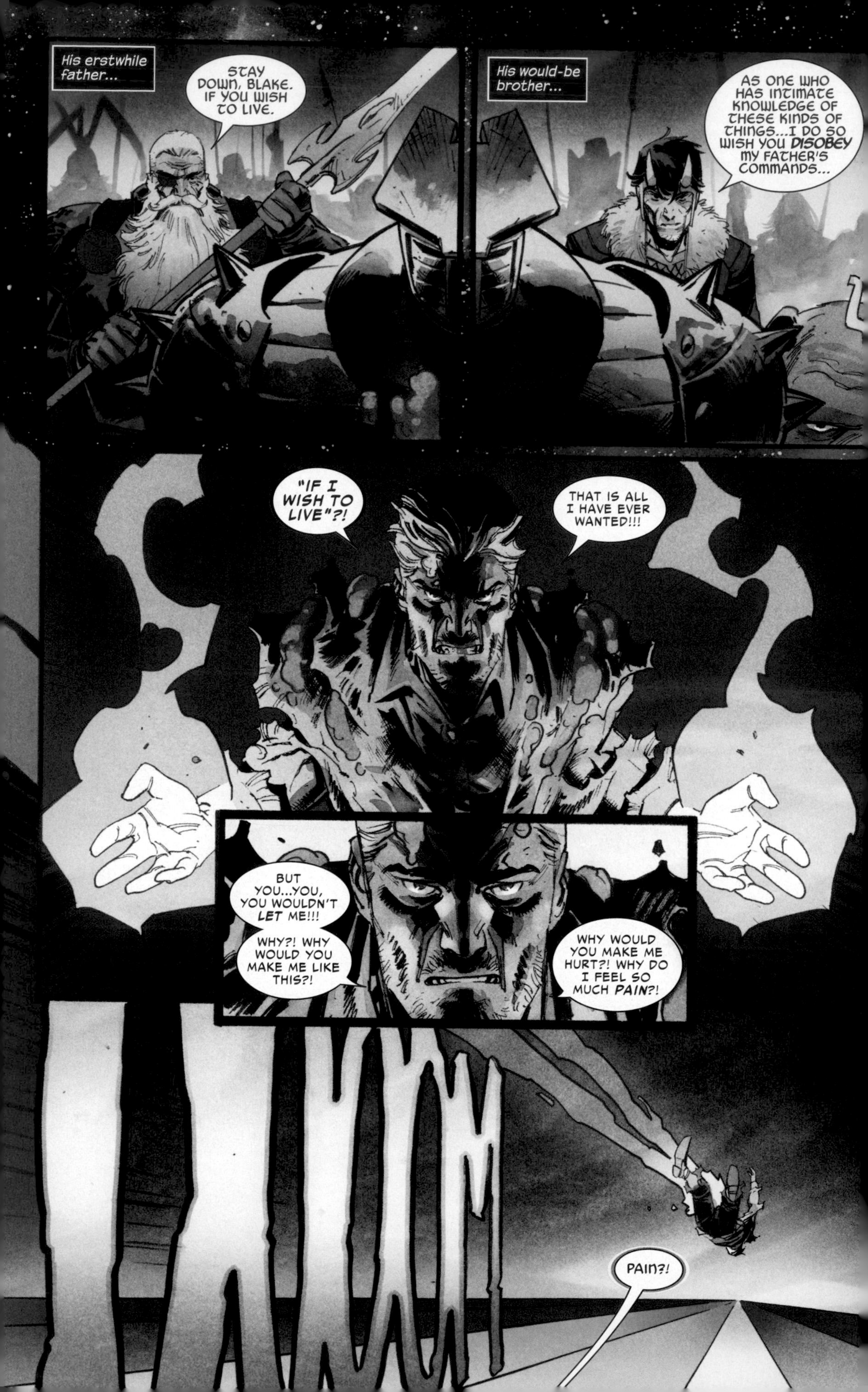
His erstwhile father...
STAY DOWN, BLAKE. IF YOU WISH TO LIVE.
His would-be brother...
AS ONE WHO HAS INTIMATE KNOWLEDGE OF THESE KINDS OF THINGS...I DO SO WISH YOU ***DISOBEY*** MY FATHER'S COMMANDS...
"IF I WISH TO LIVE"?!
THAT IS ALL I HAVE EVER WANTED!!!
BUT YOU...YOU, YOU WOULDN'T ***LET*** ME!!!
WHY?! WHY WOULD YOU MAKE ME LIKE THIS?!
WHY WOULD YOU MAKE ME HURT?! WHY DO I FEEL SO MUCH ***PAIN***?!
PAIN?!

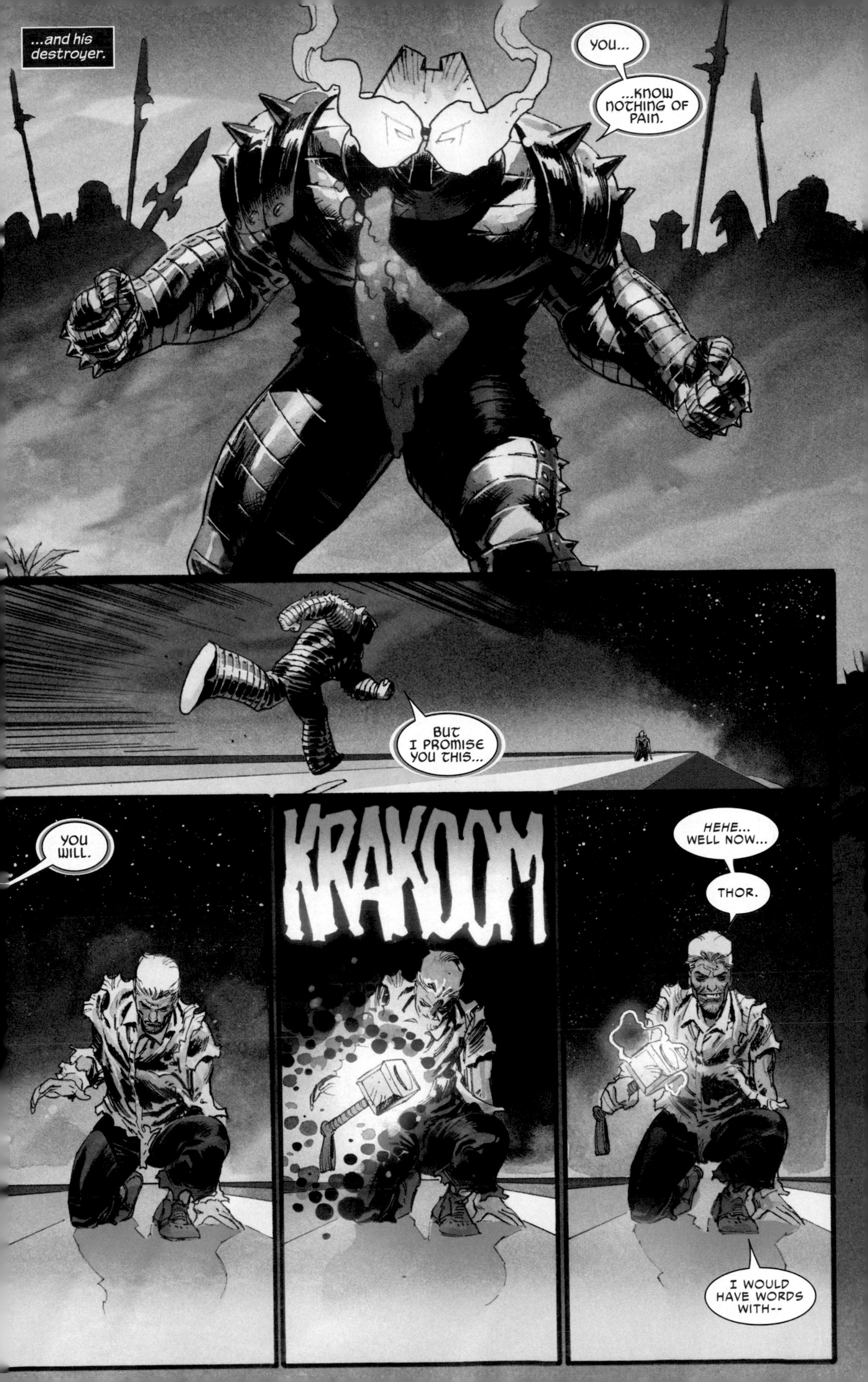
...and his destroyer.
YOU...
...KNOW NOTHING OF PAIN.
BUT I PROMISE YOU THIS...
YOU WILL.
KRAKOOM
HEHE... WELL NOW...
THOR.
I WOULD HAVE WORDS WITH--

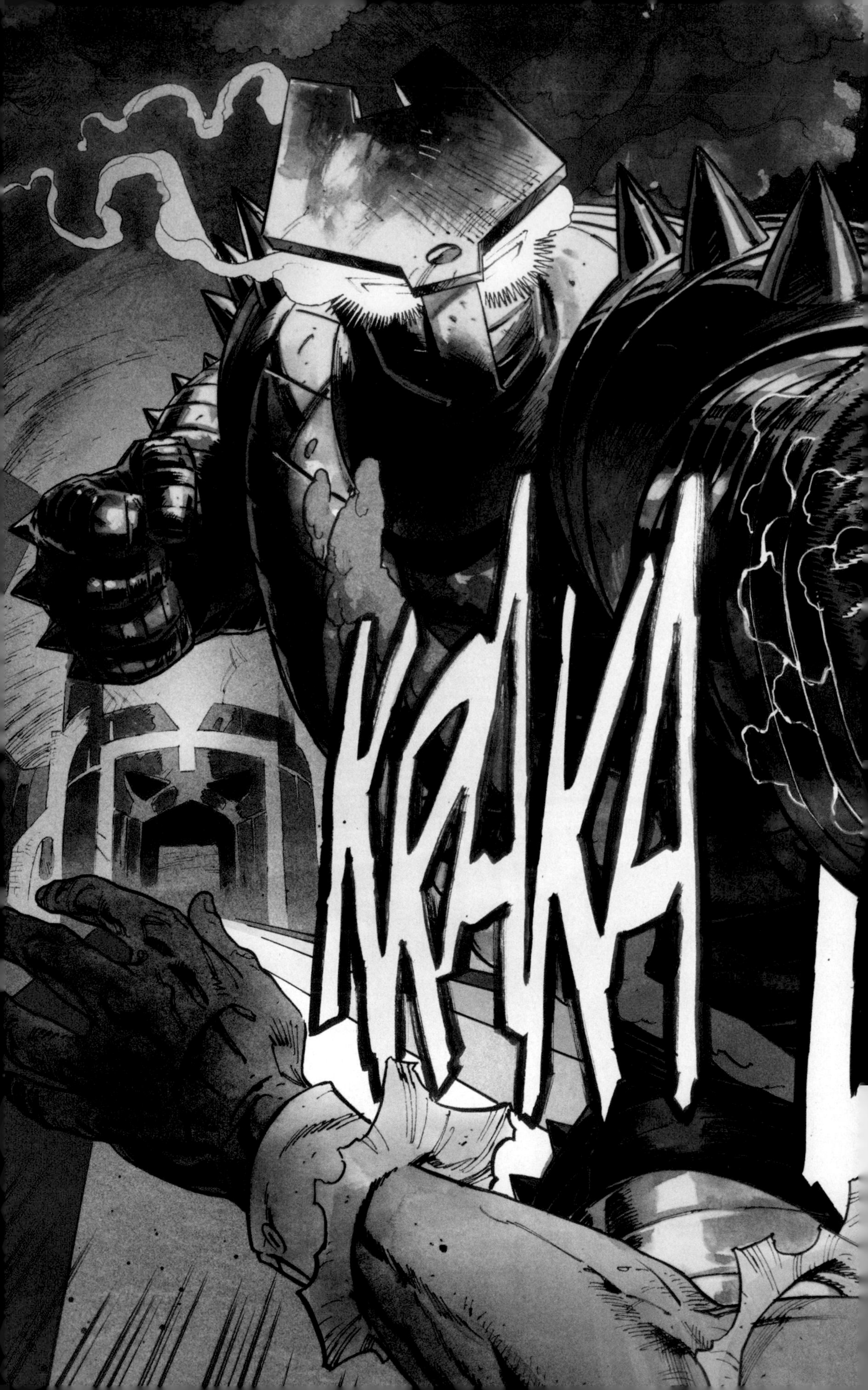

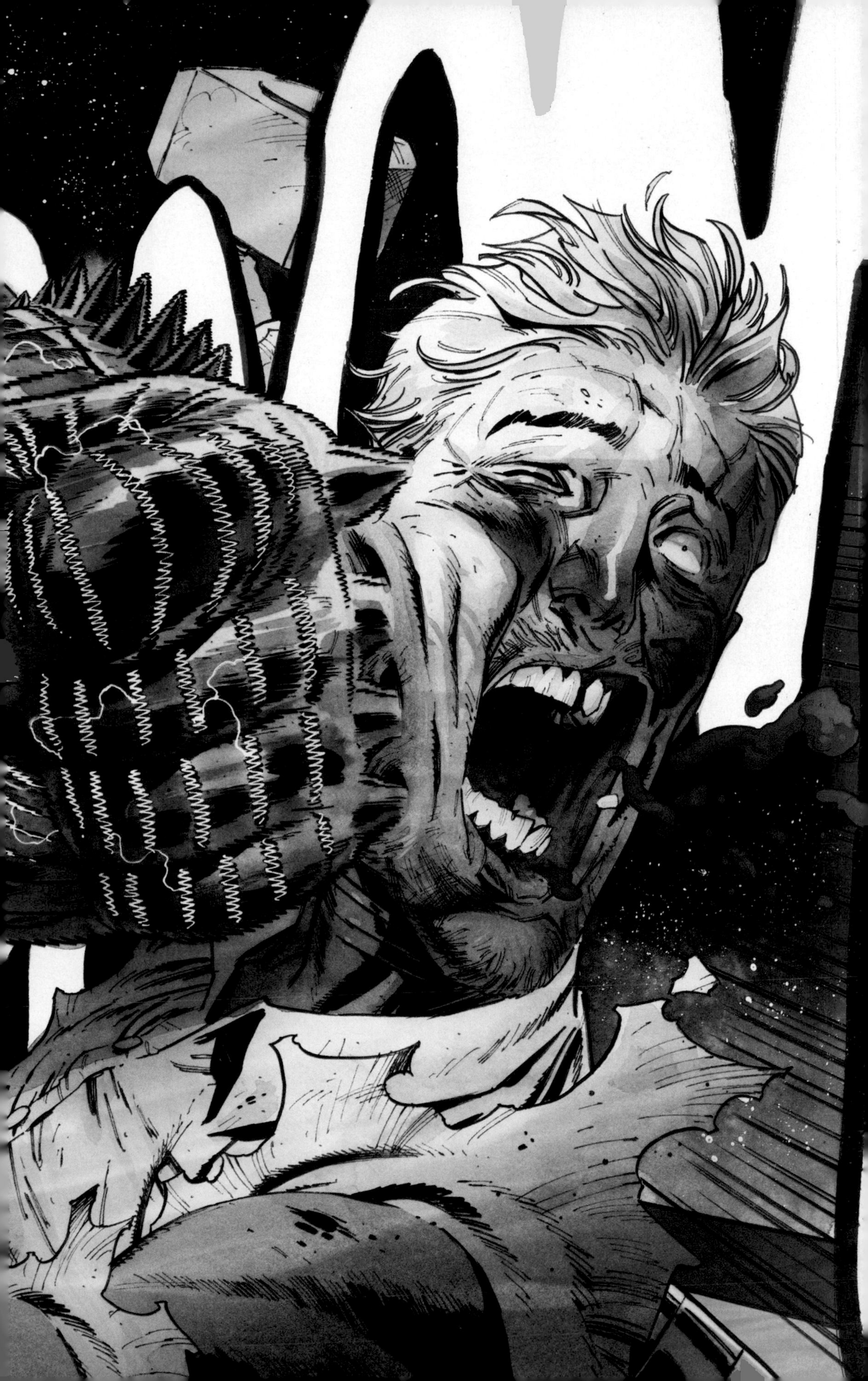

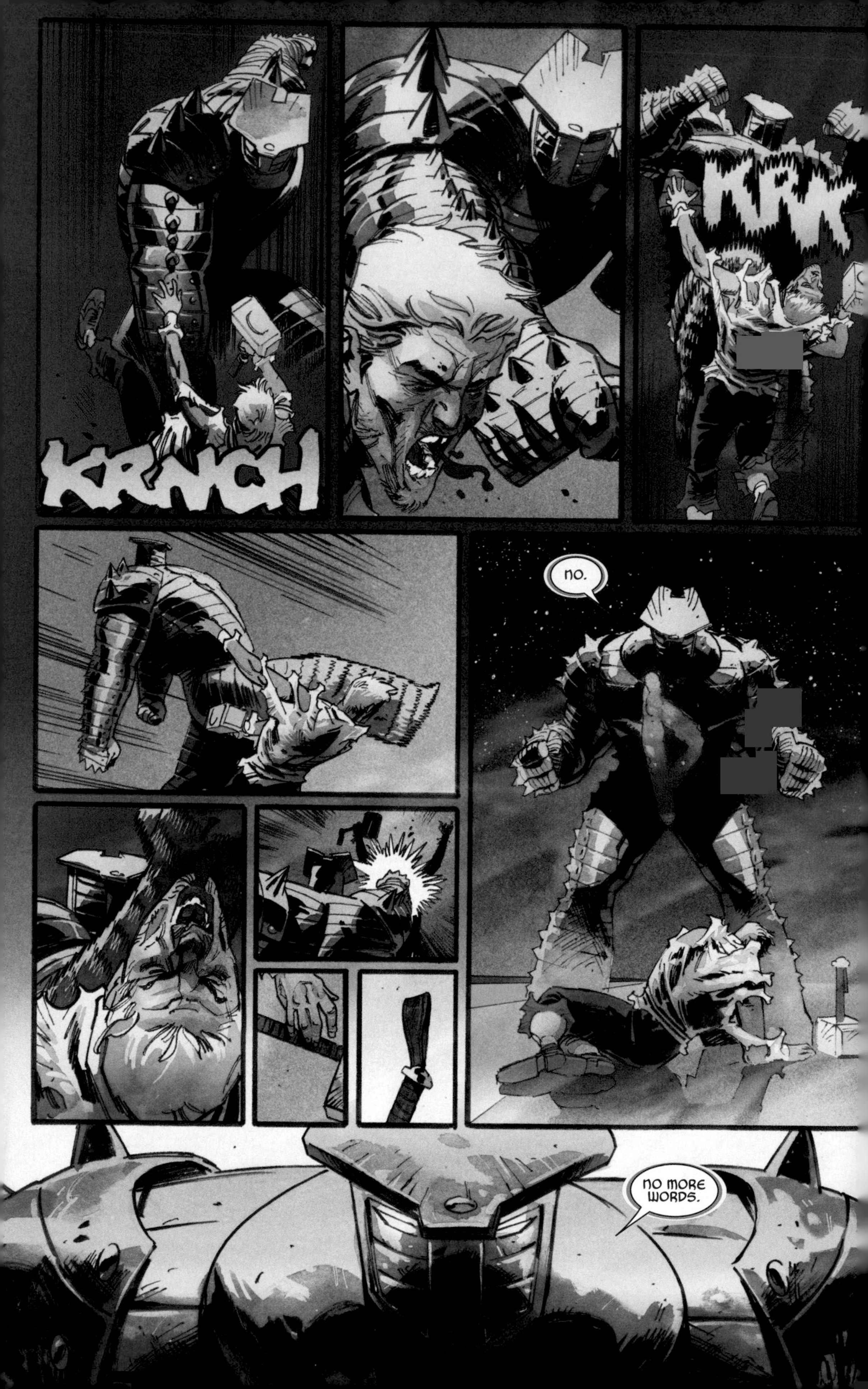
KRANCH
no.
NO MORE WORDS.

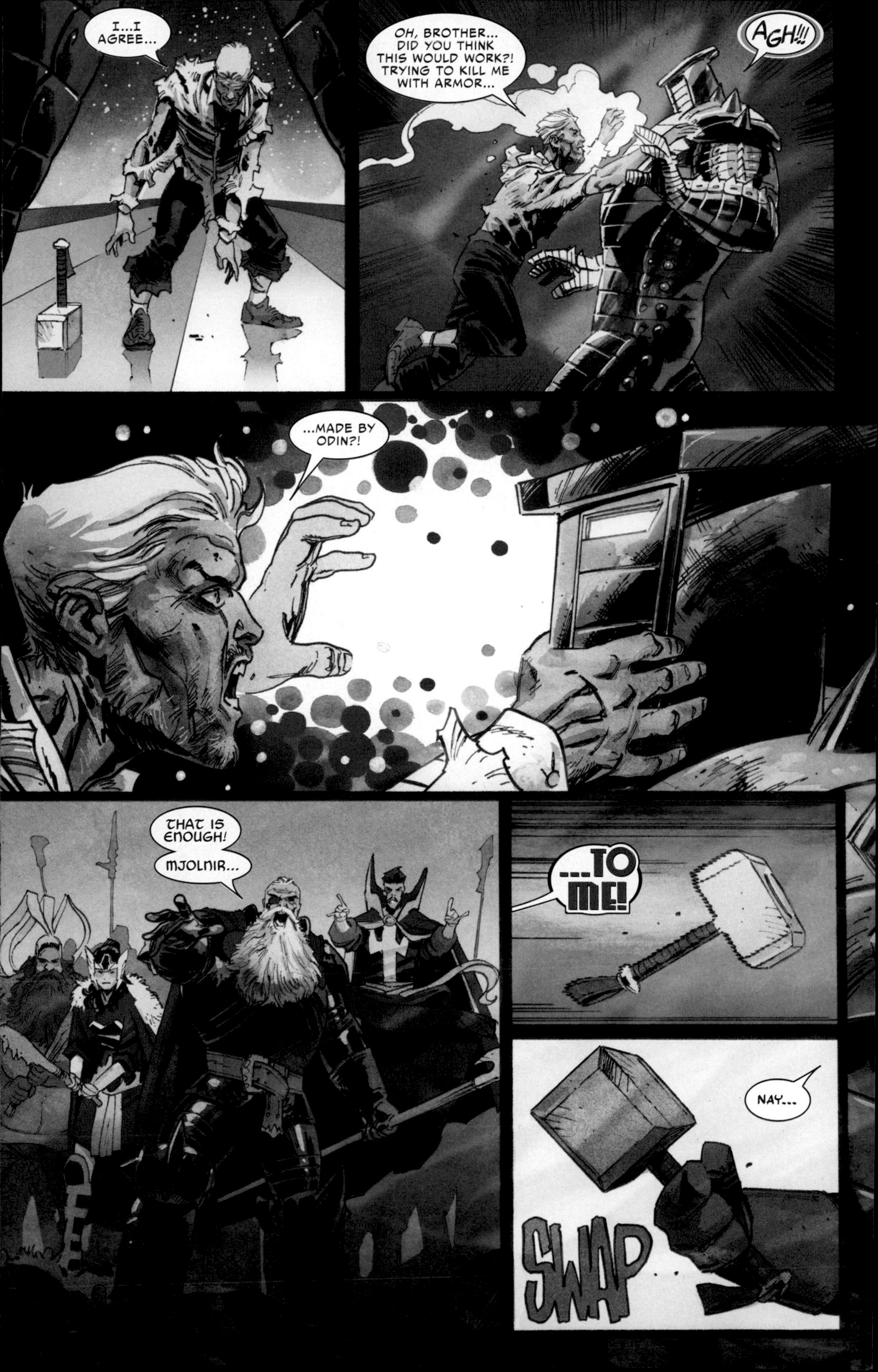

I...I AGREE...
OH, BROTHER... DID YOU THINK THIS WOULD WORK?! TRYING TO KILL ME WITH ARMOR...
AGH!!!
...MADE BY ODIN?!
THAT IS ENOUGH!
MJOLNIR...
...TO ME!
NAY...
SWAP

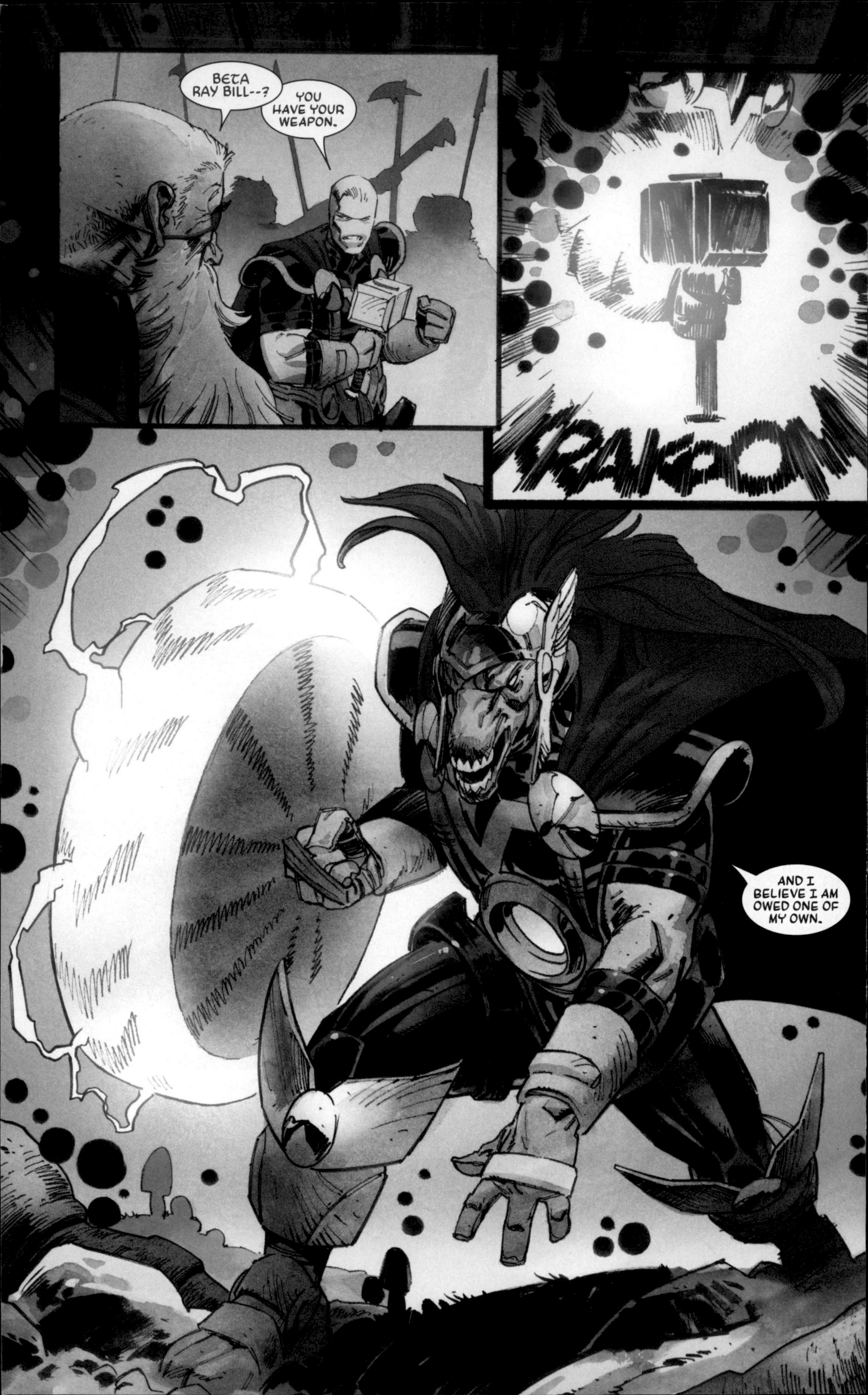
BETA RAY BILL--?
YOU HAVE YOUR WEAPON.
KRAKOOM
AND I BELIEVE I AM OWED ONE OF MY OWN.

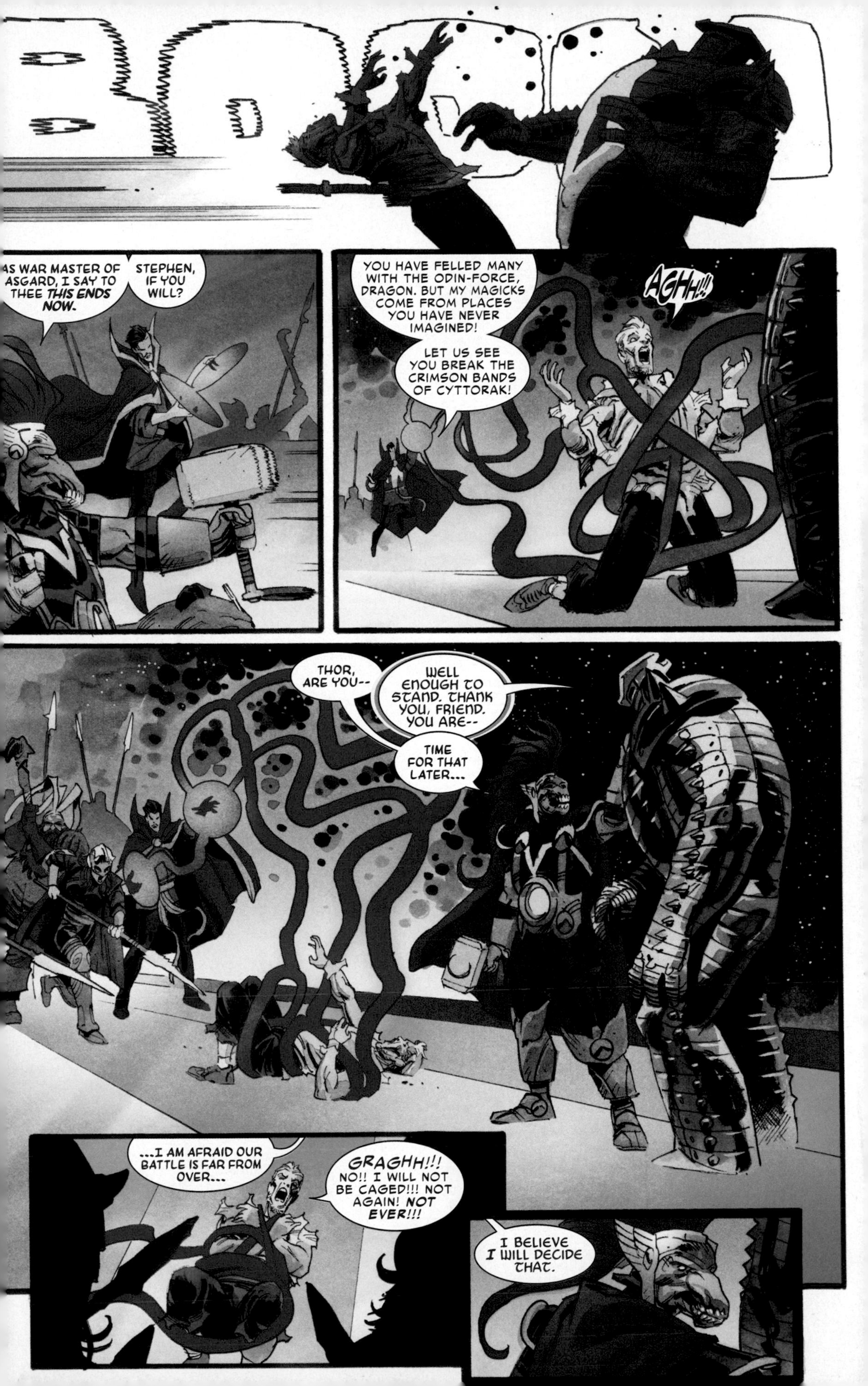
AS WAR MASTER OF ASGARD, I SAY TO THEE *THIS ENDS NOW.*
STEPHEN, IF YOU WILL?
YOU HAVE FELLED MANY WITH THE ODIN-FORCE, DRAGON. BUT MY MAGICKS COME FROM PLACES YOU HAVE NEVER IMAGINED!
LET US SEE YOU BREAK THE CRIMSON BANDS OF CYTTORAK!
AGHH!!!
THOR, ARE YOU--
WELL ENOUGH TO STAND. THANK YOU, FRIEND. YOU ARE--
TIME FOR THAT LATER...
...I AM AFRAID OUR BATTLE IS FAR FROM OVER...
GRAGHH!!!
NO!! I WILL NOT BE CAGED!!! NOT AGAIN! *NOT EVER!!!*
I BELIEVE *I* WILL DECIDE THAT.

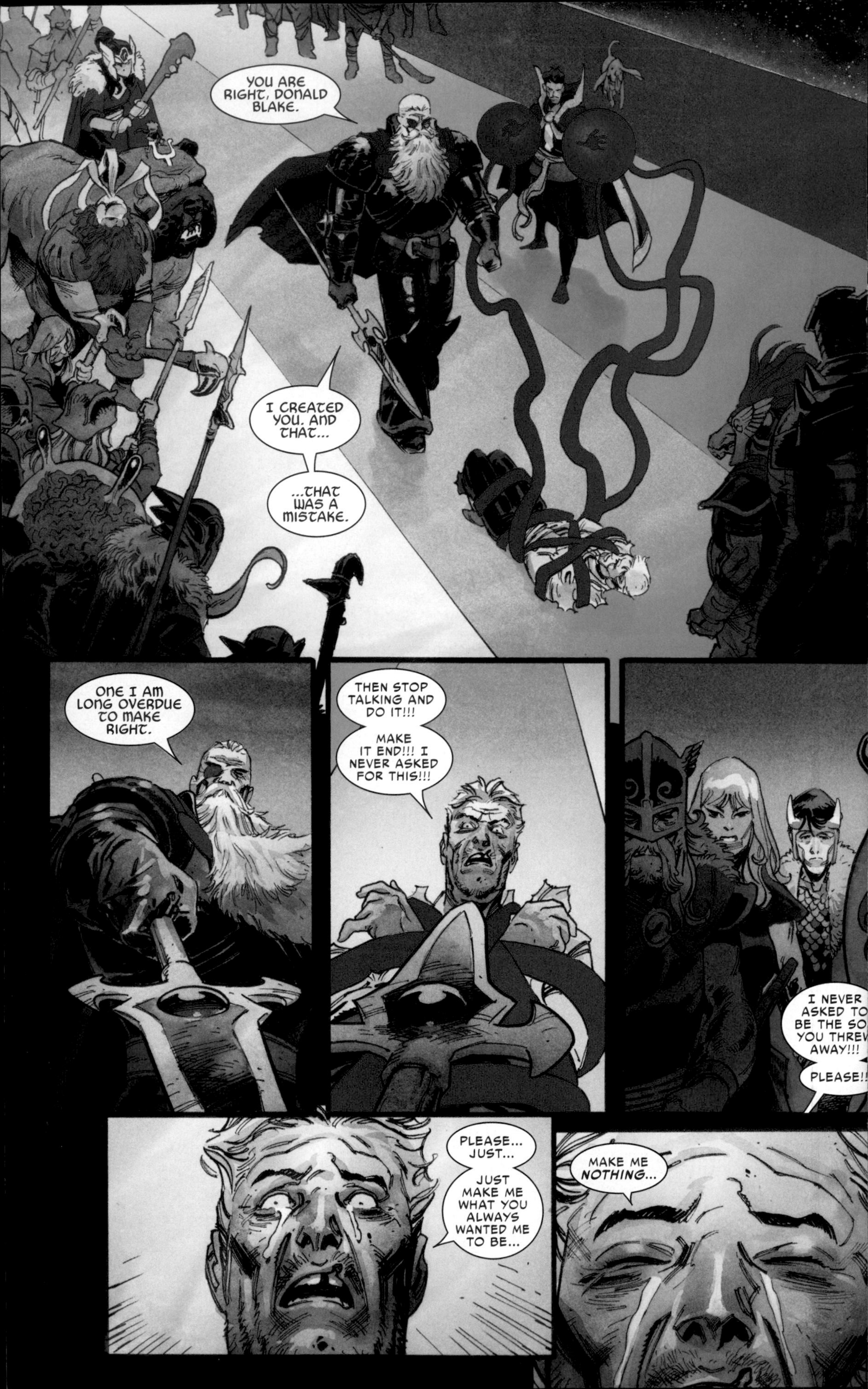
YOU ARE RIGHT, DONALD BLAKE.
I CREATED YOU. AND THAT...
...THAT WAS A MISTAKE.
ONE I AM LONG OVERDUE TO MAKE RIGHT.
THEN STOP TALKING AND DO IT!!!
MAKE IT END!!! I NEVER ASKED FOR THIS!!!
PLEASE!!
PLEASE... JUST...
JUST MAKE ME WHAT YOU ALWAYS WANTED ME TO BE...
MAKE ME *NOTHING*...

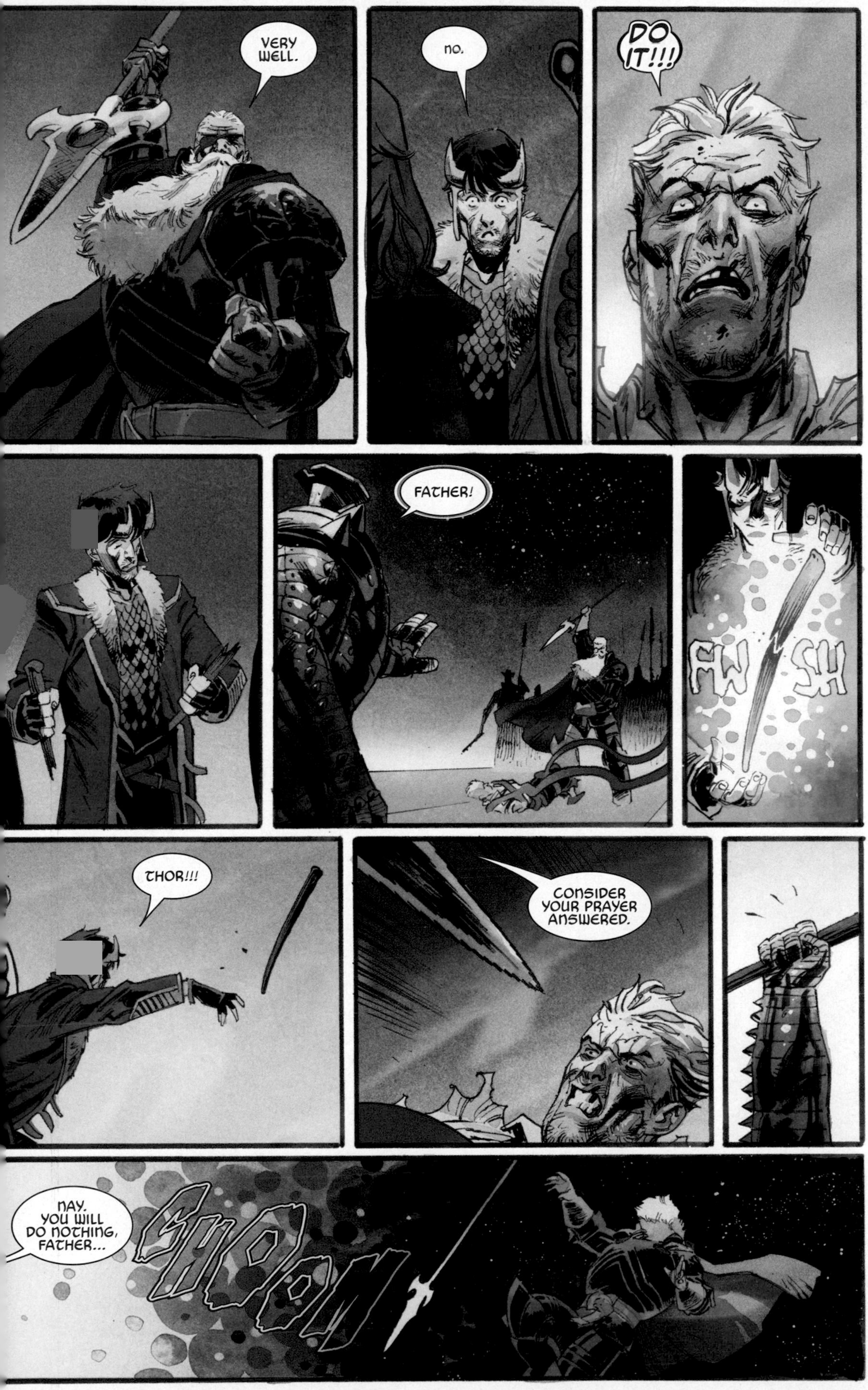
VERY WELL.
no.
DO IT!!!
FATHER!
FWSH
THOR!!!
CONSIDER YOUR PRAYER ANSWERED.
NAY. YOU WILL DO NOTHING, FATHER...
SHOOM

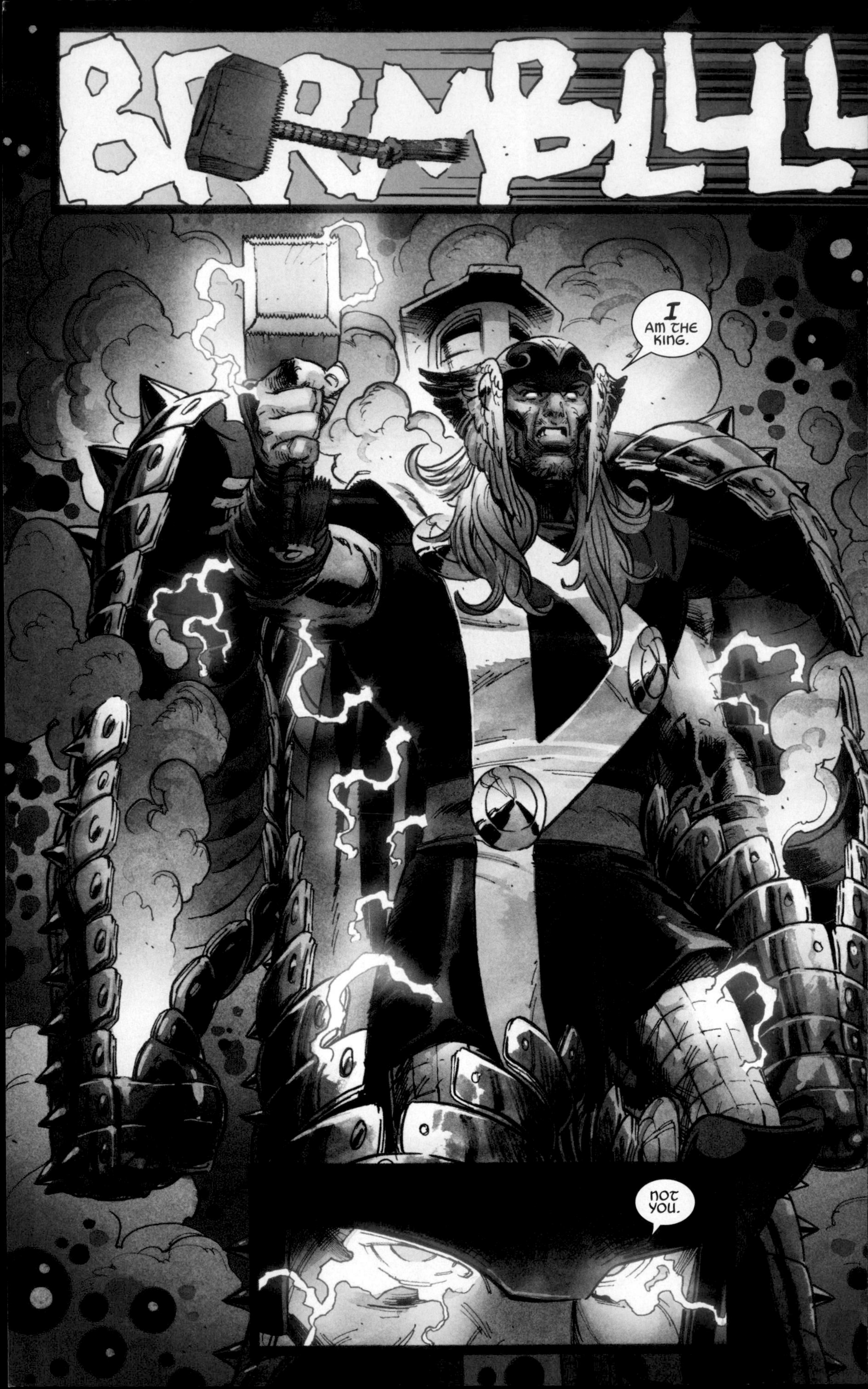
I AM THE KING.
NOT YOU.

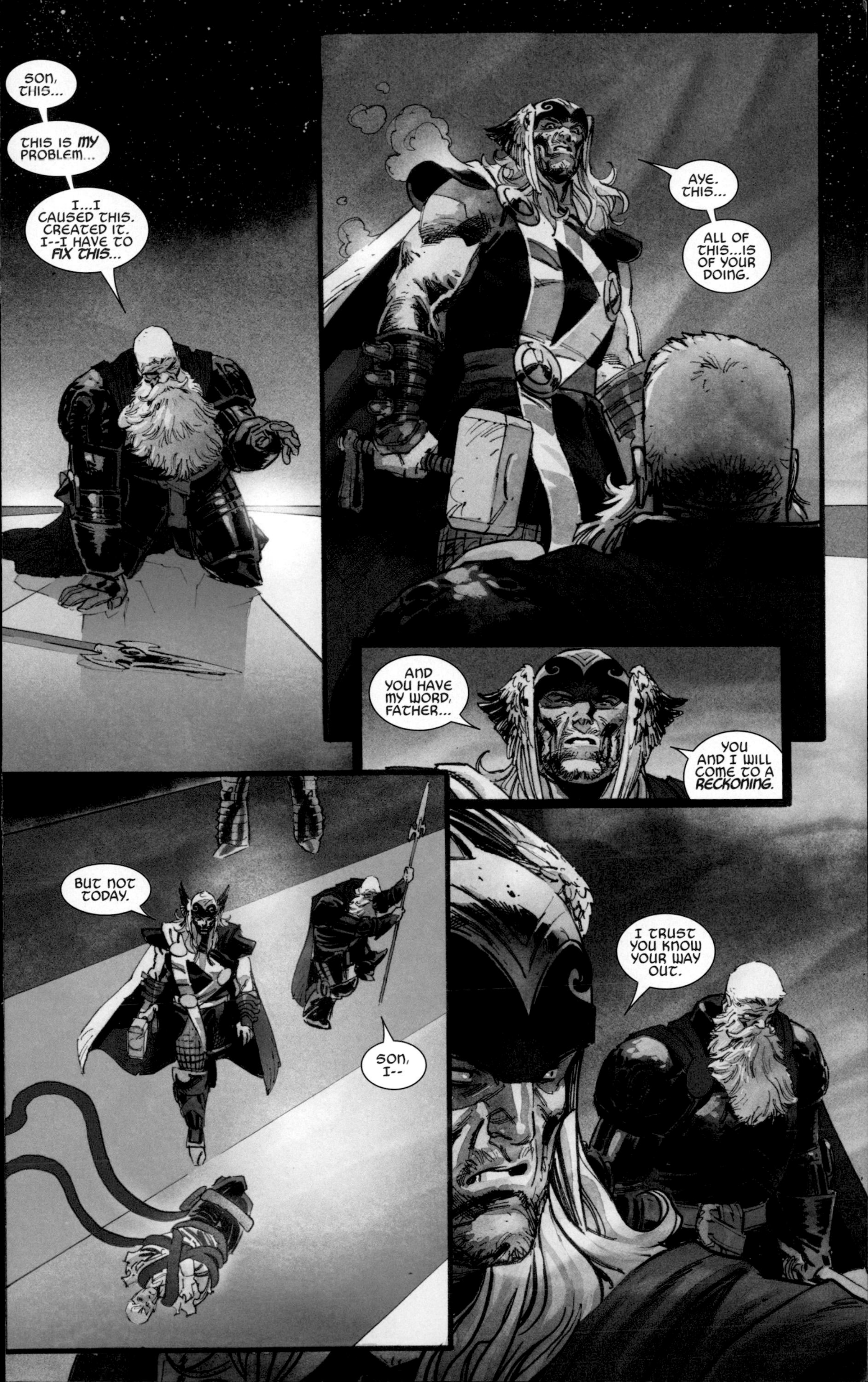
SON, THIS...
THIS IS MY PROBLEM...
I...I CAUSED THIS. CREATED IT. I--I HAVE TO FIX THIS...
AYE. THIS...
ALL OF THIS...IS OF YOUR DOING.
AND YOU HAVE MY WORD, FATHER...
YOU AND I WILL COME TO A RECKONING.
BUT NOT TODAY.
SON, I--
I TRUST YOU KNOW YOUR WAY OUT.

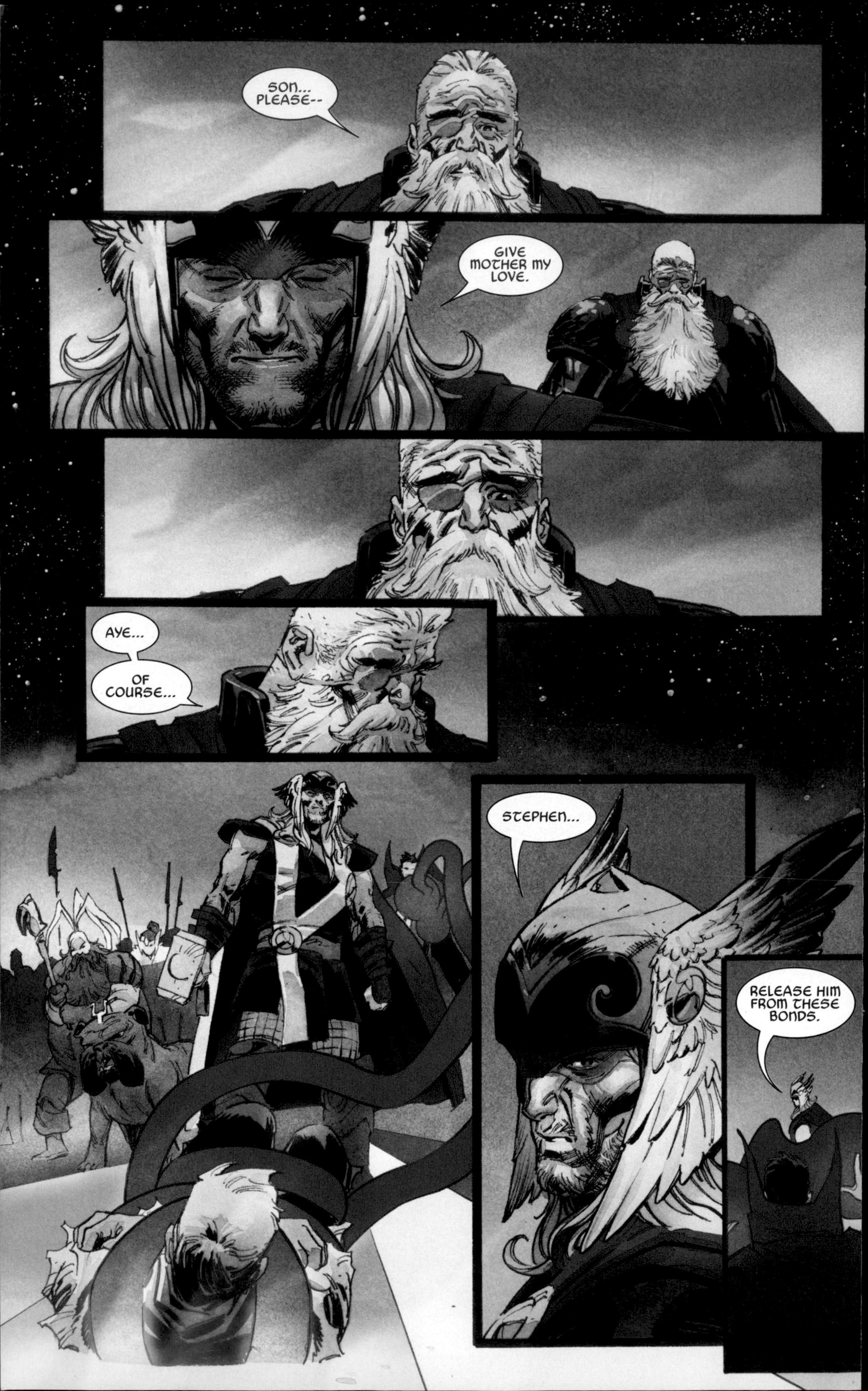
SON... PLEASE--
GIVE MOTHER MY LOVE.
AYE...
OF COURSE...
STEPHEN...
RELEASE HIM FROM THESE BONDS.

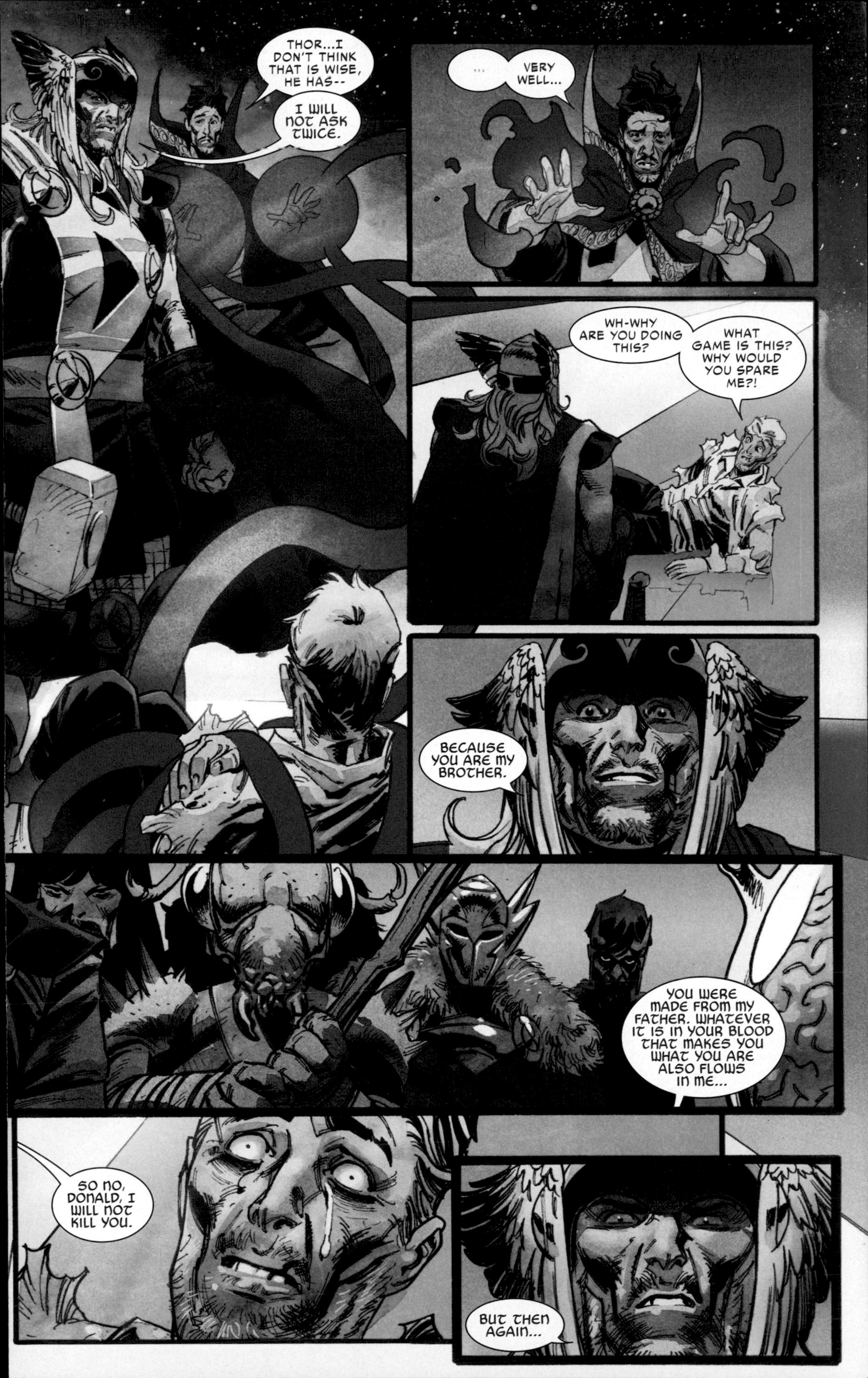
THOR...I DON'T THINK THAT IS WISE, HE HAS--
I WILL NOT ASK TWICE.
...
VERY WELL...
WH-WHY ARE YOU DOING THIS?
WHAT GAME IS THIS? WHY WOULD YOU SPARE ME?!
BECAUSE YOU ARE MY BROTHER.
YOU WERE MADE FROM MY FATHER. WHATEVER IT IS IN YOUR BLOOD THAT MAKES YOU WHAT YOU ARE ALSO FLOWS IN ME...
SO NO, DONALD, I WILL NOT KILL YOU.
BUT THEN AGAIN...

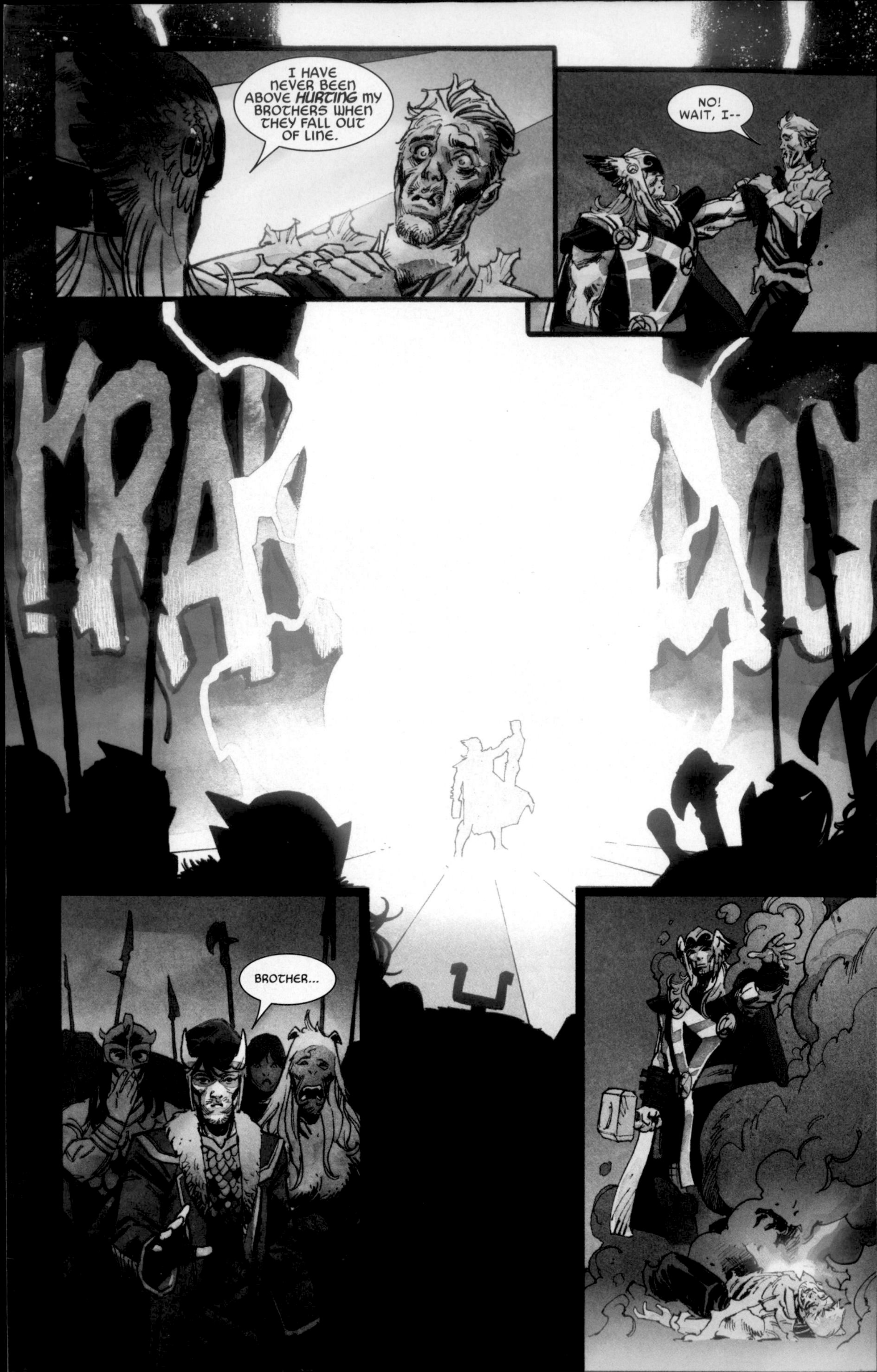
I HAVE NEVER BEEN ABOVE *HURTING* MY BROTHERS WHEN THEY FALL OUT OF LINE.
NO! WAIT, I--
BROTHER...

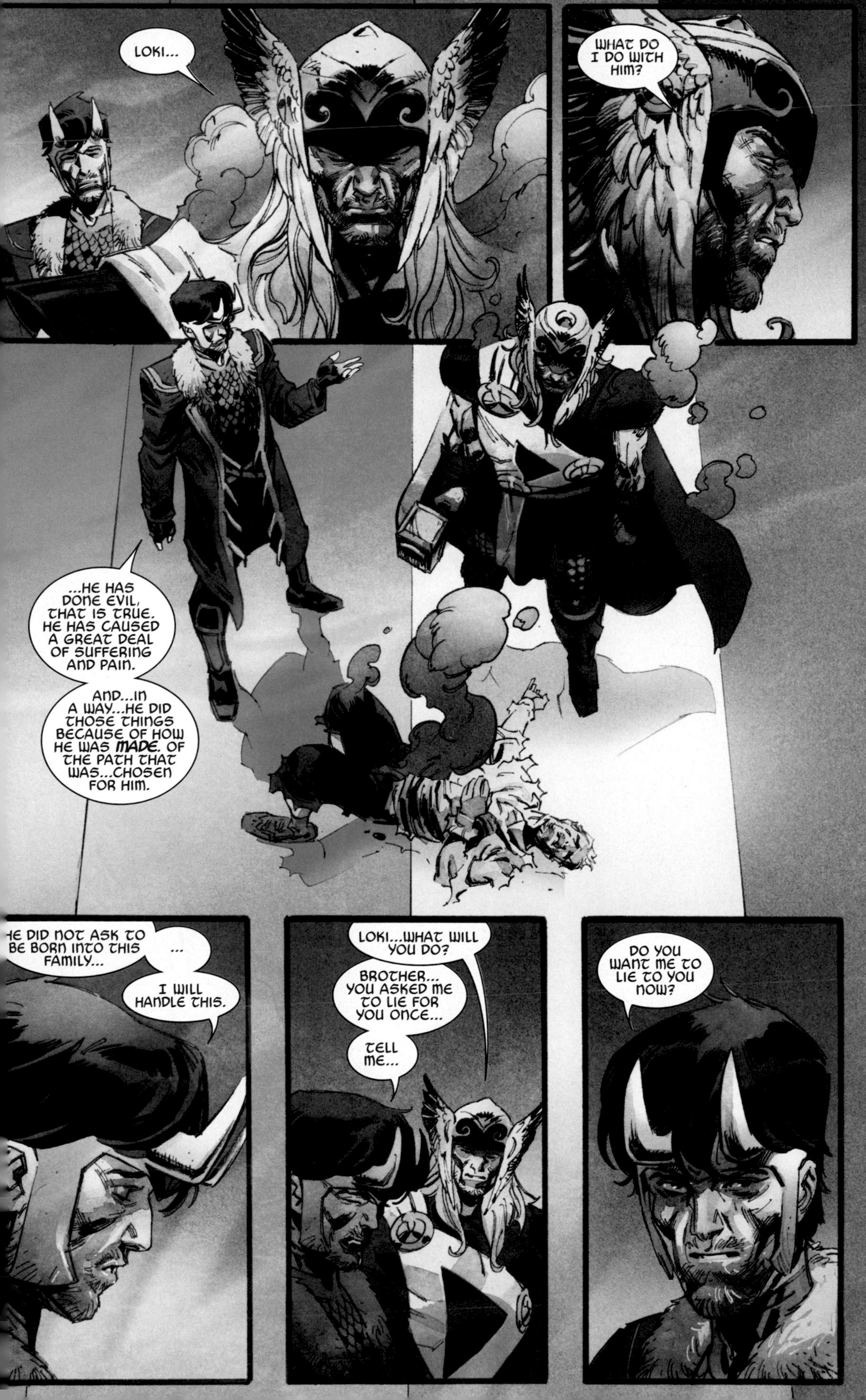
LOKI...
WHAT DO I DO WITH HIM?
...HE HAS DONE EVIL, THAT IS TRUE. HE HAS CAUSED A GREAT DEAL OF SUFFERING AND PAIN.
AND...IN A WAY...HE DID THOSE THINGS BECAUSE OF HOW HE WAS MADE. OF THE PATH THAT WAS...CHOSEN FOR HIM.
HE DID NOT ASK TO BE BORN INTO THIS FAMILY...
...
I WILL HANDLE THIS.
LOKI...WHAT WILL YOU DO?
BROTHER... YOU ASKED ME TO LIE FOR YOU ONCE...
TELL ME...
DO YOU WANT ME TO LIE TO YOU NOW?

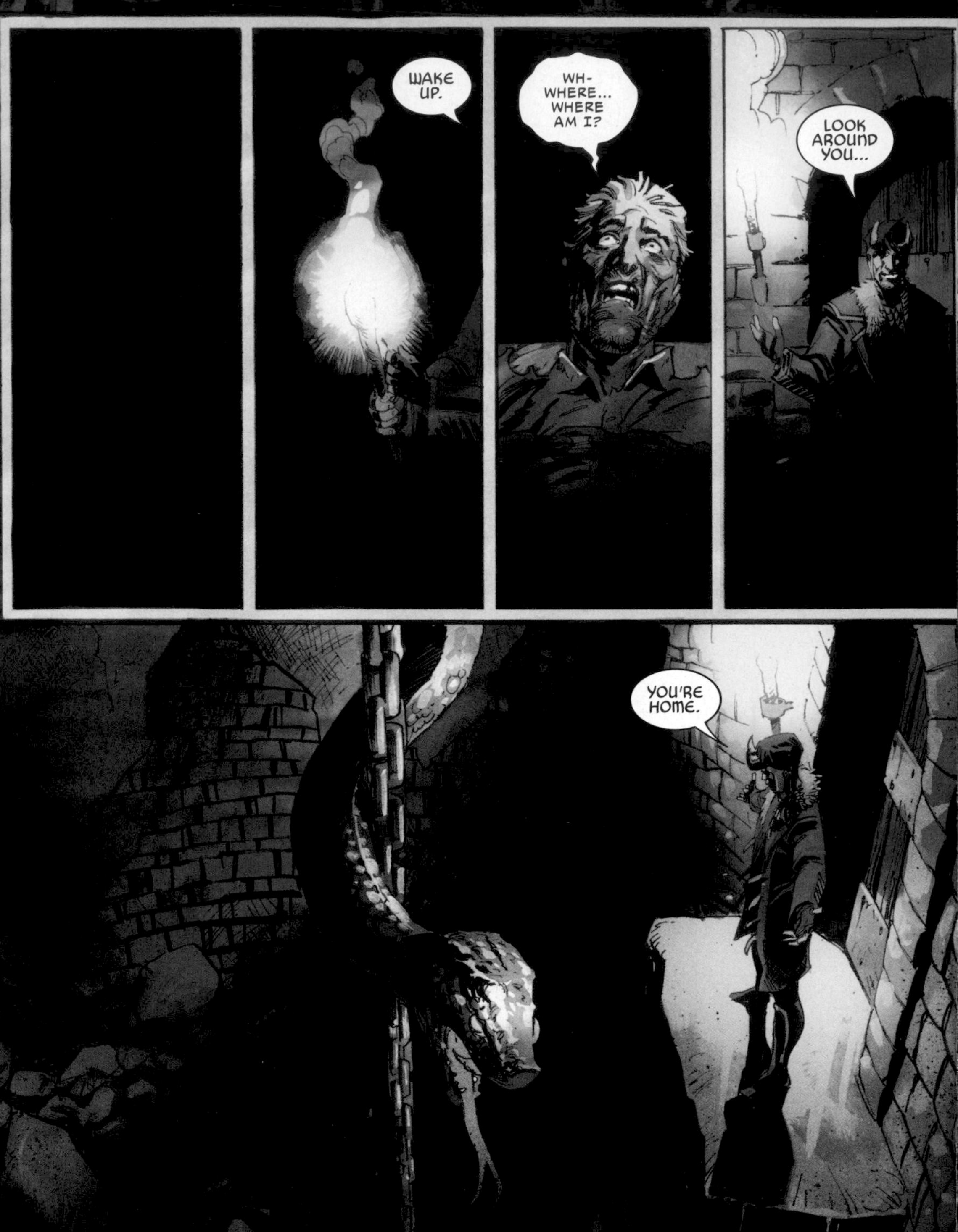
WAKE UP.
WH- WHERE... WHERE AM I?
LOOK AROUND YOU...
YOU'RE HOME.